The Military Ecosystem and Entrepreneurship in Nigeria

The Military Ecosystem and Entrepreneurship in Nigeria

Economic Growth and Security Developments

Edited by Sanya Ojo

BLOOMSBURY ACADEMIC
NEW YORK • LONDON • OXFORD • NEW DELHI • SYDNEY

BLOOMSBURY ACADEMIC
Bloomsbury Publishing Inc, 1359 Broadway, New York, NY 10018, USA
Bloomsbury Publishing Plc, 50 Bedford Square, London, WC1B 3DP, UK
Bloomsbury Publishing Ireland, 29 Earlsfort Terrace, Dublin 2, D02 AY28, Ireland

BLOOMSBURY, BLOOMSBURY ACADEMIC and the Diana logo are trademarks of Bloomsbury Publishing Plc

First published in the United States of America 2026

Library of Congress Cataloging-in-Publication Data
Names: Ojo, Sanya, 1960- editor
Title: The military ecosystem and entrepreneurship in Nigeria: economic growth and security developments / edited by Sanya Ojo.
Description: New York: Bloomsbury Academic, 2026. |
Includes bibliographical references and index.
Identifiers: LCCN 2025042438 (print) | LCCN 2025042439 (ebook) | ISBN 9781666981230 hardback | ISBN 9781666981254 paperback | ISBN 9798216201250 pdf | ISBN 9781978762909 epub
Subjects: LCSH: Defense industries–Nigeria | Entrepreneurship–Nigeria | Military-owned business enterprises–Nigeria | Veteran-owned business enterprises–Nigeria
Classification: LCC HD9743.N62 M55 2026 (print) | LCC HD9743.N62 (ebook) | DDC 338.0409669–dc23/eng/20250917
LC record available at https://lccn.loc.gov/2025042438
LC ebook record available at https://lccn.loc.gov/2025042439

ISBN: HB: 978-1-6669-8123-0
ePDF: 979-8-216-20125-0
eBook: 978-1-9787-6290-9

Typeset by Integra Software Services Pvt. Ltd.

For product safety related questions contact productsafety@bloomsbury.com.

To find out more about our authors and books visit www.bloomsbury.com and sign up for our newsletters.

Contents

Figures

Tables

Contributors

Murtala Ayinla Ahmed is a captain in the Nigerian Navy. He holds a BSc in Accounting from Bayero University Kano (1998), an MBA from Usmanu Danfodiyo University Sokoto (2001), an MSc in Military Studies from the Bangladesh University of Professionals, Dhaka, Bangladesh (2014), an MSc in Professional Accounting from the University of London (2017) and a Masters in Strategic Studies from the Nigerian Defence Academy (2025). He is a fellow of the Institute of Chartered Accountants of Nigeria (ICAN), an associate of the Association of Chartered Certified Accountants (ACCA), an associate of the Chartered Institute of Public Finance and Accounts (CIPFA), a fellow of the Chartered Institute of Taxation of Nigeria (CITN) and a fellow of the National Defence College, Nigeria (fdc). He is also a member of the Nigerian Institute of Management and a member of the Nigerian Institute of International Affairs. Ahmed has over two decades of experience in the finance field, and he is currently the Command Accounts and Budget Officer of the Nigerian Navy Special Operations Command, Makurdi. His core competencies are in budgeting, investment and portfolio management, financial accounting and public procurement.

Ayobami Oluwatoyin Ajepe is a lecturer in the Department of Accounting and is currently a doctoral degree student in Accounting at the Nigerian Defence Academy, Kaduna.

Yusuf Ali is a serving military officer at the Defence Headquarters, Abuja and a doctoral degree student in Defence and Security Studies at the Nigerian Defence Academy, Kaduna.

Aisha Yahaya Bambale is currently a doctoral degree student in the Department of Management Studies at the Nigerian Defence Academy, Kaduna. She holds a BSc in Business Administration and a Master's of Business Administration (MBA) from Ahmadu Bello University, Zaria, and an MSc in Management from Bayero University, Kano, Nigeria. She has authored and co-authored articles in reputable local and international scholarly journals. As a doctoral student, Aisha is affiliated with the Nigerian Defence Academy and can be reached at aisha.bambale2022@nda.edu.ng

Anthony Onyemaechi Chukwu is a professor at the Centre for Critical Thinking, Teaching and Learning (CCTTL), Nigeria Defence Academy, Kaduna.

Osogu Nweji Ebe Collins is a serving military personnel member with the Nigerian Army and a lecturer in the Department of Logistics and Supply Chain Management at the Nigerian Defence Academy, Kaduna, Nigeria.

Abubakar Surajo Imam (Colonel) is a professor of Mechatronics and Robotics, Nigerian Defence Academy, Kaduna, Nigeria. He is the founding director of the NDA Centre for Innovation and Creativity (CINOCRE) and has won the Nigerian Army Innovation Medal for two consecutive years. His research focuses on AI, robotics, military mechatronics and defence innovation and entrepreneurship.

Senator Iroegbu is a defence editor, security sector and governance reforms advocate, and public affairs analyst, serving as convener of the Geopolitics Series and editor-in-chief at Global Sentinel.

Irene Oka Isaac is a lecturer in the Department of Management Studies, Nigerian Defence Academy, Nigeria.

Ester Kadarko is a senior lecturer in the Department of Management Studies, Nigerian Defence Academy, Nigeria.

Shaju Meetna is head of the Research and Development Cell at LEAD College of Management, Kerala, India and serves as editor of LEADER: *International Journal of Business Management*.

Etham Bwalasom Mijah is a professor of Political Science and Defence Studies, Nigerian Defence Academy (NDA), Kaduna, a DAAD scholar, author and co-editor, with S.G. Best and N.C. Lord-Mallam of (2019). *Nigeria's Defence and Security: The Role of Military Families*. (John Archers, 2019), and with U.A. Tar and M.E.U. Tedheke of *Globalization in Africa: Perspectives on Security, Environment and Development* (Lexington Books, 2016). Etham is also widely published in local and international scholarly peer-reviewed journals: with B.E. Mijah and A.A. Adamu, 'Public Perception of Political Parties and the Consolidation of Democracy in Nigeria', in I.A. Shuaibu, H. Saliu and A.M. Okoli (eds) *Political Parties and Political Process in Nigeria - Exploring the Missing Links* (Nigerian Political Science Association, 2018).

Lateef Olumide Mustapha is a holder of a Bachelor's Degree in Accounting, a Master's in Accounting and a PhD in Accounting in 2001, 2010 and 2016, respectively. Mustapha is a member of many professional bodies, including the Institute of Chartered Accountants of Nigeria (ICAN), the Association of National Accountants of Nigeria (ANAN), the Chartered Institute of Taxation of Nigeria (CITN), and the Association of Certified Chartered System Accountants-USA (ACCA-USA). Apart from qualifying many students as Chartered Accountants in ICAN, he served on many committees of most of these bodies, both at district and national levels.

Dr Mustapha has been an associate professor since 2022 in the Department of Accounting, Faculty of Management Sciences, Nigerian Defence Academy, Kaduna. Apart from serving on various committees at the departmental, faculty and academy levels, he has successfully supervised and completed many undergraduate projects in Accounting and many theses in Accounting, Finance and Management at the postgraduate level. He has 110 publications in Accounting and Finance in reputable journals to his credit.

Sanya Ojo is an associate professor of Entrepreneurship at the Nigerian Defence Academy, Kaduna, Nigeria and a research fellow at the School of Business and Law of the University of East London, UK. His over forty years of experience in entrepreneurship (national, diaspora and transnational) informs his research interest in ethnic, transnational and diaspora entrepreneurship, and he has published papers in these areas. His other research interest extends to international business strategy and management. Sanya Ojo has the privilege of mobility in career choices, exploring options critically, establishing educational preferences, and placing bets on multiple knowledge paths, as a consequence of his capacity to benefit from high-end knowledge and research. He is a fellow of the Higher Education Academy (FHEA). As an award-winner, he has published in reputable academic journals and resources.

Ijeoma Chinyere Onuorah is a doctoral student at the Nigerian Defence Academy, Kaduna.

Onyeka Leo Onuorah is a lecturer in the Department of Political Science at the Nigerian Defence Academy, Kaduna.

Bishir Sirajo lectures at the Umaru Musa Yar'Adua University, Katsina State, Nigeria.

Adewale Abdulwaheed Soneye is currently a doctoral degree student in the Department of Management Studies at the Nigerian Defence Academy, Kaduna. He holds a BSc (Hons) in Business Administration and an MSc in Operations Research from the University of Lagos, Nigeria. He has authored and co-authored articles in reputable local and international scholarly journals. As a doctoral student, Adewale is affiliated with the Nigerian Defence Academy and can be reached at adewale.soneye2022@nda.edu.ng

Alfa Yakubu holds a PhD in Economics, with specialization in Monetary Economics, and a Master of Science (MSc) and a Bachelor of Science (BSc) in Economics. His professional qualifications include Postgraduate Diploma in Education, Postgraduate Diploma in Applied Statistics and Demography, Postgraduate Diploma in Customer Relations, and Proficiency Certificate in Management. He has published academic papers in reputable international and national journals, including the Journal of Monetary and Economic Integration, Ghana and other University-based Journals. His current areas of research cut across monetary policy and central banking, and econometrics. Alfa is currently a full-time lecturer in the Economics Department, Nigerian Defence Academy, Kaduna.

Foreword

It is a genuine pleasure to introduce *The Military Ecosystem and Entrepreneurship in Nigeria: Economic Growth and Security Developments*. This book presents a fresh and much-needed perspective in the often complex and crowded field of entrepreneurship. While significant progress has been made in deepening our understanding of the many facets of entrepreneurship, whether by expanding its theoretical frameworks or exploring its context-specific dimensions, persistent challenges remain, especially in countries like Nigeria, which are grappling with development obstacles.

Typically, the dominant narrative around entrepreneurship relies heavily on models shaped by broad economic axioms and individual market choices. Much of what we know about entrepreneurship has been filtered through the lens of open markets and individual agency. Despite advances in demystifying entrepreneurial processes, this book offers an important supplementary viewpoint: it examines entrepreneurship through the unique context of the military ecosystem.

By doing so, the book reconstructs conventional ideas and highlights the military context as a fertile ground for entrepreneurial exploration, a domain where research is still emerging. Personally, I am excited by this book's contribution for three reasons. First, it pushes the boundaries of entrepreneurial theory, exploring a field that has been largely overlooked but is becoming increasingly relevant in policy discussions. Second, it takes a practice-based approach, interrogating military entrepreneurship and its implications for sustainable nation-building. The meeting point between the military ecosystem and entrepreneurship, while still under-researched, presents a landscape rich with opportunities and inherent tensions – a reality shaped by conditions that are often ambiguous and complex. Third, the book's reconceptualization holds great potential for setting new research agendas. This is particularly significant for scholars interested in entrepreneurship as a process embedded within the power dynamics of society, attracting critical thinkers from military leaders to public officials.

These perspectives are likely to surface both contradictions and gaps in our received wisdom, strengthening existing knowledge while exposing areas for growth. By examining how entrepreneurship and the military ecosystem intersect to address Nigeria's economic and security challenges, this book opens a scholarly path filled with opportunities to challenge norms and inspire new ways of thinking about entrepreneurship. It calls for a renewed intellectual willingness to recalibrate our core assumptions in light of evolving realities.

The chapters in this volume may approach the topic from different angles, but each deepens our appreciation for the dialogue between theory and practice, revealing that much remains to be learned about the shifting landscape of entrepreneurship. The very complexity and diversity of this field, a mixture of eclectic perspectives and relative measures, are not a shortcoming but a sign of scholarly vitality.

This book could not be timelier for Nigeria's quest for sustainable development, a period marked by significant security challenges and stunted economic goals. Yet, there are signs of change. Initiatives such as the Defence Industries Corporation's successful collaborations and innovations in arms manufacturing – most notably, with indigenous firms – demonstrate a growing capacity for self-reliance and domestic industry. These efforts help reduce external dependency and boost national enterprise.

Similarly, the Nigerian Armed Forces Resettlement Centre has trained thousands of service personnel in entrepreneurship, ensuring a smoother transition to civilian life, fostering economic diversity, social cohesion, and national stability. These capacity-building efforts strengthen the civil economy while bolstering the country's broader entrepreneurial landscape.

Budget challenges and increasing security demands have made innovation and self-sufficiency an imperative. While defence allocations remain substantial, currency fluctuations and operational pressures test the limits. Even so, these hurdles catalyse reforms – spurring greater interest in research, development, technology transfer, and talent cultivation, all of which feed into the economy more broadly.

At the heart of this book is a bold and urgent claim: Nigeria's military is not only a guardian of security but also an emerging driver of economic transformation. For too long, the military has been seen chiefly through the prism of defence. Today, it is clear that security and economic progress are inextricably linked, and Nigeria's future prosperity relies on forging even stronger partnerships between military institutions, private enterprise, and entrepreneurial leaders.

Throughout the book, a consistent theme emerges – the growth of an entrepreneurial ecosystem within and around the military sector. Despite pressuring constraints like infrastructure gaps and financing challenges, Nigerian entrepreneurs in the military sector are at the forefront of innovation, building global partnerships and reinforcing Nigeria's competitive standing in fields ranging from manufacturing to cybersecurity. Often, technological advances within the military spread rapidly to civilian sectors, accelerating growth and cross-sector collaboration.

Summarizing the book's chapters is no easy task: the contributors represent a remarkable diversity of expertise and perspectives. Collectively, they extend the frontiers of entrepreneurship research, opening new avenues and introducing emergent themes that demand continuous exploration in this dynamic field.

Importantly, this book does not gloss over the obstacles – corruption, inertia and infrastructural limitations remain stubborn barriers. But it compellingly demonstrates that when military leaders, policymakers and entrepreneurs collaborate, the dividends for national development can be both substantial and transformative.

I extend my congratulations to all contributors and, above all, to the book's editor, Dr Sanya Ojo. Dr Ojo's extensive experience, research and multidisciplinary insight have been instrumental in bringing this volume to fruition. I have long admired his rigour, curiosity and commitment to bridging entrepreneurship, defence, and development studies. His efforts in curating insights from a wide range of experts have ensured that this work addresses not only the 'what' and 'how' but also the crucial 'why' of leveraging the military ecosystem for Nigeria's sustainable growth.

As someone who has witnessed Dr Ojo's academic journey first-hand, I am proud to see his vision realized in this landmark publication. The questions raised and solutions proposed here will, I believe, foster spirited debate, invigorate research and, most importantly, drive practical progress among Nigeria's policy and business leaders. May the insights contained in these pages serve both as inspiration and as a roadmap towards a more secure, innovative and prosperous Nigeria.

Azubuike Sonny Nwankwo
Emeritus Professor, University of East London, UK
Former Academy Provost, Nigerian Defence Academy

Preface

This preface to *The Military Ecosystem and Entrepreneurship in Nigeria: Economic Growth and Security Developments* highlights the growing recognition of the valuable skills and experiences that military personnel bring to the business world, as well as the potential for military organizations and stakeholders to engage in commercial activities for economic and strategic benefits. The military entrepreneurship ecosystem refers to the involvement of military organizations, personnel, veterans and their families in commercial enterprises, both within and outside of the formal military structure.

Military entrepreneurship encompasses a wide range of activities, from businesses owned and managed by military personnel themselves to ventures started by individuals with military experience or affiliation. A military experience can inspire unique business ideas and approaches to problem-solving, potentially leading to entrepreneurship/business startups. Hitherto, entrepreneurship has not only affected individuals but also the conditions for entrepreneurship in the military. As a field, military entrepreneurship is gaining increasing attention due to the unique skills and experiences people connected to the military (e.g. veterans, military spouses, military children and others) bring to the business world, as well as the potential for military units to leverage commercial activities for various purposes.

Nonetheless, entrepreneurship is full of challenges and uncertainties (e.g. entrepreneurs growing and scaling their businesses and accessing capital). Its pace and complexity do not lend themselves to mature thought on important issues. As a result, scholars and professionals who contributed chapters to this volume examine the complexity and central theme of entrepreneurial activities as rooted in the military institutions and relationships. The multiplex nature of military entrepreneurship yields varied, interesting research positions, which can be related to both individual enterprise (veterans, military spouses, and military children starting businesses) and institutional undertaking (military organizations engaging in commercial activities).

Ultimately, this book volume explores the characteristics of commercial ventures within the military ecosystem at the micro and macro levels. Whether at the individual level (micro) or the organizational level (macro), the leverage of military experience or encounter is fundamental to the character of military entrepreneurship. For instance, veterans and military families often possess a unique set of characteristics that can be highly beneficial in entrepreneurial settings. These include resilience, adaptability, strong teamwork and communication skills, a high degree of loyalty and commitment. These qualities are enhanced through the experiences of military life and relationships and can translate well into the challenges and opportunities of running a business. Invariably, the economic and strategic implications of military entrepreneurship can be deciphered in its significant commercial impacts, including job creation, revenue generation, and the development of new businesses. Yet, transitioning from a structured military environment to the more unstructured realm of entrepreneurship can present challenges for military entrepreneurs, but also opens up unique opportunities for innovation and success. Entrepreneurship often involves rapid changes, such as institutional, technical, and economic changes. Hence, the influence of entrepreneurship on institutions, individual empowerment, and its impact on the military is perhaps the most significant topic in military entrepreneurship research.

Altogether, the purpose of this book volume is largely to expound the scope of the field of military entrepreneurship and show how the military background affects businesses and business management in various ways. The contributions to the book volume explore various facets and practices of military entrepreneurship within the wider military ecosystem. The book's approach suggests that a fertile line of enquiry in the evolving field of research at the interface of military entrepreneurship research comprises the routine, everyday macro- and micro-activities and strategies of entrepreneurship within multiple, potentially conflicting logics. This approach holds promise to link diverging fields in the different, yet progressively intersecting spheres within the military entrepreneurship ecosystem. Consequently, this book could facilitate cross-fertilization between studying entrepreneurship as an everyday practice of recombining resources within military contexts in the entrepreneurship literature. As a result, the book is an interrogation of issues in innovative and creative ways that intercept perceived local necessities. Conceptually, it nudges us to consider the business enterprises incorporated in the military in terms of the variety of interconnections within the military ecosystem.

Nonetheless, this book volume does attempt to depict military entrepreneurship in a territorial specificity rather than in a universal formation. Against the background of a renaissance in military entrepreneurship studies, the book volume mainly concentrates on defining and explaining the character of military entrepreneurship in Nigeria more precisely. As such, the adopted approach is focused, rather than universal, on a broader reflection of military entrepreneurship in Nigeria. It is intentionally multi-dimensional to better mirror the diversity within the military ecosystem in Nigeria. Yet invariably, papers in the volume expose the manifold fields of entrepreneurship actions that are crucial for a varied understanding of the nuances underpinning the military entrepreneurship ecosystem, including the application of military resources in commercial ventures.

The book volume has both quantitative and narrative contributions, and the chapters are divided into six sections: overview of the military entrepreneurship landscape; technology and militarization; the social capital of military entrepreneurship; military family entrepreneurship; education and finance matters; and comparative cases/international partnership and alliances. Consequently, the book will facilitate the understanding of the phenomenon of military entrepreneurship as it helps to analyse the motivations, processes and outcomes of military involvement in commercial ventures, both from an individual and organizational perspective. In addition, it enables the exploration of the intersection of security and commerce, sheds light on the complex relationship between military power, economic activity and state formation, and identifies innovative solutions to enterprise conundrums.

The book is designed to fit easily into college curricula that span entrepreneurship, political economics, psychology and other related courses. It is pitched at students of both the undergraduate and postgraduate levels, professionals and scholars of military and security studies. Profound gratitude goes to all the contributing authors to this volume, the reviewer and the supporting staff at Bloomsbury Publishing.

Sanya Ojo (FHEA)
Nigerian Defence Academy, Kaduna, Nigeria

Introduction

The Military Ecosystem and Entrepreneurship in Nigeria: Economic Growth and Security Developments

Sanya Ojo

Background

Entrepreneurship research is a key driver to realizing economic growth and development. Scholarly research, particularly the kind that often falls outside the mainstream of attention, into all facets of entrepreneurial activities within a society's economy, is considered useful for employment and empowerment schemes in any country. Given Nigeria's youth bulge, the country must produce a critical mass of individuals and groups whose primary interest is the well-being of Nigeria and Nigerians themselves. The military's great repository of resourceful human capital in various fields of endeavours, such as business administration, engineering, architecture, logistics management, research and medicine, among others, and its reputation for discipline, ingenuity and innovation could also be part of this critical mass of individuals and groups. The heterogeneity of activities and groups that make up the military-serving personnel, veterans, military families and military-run enterprises provides an opportunity to deeply interrogate the concept of military entrepreneurship in the context of Nigerian economic growth and security development.

Against this backdrop, this book edition is mainly a collection of studies on military-affiliated entrepreneurship, examining the subject from different interpretations of entrepreneurship practices within the military ecosystem in Nigeria. The book is expected to generate and inspire studies that interrogate business enterprise articulations and entrepreneurship apparatuses in Nigeria. The chapters are a potpourri of conceptual, review and empirical papers, and interdisciplinary perspectives in the bid to provide better outcomes in the management of the military entrepreneurship ecosystem and in cross-cultural learning among practitioners, researchers, students and policymakers. Although the book's main theme is on the military entrepreneurship ecosystem, some chapters focus on security and economic topics and the international dimension of military entrepreneurship. These chapters highlight how different components of the military community interrogate business enterprise and hint at how the enterprising military network can help (re)shape socio-economic and political development in society.

Nevertheless, the contentious debate over military involvement in commercial enterprises is underscored throughout the book. On the one hand, it has been argued that military incursion into business/entrepreneurship is beneficial, given that the military officer cadre is endowed with rigour, order, probity, discipline, loyalty and adaptability, all of which are vital components for the effective administration of state institutions. On the other hand, some scholars believe that the military has little background in macroeconomic policy or the professional ethos required to achieve substantial benefits for a country's economic growth. This side of the argument contends that military involvement in business enterprise offers predatory commercial opportunities for military officers. For instance, G. Moyo (2016) concludes that military forays into commerce in Zimbabwe (a country that has had very close ties with Nigeria in the past) are significantly and robustly detrimental to that country's economic development. Also, the Zimbabwe military's unfettered access to mineral resources and other business ventures could be seen in the context of rewards and patronage to keep them on the side of the political establishment (H. Moyo, 2016).

It is pertinent to reiterate that many of the chapters in this book explore different themes, generally using secondary sources. Eventually, their findings and conclusions are drawn from their literature reviews, and they offer recommendations based on these findings.

Contextual Narrative

Several scholars (e.g. Maune, 2023; Mani, 2007; Ojo, 2023) contend that military service provides specific competencies and capabilities that are transferable to entrepreneurship. Competencies such as loyalty, duty, responsibility, selfless service, honour, integrity and personal courage are regarded as the main ingredients of success in entrepreneurship. Moreover, the military is known to possess enhanced problem-solving capacity, better ability to cope with physical difficulties and emotional tensions, enhanced independence, self-confidence and a greater willingness to take responsibility among its cadres. The chapters in this book edition are largely situated within the domains of entrepreneurship, military community, business enterprise leadership and Nigeria's economic growth, as illustrated by four main themes described below.

Military Entrepreneurship

In the literature, the phrase 'military entrepreneurship' appears to be an umbrella term for entrepreneurial activities involving the military establishment, military personnel (serving and retired), and military-affiliated persons (e.g. families of military personnel). In general, military entrepreneurship seems to replicate mainstream (civilian) entrepreneurship in many aspects in which entrepreneurship is defined, e.g. creating, finding opportunities, managing, controlling, and changing (Cunningham and Lischeron, 1991). At the macro level, many of the military establishments in Nigeria spawn off new business enterprises (e.g. manufacturing, farming, construction firms, banking, and many more) that are run and managed like any other civilian-run commercial enterprises. The various military-run enterprises have motives for profit, value stakeholders, growth, etc., like the mainstream enterprises (Ahmad and Seymour, 2008).

Nowadays, the Nigerian military establishments have built commercial ventures all around the country. According to Mani (2007: 591), military engagement in business is closely associated with the state-building process in developing countries in the twentieth century. Besseling (2015) submits that African militaries are broadening their role in the business sector, competing directly with other state-owned enterprises and private companies for the award of publicly tendered contracts.

The military has long been known as an incubator for high-tech firms started by ex-soldiers, with some entrepreneurs using their military knowledge to develop physical tools as well. It is important to note that several start-ups are emerging from the military with spill-over effects on the private sector and civilian life. Several global entrepreneurs are people who retired from the military or have indirect connections to the military. Many start-ups are based on technical innovations that originated in the military. Yet, several military entrepreneurial activities appear to generate what Baumol (1990) refers to as unproductive and destructive entrepreneurship, such as encouraging rent-seeking, illegal and shadow activities, and different forms of corruption.

Military Spouses' Entrepreneurship

Military personnel are assets to a country's national defence and their local communities. Equally, military families are vital to the health and capability of the armed forces and are good neighbours, actively engaged in making their civilian communities great places to live. The unique demands (e.g. constant deployments) of military service mean families must serve and sacrifice along with their service members, and this creates exceptional issues and challenges for the entire military family. These issues and challenges revolve around the economic welfare and well-being of military families arising from the peculiarities of military service. For instance, deployment-induced nomadic living makes it difficult for a military spouse (wife) to hold a steady job and pursue a career. Bello-Utu and DeSocio (2015) discovered that a child coping with the absence of a deployed military parent is profoundly dependent on age. Some families would have to cope with unmet family needs and depleted resources when the breadwinner is the deployed parent.

Hence, for reasons of economic survival, many military wives are opting for self-employment vis-à-vis military wives' entrepreneurship. It is then imperative to understand the nature of this phenomenon. Nevertheless, understanding the relationship between military spouses' business ownership and business outcomes as it relates to the personal characteristics, resources, network and ecosystem of the business owner is a great challenge for researchers.

Barrack Youths' Entrepreneurship

Barrack youths represent a unique subculture in Nigeria. For years, the seeming perception of barracks youths has always been one riddled with negativity. They suffer all kinds of stereotypes. Barracks youths are often wrongly perceived as rascals, miscreants, unruly and never-do-wells. This has often been attributed to the idleness and unemployment of the youths living in either military or paramilitary barracks in Nigeria (Ndace, 2022). A major factor in the plight of the barrack youths has been attributed to the stress that accompanies the absence of fathers who are frequently on deployments by their various military units. According to McFarlane (2009), just as wives' anxiety produced greater effects on the deployed husband, children and families of the deployed military personnel experienced stress. Lincoln and Sweeten (2011) establish that some children of deployed military personnel exhibit resilience, while many continue to cope with the impact of the deployed parent. Also, Lowe et al. (2012) assert that military deployment could impact parent-child relationships. Military children confront a variety of challenges at all stages of deployment. Furthermore, Faber et al. (2008) affirm that families experience three types of ambiguity: ambiguous absence (being physically absent but psychologically present), ambiguous presence (being physically present but psychologically absent), and boundary ambiguity (uncertainty about perceptions concerning family and roles and tasks within family).

In essence, families of deployed service members endure various stressors such as absenteeism of fathers, deviant children, infidelity on the part of either parent, substance abuse, psychological/mental health complications, and many others, at different periods in the deployment cycle. Consequently, the psychological consequences of deployment affect families. For example, families of service members who are deployed face the challenge of worrying about and supporting a loved one for an extended period without knowing if or when they will return (Faber et al., 2008).

Faced with the daunting challenges and increased hardship in the absence of a father (or mother), many barrack youths dig deep within and harness their entrepreneurial skills to survive and develop themselves economically. This entrepreneurship strand has not been adequately researched and presents an interesting research subject for entrepreneurship scholars.

Veteran Entrepreneurship

Retirement from the military service, according to Ojo (2023: 119), 'is not "retirement" in the actual sense of the word as many retired military personnel (veterans) go on to work a second career after leaving the military service'. Veterans can be overwhelmed by the number of adjustments and choices they must make in retirement, as they could suffer a 'selection predicament' because they are new to their present situation. Some veterans, subject to individual peculiarities and the impact of age on self-confidence, may doubt their ability to make the right decisions because there is so much at stake. Others may be unable to muster the energy needed to take pivotal actions and slip into procrastination and decision paralysis (Ojo, 2023). In essence, veterans are often faced with the challenge of building a second career after retirement from the military (Vigoda-Gadot et al., 2010).

Nevertheless, many veterans choose entrepreneurship as a career option in retirement. Veterans are usually highly skilled, qualified and adaptable people, making them effective entrepreneurs who are reliable, ambitious and able to adapt military resources to solve problems (e.g. job creation) in a civilian setting. Veteran entrepreneurs, aside from providing jobs for themselves, create employment for others, thus giving back to the society they once served as military personnel and serving again as civilians. Veteran entrepreneurship has certain peculiarities that underpin its characteristics, which differentiate it from 'civilian' entrepreneurship. It is clear that veteran entrepreneurs bring some of the acquired military skills and experiences into their business enterprises, and these have both positive and negative impacts. Military training supports veteran entrepreneurs in their enterprises, but the difference between the highly structured military environment and the less structured civilian environment creates challenges in organizing veteran entrepreneurship on some occasions. Veterans' military experience could also become an issue in retirement. For instance, Pincus et al. (2005) identified the potential challenges and mental health consequences of wartime deployments on service members and veterans. Even though the skill sets veterans acquired in the military promote veteran entrepreneurship, the same skill set could also create an impediment for an unwary veteran entrepreneur (Ojo, 2023).

General Information on the Book

This comprehensive publication is intended as a corpus of research resources that will form a vital reference base, building on the extant literature in the entrepreneurship, military, military family and military-affiliated enterprise fields. Chapters in the book bring together new thinking and insights into the fields and offer essential resources to researchers, practitioners and policymakers. The book has the potential to provide a vision for progressing and improving learning in entrepreneurship and military-affiliated enterprise matters in countries around the world.

The chapters in the book research and report on entrepreneurship and military enterprise activities in Nigeria as a cynosure of the business activities of the military and military affiliations in the country. The contributors' compilation covers multiple aspects of the entrepreneurship and military framework, utilizes lessons from different perspectives and meets multidisciplinary requirements. In acknowledging the critical roles entrepreneurship plays in the economic growth of any nation, one key accomplishment of the book is the assemblage of multidisciplinary knowledge and expertise of contributors in entrepreneurship practice. Their contributions serve as a catalyst for effective empowerment of the military ecosystem in Nigeria as well as other countries. Another objective is the exploitation of the manifest multidisciplinary competence of contributors to explore and cross-fertilize the core themes of interest: military, entrepreneurship, economy, enterprise and leadership.

Value and Target Audience

The book will undoubtedly be valuable in generating useful conversations on the dynamic processes of entrepreneurship from the contextual lenses of the military ecosystem in Nigeria and elsewhere. The chapters demonstrate a wide variety of intellectual purposes and practice approaches. In many ways, they stretch the theoretical and discursive aspects of military entrepreneurship. Justifiably eclectic, the chapters collectively advance the appreciation of inter-subjective discourses and situated practices in entrepreneurship and enterprise matters.

Researchers, advanced-level students, practitioners, managers and policymakers are the primary target audiences of this book. Other stakeholders, who are interested in the idea of effective entrepreneurial competencies within the military and its affiliations, will also find the book useful.

Organization of Chapters

This book is structured into six sections. Part I contains chapters that give an overview of the military entrepreneurship landscape in Nigeria. A synopsis of each chapter is as follows:

Chapter 1: The Nature of Military Entrepreneurship in the Armed Forces of Nigeria

This chapter focuses on commercial enterprises of the three arms of the Nigerian military (Nigerian Army, Nigerian Navy, and Nigerian Air Force) with the aim of capturing the unique local dynamics that serve as impetus for military entrepreneurship and the attendant socio-economic implications. Issues revolving around management, economic, political and military impacts of military commercial ventures on the Nigerian economy are extracted from various literature sources.

Two strands of military entrepreneurship in Nigeria, namely welfare-oriented ventures and profit-oriented commercial ventures, are identified. Both are structured to compete for prestige, be profit-oriented and promote economic development that can foster social development and cohesion in the services. However, the viability and profitability of many of these ventures are in doubt partly because of weak management, lack of robust accountability and inadequate legislative oversight.

Chapter 2: Military Entrepreneurship in Nigeria: Economic Growth and Security Developments

This chapter explores issues relating to the contributions, prospects and strategies of defence enterprises in Nigeria's economic growth and security developments. The chapter adopts the Resource Dependency Theory, analysing the military's involvement in commercial ventures to bridge resource gaps and ensure national security. The observed issues in defence and security enterprises' networks include resource imperatives, public perception, legal status, and self-reliance, as well as their impact on private-sector growth and competition. The chapter reveals that defence enterprises have contributed significantly to national economic development, creating jobs, enhancing food security and promoting sustainable cities and communities. Key prospects identified for enhancing defence enterprises include unmet national needs, the National Development Plan 2021–2025 and the evolving role of the military in economic affairs.

The chapter concludes that defence enterprises in Nigeria have played a crucial role in shaping the country's economic landscape. Thus, addressing concerns around legal status, governance and transparency is essential to ensure their continued contribution to national economic development. It was therefore recommended that strategies to enhance defence enterprises, which include process optimization, governance optimization and strategic partnerships, should be executed.

Chapter 3: Organizing for Entrepreneurship in the Nigerian Armed Forces: Analysis of Welfare and Commercial Ventures

This chapter draws attention to the increasing occurrence of the Nigerian armed forces taking on roles as owners and managers of economic enterprises that constitute an important source of financial and institutional autonomy from the state and society. By engaging in business activities, the military inevitably introduces profit incentives into its daily operations. Increasingly, the military competes with an unfair advantage to crowd out civilian enterprises in the marketplace. Thus, the armed forces' search for cost savings, efficiencies and quality makes the business case for further outsourcing and privatization more compelling. The armed forces in parts of Africa expect these new relationships to improve their performance by introducing corporate resources and capabilities. Furthermore, the chapter looks at how military enterprises are evolving and how privatization could help meet military needs through recapitalizing programmes that cannot be adequately funded through annual budgets.

Part II has chapters that focus on technology and militarization as depicted below:

Chapter 4: The Role of Artificial Intelligence in Enhancing Defence and Security Enterprise Networks

This chapter explores the integration of artificial intelligence (AI) into Nigeria's defence and security enterprise networks, focusing on its potential to enhance threat detection and response capabilities. As global security challenges grow increasingly complex, AI offers significant opportunities to improve surveillance, cybersecurity and predictive analytics within defence systems. However, the successful implementation of AI in Nigeria faces several challenges, including infrastructural limitations, data quality and privacy concerns, and a shortage of skilled personnel. These challenges are examined alongside the opportunities that AI presents, such as automated decision-making, resource optimization and proactive threat management.

In addition, the chapter highlights the importance of addressing ethical and legal issues associated with AI, particularly concerning autonomous systems and data privacy. By investing in technological infrastructure, enhancing data management practices and developing a skilled workforce, Nigeria can overcome these obstacles and fully realize the benefits of AI integration. The chapter concludes that AI has the potential to significantly strengthen Nigeria's defence and security networks, provided that strategic investments and international collaborations are pursued to address existing challenges. The findings underscore the need for a balanced approach that leverages AI's capabilities while ensuring ethical and responsible use, thereby enhancing national security in an increasingly digital world. This chapter contributes to the broader discourse on the role of AI in national security, offering insights relevant to policymakers, security professionals and AI practitioners in Nigeria and beyond.

Chapter 5: Robotics and Artificial Intelligence in Military Entrepreneurship: A Case Study of the Armed Forces of Nigeria

This chapter focuses on the integration of robotics and artificial intelligence (AI) in military entrepreneurship, which presents a significant opportunity for the Armed Forces of Nigeria to enhance operational effectiveness, self-reliance and economic sustainability. It thus explores how robotics and AI-driven solutions are being deployed within the Armed Forces of Nigeria for various military and non-military applications, fostering indigenous technological advancements and defence entrepreneurship. Case studies highlight ongoing initiatives, challenges and prospects. Additionally, this chapter provides a thorough review of military entrepreneurship, focusing on defence innovation, economic implications and technological advancement.

Chapter 6: The Concepts of Enterprise, Innovation and Entrepreneurship in the Context of the Military Ecosystem

This chapter explores the significance and applicability of three key concepts commonly found in the corporate business world, within the context of the military ecosystem. Rarely is it believed that military personnel should possess and exhibit skills primarily associated with the civilian business world. The chapter emphasizes the applicability of the concepts, regardless of the perception that they are not exactly applicable to the military ecosystem. The applicability of these concepts within the military ecosystem is explored by delving into what each concept implies, taking a quick journey into Nigeria's military ecosystem and examining the views held about these concepts.

The chapter also includes sections that investigate the interconnectedness of these concepts, the transition from military to civilian domains and the reflection of these concepts in the Nigerian military ecosystem in comparison to developed countries. Last, the chapter presents several recommendations for policy reforms and practice enhancements. The anticipated outcomes of the implementation of these suggestions include the emergence of a Nigerian military with a stronger ecosystem for enterprise, innovation and entrepreneurship.

Part III chapters are on the social capital of military entrepreneurship, as listed:

Chapter 7: The Role of Religion and Faith in Military Entrepreneurship

This chapter presents a unique perspective on how religion influences military entrepreneurship, particularly in Africa. It underscores the deep-rooted religious beliefs held by Africans, including those within the military, which significantly impact their actions. Religion is interwoven into every aspect of the defence and security sectors, forming an integral part of the military landscape that encompasses tradition, warfare, the defence community and military entrepreneurship. The concept of spiritual readiness in the military extends beyond merely the ability to conduct combat operations. It includes the overall capability of the armed forces, such as their equipment, personnel, training, preparedness and entrepreneurial initiative.

Chapter 8: Conceptualizing the Warrior Ethos in Military Entrepreneurship

This chapter explores the concept of the warrior ethos in military entrepreneurship through the lens of Clausewitz's trinity of society, state and soldier. It emphasizes the soldier's role in using coercive power to protect the state from external threats, in line with McNamara's security model for state modernization. The chapter argues that the warrior ethos, rooted in the readiness to sacrifice for public security, intersects with entrepreneurial endeavours often driven by profit maximization. It contends that the mental, physical and psychological traits soldiers develop, such as tolerance, selflessness, compassion and courage, are crucial for successful entrepreneurship, particularly in high-risk and uncertain environments.

Part IV chapters are on themes of military family entrepreneurship as indicated below:

Chapter 9: Military Spouses' (Wives) Entrepreneurship

The chapter looks at the entrepreneurial activities of military spouses, which often result from the transient lifestyle of military life and its demands. This lifestyle induces military spouses, particularly wives, to pursue entrepreneurial activities and business ventures that serve their various interests, skills and people's needs within the military base. The chapter, through a case study methodology, examines the entrepreneurial endeavours of military spouses (wives) at the Nigerian Air Force base, Kaduna. Examining the motivations, the challenges and support systems that influence and impact their business ventures. Findings show that entrepreneurship offers military spouses (wives) a pathway to financial independence and community contribution. The chapter concludes that military spouses' (wives') entrepreneurship greatly enhances the personal and economic well-being of military families. It recommends providing more business opportunities through offering financial support and organizing training and mentorship programmes on entrepreneurship, to help maintain, grow and overcome challenges in their entrepreneurial activity within the Nigerian Air Force base, Kaduna.

Chapter 10: Empowering the Barrack Boys Through Entrepreneurship in Nigeria

This chapter is interested in the ordeal of young men who reside in barracks, particularly their limited access to education, property and business in Nigeria. The chapter examines the determinants of barrack boy entrepreneurship with respect to skill development, access to resources and guidance. Results show that while training schools have been recording enhanced skill development and management of money, access limitations on long-term resources hinder the entrepreneurial successes of the barrack boys in Nigeria. The chapter concludes that the empowerment of barrack boys through business entails a comprehensive process incorporating skill formation, provision of resources and continuous mentorship. The central recommendation is the establishment of long-term funding arrangements in mentorship programmes to foster sustainability and participation of these future entrepreneurs and coordinate the vision of training institutions, resource persons and youths to long-term success.

Chapter 11: Military Family Lifestyle, Military Spouse Career Progression and Readiness: A Nigerian Perspective

This chapter examines how military family lifestyle affects military spouse career progression, and how that can contribute to the state of readiness of the Nigerian armed forces to counter and defeat present and future threats to Nigeria's national security. It relies on secondary data using previous research and published works, but also benefited from discussion and interaction with military families in Kaduna, mainly, who have experienced the problem under discussion. The argument is made in the chapter that military spouses, by their affiliation with the military, do face adverse challenges of family and work. Also, at work, the career progression of military spouses is stunted. Therefore, the military should do all within its power to protect career spouses seeking to secure and retain jobs within the context of the demands of the military profession.

Part V chapters focus on the themes of education and Finance matters.

Chapter 12: Veteran Entrepreneurship Training in Nigeria: A Review and Future Research Directions

This chapter provides a review of veteran entrepreneurship as well as entrepreneurship training, job creation and veteran empowerment in the Nigerian military through the lens of the Nigerian Armed Forces Resettlement Centre. The chapter applies qualitative and analytical approaches and typically obtains data from secondary sources, including journal articles, books, monographs and institutional records. Entrepreneurship training for veterans is recognized as a valuable vehicle for setting retiring/retired military personnel on a solid foundation for entrepreneurial success. However, the entrepreneurship training must be carefully rejigged to provide value for the veteran entrepreneurs for whom it was designed.

Chapter 13: Impact of Monetary Policy on Entrepreneurial Financing in Nigeria

This chapter uses annual data to investigate the impact of monetary policy on entrepreneurial financing in Nigeria over the period from 1990 to 2023. Data obtained from the Central Bank of Nigeria Statistical Bulletin were analysed using the autoregressive distributed lag (ARDL) model. Findings reveal that monetary policy impacts entrepreneurial financing in Nigeria both in the short run and in the long run. However, the estimates are significant only in the long run. Results show that lending rate and monetary policy rate have negative impacts on entrepreneurial financing, both in the short and long run. However, broad money supply has a positive impact on entrepreneurial financing in both the short and long run. The chapter, therefore, concludes that entrepreneurial financing is enhanced when there is enough liquidity available in the economy. Based on the findings, the chapter recommends that the monetary authorities keep the monetary policy rate and lending rate as low as possible in order to encourage entrepreneurs to borrow more for investment in Nigeria. Also, expansionary monetary policy should be used to inject more money into the economy.

Part VI has two chapters on comparative cases/international partnerships/alliances issues.

Chapter 14: Military Entrepreneurship in India and Nigeria: A Comparative Review and Future Research Agenda

Against the background of the British colonial experiences shared by India and Nigeria, this chapter explores the connections and complementarities between the Nigerian and Indian military establishments and their military entrepreneurship arrangements. This complementarity is appraised in the chapter through an assessment of military entrepreneurship formation and practices in both countries' military establishments. Attention is also paid to issues such as the contextual parallel between the military entrepreneurship of both countries and the influence the national culture of each country has on their entrepreneurship cultures. A comprehensive literature review of military entrepreneurship in both countries is undertaken to interrogate these issues. Findings highlight challenges around military entrepreneurship in both countries, and recommendations are offered to confront those challenges.

Chapter 15: War Entrepreneurship: Analysing the Wagner Group's Military Activities in Africa

The chapter appraises the concept of war entrepreneurship through the lens of the Wagner Group, a private military contractor, operations in Africa. This is done within the overlapping network of businesses and private military forces. Primary data are collated from research articles published in scholarly journals, the internet and newspaper sources. Findings elaborate on the main themes of war entrepreneurship and geopolitics in war and conflict areas in some parts of Africa. The implications unravelled to suggest that war entrepreneurship activities embedded in Wagner's services to state clients in Africa generate unproductive and destructive entrepreneurship that activates the weakening of the military forces, human rights abuses, plundering of resources and state capture of the clients.

Summary

The chapters in this book have been carefully picked to expand the field of military entrepreneurship. The book aspires to enhance current research on the nature, process and outcomes of military entrepreneurship and military entrepreneurs' economic activities in different contexts, backgrounds and ontological directions. The significance resides in its capacity to broaden our knowledge of the military entrepreneurship ecosystem within the Nigerian socio-economic and political contexts.

References

Ahmad, N., and R.G. Seymour (2008). 'Defining Entrepreneurial Activity: Definitions Supporting Frameworks for Data Collection', OECD Statistics Working Paper STD/ DOC (2008): 1, 5–6.

Baumol, W. (1990). 'Entrepreneurship: Productive, Unproductive, and Destructive', *Journal of Political Economy*, 98(5): 893–921.

Bello-Utu, C.F., and J.E. DeSocio (2015). 'Military Deployment and Reintegration: A Systematic Review of Child Coping', *J Child Adolesc Psychiatr Nurs.*, 28(1): 23–34. Available at: https://doi.org/10.1111/jcap.12099.

Besseling, R. (2015). 'African Militaries Expand Role in Business Sector'. SPGlobal. Available at: https://www.spglobal.com/marketintelligence/en/mi/research-analysis/q22-african-militaries-expand-role-in-business-sector.html

Cunningham, J.B., and J. Lischeron (1991). 'Defining Entrepreneurship', *Journal of Small Business Management*, 29: 45–61.

Faber, A.J., E. Willerton, S.R. Clymer, S.M. MacDermid and H.M. Weiss (2008). 'Ambiguous Absence, Ambiguous Presence: A Qualitative Study of Military Reserve Families in Wartime', *Journal of Family Psychology*, 22(2): 222–30. Available at: https://doi.org/10.1037/0893-3200.22.2.222

Lincoln, A.J., and K. Sweeten (2011). 'Considerations for the Effects of Military Deployment on Children and Families', *Soc Work Health Care*, 50(1): 73–84. Available at: https://doi.org/10.1080/00981389.2010.513921.

Lowe, K.N., K.S. Adams, B.L. Browne and K.T. Hinkle (2012). 'Impact of Military Deployment on Family Relationships', *Journal of Family Studies*, 18(1): 17–27. Available at: https://doi.org/10.5172/jfs.2012.2003

Mani, K. (2007). 'Militaries in Business: State-Making and Entrepreneurship in the Developing World', *Armed Forces & Society*, 33(4): 591–611.

Maune, A. (2023). 'Role of Military in the Entrepreneurial Ecosystem'. Newsday. Available at: https://www.newsday.co.zw/theindependent/opinion-analysis/article/200011603/role-of-military-in-the-entrepreneurial-ecosystem

McFarlane, A. (2009). 'Military Deployment: The Impact on Children and Family Adjustment and the Need for Care', *Current Opinion in Psychiatry*, 22(4): 369–73. Available at: https://doi.org/10.1097/YCO.0b013e32832c9064

Moyo, G. (2016). 'The Curse of Military Commercialism in State Enterprises and Parastatals in Zimbabwe', *Journal of Southern African Studies*, 42(2): 351–64. Available at: https://doi.org/10.1080/03057070.2016.1145981

Moyo, H. (2016). 'Should Military Be Involved in Business?' Zimbabwe Situation. Available at: https://www.zimbabwesituation.com/news/zimsit-m-should-military-be-involved-in-business-the-zimbabwe-independent/

Ndace, J.B. (2022). 'COAS, NAOWA and Future of Barracks Youths'. Blueprint. Available at: https://blueprint.ng/coas-naowa-and-future-of-barracks-youths/

Ojo, S. (2023). 'Exploring Veteran Entrepreneurship in Nigeria', *Journal of Enterprising Communities: People and Places in the Global Economy*, 17(3): 644–63. Available at: https://doi.org/10.1108/JEC-10-2021-0148

Pincus, S., R. House, J. Christenson and L. Adler (2005). 'The Emotional Cycle of Deployment: A Military Family Perspective', *US Army Medical Department Journal*, 4(5): 6–15.

Vigoda-Gadot, E., Y. Baruch and S. Grimland (2010). 'Career Transitions: An Empirical Examination of Second Career of Military Retirees', *Public Personnel Management*, 39(4): 379–404.

Part I

Overview of the Military Entrepreneurship Landscape in Nigeria

1

The Nature of Military Entrepreneurship in the Armed Forces of Nigeria

Sanya Ojo

This chapter examines the characteristics and motives of military entrepreneurship in Nigeria by illuminating the features of military commercial enterprises and the impact on the Nigerian economy, civil-military relations and the overall defence capabilities of armed forces. In other words, the chapter focuses on registered business enterprises of the three arms of the Nigerian military (Nigerian Army, Nigerian Navy and Nigerian Air Force), intending to capture the unique local dynamics that serve as an impetus for military entrepreneurship, and the attendant socio-economic implications.

Military involvement in commercial activities, otherwise known as military entrepreneurship, is common in many societies, both developing and developed. Mani (2011: 29) described military entrepreneurship as 'the innovative creation of resources and new means of production by commissioned military officers acting in an institutional capacity as formal owners, managers, and stakeholders of enterprises that generate financial resources or goods directly benefiting the military'. Accordingly, military participation in commercial activities comes in two formats. The first, often practised in developed economies, is through the privatization of security, which involves privileged members of the military offering services such as training or weapons production to generate profit that is shared with the investors who provide capital for the venture. The other format, often prevalent in developing economies, is military engagement in business ventures (e.g. farming, hotels, airlines, banks or real estate agencies). These are neither non-conventional roles nor related traditional functions (e.g. security), which the military is set up to perform. These two types of military commercial venturing are differentiated, not just by the volume of financial dividends earned but also by the extent of penetration of the military in its society and economy. Furthermore, the first type is conducted abroad, but the second type takes place in the military homeland (Siddiqa, 2007).

Military commercial enterprise structures and manifestations differ from country to country. For example, military business in central Africa is usually on an individual basis rather than on a collective basis. Individual soldiers engage in illegal activities to supplement their meagre incomes (Brömmelhörster and Paes, 2003). In some countries (e.g. the USA, the UK, France, Israel and South Africa), military entrepreneurship is operated in partnership with the civilian corporate sector and the government. In other places (e.g. Iran, Cuba and China), military entrepreneurship is manifested through partnership with the dominant ruling party or individual leader, and in countries such as Turkey, Indonesia, Pakistan, Myanmar and Thailand, the military is the sole driver of military business enterprise. In this last category, military entrepreneurial activity is caused by the military's involvement in politics (Siddiqa, 2007). The Russian military is involved in many sectors of the economy, stretching from transportation to health care, and later expanding into new sectors, such as the sale of surplus weapons, insurance and marketing. The Egyptian military owns business enterprises that are in almost every industry and produces a vast range of services and goods. The military in Egypt operates hotels, sea resorts, apartment buildings and luxurious villas. It owns cement, steel, Jeep, fertilizer, home appliances, pasta and other factories; runs gas stations; and constructs toll highways. Moreover, ex-generals occupy the top civilian positions in the state's administrative apparatus in control of key sectors, from public transportation systems to water and sewerage services, Internet lines, social housing projects and more (Abul-Magd, 2015). The military business in Pakistan is vast and highly intertwined with the country's economy (Ojo, 2021). The Pakistani military owns 12 per cent of Pakistan's fertile land, with two-thirds of that land in the hands of senior serving and retired officers (Siddiqa, 2007). The deficit in budgetary allocation incentivized the Indonesian military to engage in entrepreneurship as a source of income. Though this has provided some benefits, it has also weakened accountability and professionalism. Moreover, military establishments operate a system of 'welfare organizations', which are in the form of businesses run by the organizations and often used to divert resources earmarked for the armed forces to survive in the market.

In general, military entrepreneurship can be interrogated along a broad spectrum of positive and negative effects. The cases of Egypt and Israel readily come to mind when interrogating the mixed fortune of military entrepreneurship, as both are at the ends of the spectrum. First, it is estimated that the Egyptian military controls 25–40 per cent of Egypt's economy. Military-run firms gain competitive advantages from having a ready supply of free labour (in the form of conscripts) and having other exceptional rights granted to them by law, most importantly, the right to acquire public land. Yet, military production is non-competitive because it is forced to sell its products to government agencies. For instance, some public universities are compelled to buy food products from the army (Naguib, 2012). The reliance of military business on compulsory drafting causes many youths in their prime to be deployed to military firms to work as forced labour for free. This also has a knock-on damaging effect on the Egyptian economy. Workers in military-run factories, farms and service enterprises are also deprived of basic rights (Naguib, 2012). Military-owned firms in Egypt also enjoy tax and other advantages granted to military-owned firms. For example, the military and other security institutions were given exemptions in the value-added-tax (VAT) law enacted in 2016 as part of reforms inspired by the International Monetary Fund (IMF) (Reuters, 2018). In 2017, the IMF expressed a concern that private sector development and job creation 'might be hindered by involvement of entities under the Ministry of Defence' (Reuters, 2018).

Second, Israel has emerged as a start-up nation, or innovation nation, due to numerous start-ups and the innovation ecosystem created by the military. The

Israeli military is noted for the establishment of many high-tech firms by ex-military personnel, and several of these start-ups have spillover effects on Israel's overall economy. As expected, most Israeli technology firms trading on the NASDAQ are either founded by a military officer or have alumni serving in key military units (Avin, 2021; Komash, 2020).

Military entrepreneurship (in one form or the other) in Nigeria has been examined in a few studies (e.g. Madichie and Ayasi, 2018; Ojo, 2021; Ojo, 2023; Iroegbu, 2023; Olawuyi and Amakom, 2023). The Nigerian military establishment, as embedded in the Armed Forces of Nigeria (AFN), engages in commercial activities through the services (i.e. the Nigerian Army, the Nigerian Navy and the Nigerian Air Force). This chapter investigates their entrepreneurial modus operandi and seeks to answer two essential questions: (1) What is the rationale behind the establishment of business enterprises by the services in the AFN? (2) What are the implications of military entrepreneurship on the Nigerian economy? While addressing these questions, insights from the existing literature that has developed theoretical frameworks in the analysis of military business were harvested from many reputable resources such as academic journals, books, newspaper reports, professional papers, case studies, internet sources and many more.

In this paper, some contiguous concepts and expressions were applied interchangeably just to keep in line with the literature from which they are extracted. Concepts like military entrepreneurship and military commercial enterprises/ventures are used as such. The study is structured into five parts. This introduction constitutes the first part, while the second outlines the contextual framework. The third and fourth parts probe the conceptual background and the analysis/discussion, respectively. The last part provides the summary and implications.

Contextual Outline

In this section, a summary of the background of each arm of the AFN is given. The AFN represent the military forces of Nigeria, consisting of three service branches: the Nigerian Army (NA), Nigerian Navy (NN) and Nigerian Air Force (NAF). The president of Nigeria functions as the commander-in-chief of the armed forces, exercising his constitutional authority through the Ministry of Defence, which is responsible for the management of the military and its personnel. The operational head of the AFN is the Chief of Defence Staff (CDS), who is subordinate to the Nigerian Defence Minister. According to Global Firepower, the AFN are the most powerful military in sub-Saharan Africa, the third-most powerful military in Africa, and ranked 31st on its list, internationally (GlobalFirePower, 2025).

The Nigerian Army (NA)

The NA is the largest among the AFN, and its history dates back to 1863, when Lt Glover of the Royal Navy drafted eighteen indigenes from Northern Nigeria and organized them into a local force, known as the 'Glover Hausas'. The force later underwent a series of metamorphoses from ‘Hausa Constabulary’ to ‘Lagos Constabulary’ to ‘Royal West African Frontier Force (RWAFF)’ to ‘the Queen’s Own Nigerian Regiment (QONR)’ to the Nigerian Military Force (NMF) in 1956 and the Royal Nigerian Army in 1960. The NA, as of 2019, consists of 223,000 enlisted personnel (Dike, 2023), and it is the largest in West Africa. The NA is often headed by a general and is addressed as the Chief of Army Staff (COAS). The NA is functionally structured into combat arms (infantry and armoured); combat support arms (artillery, engineers, and signals); combat support services (medical, supply and transport, ordinance and finance). Others include the military police, intelligence, physical training, chaplains, public relations and band. Also, the Training and Doctrine Command (TRADOC) oversees doctrinal, training and combat development with an R&D outfit. There are seventeen Corps Training Schools and an NA College of Logistics (NACOL) (GlobalSecurity.org, 2025).

The Nigerian Navy (NN)

The Naval Defence Force (NDF), which was the precursor of the NN was officially established in 1956 even though its origin could be traced to the Marine Department of the Royal Navy established in 1887 (a quasi-military organization), which combined the duties of the present-day Nigerian Ports Authority (NPA), the Nigerian Inland Waterways Authority and the NN. The NN is presently organized into eleven branches at the naval headquarters, six commands and several autonomous units. The six commands are made up of three operational commands – Western Naval Command, Central Naval Command and Eastern Naval Command, with headquarters located at Apapa, Yenagoa and Calabar, Naval Training Command with headquarters at Onne, as well as the Logistics and Naval Doctrine Commands with headquarters at Oghara and Lagos respectively. Additionally, the NN autonomous units include the Naval Ordnance Depot (NOD), Naval Doctrine and Assessment Centre (NDAC) and Navy Holdings Limited (NHL) (Nigerian Navy, 2024). The NN is headed by a rear admiral and titled Chief of Naval Staff (CNS).

The Nigerian Air Force (NAF)

The NAF was formally established on 18 April 1964 with the passage of the Air Force Act 1964 and received technical assistance from Germany (Nigerian Air Force, 2011). The NAF is usually headed by an air marshal and designated Chief of Air Staff (CAS). NAF includes a service headquarters, seven principal staff branches, four direct reporting units and four operational commands. The seven staff branches formulate policies, including Policy and Plans, Training and Operations, Aircraft Engineering, Logistics and Communications, Administration, Standards and Evaluations and Air Secretary. Each staff branch is headed by a branch chief, who is directly responsible to the CAS. The NAF’s four commands include the Tactical Air Command (in Makurdi), Mobility Command (in Yenagoa), Training Command (in Kaduna), and Logistics Command (in Lagos) (Nigerian Air Force, 2011).

Conceptual Background

This section appraises the different concepts employed in this paper, including military entrepreneurship, consequences of military entrepreneurship and military entrepreneurship in Nigeria.

Military Entrepreneurship

The concept of military business enterprise is not a new one (Brömmelhörster and Paes, 2003), and it is firmly rooted in military history and continually expressed in the contemporary era in the form of the state-building process, particularly in developing countries (Mani, 2007). For instance, in countries such as Pakistan, Indonesia, Turkey, Egypt and Ethiopia, the military has built multi-billion-dollar business empires (Abebe, 2018). Two strands of conceptualization are evidenced in the literature of military entrepreneurship. The first relates to the positive effects of the military involvement in entrepreneurship (i.e. commercial enterprise) and the second considers the negative impacts of military entrepreneurship.

The motives behind the military engagement in commercial ventures, which is a clear departure from its main mandate of protecting the state and its people, could be linked to a variety of factors that range from personal selfishness and gratification to a desire to contribute to the economic development of the country. Nevertheless, researchers (e.g. Siddiqa, 2007) generally agree that the raison d'être for military incursion into business and commercial activities is neither linear nor simple. Meanwhile, Brömmelhörster and Paes (2003: 4) refer to a multiplicity of factors by observing that military entrepreneurship is 'a complex combination of material, ideological and political factors'.

Material factors implicate the often-imbalanced relationship between the budgetary needs of the military and the budget allocation from the government. Budgetary allocation for defence/military expenditure, especially in developing countries, is barely enough to cater for military needs. Budgetary deficit could be further exacerbated by the constantly changing geopolitical contexts. The difficult task of allocating resources among competing needs (e.g. military spending and education/health care) is always a source of frustration for governments, particularly in developing countries. In such a situation, military commercial enterprises are avenues to rake in money to fill the gaps in budgetary allocation. Thus, opting for off-budgetary means such as military entrepreneurship becomes imperative (Brömmelhörster and Paes, 2003). Furthermore, personal economic considerations also provide impetus for military commercial activities. According to Siddiqa (2007), the military capital derived from military business is used for the personal benefit of the military fraternity, particularly the officer cadre, but is outside the defence budget. Siddiqa (2007) also contends that military commercial enterprising diverts resources from the public sector to individuals or groups of people linked with the top stratum of the military. Although the prevalence and predatory nature of military business vary considerably across different locations, personal greed remains one material factor at the heart of the emergence of military entrepreneurship in many countries.

Ideology underpins the military doctrine and its role in society (Mani, 2010). Consequently, the military is usually at the forefront of the struggle to develop through industrialization and economic transformation in many developing societies. The military's reputation for advanced technical skills in modern technologies, high discipline and effective organizational culture positioned the military to be in pole position to lead development initiatives (Prina, 2017). This is especially true in countries that practice state-led economic ideology, such as when China used its military during the transitional period from a socialist to a market-oriented economy (Lee, 2006).

Political factors are also adduced as responsible for the military commercial engagement. Prina (2017) argues that political elites encourage military entrepreneurship as a means of keeping the military 'busy' – a kind of material invention to distract them from getting involved in politics. According to the author: 'Military commercial enterprises are the result of political activity by political leaders to limit the likelihood of the most disruptive military behaviour in politics: the coup d'état' (Prina, 2017: 3). Civilians have little control over the military in most fledgling developing societies' democracy, hence, the threat from the military is attenuated by allowing the military to engage and prosper in entrepreneurship. This is, in fact, one of the reasons why military entrepreneurship easily flourishes in non-democratic settings (Abebe, 2018).

Although several reasons have been adduced for military engagement in entrepreneurship, Abul-Magd (2015) refer to a few common factors identified in military entrepreneurship. These factors include (a) the access the military has to material and human resources that are not available to civilians and which enable them to carry out other tasks; (b) the military usually engages in commercial enterprise to fill the deficit in defence budgets; (c) weak state and poor civilian oversight and control of the military encourage the military high command to commence commercial ventures; (d) the origins of some military enterprises can be traced back to measures taken for insurgent forces to be self-sufficient; and (e) even in the absence of security threats, downsizing of the armed forces is difficult to achieve and militaries are consequently used in secondary roles (Abul-Magd, 2015).

Consequences of Military Entrepreneurship

The consequences of military entrepreneurship have been interrogated in climes such as China, Pakistan, Turkey and Egypt (e.g. Mulvenon, 2001; Siddiqa, 2007; Marshall, 2015). Many of these studies reveal both positive and negative ramifications of military entrepreneurship. Insights from studies into commercial enterprises run by military establishments in various countries around the world show that the armed forces in several Central American countries own or control large numbers of business ventures that enjoy political protection and have weak legislative control, but there is increasing awareness that military entrepreneurship is problematic (Mani, 2007). For instance, it is commonly accepted that Indonesian military involvement in commercial enterprise is harmful as it undermines civilian control over the armed forces, encourages human rights abuses and promotes corruption (Human Rights Watch, 2007). Like in many other countries, the Iranian military (guards) entrepreneurship is marred by corruption and its stranglehold on the Iranian economy (Bozorgmehr, 2017). The Chinese military business complex used to have preferential access to resources and infrastructure, which created problems for the liberalization of the economy, thus prompting the government to reduce the military business empire in the 1990s (Rathi, 2024). Likewise, Mani (2007) indicates the negative repercussions of military entrepreneurship on military professionalism, market economy and democracy. Ojo (2021) distils both the positive and negative consequences of military entrepreneurship as shown in Table 1.1:

Table 1.1 Consequences of Military Entrepreneurship

Advantages of Military Entrepreneurship	Disadvantages of Military Entrepreneurship
Economic Stimulation – contributes to the national economy through employment and research & development (R&D).	**Weakens Military Professionalism** – undermines military professionalism.
Spillover Effects – stimulates spillover effects in the informal sector.	**Incite Shadow Economy** – encourages a 'black economy' and loss of tax revenue.
Entrepreneurial Skills – provides entrepreneurial skills and training for members.	**Promote Corruption** – Incites corruption and official malfeasance.
Welfare Packages – delivers welfare benefits for veterans and serving members.	**Crowding out Civilian Investment** – crowds out civil commercial enterprises.
Stimulate Efficiency – inspires proficiency and disciplined enterprise organizing and structuring.	**Encourage Externalities** – exploits labour and promotes 'public bads' (e.g. prostitution, racketeering).
Promote Civil-Military Relationships – facilitates military–civilian interface and association.	**Anti-competition** – stifles competition in the economy.
Pathway to Innovation – provides an avenue for creativity and innovation in the military.	**Suppression of Democracy** – subverts the democratic process in some countries.
Provides Extra-budgetary income – source for financial allocation not approved in the annual budget to fill financial gaps in the military.	**Diminish Government Control** – reduces the 'power of the purse', undermining the authority of elected officials to oversee the military via budgetary allocation.
Boosts Inter-governmental Cooperation – through arms sales and joint ventures in arms production.	**Interrupt Global Peace** – disturbs world peace through arms sales to warring parties around the globe.
Technology Transfer – military enterprises often pioneer technologies (e.g. aviation, telecommunications, cybersecurity) that spill over into civilian use.	**Conflict of Interest** – blurs the line between defence priorities and profit motives, potentially misaligning national security with commercial interests.

Advantages of Military Entrepreneurship	Disadvantages of Military Entrepreneurship
National Security Support – revenue from military enterprises can help reduce dependence on foreign arms imports, supporting self-reliance in defence.	**Erosion of Civil-Military Relations** – increased economic power may lead to military overreach in politics and governance.
Crisis Response Capacity – military-owned logistics and supply chains can be mobilized quickly during emergencies or disasters.	**Accountability Challenges** – military businesses may operate with less transparency and weaker oversight than civilian firms.
Capacity Building – provides continuous training and development opportunities for personnel, improving both military readiness and employability post-service.	**Inefficiency and Waste** – some enterprises may become monopolistic and underperform due to a lack of competition, wasting public resources.
Foreign Exchange Earnings – arms exports and defence-related services can bring in foreign exchange, boosting the national balance of payments.	**Dependence Risk** – over-reliance on military enterprises may discourage private sector development and innovation.

Source: Author's Literature Review (2025).

Military Entrepreneurship in Nigeria

This section focuses on welfare and commercial ventures formed by the components of the AFN to interrogate military entrepreneurship in Nigeria. Each arm of the AFN, comprising the NA, NN and NAF, engages in various commercial enterprises. However, these enterprises can be classified into two distinct categories, namely welfare and business ventures. The need to improve personnel welfare and to profit financially were some of the reasons that made the AFN get involved in commercial ventures. According to Bashir (2013), these multi-dimensional business enterprises have motivated personnel and cemented civil-military relations because they are being carried out in conjunction with civilians. Each of the services of the AFN has established a body to oversee the accomplishment of its commercial ventures to avoid duplication of duty and guarantee efficiency. The NA has established the Army Welfare Holdings (AWHL) and registered it with the Corporate Affairs Commission (CAC) as a company to administer all other ventures. The NN has the Nigerian Navy Holdings Limited, while the NAF established the Nigerian Air Force Holdings Company (NAFHC) (Bashir, 2013). However, it must be noted that the military business in Nigeria could be classified into two broad categories, welfare ventures and commercial ventures. The former is supposed to be non-profit, while the latter is for-profit. However, both categories are profit-oriented in practice. There is a thin line between welfare schemes and commercial ventures in terms of scope and objectives. Ostensibly, the Nigerian military's commercial ventures are established for profit-making reasons, while welfare schemes are gratuitous in nature and outlook.

According to Iroegbu (2023), military organizations that are established for welfare purposes sell at a margin fairly above the cost of production or break-even point. The core objective of military welfare organizations (e.g. schools, hospitals, housing, etc.) is to cater to the immediate needs of the rank and file of the armed forces. For example, the various housing schemes are aimed at providing accommodation to officers and personnel at subsidized rates. Schools (primary and secondary) are originally set up to cater for children of military personnel at the various barracks/bases, particularly bases that do not have local community schools. The military schools were to be situated a few miles away from the barracks/bases. Likewise, opening a medical unit is based on identified needs, which consider the number of military personnel and their families that do not have access to healthcare facilities in the area (Iroegbu, 2023).

The avenues through which most military commercial ventures are executed are recorded in some key major revenue-generating commercial interests, including education, hospitality, health centres, real estate and others. In education, all three arms of the AFN have founded various schools from primary to secondary (command schools) to tertiary institutions (e.g. army, naval and air force universities in Nigeria). According to Iroegbu (2023), military schools such as the army day secondary schools, air force secondary schools and command secondary or primary schools were to be located some 5–10 kilometres from the barracks, particularly in areas where there are no existing local community schools. This is purely to serve children and wards of soldiers living in the barracks, and an allowance of 20–30 per cent allotments for the local community as part of the military's Corporate Social Responsibility (CSR) is factored in. However, in practice, there is a proliferation of military schools purely for commercial purposes, and some are even situated completely outside the barracks. These schools are funded with government money, but they still get free or subsidized services from personnel (e.g. teachers, guards) and utility bills paid for from military budgeted sources. This put the military schools at an enviable advantage compared to private schools, where proprietors pay for teachers, power, water and every other expense from their pockets.

In the hospitality sector, all the tri-services of the AFN have one form of hospitality venture or another. These include the NAF clubs and command guest houses, which are meant for the members of the AFN. It was argued in Iroegbu (2023) that these military hospitality institutions are now increasing in numbers and could potentially run their private competitors out of business without necessarily contributing much to the economy in an accountable way. They can afford to charge highly subsidized rates, far below the market value, for their rooms and other services because it is the military officers and personnel who are ordinarily employed to serve in the military that are being made to work (e.g. administrative, guard duty and other jobs) in these hospitality outfits. In the real estate sector, the military services are actively engaged in property business and real-estate development. Even though the primary purpose of various housing schemes is to provide accommodation for their officers and personnel at subsidized rates, these are increasingly being built with civilians as potential buyers and at a highly lucrative rate. The AFN's real estate projects have become a money-making enterprise. Likewise, all the services have their medical centres. Like the rules that guide the establishment of schools at bases/barracks, opening a medical unit is supposed to be based on identified needs – that is, how many officers, soldiers and their families are in an area that does not have healthcare facilities. Primarily, medical centres are not established for making money, as is the case today (Iroegbu, 2023). Other commercial ventures operated by the military include catering and events management, private guards' firms, gas stations, water-making factories and engineering companies, among others. By and large, the AFN's commercial ventures are profit-oriented, positioned to generate internally generated revenue (IGR) as their counterparts in other armies in many parts of the world.

A common thread in all the military commercial ventures is the management cadre that always has serving military officers seconded to manage those business units. Often, selection may not be based on capacity but on other considerations such as cronyism. However, more detrimental is the issue of tenure, which is not stable due to the constant deployment of personnel. Military postings are regular exercises carried out within the military to bolster the system for greater performance. In the Nigerian military, the length of postings ranges between six months and two years, depending on the mission (Tade, 2021). In such a situation, a chief executive of a military commercial entity may not be able to initiate or maintain a consistent business policy that could have a long-term benefit to the organization. It is also observed that most of these business units do not publish their accounts, and their websites are not adequately maintained or are even non-existent in many cases, such that their activities are shrouded in mystery. The opaqueness of most military enterprises' security (e.g. Brömmelhörster and Paes, 2003) allows military officers to use their privileged position to influence the mechanisms of the redistribution of economic resources and the pursuit of rents that have an indirect impact on the private sector economy and the state. As Iroegbu (2023) puts it, this is like a case of stealing from the government or using the money allocated for other projects, programmes and procurement purposes that are being re-channelled (sometimes illegally) to these ventures (military commercial entities). The implication is that other aspects of defence and security suffer from regular complaints that the money is never enough for internal security operations.

Some businesses under the aegis of military entrepreneurship in Nigeria are discussed below.

The NA, being the largest and the oldest of the three arms of the AFN, has more commercial ventures, and the other two services tend to emulate or replicate its actions. The Nigerian Army, under the umbrella of AWHL, operates the following business entities: Directorate of Non-Public Funds (DNPF), Nigerian Army Properties Limited (NAPL) Group, Post-Service Housing Development Limited (PHDL), Command Guest House (CGH) Limited and the Nigerian Army Drug Manufacturing Company (NADMACO) Limited. Others include Command Guest House (CGH) Limited, Nigerian Army Farm and Ranches Limited (NAFARL), ST Foods Limited, Nigerian Army Vehicle Manufacturing Company (NAVMC), Nigerian Army Post Exchange (NAPEX) Supermarket, Nigerian Army Shopping Arena and the Central Engineering Depot (CED). Additional business ventures that were also established are the Nigerian Army Driving School (NADS), Nigerian Army Green Security (NAGS) Limited, Sappers Engineering Nigeria Limited (SENL), Nigerian Army Pronto Technical Company (NAPTC), Nigerian Army Ordnance Tailoring Factory (NAOTF) and Buffalo Engineering Technical Services Ltd (BETSL).

The Nigerian Navy Holdings includes nine subsidiary companies. These include Naval Dockyard Limited (NDL), Naval Shipyard Limited (NSYL), Naval Building & Construction Company Limited (NBCCL), Navy Hotels & Suites Limited (NHSL), Navy Micro Finance Bank Limited (NMFBL), Navy Maritime Services Limited (NMSL), Naval Exchange (NAVEX), Naval Engineering Services Limited (NESL) and Navy Clearing and Forwarding Services Limited (NCFSL). The autonomous units and support facilities enable the NN to maintain the fleet and personnel for sustained operations. The NN has also recently established a Project Implementation, Monitoring and Evaluation Directorate at the NHQ for better management of NN projects (Nigerian Navy, 2024).

Nigerian Air Force Holding Company (NAFHC) has business-oriented formations that are directly accountable to HQ NAF. These businesses are the Aeronautical Engineering and Technical Services Limited, Nigerian Air Force Post-Service Housing Development Limited, Nigerian Air Force Investment Limited, Nigerian Air Force Properties Limited, the Pay and Accounting Group, the Personnel Management Group and the Air Force Institute of Technology (Nigerian Air Force, 2011). Others are the NAF garment factory and NAF cooperatives, among others.

Having listed the commercial ventures under the purview of the tri-service components of the AFN, some germane issues become apparent. First is the viability and profitability of those military ventures. Second is the accountability of the military managers in the management of those ventures. Third is the question of how these ventures can be better regulated and overseen. These issues are resolved in the next section.

Analysis and Discussion

Three main problematic issues were identified during the review of data gathered for this study. These include the viability and profitability of military commercial ventures, accountability and management issues, and oversight and regulatory processes of the military commercial ventures.

Viability and Profitability Issues

Military commercial businesses in Nigeria benefit from unaccounted funding and can leverage on a free, cheap labour force (military personnel are mostly seconded to the businesses). In other words, military commercial enterprises have a competitive advantage over the private (civilian) sector/enterprises due to funding received from taxpayers' sources (i.e. defence budget), and there is a sense of durability because many of the military ventures can adapt to prevailing market conditions and therefore can weather major shifts in the market. A similar crowding-out effect on civil enterprises in Nigeria was identified in other climes such as Pakistan, Egypt and Ethiopia (e.g. Mani, 2007).

Studies (e.g. Abul-Magd, 2015; Ojo, 2021; Mani, 2007; Siddiqa, 2007) have revealed that militaries in the developing world adopted roles as owners and managers of economic enterprises that constitute an important source of financial and institutional autonomy from the state and society. Likewise, several distinct types of military commercial ventures were identified in this paper. The number and state of development of these military business ventures seem to depend on the capacity of the arm (service) of the military concern. The NA, perhaps due to its size, has the largest business enterprises in the country. As in other developing countries (e.g. Egypt, Ethiopia and Pakistan), military entrepreneurship seems to be harmful, at least in terms of the crowding-out effect it has on the private sector of the economy.

Accountability and Management Issues

For starters, the military as an institution is globally known to be hierarchical and to instil core leadership values including loyalty, duty, responsibility, selfless service, honour, integrity and personal courage. These virtues are regarded as the main ingredients that account for success in entrepreneurship. Furthermore, the military is credited with improved problem-solving capacity, better ability to cope with physical difficulties and emotional tensions, enhanced independence, self-confidence, and a greater willingness to take responsibility among its cadres (Ojo, 2021). Experience with critical events, encounters with more dilemmas and exposure to different ethnic cultures broaden the soldiers' personal and social horizons. Consequently, the military institution provides specific competencies that are transferable to entrepreneurship (Maune, 2023).

However, the issues of accountability and managerial competency in the running of military commercial ventures could be negotiated in the tradition and ethos of the military. In the Nigerian military, the deployment of officers and soldiers regularly occurs between six months and two years, depending on the mission (Tade, 2021). Given that situation, the chief executive of a military commercial entity (usually a senior military officer) may not stay long in the job to implement cogent reforms or sustain useful programmes that may have a long-term positive impact on the organization. Added to this is the appointment process, which in most cases is handled by the top hierarchy of the tri-service arms of the AFN (i.e. the service chiefs). Hence, appointment (or secondment) to manage any military commercial entities may not necessarily be based on merit and could be open to favouritism – a sort of 'job-for-the-boys' affair, which on many occasions compromised competency and accountability.

Moreover, the hierarchical nature of the military often deters a junior officer from querying his/her predecessor in office, thus allowing fraud and sleaze to fester. Military personnel act under command since their professional role implies compliance with hierarchical authority. The structure of most armies is based on strict hierarchies where people have a professional legal duty to follow orders (Caspar et al., 2020). Furthermore, the emphasis on seniority and rank can sometimes stifle the contributions of junior personnel who may have valuable insights or ideas to offer but feel constrained by the hierarchical system (MilitarySphere.com, 2024).

It is also observed that most of these military business units do not publish their accounts, and their websites are not adequately maintained or are even non-existent in many cases, rendering their activities shrouded in obscurity. Such opaqueness in many military enterprises allows military officers to use their privileged position to influence the mechanisms of the redistribution of economic resources and the pursuit of rents that have an indirect impact on the economy in the private sector.

Oversight and Regulatory Issues

It seems the case that military entrepreneurship in Nigeria opens a channel of opportunity to maintain disproportionate institutional autonomy and weakens the civilian control mechanisms of the military. This offers the military additional instruments of economic influence and serves as a patronage scheme for serving and retired military officers. According to Iroegbu (2023), there are key challenges militating against effective oversight of the military commercial enterprise sector. These are (1) lack of legal backing – those ventures do not exist legally as they were not legislated upon, and that makes it difficult to prosecute or hold anyone liable for infractions. In addition, the official information is protected through the Official Secrets Act, which prohibits the collection, possession or dissemination of official information and state secrets. (2) Lack of capacity for legislative oversight – the general lack of capacity or even connivance on the part of the legislators in their oversight functions is a palpable obstacle to effective tracking and monitoring of the defence budget. Oftentimes, legislators lack basic knowledge of their roles to hold security chiefs accountable for the use of public funds, and in some cases, they are either intimidated or prevented from investigating. (3) Lack of political will – likewise, the absence of political will on the part of the Commander-in-Chief of the armed forces to hold the security chiefs liable is a key challenge. (4) Esprit de corps/military culture – the reportage cases of corruption within the defence and security sector are difficult because of the solidarity among officers and officials who often hide under the oath of secrecy in matters relating to defence budgeting and expenditures. Invariably, secrecy requirements are often used as a pretext to hide unlawful activities like the establishment, earnings and management of the military commercial entities in Nigeria. Thus, the opaqueness of most military enterprises allows military officers to use their privileged position to influence the mechanisms of the redistribution of economic resources and the pursuit of rents that have an indirect impact on the economy in the private sector. In this way, military entrepreneurship's pattern of complemented interventions indirectly stimulates vices such as corruption and the distortion of the economic process.

Summary and Implications

Summary

This chapter identifies two strands of military entrepreneurs in Nigeria, namely welfare-oriented ventures and profit-oriented commercial ventures. Both are structured to compete for prestige, be profit-oriented and promote economic development that can foster social development and cohesion in the services. The AFN established many welfare schemes and business ventures to improve the welfare of personnel as well as generate revenue for the military. The welfare and business ventures are set up in the belief that they provide empowerment opportunities for officers and men of the armed forces. However, the military welfare-oriented organizations appear to have morphed into profit-oriented commercial ventures; that is, hardly a line of distinction between these two categories of ventures. It is generally accepted that military entrepreneurship, in any format, has certain peculiarities such as the enjoyment of privileges, preferential access to infrastructure and the use of resources meant for the armed forces, which could lead to severe market distortions.

Among the key challenges that hinder military commercial ventures is the regular military postings/deployments in the military, which are carried out to bolster the system for greater performance. This exercise creates an atmosphere of instability that hampers continuity, efficiency and effective performance of the military business in Nigeria. Altogether, the military commercial ventures in Nigeria play a vital role in the country's economic development, as they are involved in a wide range of activities, including construction, telecommunications and transportation. They also provide job opportunities for Nigerians and contribute to the growth of the country's economy (Aeroleas, 2024).

Implications

The existence of extra and off-budgetary sources of revenue, in the form of military entrepreneurship, enables the armed forces to become more independent of civilian oversight and, thus, less accountable to government controls. When a substantial part of the armed forces is engaged in commercial activities, training and combat readiness necessarily get compromised (Brömmelhörster and Paes, 2003). Arguably, military commercial activities will generally have several impacts on professionalism, the economy and society. The first impact is related to civil-military relations and the democratization process. Budgetary control is considered one of the oversight mechanisms that civil authorities employ to control the military. Off-budgetary earnings, such as from military entrepreneurship, will give more autonomy and leverage to the military against the civilian authorities. This will seriously damage civilian authority over the military (see Siddiqa, 2007; Brömmelhörster and Paes, 2003). A case in point is the Chinese People's Liberation Army (PLA). The growing autonomy of the PLA, concomitant with the expansion of its economic empire, was perceived to overshadow the supremacy of the Chinese Communist Party, a perception that eventually led to its divestiture at the end of the 1980s (Char and Bitzinger, 2017). As Siddiqa (2007: 17) justifiably noted, 'pervasive military business is also a barrier to the democratization process because of the general tendency to perpetuate the army's hegemony in the society'.

The second is the negative impact on the national economy. The fact that the armed forces gain unfair advantages (tax cuts, easy access to state resources, favoured bids on government projects, elevated social status, lack of transparency) over the private sector leads to market distortion or even market monopoly. According to a study by Transparency International (Goh and Muravska, 2012), commercial activities by the military jeopardize the economic prospects as free competition is inhibited, the private sector is strangled, and foreign investments are impeded.

The third impact is the high corruption risk it poses to society. There appears to be a consensus among scholars about the military's tendency for corruption when it is involved in commercial activities. Transparency International (Goh and Muravska, 2012) study a variety of military business cases and succinctly conclude that corruption is highly likely to occur either at an institutional or an individual level across the different spectrum of military professionalism. Again, the Chinese PLA provides a good example where the high degree of professionalism did not prevent corruption in its system. It is of little surprise, given the opacity that surrounds military business, the low or non-existent oversight mechanisms and its privileged position in society.

The fourth impact relates to military professionalism. Commercial engagement of the military often undermines the esprit de corps and its institutional cohesiveness. The struggle to profit from the lucrative revenue that comes from the military business unleashes patron-client relations and factionalism. Also, the struggle for 'juicy appointment' to manage the military business ventures among top military generals tends to subvert camaraderie in the military. In this regard, Mani (2007) argues that personal and factional gains eclipse institutional interest, thus eroding the professional ethos of the armed forces. It also significantly affects combat readiness when a large number of the armed forces become part of the business (Brömmelhörster and Paes, 2003)

Further Studies

Further studies will be needed to investigate questions surrounding the constitutional mandate of military ventures, the sources of funding for these ventures, how the money accrued is expended, the source of business funding and whether accountability mechanisms are embedded within those commercial organizational structures. If they are, how do the accountability instruments work and how effective are they?

References

Abebe, Z.B. (2018). 'The Failed Experiment of Military Business in Ethiopia: The Case of METEC'. SSRN. Available at: https://ssrn.com/abstract=3655184 or http://dx.doi.org/10.2139/ssrn.3655184

Abul-Magd, Z. (2015). 'Egypt's Military Business: The Need for Change'. Middle East Institute. Available at: https://mei.edu/ar/publication/egypts-military-business-need-change

Aeroleads (2024). 'List of Government and Military Companies in Nigeria in 2025'. Aeroleads. Available at: https://aeroleads.com/list/top-government-and-military-companies-in-nigeria.

Avin, S. (2021). 'The Israeli Tech Ecosystem: Veterans, Startups, and Innovation', *Journal of Technology and Defense*, 38(2): 101–15.

Bashir, M. (2013). 'Nigeria: Now Military Means Business'. allAfrica. Available at: https://allafrica.com/stories/201304010459.html

Bozorgmehr, N. (2017). 'Iran Cracks Down on Revolutionary Guards Business Network'. *Financial Times*. Available at: https://www.ft.com/content/43de1388-9857-11e7-a652-cde3f882dd7b

Brömmelhörster, D.J., and W. Paes (2003). *The Military as an Economic Actor: Soldiers in Business*. Basingstoke: Palgrave Macmillan.

Caspar, E.A., S. Lo Bue, P.A. Magalhães De Saldanha da Gama, P. Haggard and A. Cleeremans. (2020). 'The Effect of Military Training on the Sense of Agency and Outcome Processing', *Nature Communication*, 11: 4366. Available at: https://doi.org/10.1038/s41467-020-18152-x

Char, J., and R.A. Bitzinger (2017). 'A New Direction in the People's Liberation Army's Emergent Strategic Thinking, Roles and Missions', *China Quarterly*, 232: 841–65.

Dike, C. (2023). 'The Nigerian Army: A Century of Service'. Zikoko. Available at: https://www.zikoko.com/citizen/the-nigerian-army-a-century-of-service/

GlobalFirePower (2025). '2025 Nigeria Military Strength'. GlobalFirePower. Available at: https://www.globalfirepower.com/country-military-strength-detail.php?country_id=nigeria

GlobalSecurity.org (2025). 'Nigerian Army Order of Battle'. GlobalSecurity.org. Available at: https://www.globalsecurity.org/military/world/nigeria/army-orbat.htm

Goh, K., and J. Muravska (2012). 'Military-Owned Businesses: Corruption and Risk Reform: An Initial Review, with Emphasis on Exploitation of Natural Resource Assets'. Transparency International UK. Available at: http://ti-defence.org/wp-content/uploads/2016/03/2012-01_MilitaryOwnedBusinesses.pdf (accessed 11 March 2025).

Human Rights Watch (2007). 'Indonesia: Reform of Military Business'. Human Rights Watch. Available at: https://www.hrw.org/news/2007/02/16/indonesia-reform-military-business

Iroegbu, S. (2023). 'Special Report: Tracking Nigerian Military's Commercial Ventures?' Available at: https://crossriverwatch.com/2023/01/special-report-tracking-nigerian-militarys-commercial-ventures

Komash, S. (2020). 'Israel's Military Industrial Complex'. Ideas for Peace. Available at: https://ideasforpeace.org/wp-content/uploads/2020/06/israel.pdf

Lee, D. (2006). 'Chinese Civil-Military Relations: The Divestiture of People's Liberation Army Business Holdings', *Armed Forces & Society*, 32(3): 437–53.

Madichie, N.O., and K. Ayasi (2018). 'Entrepreneurial Opportunities and Challenges for Retired Senior Military Officers in Nigeria', in L.P. Dana, V. Ratten and B. Honyenuga (eds), *African Entrepreneurship. Palgrave Studies of Entrepreneurship in Africa*, 131–51. Cham: Palgrave Macmillan.

Mani, K. (2007). 'Militaries in Business: State-Making and Entrepreneurship in the Developing World', *Armed Forces & Society*, 33(4): 591–611.

Mani, K. (2010). 'Militares Empresarios: Approaches to Studying the Military as an Economic Actor', *Bulletin of Latin American Research*. Available at: https://doi.org/10.1111/j.1470-9856.2010.00445.x

Mani, K. (2011). 'Military Entrepreneurs: Patterns in Latin America', *Latin American Politics and Society*, 53(3): 25–55.

Marshall, S. (2015). *The Egyptian Armed Forces and the Remaking of an Economic Empire*. Carnegie Middle East Centre.

Maune, A. (2023). 'Role of Military in the Entrepreneurial Ecosystem'. *Zimbabwe Independent*. Available at: https://www.newsday.co.zw/theindependent/opinion-analysis/article/200011603/role-of-military-in-the-entrepreneurial-ecosystem

MilitarySphere.com (2024). 'Understanding the Hierarchical Military Rank Structure'. MilitarySphere. Available at: https://militarysphere.com/military-rank-structure-2/

Mulvenon, J. (2001). *Soldiers of Fortune: The Rise and Fall of the Chinese Military-Business Complex, 1978–1999*. New York: East Gate.

Naguib, R. (2012). 'Boycott Them: Activists Raise Awareness About Military's Economic Empire'. *Egypt Independent*. Available at: https://www.egyptindependent.com/boycott-them-activists-raise-awareness-about-militarys-economic-empire/

Nigerian Air Force (2011). 'About Nigerian Air Force'. Nigerian Air Force. Available at: https://airforce.mil.ng

Nigerian Navy (2024). 'History'. Nigerian Navy. Available at: https://navy.mil.ng/history/

Ojo, S. (2021). 'Military Enterprises and Entrepreneurship: A Critical Perspective', in Ojo, S. (ed.), *Global Perspectives on Military Entrepreneurship and Innovation*, 17–44. Hershey: IGI Global.

Ojo, S. (2023). 'Exploring Veteran Entrepreneurship in Nigeria', *Journal of Enterprising Communities: People and Places in the Global Economy*, 17(3): 644–63. Available at: https://doi.org/10.1108/JEC-10-2021-0148

Olawuyi, I.B., and U. Amakom (2023). 'Pre-Retirement Entrepreneurship Training and Veterans' Occupation: A Tracer Study of Nigerian Armed Forces Resettlement Centre (2002–2023)', *International Journal of Economics, Environmental Development and Society*, 4(4): 468–91.

Prina, D. (2017). 'Taking Care of Their Own: The Causes and Consequences of Soldiers in Business', PhD dissertation, Faculty of the Graduate School of the University of Maryland, College Park.

Rathi, P. (2024). *China's Military-Industrial Complex: Nature and Reforms Under Xi Jinping*. Available at: https://www.researchgate.net/publication/385648387_CHINAS_MILITARY-INDUSTRIAL_COMPLEX_NATURE_AND_REFORMS_UNDER_XI_JINPING.

Reuters (2018). 'From War Room to Boardroom. Military Firms Flourish in Sisi's Egypt'. Reuters. Available at: https://www.reuters.com/investigates/special-report/egypt-economy-military/

Siddiqa, A. (2007). *Military Inc.: Inside Pakistan's Military Economy*. Oxford: Oxford University Press.

Tade, O. (2021). 'Military Postings Put Strains on Nigerian Families: Here's What Some Told Us'. *The Conversation*. Available at: https://theconversation.com/military-postings-put-strains-on-nigerian-familiesheres-what-some-told-us-169275

2

Military Entrepreneurship in Nigeria: Economic Growth and Security Developments

Murtala Ayinla Ahmed

The Nigerian military has progressively expanded its role beyond traditional security responsibilities to include commercial ventures, thereby contributing to the nation's economic development. This study examines the issues, contributions, prospects and strategies associated with defence enterprises and their impact on Nigeria's economic growth and security dynamics. Grounded in the resource dependency theory, the analysis interprets military engagement in commercial activities as a mechanism for bridging resource gaps while reinforcing national security.

Several critical issues emerge within the networks of defence and security enterprises, including the imperatives of resource mobilization, public perception of military-led business activities, questions around their legal status, the pursuit of self-reliance and the implications for private sector growth and competition. Despite these challenges, the study finds that defence enterprises have made significant contributions to national development by generating employment opportunities, enhancing food security and supporting the creation of sustainable cities and communities.

Looking ahead, a number of prospects are identified for strengthening the role of defence enterprises. These include addressing unmet national needs, leveraging the opportunities embedded in the National Development Plan (2021–2025), and responding to the military's evolving role in national economic affairs. This chapter focuses on how defence enterprises have been instrumental in shaping Nigeria's economic landscape, and emphasizes how sustained impact requires addressing lingering concerns over legal frameworks, governance and transparency. To this end, the implication for targeted strategies such as process optimization, governance reform and the establishment of strategic partnerships to enhance efficiency and ensure the continued relevance of defence enterprises in national economic development unravels.

Classical military theorists like Sun Tzu and Clausewitz have largely constrained the role of the military to state-centric national security along the lines of defence of territory and protection of national interests (Tzu, 1994; Clausewitz, 2021). Thus, it is seen as a sort of anomaly for the military to transcend its traditional role and become involved in commercial, for-profit ventures. However, the redefinition of national security across a broad spectrum of dimensions has brought in the need to rethink the role of the military as a critical lever and facilitator of national development beyond kinetic military operations alone (National Coordinator for Counterterrorism and Security (NCTV), 2019).

The aforementioned imperatives consequently account for the involvement of the Pakistan and Egyptian military in commercial enterprises. Notably, the Pakistan Army Welfare Trust (PAWT) and Fauji Foundation have evolved into successful diversified conglomerates, covering sectors like bakeries, hospitals, airlines, insurance companies, banks, oil and gas, cement, fertilizer, power generation, security consultancy, hotels, farms and ranches, cereals and supermarket chains, amongst others (PAWT, 2024 and Fauji Foundation, 2024). In 2020, they generated a net income of USD$9 billion, providing employment to over 28,000 people and benefiting 7 per cent of Pakistan's population daily (PAWT, 2024; Fauji Foundation, 2024).

Similarly, Egypt's military commercial ventures are another model worthy of mention. The ventures are managed by the Ministry of Military Production, the Ministry of Defence, and the Arab Organization for Industrialization, and they contribute significantly to the country's gross domestic product (GDP). These ventures include construction, food provision, petrochemicals, hotels, aviation and textiles. Estimates suggest military ventures could account for between 20 and 50 per cent of Egypt's GDP, demonstrating their efficiency and effectiveness (Presidency of the Republic of Egypt, 2024). Thus, both Pakistan and Egypt's military commercial ventures are critical to job creation, economic growth and national development.

In Nigeria, the Armed Forces of Nigeria's (AFN) commercial ventures have become diversified conglomerates catering to a wide variety of needs whilst being major players in critical sectors of the economy (Navy Holdings Limited, 2025). The contributions of the defence enterprises to national economic development notwithstanding, concerns have been raised about their legal status, governance and justification for their existence. Hence, this paper seeks to explore the issues in defence and security enterprises' networks and their tie-in to national economic development. Accordingly, the paper will cover conceptual definition, overview, theoretical framework, issues, contributions, prospects and strategies.

Conceptual Definition

The three key variables in this study are defence entrepreneurship as the independent variable, economic growth as the dependent variable and the associated issues in defence entrepreneurship as the rider. The variables are defined, and their relationship is conceptualized subsequently.

Defence Entrepreneurship

Defence entrepreneurship refers to businesses or corporations either wholly or partially owned and managed by the AFN or its affiliates (Iroegbu, 2022). In Nigeria, these enterprises are typically involved in sectors such as real estate, construction, engineering, consultancy, banking, mercantile, pharmaceuticals and agriculture, amongst others (Iroegbu, 2022).

Economic Development

This refers to the process by which a nation improves the economic well-being and quality of life of its citizens (Federal Ministry of Finance, Budget and National Planning (FMFBNP), 2021). In the context of Nigeria, economic development includes improving GDP, employment, infrastructure and general welfare through various sectors, including oil, agriculture and services (FMFBNP, 2021).

Relationship Between Defence Entrepreneurship and Economic Development

Based on the ownership and management structure of defence enterprises, it follows that the effective and efficient management of defence enterprises would lead to improvement in their financial and operating performance, whilst contributing to overall economic development. Conversely, sub-optimal management of the defence enterprises would impair their financial and operating performance, as well as impinge on national economic development. Thus, there is a direct relationship between defence entrepreneurship and economic development.

Overview of Defence Entrepreneurship and Economic Development in Nigeria

Defence entrepreneurship has played a significant role in Nigeria's economy. Over the years, the AFN has established a presence in various commercial sectors, ranging from defence and infrastructure to agriculture, banking and pharmaceuticals, amongst several others (Iroegbu, 2022). In the last two decades, the AFN's involvement in commercial activities was on account of the need to ensure national security, self-sufficiency and economic stability.

Notably, the AFN's commercial enterprises are driven by the respective service's holding company. For the Nigerian Army (NA), it is the Nigerian Army Welfare Limited/Guarantee (NAWL/G). The Nigerian Navy's (NN) commercial entities come under the Navy Holdings Limited (NHL), whilst the Nigerian Air Force (NAF) commercial operations are handled by the Nigerian Air Force Holding Company Limited (NAFHCL). The NAWL/G was established in 2007 for the purpose of coordinating the activities of the subsidiaries under the group in a bid to improve the welfare of Nigerian Army personnel (Ugbong, 2021). The NHL was set up in 2012 with a view to achieving efficiency in-service delivery as well as effective coordination of the internally generated revenue (IGR) of the subsidiaries. This was in a bid to enhance accountability, as well as to foster effective management and ease of administration (NHL, 2025). Similarly, the NAFHCL was established in 2014 to coordinate the activities of the four subsidiaries in the group (NAFHCL, 2024). These are the Nigerian Air Force Investment Limited, the Nigerian Air Force Properties Limited, the Nigerian Air Force Housing and Construction Company Limited, as well as the Aviation Engineering and Technology Services Limited.

One of the most visible sectors in which the AFN's commercial enterprises have thrived is real estate and construction. This is spearheaded by the NA Engineering Corps, the Naval Building Construction Company Limited and the NAF Properties Limited. The activities of the companies have significantly contributed to housing security and national infrastructure development. In the area of defence and military hardware production, military enterprises have been instrumental. The Defence Industries Corporation (DICON) and Naval Dockyard Limited have played major pioneering roles in the nation's military-industrial complex.

The NA's involvement in agriculture through the Nigerian Army Farms and Ranches Limited (NAFARL) also emerged as a means to ensure food security and self-sufficiency. Farms have been established in several parts of Nigeria, focusing on crop cultivation, livestock farming and food production. These ventures are often linked to broader national goals of achieving self-sufficiency and reducing dependence on imports. Other areas include micro-finance banking, cooperatives, engineering consultancy, blue economy, oil and gas, fast-moving consumables and pharmaceuticals, amongst several others.

Theoretical Framework

Certain theories could be adopted to proffer the theoretical underpinning for this article. The theories include the security theory, public goods theory, defence industrial base theory and the resource dependency theory. However, considering the variables of the study as well as their key attributes, the theory used for this paper is the resource dependency theory. The theory rests on the government's recognition of the reality of the external domiciliation of critical resources and the essential facilitation role that defence and security business enterprises play in liaising with the external stakeholders to mobilize capabilities and resources essential for national security and national defence, whilst bridging appropriation inadequacies (Pfeffer and Salancik, 1978).

The resource dependency theory was advocated by Pfeffer and Salancik (1978). The theory posits that the realities of external resource dependencies affect the behaviour, actions and strategies adopted by the military. Hence, the military would seek to minimize appropriation funding uncertainties by proactive business engagement with external stakeholders via alliances, integration and a host of other business initiatives.

Casciaro and Piskorski (2005), however, criticized some of the assumptions underpinning the resource dependency theory. This was on account of the complex interplay of power dynamics between and amongst organizations. Notably, power dynamics were averred not to be a binary issue but rather, unfolding across a broad spectrum from complementary to competing interests. Thus, adopting a binary approach to power dynamics tends towards oversimplification of the issue. The reservations and criticisms expressed notwithstanding, the resource dependency theory is deemed to be suitable for this study on account of its core thrusts and its explicit capability to directly address the variable of this study. Hence, it is adopted as the theoretical framework for this paper.

Pertinently, the application of the resource dependency theory to issues in defence and security enterprise networks in Nigeria would contextualize the emergence of military enterprises whilst enabling the identification of the legal and institutional lacunae as well as the external environmental drivers for the enterprises. This would consequently aid the generation of suitable, acceptable, feasible and ethical strategies for the resolution of the resultant challenges.

Issues in Defence and Security Enterprise Network

The issues in defence and security enterprises' networks include resource imperatives, public perception, legal status, self-reliance and their impact on private-sector growth and competition. Highlights are provided subsequently.

Resource Imperatives

The subordination of the military to civil control implies that the financial resources to equip and maintain the armed forces, as well as sustain their operations, devolve upon the government. In this regard, a consideration of the annual budgetary appropriation to fund the AFN's capital and recurrent expenditures between 2019 and 2024, as provided on the website of the Budget Office of the Federation (2024), shows that the appropriation is less than one per cent of GDP. The systemic issues leading to the resource challenge are not unconnected with the fiscal challenges of the nation, which witnessed a low tax-to-GDP ratio of 9.4 per cent as of 2023 (Okon, 2024). The implication of this is that there are multiple contending needs for the available resources. Hence, the Federal Government of Nigeria (FGN) is constrained to allocate available resources as best as it can, considering the contending sectoral requirements whilst balancing the need for security, economic growth and national development.

Arising from the foregoing, it is therefore an expression of the resilience and proactivity of the AFN that it sought to contribute its quota to national development through the establishment of defence enterprises. This achieves two key imperatives: meeting the personnel welfare needs of the AFN and facilitating the activities of the services. Thus, the AFN's involvement in commercial ventures has been a civic-minded and proactive initiative to further the achievement of its constitutional mandate.

Public Perception

In the court of public opinion, the fact that funds have been appropriated to the AFN automatically translates to the perception that the military's needs have been met in full, and as such, the AFN ought to be operating effectively, efficiently and at full capacity. This assumption, however, does not take into consideration the range of the military's operations or emerging security imperatives. Notwithstanding, the FGN prioritizes the AFN and makes assiduous efforts to adequately fund the military despite the fiscal challenges. Considering the revenue challenges of the nation, which constrain the resources available for disbursement to ministries, departments and agencies for national development initiatives, the onus consequently returns to the public to be civic-minded and shun tax evasion and blatant tax avoidance manoeuvers that sub-optimize government revenue. This would ensure that all sectors of the economy are appropriately resourced to ensure their optimal functionality.

Legal Status

A review of some of the AFN's commercial enterprises shows that they are incorporated entities registered under the Corporate Affairs Commission. For instance, the cooperative societies are funded by contributions from personnel. Hence, they are effectively not government-owned enterprises (GOE). Rather, they are answerable to their de facto shareholders: in this case, the personnel themselves. However, there exists a perception gap that all military commercial enterprises are, in effect, GOEs. While this assertion is true for some of the enterprises, it is not necessarily so for the cooperative societies and businesses whose capital is funded by such cooperative societies and sundry contributions from AFN personnel's salaries.

Self-Reliance

Nigeria runs a mixed economy with a greater inclination to the capitalist model (Ogunde, 2019). Hence, the expectation is that a private-sector-led military-industrial complex ought to drive the needs and requirements of the AFN. While this is a laudable objective, the reality, however, is that the nation's military-industrial complex is still developing. Hence, the AFN has to step in to bridge the capacity gap in the nation's military-industrial complex. To this end, the AFN's engineering and maintenance commercial entities have been critical not only to the maintenance, repair and overhaul (MRO) of the AFN's platforms, but they have also ventured into the construction of some of the platforms and equipment required by the AFN. This has not only aided in improving the AFN's order of battle (ORBAT), but it has also enhanced functional surveillance, response and enforcement capabilities of the services. This is aside from creating a culture of autonomous self-reliance, whilst helping to make substantial foreign exchange savings that would otherwise have been devoted to procuring these capabilities from foreign nations. Thus, this consideration needs to temper some of the discussions regarding the AFN's foray into commercial enterprises.

Impact on Private Sector Growth and Competition

The Public Procurement Act (PPA) 2007 directs that procurements in the public sector are to be executed in accordance with the Act. The popular impression is that the AFN's commercial enterprises exercise a virtual monopoly on procurements in the military to the exclusion of the private sector, thereby stifling growth and competition.

The reality, however, is that the AFN's budget is executed under the PPA 2007. This is particularly so when it comes to the procurement of platforms, equipment and sensors. Accordingly, the operations of the AFN's commercial ventures do not hinder private-sector growth, nor impair competition.

Contributions of Defence Enterprises to National Economic Development

The AFN's commercial enterprises contribute significantly to national economic development. The ventures touch on practically every facet of the United Nations' Sustainable Development Goals (SDGs) and others. The SDGs aim to ensure people's overall well-being while enabling sustainable economic growth and development.

In the areas of food security/SDG Goal 2 (Zero Hunger), the operations of the NAFARL have contributed significantly to advancing climate-smart agriculture, mechanization and improved crop yields. This is in addition to the company's agricultural extension services training it offers to civilians (National Youth Service Corps members and IT students) as part of capacity building for enhanced food security in the nation.

The achievement of SDG 11 – Sustainable Cities and Communities and SDG 13 – Climate Action is being advanced by the Naval Building Construction Company Limited (NBCCL) through its adoption of the compressed earth bricks (CEB) building technique. This is an eco-friendly building method with significant cost savings relative to the sandcrete method of construction (NBCCL, 2024). It is not only thermodynamic, but it also has the capacity to significantly resolve the housing deficit in the country through its mass adoption.

The AFN's commercial ventures have also created thousands of direct and even greater numbers of indirect jobs. This runs through the various sectors they have core competencies in, such as engineering, construction, fabrication, agriculture, investment advisory and cooperatives. This has helped in reducing the nation's unemployment levels to just 5.3 per cent (National Bureau of Statistics (NBS), 2024).

The Nigerian Army Small Drug Manufacturing Units (NASDMU) is playing a major role in enhancing the achievement of SDG 3 – Good Health and Well-being. The company is involved in the local manufacture of high-quality drugs at an affordable cost. This not only enhances healthcare for NA personnel, but it also has a positive impact on the host communities where the NA's medical hospitals are located, as they benefit too.

Perhaps the most important contribution of the AFN's commercial ventures is the MRO services they offer to the services themselves. This has helped to ensure the optimal availability for tasking of AFN's platforms whilst aiding in the induction of new platforms and equipment. For instance, since the NN started docking its ships at the Naval Dockyard Limited (NDL), foreign dry docking of ships has stopped. Hence, the NDL is strategically important to the Nigerian economy in curtailing capital flight while promoting indigenization. Additionally, as a fully integrated dockyard that operates the full spectrum of the marine MRO value chain, the NDL also offers MRO and construction services to merchant vessels and stakeholders in the Nigerian maritime domain (NDL, 2024).

The AFN's commercial entities have also contributed significantly to youth capacity development in the nation. Over the years, thousands of NYSC members, as well as students on industrial training attachments, have been trained by the ventures across various specializations. These include agriculture, marine MRO, fabrication and construction value chain. Additionally, the commercial ventures have played host to technical visits from various organizations, such as research institutes, professional associations, colleges, polytechnics and universities. This is in a bid to facilitate knowledge sharing and skills transfer in engineering, construction and other vital sectors that the ventures have core competences in. The aforementioned activities have further underscored the AFN's commercial ventures' importance in the development of technical and other specialist capacity amongst the nation's youths.

Prospects

The National Development Plan 2021–2025

The National Development Plan (NDP) 2021–2025 intends to grow the Nigerian economy to have a GDP of US$4 trillion by 2035 (Federal Ministry of Finance, Budget and National Development (FMFBNP), 2021). This is a 970 per cent increase from the nation's 2023 GDP of US$374 billion. The sheer ambitiousness of the NDP's objective behoves keen and active participation by all stakeholders to see to its fruition. Thus, the active participation of the AFN's commercial entities in most sectors of the company makes them key facilitators of national economic growth and development. Accordingly, the NDP 2021– 2025 is a major prospect for AFN commercial entities to leverage, to reinforce and deepen their relevance and credibility to national economic development.

Changing Political Dynamics and the Evolving Role of the Military in Economic Affairs

The activities of the military had hitherto been confined to a narrow state-centric interpretation of national security, which just speaks to territorial defence and other kinetic military operations. However, the adoption of the new concept of national security, which adopts a broader perspective, is gaining more currency. Thus, governments the world over begin to see the utility of the military not only in physical security but also in economic security, energy security, food security, cyber security, environmental security and border security. These areas consequently give the AFN the will and freedom of action to explore how best they could also contribute to national security beyond the confines of the border and physical security.

Unmet National Needs

The AFN's commercial ventures are not superfluous entities. Rather, they are a proactive initiative to fill unmet needs and requirements. In this regard, there are substantial gaps in housing, agriculture, construction, engineering, MRO and fabrication, and pharmaceuticals, amongst others, in the country that the AFN's pool of talents and commercial ventures could help ameliorate. These offer significant prospects for the AFN's involvement in commercial ventures in the country for enhanced national development.

Strategies to Enhance Defence Enterprises for Economic Development

Process Optimization Strategy

The implementation of a process optimization would help reinforce the culture of resource utilization efficiencies to deliver improved financial and operating performance. The objective is to foster a spirit of continuous improvement of core competencies that confer competitive advantage. To this end, the respective holding companies of the AFN's commercial ventures could impose financial and operating targets and key performance indicators (KPI) for each of their subsidiaries. This is with the understanding that the execution of the KPIs would engender the desired process optimization. The funding for the strategies could be drawn from the operating capital of the ventures to enable implementation by the first quarter of 2026.

Governance Optimization Strategy

The Governance Optimization Strategy would mitigate the public perception gap around accountability and transparency. The objective is to enhance the public's perception of the degree of compliance of the AFN's commercial ventures with the Nigerian Code of Corporate Governance. To this end, the ventures could identify key corporate governance activities that do not comprise national security or lead to inadvertent disclosure of classified information and, thereafter, invite select members of the public as observers. This would display the AFN's commitment to transparency whilst improving public confidence. The resources for the execution of the strategy could be sourced from the ventures' operating capital to enable commencement by the first quarter of 2026.

Strategic Partnerships

The pursuit of strategic partnerships will ensure the contemporary relevance and competitiveness of the AFN's commercial ventures. The objective is to ensure that ventures continuously implement capabilities that would keep honing their core competencies for sustained competitive advantage. To this end, the ventures could seek strategic partnerships with credible original equipment manufacturers (OEM), companies, research institutes and academia relevant to their area of specialization. If diligently pursued, this line of effort carries the potential of emplacing essential capabilities for the ventures without the onerous challenge of the AFN ventures solely financing capacity upgrades.

Conclusion

Defence enterprises in Nigeria have continued to play a major role in shaping the country's economic landscape. Concerns have been raised regarding their legal status and governance. However, it was observed that the concerns arose due to public perception gaps regarding their source of capital as well as the extent of their compliance with corporate governance codes. Notably, some of the enterprises are mainly financed from non-public fund sources whilst having robust internal financial controls, a board of directors and management structures. Furthermore, they not only pay taxes as due as responsible corporate citizens, but they are also accountable to their shareholders. The prospects for enhancing the ventures include key unmet needs, the imperatives of the NDP 2021–2025 and the evolving role of the military in the economic affairs of nations. These made strategies such as strategic partnerships, process and governance optimization key to enhancing the financial and operating performance of the ventures.

Recommendations

It is recommended that:

a. the AFN commercial ventures should execute the process optimization strategy by the first quarter to deliver improved financial and operating performance.
b. the AFN commercial ventures should execute the process Governance Optimization Strategy by the first quarter of 2026 to mitigate the public perception gap around accountability and transparency.
c. the AFN commercial ventures should initiate strategic partnerships with credible OEMs, organizations, research institutes and academia relevant to their area of specialization by the first quarter of 2026 to ensure contemporary relevance and competitiveness of the AFN's commercial ventures.

References

Budget Office of the Federation (2024). *Budget Documents*. Federal Government of Nigeria. Available at: https://budgetoffice.gov.ng/index.php/resources/internal-resources/budget-documents

Casciaro, T., and M. Piskorski (2005). 'Power Imbalance, Mutual Dependence, and Notes Constraint Absorption: A Closer Look at Resource Dependence Theory'. *Administrative Science Quarterly*, 50(2): 167–99.

Clausewitz, C.V. (2021). *On War*. Produced by C. Keller and D. Widger. Project Gutenberg. Available at: https://www.gutenberg.org/files/1946/1946-h/1946-h.htm

Fauji Foundation (2024). 'About Us'. Available at: http://www.fauji.org.pk

Federal Ministry of Finance, Budget and National Planning (2021). *National Development Plan 2021–2025*. Abuja: Federal Ministry of Finance, Budget and National Planning.

Iroegbu, S. (2022). *Special Report: Tracking Nigerian Military's Commercial Ventures?* Global Sentinel. Available at: https://globalsentinelng.com/special-report-tracking-nigerian-militarys-commercial-ventures/

National Bureau of Statistics (2024). *Unemployment Statistics*. Federal Government of Nigeria. Available at: https://microdata.nigerianstat.gov.ng/index.php/catalog/151

National Coordinator for Counterterrorism and Security (2019). *National Security Strategy*. Government of the Netherlands. Available at: https://www.government.nl/topics/counterterrorism-and-national-security/preventing-crises-and-disasters#:~:text=The%20National%20Coordinator%20for%20Counterterrorism,for%20security%20in%20the%20Netherlands

Naval Building Construction Company Limited (2024). 'About Us'. Available at: https://navalbuilding.com/about-us/

Naval Dockyard Limited (2024). 'About Us'. Available at: https://navaldockyard.com/about-us/

Navy Holdings Limited (2024). 'About Navy Holdings Limited'. Available at: https://navyholdings.org/about

Navy Holdings Limited (2025). *Navy Holdings Limited*. Instagram. Available at: https://www.instagram.com/navyholdingsltd/

Nigerian Air Force Holding Company Limited (2024). 'About the NAFHCL'. Facebook. Available at: https://web.facebook.com/p/Nigerian-Air-Force-Holding-Company-100067606215365/?_rdc=1&_rdr#

Ogunde, F. (2019). 'Is the Nigerian Economy Capitalist, Socialist or Mixed?' Stears. Available at: https://www.stears.co/article/is-the-nigerian-economy-capitalist-socialist-or-mixed/

Okon, D. (2024). 'IMF: At 9.4% in 2023, Nigeria's Tax Revenue to GDP Ratio Among Lowest in the World'. *The Cable*. Available at: https://www.thecable.ng/imf-at-9-4-in-2023-nigerias-tax-revenue-to-gdp-ratio-among-lowest-in-the-world/

Pakistan Army Welfare Trust (2024). 'About Us'. Available at: https://awt.com.pk/aboutus

Presidency of the Republic of Egypt (2024). *Ministry of Military Production*. Available at: https://www.presidency.eg/en

Salancik G.R., and J. Pfeffer (1978). *The External Control of Organisations: A Resource Dependence Perspective*. New York: Harper & Row.

Tzu, S. (1994). *The Art of War*. Translated by Samuel B. Griffith. Oxford: Oxford University Press.

Ugbong, M.U. (2021). 'Enhancing Nigerian Army Welfare Schemes Toward Improved Personnel Motivation'. Coleção Meira Mattos. Available at: https://doi.org/10.52781/CMM.E029

3

Organizing for Entrepreneurship in the Nigerian Armed Forces: Analysis of Welfare and Commercial Ventures

Senator Iroegbu

This chapter calls attention to the growing occurrence of the Nigerian armed forces taking on roles as owners and managers of economic enterprises, which constitutes an important source of financial and institutional autonomy from the state and society. By engaging in business activities, the military inevitably introduces profit incentives into its daily operations. Increasingly, the military enjoys an unfair advantage over civilian enterprises in the marketplace. Thus, the armed forces' search for cost savings, efficiencies and quality makes the business case for further outsourcing and privatization more compelling. The armed forces in parts of Africa expect these new relationships to improve their performance by introducing corporate resources and capabilities. Furthermore, the chapter looks at how military enterprises are evolving and how privatization could help meet military needs through recapitalizing programmes that cannot be adequately funded through annual budgets.

The interconnectedness between state-making and entrepreneurship is also important for understanding military involvement in business enterprises in today's developing world. The nature of national security and the need for resource acquisition to execute projects have put war-makers in the spotlight of self-seeking entrepreneurs. Over the years, military institutions have assumed primary roles as entrepreneurs, owning and running a range of enterprises (Tilley, 1985).

Military entrepreneurship is significant for the potential economic impact it can have on the armed forces and their relations with civil and political society. While entrepreneurship building may well improve the welfare of the rank and file based on accrued profits, it tends to introduce a motivation for profit and competition that challenges the professional integrity and institutional cohesion of the military. In some cases, entrepreneurship-building enhances the political power of the military institution and its officer in charge, making them less dependent on and therefore less accountable to civil and political society. Military entrepreneurs are doubly powerful: not only do they have a near monopoly on the state's power of coercion, but they are also stakeholders in lucrative non-market enterprises run with minimal oversight from government officials or society at large. Thus, where a legacy of military entrepreneurship exists, civilians seeking to establish responsible political control over the institution may face the daunting task of eroding a discreet, but established, prerogative to economic power and autonomy.

These developments are not lost on policymakers, who see military entrepreneurship as injurious to the development of a strongly professional military and antithetical to civil-military relations based on democratic accountability. Yet, while several theoretical and policy studies have examined the privatized military industry, to date, only journalistic accounts and single case studies exist on the corollary topic of the militarized private sector.

For example, during the twentieth century, in some developing countries, economic resources were held in the name of the institution of the armed forces, while in others, officers collected profits for personal enrichment. With few exceptions, however, once military entrepreneurship takes hold, it grows, providing its protagonists with an important and often autonomous resource base. For example, in Indonesia, the military engaged in numerous businesses ranging from mining, oil, manufacturing and protection for multinationals, including assets estimated at more than US$10 billion (Australian Associated Press, 2004). By the 1990s, China's People's Liberation Army (PLA) had incorporated more than twenty thousand enterprises, employed several million workers, and demanded state compensation of US$24 billion upon divestiture in 1998 (Mulvenon, 1999). In a similar manner, the Thai military controlled national radio and television broadcast industries in a tax-free monopoly that generated more than US$1 billion until privatization in 1999 (Asian Economic News, 1999). Also, Pakistan's military holds assets and investments worth US$5 billion, including stakes in industries ranging from airlines to the most important private bank in the country (Harrison, 2002). Turkey's military owns stakes in construction, banking and supermarkets, as well as in the automobile joint venture Oyak-Renault; Oyak, the armed forces pension fund, employs about thirty thousand, with profits earned tax-free (Frantz, 2001). In El Salvador, Guatemala, Honduras and Nicaragua, militaries maintain pension funds and ownership of corporations, including radio stations, resorts, banks, construction companies and hospitals (Mani, 2007).

In Nigeria, the major avenues through which most of the commercial ventures are executed by the military are circumscribed into four key revenue-generating commercial interests: education, hospitality, health centres and real estate. All the tri-services of the Armed Forces of Nigeria (AFN) – that is, the Nigerian Army, Nigerian Air Force and Nigerian Navy – have one form of hospitality platform or another, including NAF clubs and command guest houses. Report has it that these military hospitality institutions, which are now increasing in numbers, could potentially run their private competitors out of business without necessarily contributing much to the economy in an accountable manner. Also, the military services, including the Defence Headquarters (DHQ) have established various school platforms right from primary to tertiary institutions. There are today, army, naval, and air force universities in addition to the Nigerian Defence Academy (NDA) and related institutions. Findings reveal that the concept of schools in the AFN, like the army day secondary schools, air force secondary schools and command secondary or primary schools, were to be situated between 5 and 10 kilometres from the barracks. However, today, this basic concept is not observed but abused with the mushrooming of military schools purely for commercial purposes, and some are even situated completely outside the base.

The military services are actively engaged in property business and real estate development. Even though the primary purpose of various housing schemes is to provide accommodation to their officers and personnel at subsidized rates, these are increasingly being built with civilians as potential buyers and at a profitable rate. The real estate schemes by the AFN have blossomed into money-making ventures. The military also operates other commercial ventures. For instance, the Nigerian Army run catering and events management, private guards' firms and engineering companies, among others.

It is against this background that this chapter will take a more comprehensive approach to entrepreneurship in the Nigerian armed forces through a grounded comparative analysis of welfare and commercial ventures. The military's organizational features determine whether the economic activities will serve the military institution or officers' gain; the more professional the armed forces, the more likely it is that the enterprises will serve institutional needs.

Conceptual Clarification

Richard Cantillon, a French economist, is acknowledged to have introduced the term entrepreneurship. Cantillon sees the entrepreneur as the agent who buys means of production at certain prices to combine them into a new product. Also, he defined entrepreneurship as self-employment of any sort where the entrepreneur is the bearer of uncertainty and risk (Sautet, 2014). In addition, Steinfioff and Burgers (1993) posited that entrepreneurship is 'the ability to develop a new venture or apply a new approach to an old business'. The new approach can be in terms of marketing, packaging or production by way of using resources in a new way. Suleiman (2006: 6) is of the view that entrepreneurship is 'the willingness and ability of an individual to seek investment opportunities to establish and run an enterprise successfully'. One can deduce from these definitions that entrepreneurship is a valuable strategy for creating jobs and improving livelihood and economic self-reliance. We can deduce from these definitions that certain features of entrepreneurship are necessary for a successful, self-reliant business. Another important ingredient for successful entrepreneurship is the willingness to take responsibility and sense opportunities, which must be re-conceptualized by starting in a new form.

A Brief on the Development of Military Entrepreneurship

Scholars of European descent have argued that the emergence of strong modern state-building is typically linked to the establishment of standing professional militaries. From the seventeenth century on, strong states were the ones that maintained substantial armed forces because they could afford to do so primarily through an administrative apparatus enabling the extraction of resources from citizen-taxpayers and the promotion of allegiance to the national state (Hintze, 1975). In the developing world, this pairing of strong states and professional militaries was uncommon. Through colonial rule, European influence in Asia and Africa distorted the process, generally creating strong militaries in weak states. In many post-colonial countries, militaries were among the best-organized public entities, with nascent institutional interests of their own. This phenomenon also holds for many African countries, where, despite early independence from colonial rule, European influence in the form of military missions to professionalize local armies in the late nineteenth century helped to create strong militaries while states remained underdeveloped (Skocpol, 1985).

The emphasis point is that, like other organizations within the state, militaries compete for resources distributed through the state. Although what should be obtainable is that national armies were created as tools of the state to be maintained by it, the developing world generally lacked the investment capital required to fund either national development projects or militaries consistently (Tilly, 1992). Competition within the developing state for resources was therefore fiercer, as substantial armed forces already existed, but available resources were limited.

To understand how military interests and behaviour evolve toward entrepreneurship, we need to examine the features of two institutions: the state and the military organization itself. In addition, we must consider threat conditions, which accelerate efforts to secure economic resources to enhance defence capabilities. States have the potential to be society-shaping structures when they develop an administrative apparatus to configure relations both within society and between society and public authorities (Stepan, 1978). States can set the parameters for the behaviour of various groups, including the military, within their jurisdiction by setting national goals and instituting policies intended to achieve these goals (Scott, 1999). Nonetheless, there is great variation regarding whether state actions encourage, check or are overwhelmed by national groups. To sort out such differences, it helps to conceptualize states as being either strong or weak. In Migdal's definition, strong states have 'the capacities to penetrate society, regulate social relationships, extract resources, and appropriate or use resources in determined ways'. Weak states, by contrast, lack these capabilities (Migdal, 1988).

State capacity dynamics function similarly concerning the military. Just as strong states are better than weak ones at structuring societal behaviour, they are also more successful at guiding and controlling military behaviour. State capacity is therefore relevant in the evolution of military entrepreneurship: the stronger the state, the more beholden the military will be to needs and goals determined by state officials, rather than to its interests.

Put differently, militaries are commonly categorized based on their level of professionalization. At the extremes, militaries are expected to be professionals. In Huntington's classic formulation, professional militaries are trained and organized to possess specially learned skills designed to protect the state and nation, generating a sense of in-group identity (Huntington, 1957). The professional is important because it indicates the ends to which soldiers are likely to apply their entrepreneurial activities: the more professional militaries are, the more likely they are to pursue economic activities for institutional rather than personal ends. Yet several factors drive militaries to pursue economic enterprise intensively. The existence of a viable threat to the established order, either through a foreign adversary or the potential for civil war, encourages rigorous military entrepreneurship when existing resources provided through the state are insufficient. In weak states, military leaders will take the initiative, while in strong ones, state authorities will be the ones to sanction the practice; in either case, the intention is to secure resources needed to defend against the threat.

Professional militaries will seek resources on behalf of the institution and the general stability of the country. In short, the greater the level of threat, the more prevalent military-economic activity will be. Brought together, the degree of state capacity and the nature of military organization determine the kinds of military entrepreneurship (Mani, 2007).

Theoretical Framework

The paper adopts the opportunity-based theory. The theory was proposed by Peter Drucker in 1985. He argued that entrepreneurs thrive by identifying and taking advantage of opportunities produced by social changes. This advantage is also regarded as an opportunity-based theory. Contrary to the Schumpeterian position that entrepreneurs seldom effect change but rather utilize opportunities available due to a change in customer preference. The theory posits that the entrepreneur is defined by a quest for change, responding to the change and equally exploring the change as a given opportunity. Drucker's opportunity construct fundamentally entails that entrepreneurs have an eye more for potential fashioned by change than problems. In extending the view of Drucker, Stevenson (1990) opined that the opportunity-based construct includes resourcefulness based on research to determine the differences between entrepreneurial management and administrative management. Nevertheless, the entrepreneurial process originates with opportunities; it also involves other significant rudiments. Such rudiments include gathering resources, handling a going concern, developing a business venture, etc. The opportunity-based theory is not envisioned to apply to those elements that entail different kinds of phenomena, but only to opportunities in emerging stages. Entrepreneurship starts with the formation of opportunities, which is the domain of the entrepreneur (Shane, 2000; Katz and Shepherd, 2003), while opportunity exploitation, a process hinged on the entrepreneur's decision, is archetypally the jurisdiction of the organization, which, through its capabilities, turns opportunities into market outcomes (Whittaker et al., 2009).

Applying the opportunity-based theory to organizing for entrepreneurship in the Nigerian armed forces, it proposes that its research focus should not be limited to the aspect of opportunity exploitation but on why entrepreneurial opportunities are formed, and the decision is taken to explore the opportunities within the military sphere. However, Alvarez and Barney (2007) argued that opportunities are not assumed to be objective phenomena formed by exogenous shocks to an organization. Rather, opportunities are created endogenously by the activities, responses and depiction of entrepreneurs exploring ways to introduce new services. In the world today, we live in an era of a global economy wherein rivalry has become knowledge-based.

There are various potential, imaginable future inventions based on the informed reflections of the Nigerian armed forces. The Nigerian armed forces are expected to realize the full potential created by the identified changes in the opportunity-based theory of military entrepreneurship. For the reason that entrepreneurship entails the identification of business opportunities and acquiring and deploying the necessary resources needed to exploit them, sustainable military entrepreneurship can be assured within the Nigerian armed forces through a thorough comparative analysis of officers' welfare and their commercial ventures, with the aim of achieving potential innovations. Hence, innovative analysis of welfare and commercial ventures should form the centre stage in military entrepreneurship in the Nigerian armed forces. Moreover, there has been a developing interest in the nexus between the Nigerian armed forces, welfare and entrepreneurship.

The Welfare and Commercial Ventures of the Armed Forces

This paper identifies various ways in which military entrepreneurship develops, focusing on military enclave-building in the Nigerian armed forces. Patterns of state capacity and military organization, along with the intensifying effect of a threat to the established order, are determining features of how and why military entrepreneurship takes hold. Having considered these dynamics in the case of the Nigerian armed forces, it is possible to draw some comparisons concerning the effect of entrepreneurship on military welfare and the potential durability of military entrepreneurship. Concerning welfare, military entrepreneurship is likely to undermine the integrity of even the most skilled and cohesive forces. The potential is great for entrepreneurship to lure motivations away from professional corporate interests toward individual or factional gain, even when the original purpose of military entrepreneurship is for institutional gain.

A striking feature of all of the cases of military business involvement examined in this article is that economic stakeholder involvement challenges the professional reliability and institutional cohesiveness of the armed forces. Thus, the decision to establish military-economic enclaves should be considered with care. Professional militaries, in particular, have much to lose if the achievements of integrity and cohesiveness are put at risk. Similarly, civilian leaders have much to lose if the armed forces not only establish a basis for autonomy but also lose the ability to become or remain professionally oriented. Concerning durability, it appears that military entrepreneurship is quite resilient, even under conditions of democratization and marketization. This is remarkable because the spread of the market economy and democracy should discourage military entrepreneurship: increased competition in markets should cause military-economic empires to crumble in bouts of democratic divestiture and privatization.

The adaptability of the military to identify new areas of economic engagement is notable and dispels the notion that military entrepreneurship is either inflexible or focused on ventures with applications for national defence. This is significant because behaviour that is adaptable and flexible is also more likely to survive well. The emergence and evolution of military entrepreneurship should be considered in this broader conceptual context. Considering the scale and frequency of military entrepreneurship in the contemporary period, there is ample ground for further attention to this topic from both scholars and policymakers.

For instance, *Global Sentinel* (Iroegbu, 2024) was able to obtain a paper in 2021 by Gen. JD Bulus, titled 'Welfare and Commercial Ventures of the Nigerian Army', where he argued in favour of the military establishing welfare and commercial entities, like most South Asian militaries. According to Bulus, some Asian and Middle Eastern militaries have, through these schemes, developed home-grown welfare schemes and are now running lucrative commercial ventures that rival private businesses. He noted that their welfare schemes and businesses are not only doing well but have contributed a commendable proportion to the gross domestic product (GDP) of such nations. Some of the countries include Pakistan, Sri Lanka, Bangladesh, China and India, to mention a few. 'While some of the welfare schemes and commercial ventures are run by their armed forces, others are wholly owned by the Army. They have provided investment opportunities for their military personnel to own shares in them,' he added.

To this end, the senior officer stressed that the Nigerian Army established 'numerous welfare schemes and business ventures to improve the welfare of personnel as well as generate revenue for the system', adding that the welfare and business ventures, though still at their infant stage, are capable of providing massive investment opportunities for officers and men. Bulus listed some of these ventures, including Nigerian Army Welfare Limited by Guarantee (NAWL/G), Directorate of Non-Public Funds (DNPF), Nigerian Army Properties Limited (NAPL) Group, Post-Service Housing Development Limited (PHDL), Command Guest House (CGH) Limited and Nigerian Army Drug Manufacturing Company (NADMACO) Limited, among others.

He highlighted that there is a thin line between welfare schemes and commercial ventures, otherwise known as business ventures, in terms of scope and objectives. Ordinarily, he said, Nigerian army business ventures (NABVs) are set up for profit motives while welfare schemes are gratuitous in nature and outlook. Usually, entities that are set up for welfare purposes sell at a margin fairly above the cost of production or the break-even point (BEP). He listed some of the Nigerian Army Welfare Scheme (NAWS), including the Nigerian Army Welfare Limited by Guarantee (NAWL/G), Nigerian Army Finance Corporation (NAFIC), Nigerian Army Welfare Insurance Scheme (NAWIS), Nigerian Army Benevolent Fund (NA BENFUND) and Directorate of Non-Public Funds (DNPF). Other welfare schemes include Nigerian Army Mammy Markets (NAMM), Nigerian Army Hospitals (NAH), and Command Secondary Schools (CSS), among others.

On the other hand, the paper said the establishment of NABV for profit-making is still evolving as the Nigerian Army is still working on its modalities to 'ensure that they do not only provide welfare services to its personnel but is repositioned to generate IGR as their counterparts in other armies of the world'. These outfits include Nigerian Army Properties Limited (NAPL) Group, Post-Service Housing Development Limited (PHDL), Command Guest House (CGH) Limited, and Nigerian Army Drug

Manufacturing Company (NADMACO) Limited. Others are Nigerian Army Farm and Ranches Limited (NAFARL), ST Foods Limited, Nigerian Army Vehicle Manufacturing Company (NAVMC), Nigerian Army Post Exchange (NAPEX) Supermarket, Nigerian Army Shopping Arena, and Central Engineering Depot (CED). Additional business ventures that were also established are Nigerian Army Driving School (NADS), Nigerian Army Green Security (NAGS) Limited, Sappers Engineering Nigeria Limited (SENL), Nigerian Army Pronto Technical Company (NAPTC), Nigerian Army Ordnance Tailoring Factory (NAOTF) and Buffalo Engineering Technical Services Ltd (BETSL).

Even though *Global Sentinel* (Iroegbu, 2024) was not able to obtain further materials, it gathered that the same situation in the army applies to other sister services of the air force and navy, as well as other security and intelligence agencies. But responding to inquiries, security expert and former Director of Information and Public Relations (DOPRI), Nigerian Air Force (NAF), and Group Captain Sadeeq Shehu (rtd) disagreed with the justification for setting up these ventures. According to Shehu, 'Every job has its global best practices. Global best practices, as espoused by international agencies that are renowned for how the military should be run, especially in a democracy, is that military organizations should not be involved in business'. He said the argument by some proponents of this venture is throwing Pakistan and the Middle East military at you. 'Some even throw in China, of course, China doesn't even apply because they run a communist government. Military officers who are convicted of financial corruption are hanged,' he added while noting: 'although every country has its peculiarities, the general acceptance is that the military should not be involved in business'.

Four Main Avenues

A military source confided to *Global Sentinel* (Iroegbu, 2024) the major avenues through which most of the commercial ventures are executed. He listed four key major revenue-generating commercial interests: education, hospitality, health centres and real estate.

Hospitality: All the tri-services of the Armed Forces of Nigeria (AFN) – that is, the Nigerian Army, Nigerian Air Force and Nigerian Navy, all have one form of hospitality platform or the other, including NAF clubs and command guest houses. However, there are downsides to this, as explained by one security sector reform stakeholder. According to the expert, these military hospitality institutions that are now increasing in numbers could potentially run their private competitors out of business without necessarily contributing much to the economy in an accountable manner. 'They can afford to charge their rooms and other services at highly subsidised rates far below the market value because it is the military officers and personnel who are being paid to work for Nigerians that are being taken there, to do guard duty, and other jobs', the source said.

Education: The Nigerian military has developed a range of educational institutions from primary to university levels, including specialized service universities. Military schools are strategically situated near barracks, particularly where local communities lack schools. A senior military officer explained,

> So, in a situation like that, the Army can make a case for opening a primary or a secondary school purely to serve soldiers that are in that barracks, but it is also encouraged that 20–30 per cent allotments for the local community as part of corporate social responsibility. But the expected practice is that if there is a government school there, they should not be permitted to open another school.

But the reality today is that this basic concept is not observed but abused with the mushrooming of military schools purely for commercial purposes, and some are even situated completely outside the base. 'I can tell you that after finance people, the other people that have money are the education people, just like I told you about the hotels. When you come to the education sector, there is the same issue.'

He continued:

> Just like I told you about the hotels, when you come to the education sector, this is the same issue. For example, if you are the proprietor of a private school, you will have to pay for teachers, power, water, and everything from your pocket. On the other hand, the military builds and funds these schools with government money, yet gets free or subsidized services from personnel such as teachers, guards and pays bills from budgeted funds. The implication is that if a private school proprietor charges, for example, N10,000 per pupil in your school, the military schools can comfortably charge N2,000 without blinking.

Medical Centres: The same rules that guide the establishment of schools at bases also apply to hospitals. One soldier said:

> Till I die, I will oppose why the Air Force went to open a specialist hospital in Daura. The same concept for school is the same concept for opening a medical unit; it is based on identified needs, based on how many officers, soldiers, and their families are in that area that does not have healthcare. It is not to open it for making money, but today that is what these medical centres are for.

Real Estate: The military services are actively engaged in the property business and real estate development. Even though the primary purpose of various housing schemes is to provide accommodation to their officers and personnel at subsidized rates, these are increasingly being built with civilians as potential buyers and at a profitable rate. The real estate schemes by the AFN have blossomed into money-making ventures.

Others: The military also operates other commercial ventures as revealed in the document from the Nigerian Army, including catering and events management, private guards' firms and engineering companies, among others.

The Issues Militating Against Welfare and Commercial Ventures in the Nigerian Armed Forces

The essence of this aspect is to beam the searchlight on the funding and financial management of the commercial ventures by the Nigerian military because it is largely unaccounted for and hardly talked about, yet it has a great consequential effect on national security, economy and development. Even though the discussion about monitoring and tracking the defence budget has barely scratched the surface, it is, however, mostly focused on first, the funds allocated in the annual budget. Whereas further efforts by the media as well as the governmental and non-governmental anti-corruption agencies like Transparency International (TI) and its Nigerian affiliate, the Civil Society Legislative Advocacy Centre (CISLAC), are focused to unravel the extra and off-budgetary allocations like the controversial $1 billion Excess Crude Account funds, the infamous security votes and much talked about $2.1 Dasukigate scandals; no one has bothered to find out the revenue churning and spinning commercial ventures by security agencies. Discussing them has become imperative for the following reasons:

Black Hole

There is concern by some security experts and stakeholders that the growing penchant for the establishment of commercial ventures could be a black hole that sucks defence funding without a trace or accountability. This means that billions that could be ploughed back into the economy, especially the defence and security sector, are largely unaccounted for. A senior military officer who spoke to *Global Sentinel* (Iroegbu, 2024) on the condition of anonymity revealed that most of these ventures are built and sustained with government money, and they cannot be traced to any budgetary overhead.

One security source stressed:

> What will astonish you is that if you take all the military budget, you will not see where they make provisions for the running of the NAF Club. The big question is, where is the money coming from? This means they have a lot of loose money in the budget; they don't put it on paper because if it appears that the military is budgeting money to run a hotel, people will start asking questions. It is not reflected in the budget, but every year, they get money. It is a big question.

Off-Budget and Unconstitutional

Also, alarming is the fact that monies made from these ventures are never accounted for and remitted to the government coffers. These are off-budget earnings and expenditures that distort the overall defence budget allocation and procurement processes. This is also added to the fact that these ventures and the money earned from them are outside the realm of legislative oversight and, hence, unconstitutional.

Robbing Peter to Pay Paul

This is like a case of stealing from the government or using the money allocated for other projects, programmes and procurement purposes that are being re-channelled (sometimes illegally) to these ventures. The implication is that other aspects of defence and security suffer from regular complaints that the money is never enough for internal security operations.

Impacts on CTCOIN/Insecurity

One of the probable impacts is that it could negatively impact internal security operations, counterterrorism and counterinsurgency (CT-COIN) operations by diverting the attention of the military from the core issues of national defence and security to money-making ventures.

Impacts on the Economy

There is an argument that this could also negatively impact the economy, as the highly (and illegally) subsidized military ventures ruin and run private competitors out of business. And since most of the earnings from these establishments are never remitted or taxed, they eventually drain from and distort the economy. According to a counterterrorism expert, there is an economic and social problem attached to that. He said:

> So, in other countries that I have studied, the commercial venture is protected from these people. While the businessmen are hiring workers, they are taking government money and will run that man out of business. People mustn't lose their jobs, and it's also important to protect the hotel business. You cannot use government money to subsidize rates while others cannot compete.

Copycat Effect

Since money is involved, which is largely unregulated, unaccounted for and at the whims and caprices of military top brass, there is a danger of such practices being abused. Since every new service chief is at liberty to set up their legacy project, there is now a growing trend – a race to establish more commercial ventures by the service chiefs. The growing copycat effect could grow out of control.

State-Within-a-State

The most prominent danger is the fear of the emergence of a military-industrial complex, as warned by the 34th United States president, Dwight Eisenhower, that could be detrimental to national security itself. This is when a military grows so powerful that it becomes a state within a state, as seen in the case of Egypt and Pakistan, where this practice of commercial ventures is entrenched. The fear is that since the money is accounted for and unregulated, the military could grow so rich and powerful that it can no longer be controlled by civil authority.

Security Chiefs as the Accountants

Our investigation revealed that the security chiefs are the top dogs when it comes to the overall funding and financial management of these entities. A senior military officer who spoke to *Global Sentinel* (Iroegbu, 2024) on this issue explained how it works, saying:

> Another issue is that when it comes to accountability, there is no external accountability. In the military, because there is no external oversight, every financial decision rests solely on the decision of the service chief. The issue of promotion also rests with the chief, who decides who should be promoted or not, so it's not based on merit. So, the issue is that business ventures are prevalent among military chiefs. They bring in their sycophants to fill positions that are beneficial to them. That is not accountability, as they call themselves general managers, MDs, GMs, etc. They give funny names to generals in the military.
>
> He continued:
>
> This is why we are having an excess of major generals. The 'kudi-kudi' (meaning money-making offices) are only for major generals. Let me be honest with you; this is why some of the most crooked officers we see today are mainly major generals. You will be shocked that the US Armed Forces, with over 1,000,000 in strength, has just about 1,000 while the AFN, with barely 200,000 personnel, has almost 900 generals. So, you can imagine.

However, a former service chief, who spoke to *Global Sentinel* (Iroegbu, 2024) on the issue, did agree with Eisenhower on the need to be careful with the military-industrial complex but argued that every environment is unique in its own needs. According to him, there is a genuine rationale for setting the Nigerian military establishment the way it is, including the welfare and commercial ventures. He noted that it's wrong to compare Nigeria with an advanced democracy, as the country is still in the process of nation-building and should be allowed to grow through the process without being cajoled.

Silence or Fear?

Unfortunately, other stakeholders contacted by *Global Sentinel* (Iroegbu, 2024), including military spokespersons, security experts, legislators, and members of civil society organizations (CSOs), either refused to respond to our inquiries or lacked the requisite knowledge and information about the topic. Most of those who eventually spoke did so under the condition of anonymity, except a few who agreed to be quoted. Accordingly, this medium reached out to the Director of Defence Information (DDI), Maj-Gen. Ohwonigho Akpor, Director of Army Public Relations (DAPR), Brig-Gen. Onyema Nwachukwu, Director of Information Navy (DINFO), Commodore Adedotun Ayo-Vaughan, and Director of Public Relations (DOPRI), Air Commodore Edward Gabkwet, but received the silent treatment. But Ayo-Vaughan redirected us to a senior officer to speak on the matter, but the officer never responded.

Also contacted was the chairman of the House Committee on Army, the Hon. Abdulrazak Namdas, and another legislator with knowledge of the defence sector, the Hon. Jimi Benson, who could not respond to calls and messages sent to them. Other members of CSOs and security experts also did not respond to inquiries put forward to them, while those who responded explained a lack of knowledge on the subject. They were questioned about:

- How viable and profitable the ventures are
- How accountable the military is with the management of these ventures
- How can it be regulated and overseen
- Any other resources and recommendations

The investigation was also aiming to 'know the constitutional mandate of the ventures' and asked the following questions: What are the sources of funding for these ventures? How do they spend the money they make? Are they responsible for their funding? Do they have accountability mechanisms embedded within their organizational structure? If they do, how do the accountability instruments work and how effective are they?

There were, however, some insights provided by Mr Vahyala Kwaga, a Senior Research and Policy Analyst with BudgIT, who shared a document that gave a four-year insight into the nature of security budgeting and expenditure in Nigeria (2014–2018), none of which captured or factored in the plethora of 'welfare and commercial ventures'. The document, however, highlighted that 'an increasing share of Nigeria's security budget is being dedicated to the payment of salaries and emoluments of its personnel. Capital expenditure – including investments in weapons systems, communication systems, logistics infrastructure, physical infrastructure, housing, among others – is decreasing relatively in comparison to the rest of the budget.'

Challenges

In the course of this research, *Global Sentinel* (Iroegbu, 2024) discovered that there are key challenges militating against effective oversight of this sector.

Lack of legal backing: These ventures are not legislated upon and therefore, in the eyes of the law, do not exist. Just like this proved to be the albatross of various corruption cases involving defence and security procurement, it makes it difficult to prosecute or hold anyone accountable. This is also added to the fact that the official information is protected through the Official Secrets Act, which prohibits the collection, possession or dissemination of official information and state secrets.

Lack of capacity for legislative oversight: One of the major impediments to effective tracking and monitoring of the defence budget is the general lack of capacity or even connivance on the part of the legislators in their oversight functions. Most times, these legislators lack basic knowledge of their roles to hold government officials, including the security chiefs, accountable for the use of public funds. In some cases, they either get intimidated or are compelled to look the other way.

Lack of political will: Similar to the lack of capacity for legislative oversight is also the absence of political will on the part of the commander-in-chief of the armed forces to hold the security chiefs accountable. Most times, the president and other arms of government are beholden to the security chiefs, so that they hardly monitor their activities or hold them accountable.

Esprit de corps/military culture: Reporting issues of corruption within the defence and security sector is an enormous task because they often hide under the oath of secrecy in matters concerning defence budgeting and expenditures. The closeness of the security sector often allows the parties in power to easily abuse their positions in these sectors. Indeed, the ability to classify security budgets and funding provides an opportunity for various cases of abuse. In addition, organizational culture in the defence sector carries a considerable risk of solidarity among the officers and men to the extent of covering up the corrupt practices of colleagues, despite being aware of the case. More so, the defence sector stakeholders, particularly military forces, have a strong inclination towards secrecy. The military and other security and intelligence actors often try to limit the amount and quality of the information they release. Some part of military planning and activity is compromised if it becomes publicly available, which justifies a certain degree of confidentiality in some areas. However, secrecy requirements are often used as a pretext to hide unlawful activities like the establishment, earnings and management of the business platforms in the AFN.

Way Forward

Reforms

If the issue of transparency and accountability is to be achieved in the security and defence sector, then it must be backed with aggressive and sustainable reforms, including updating, repealing and enforcing some relevant laws. For example, the Freedom of Information Act has, by its very nature, repealed the often-cited Official Secrets Act, but the reality is different. Similarly, efforts should be made to implement various recommendations by various defence and security sector reform committees.

Presidential Declarations

As the number one chief security officer of the state and commander-in-chief of the armed forces, the president could abolish, nullify, repeal and reform some practices within the military that lack legislative backing with a just pronouncement or executive order. A member of one of the reform committees told *Global Sentinel* (Iroegbu, 2024) that one of their key recommendations was to abolish these commercial ventures or at the very least ensure effective regulation, monitoring and accountability. The source said:

> There is no special law that says that the military should do business. They are only operating in the absence of anyone looking into them. So, this could be stopped today with an announcement directing the military not to do business; it is an instruction. The business is distracting them from their job. I have read some research that says, apart from distracting the military from their primary duty, it is an abuse of a general's rank, especially a combatant who is put in charge of managing a hotel. Do you know how many generals we have? We have over one thousand generals, too many generals, that's why all the people conducting business in the army and navies are generals. It is bad, apart from affecting the work, there are socio-economic issues.

Effective Oversight

Similar to the presidential declaration, the legislators could be encouraged to ensure effective oversight of the sector. However, they cannot do this without the needed capacity. To this end, it is either the National Assembly embarks on capacity-building training, engages the services of experts and consultants or the political system is reformed in such a way that ensures those with the requisite experience, knowledge and capacity are either elected into the legislative chambers or appointed into the committees and relevant ministries, departments and agencies (MDAs).

Transparency and Accountability with the AFN

Also, crucial is to create a mechanism that encourages internal transparency and accountability of the funding, financial management and procurement process within the security and military services. This will also cascade down their various units and platforms, including the welfare and commercial ventures.

Conclusion

The security and defence sectors are crucial to both the internal and external security of Nigeria as well as the overall development of the country and the well-being of its citizens. And because a lot of funds go into this critical sector, it is imperative that there is adequate monitoring of these funds of the armed forces to enable them to purchase modern military equipment to fight various security threats as enunciated by BudgIT in its four-year security sector analysis in 2018, including a threat to oil installations, Boko Haram, kidnappings, Niger Delta militancy, armed robbery, herdsmen-farmers clashes, cattle rustlers, pipeline vandalism, inter-tribal clashes, cultism, extortion and hooliganism, religious clashes and tensions, piracy and extra-judicial killing.

Monitoring and tracking of funds allocated to this sector have proved very difficult because of so many factors, chief among them being the opaque nature of the defence and security sector. Nevertheless, spirited efforts are being made by the media in fulfilment of its watchdog role, which is also complemented by active inputs by the anti-graft agencies and CSOs like BudgIT, TI and CISLAC, among others.

However, the focus of this research and investigation by *Global Sentinel* (Iroegbu, 2024) helped to show that while a lot of efforts are focused on tracking the legislated budgetary allocations to ensure accountability and transparency, most of the corruption cases are from off-budget or extra-budgetary sources, like the security votes and the controversial Excess Crude Account $1 billion security fund. But more glaring gaps remain in the inability of the government, especially the legislators and other stakeholders, to oversee the multi-billion Naira 'welfare and commercial ventures' of the Nigerian military.

The implication of the unregulated nature of this practice is, however, lost on most Nigerians, including its negative impact on the economy and its potential to jeopardize national security in the long run. As a solution, a senior military source suggested: 'If today I become president or I become a minister and the government gives me power, I will transfer those universities from the place where they are. I will give them to the state government. It is another source of money not accounted for, so when we say business ventures, think of schools, hotels, and medical centres'.

References

Alvarez, S.A., and J.B. Barney (2007). 'Discovery and Creation: Alternative Theories of Entrepreneurial Action', *Strategic Entrepreneurship Journal*, 1(1–2): 11–26. Available at: https://doi.org/10.1002/sej.2

Asian Economic News (1999). 'Thai Military-Controlled Media Business Scrutinized', *Asian Economic News*, 31 May. Available at: https://www.thefreelibrary.com/Thai+military-controlled+media+business+scrutinized.-a054888651

Australian Associated Press (2004). 'Indonesian Military to Lose Business Empire', Australian Associated Press, 9 December.

Cohen, S.P. (1998). *The Pakistan Army*. New York: Oxford University Press.

Fayemi, J.K. (2000). 'Soldiers in Business: Entrenched Military Interests and Nigeria's Political Economy' (paper presented at the International Conference on Soldiers in Business, Jakarta, Indonesia, 17–19 October).

Frantz, D. (2001). 'Military Bestrides Turkey's Path to the European Union', *New York Times*, 14 January. Available at: https://www.nytimes.com/2002/05/10/opinion/IHT-corruption-and-extremism-in-pakistan-why-musharraf-clings-to.html

Frederick, M.N. (1983). *Yesterday's Soldiers: European Military Professionalism in South America, 1890–1940*. Lincoln: University of Nebraska Press.

Harrison, S. (2002). 'Why Musharraf Clings to Power', *International Herald Tribune*, 10 May. Available at: https://www.smh.com.au/world/indon-military-to-lose-business-empire-20041210-gdkaay.html

Hintze, O. (1975). 'The Territorial State', in K. Wittfogel and L. Manning (eds), *Studies in the Institutional History of Early Modern Russia*, 25–55. Chicago: University of Chicago Press.

Huntington, S. (1957). *The Soldier and the State*. Cambridge, MA: The Belknap Press of Harvard University Press.

Iroegbu, S. (2024). Special report: Tracking Nigerian military's commercial ventures? *Global Sentinel*. Available at: https://globalsentinelng.com/special-report-tracking-nigerian-militarys-commercial-ventures/

Katz, J., and D.A. Shepherd (2003). *Entrepreneurial Small Business: An International Perspective*. Upper Saddle River, NJ: Prentice Hall.

Mani, K. (2007). 'Militaries in Business: State-Making and Entrepreneurship in the Developing World', *Armed Forces & Society*, 33: 591–611. Available at: https://doi.org/10.1177/0095327X06291348

Migdal, J.S. (1988). *Strong Societies and Weak States*. Princeton, NJ: Princeton University Press.

Mulvenon, J. (1999). 'Soldiers of Fortune: The Rise and Fall of the Chinese Military-Business Complex, 1978–1999', in BICC Paper #15. Bonn, Germany: Bonn International Centre for Conversion, October.

Sautet, F. (2014). *Entrepreneurship and the Market Process*. London: Routledge.

Scott, J.C. (1999). *Seeing like a State: How Certain Schemes to Improve the Human Condition Have Failed*. New Haven, CT: Yale University Press.

Shane, S. (2000). 'Prior Knowledge and the Discovery of Entrepreneurial Opportunities', *Organization Science*, 11(4): 448–69. Available at: https://doi.org/10.1287/orsc.11.4.448.12516

Singer, P.W. (2004). *Corporate Warriors: The Rise of the Privatized Military Industry*. Ithaca, NY: Cornell University Press.

Skocpol, T. (1985). *States and Social Revolutions*. Cambridge: Cambridge University Press.

Steinfioff, S., and J. Burgers (1993). 'Entrepreneurship: The New Venture', *Journal of Business Venturing*, 8(2): 105–21.

Stepan, J. (1978). 'The State and Society: Peru in Comparative Perspective', *American Political Science Review*, 72(3): 852–66.

Stevenson, H.H. (1990). 'A Perspective on Entrepreneurship', Harvard Business School Working Paper, 9-390-020.

Suleiman, M. (2006). *Entrepreneurship and Small Business Management*. Beirut: Dar El Fikr.

Sven, S., K. Thelen and F. Longstreth (eds) (1992). *Structuring Politics: Historical Institutionalism in Comparative Analysis*. Cambridge: Cambridge University Press.

Tilly, C. (1985). 'War Making and State Making as Organised Crime,' in P. B. Evans, D. Rueschemeyer and T. Skocpol (eds), *Bringing the State Back In*, 169–91. Cambridge: Cambridge University Press.

Tilly, C. (1992). *Coercion, Capital and European States, AD 990–1992*. Cambridge, MA: Blackwell.

Whittaker, C.A., R. McKee and C. Simms (2009). 'The Process of Opportunity Exploitation: An Entrepreneurial Perspective', *Journal of Business Venturing*, 24(1): 1–17. Available at: https://doi.org/10.1016/j.jbusvent.2008.01.002

Part II

Technology and Militarization

4

The Role of Artificial Intelligence in Enhancing Defence and Security Enterprise Networks

Onyeka Leo Onuorah and Ijeoma Chinyere Onuorah

This chapter explores the integration of artificial intelligence (AI) into Nigeria's defence and security enterprise networks, focusing on its potential to enhance threat detection and response capabilities. As global security challenges grow increasingly complex, AI offers significant opportunities to improve surveillance, cybersecurity and predictive analytics within defence systems. However, the successful implementation of AI in Nigeria faces several challenges, including infrastructural limitations, data quality and privacy concerns and a shortage of skilled personnel. The chapter examines these challenges alongside the opportunities that AI presents, such as automated decision-making, resource optimization and proactive threat management. Additionally, the chapter highlights the importance of addressing ethical and legal issues associated with AI, particularly concerning autonomous systems and data privacy. By investing in technological infrastructure, enhancing data management practices and developing a skilled workforce, Nigeria can overcome these obstacles and fully realize the benefits of AI integration.

The rapid advancement of AI has significantly impacted various sectors globally, including defence and security. AI technologies are being integrated into military operations, cyber defence and strategic decision-making processes to enhance the capabilities of defence networks. According to the International Institute for Strategic Studies (IISS) (2020), AI has the potential to revolutionize military operations by improving the speed and accuracy of data analysis, enabling real-time decision-making and enhancing the overall effectiveness of defence systems. AI-driven systems, such as autonomous drones, predictive analytics, and AI-based cybersecurity tools, are now essential components of modern military arsenals.

One of the most critical applications of AI in defence is in cybersecurity. With the increasing complexity and sophistication of cyber threats, traditional defence mechanisms have become inadequate. AI provides advanced tools for threat detection, response and mitigation, making it a cornerstone in the defence against cyberattacks. For instance, NATO has emphasized the importance of AI in bolstering cybersecurity measures, particularly in identifying and countering state-sponsored cyber threats (NATO, 2021). Furthermore, AI's ability to process and analyse vast amounts of data has enabled the development of predictive analytics that can forecast potential threats and vulnerabilities, thus allowing for pre-emptive measures to be taken.

In addition to cybersecurity, AI plays a crucial role in enhancing the operational efficiency of military networks. The U.S. Department of Defence (DoD) has been at the forefront of adopting AI for network management, particularly in optimizing communication systems, automating routine tasks, and improving the resilience of military networks against disruptions (DoD, 2019). The global defence community recognizes that the integration of AI into military networks not only enhances operational capabilities but also ensures that these networks remain secure, resilient and adaptable to the ever-evolving nature of modern warfare.

In Africa, the adoption of AI in defence and security is still in its nascent stages, but it is gaining momentum as countries recognize the strategic importance of AI in modern military operations. The African Union (AU) has acknowledged the potential of AI to address the continent's unique security challenges, including terrorism, cybercrime and border security (AU, 2020). Countries such as South Africa and Egypt have started investing in AI research and development to enhance their defence capabilities, particularly in areas such as surveillance, cybersecurity and intelligence gathering. The use of AI in cybersecurity is particularly relevant for African countries, which have seen a significant increase in cyber threats in recent years. The African Cybersecurity Report (2021) highlighted the growing concern over cyberattacks targeting critical infrastructure in several African nations. AI-based solutions are being explored to strengthen the cybersecurity frameworks of these countries, to mitigate the risks associated with cyber threats.

Despite these advancements, the adoption of AI in defence across Africa is hindered by challenges such as limited technological infrastructure, lack of skilled personnel and insufficient funding for AI research and development. However, regional collaborations and partnerships with international organizations are helping to bridge these gaps, enabling African countries to leverage AI for defence and security purposes.

In Nigeria, the integration of AI into defence and security networks is increasingly recognized as a crucial element in addressing the country's complex security challenges. Nigeria faces a range of security threats, including terrorism, insurgency, cybercrime and piracy. The Nigerian government has acknowledged the role of technology, particularly AI, in enhancing the effectiveness of its defence and security apparatus. The National Information Technology Development Agency (NITDA) has been at the forefront of promoting AI adoption in various sectors, including defence and security (NITDA, 2022). AI's potential to enhance Nigeria's defence capabilities is evident in several areas. For instance, AI-driven surveillance systems can improve border security by detecting and responding to unauthorized movements and activities in real-time. Similarly, AI-based predictive analytics can help security agencies anticipate and respond to threats more effectively, thereby reducing the risk of attacks and improving overall security.

In the realm of cybersecurity, Nigeria has faced a growing number of cyber threats targeting both government and private sector entities. The Nigerian Communications Commission (NCC) has highlighted the importance of AI in strengthening the country's cybersecurity framework, particularly in detecting and mitigating cyber threats (NCC, 2021). AI's ability to analyse large datasets and identify patterns makes it a valuable tool in the fight against cybercrime, which poses a significant threat to Nigeria's national security. Despite these advancements, Nigeria still faces challenges in fully integrating AI into its defence and security networks. Issues such as limited technological infrastructure, lack of skilled AI professionals and insufficient funding for AI initiatives continue to hinder progress. However, with the government's growing emphasis on technology-driven solutions and increasing collaboration with international partners, there is potential for significant advancements in the use of AI in Nigeria's defence and security sector.

The growing complexity of security threats in Nigeria, ranging from terrorism and insurgency to cybercrime and piracy, has exposed significant vulnerabilities in the country's defence and security networks. Traditional approaches to managing these threats have proven inadequate, given the increasing sophistication of adversaries who leverage advanced technologies to outmanoeuvre conventional security measures. Despite the global recognition of AI as a transformative tool for enhancing defence and security, Nigeria's adoption of AI-driven solutions remains limited. This gap has left the country's critical infrastructure and national security assets exposed to various threats, undermining the effectiveness of its security operations. There is a pressing need to explore how AI can be effectively integrated into Nigeria's defence and security networks to address these challenges, enhance threat detection and response capabilities and improve the overall resilience of the country's security apparatus.

Given this stated problem, the study attempts to examine the potential impact of AI on the enhancement of threat detection and response capabilities within Nigeria's defence and security networks. As well as to assess the challenges and opportunities associated with integrating AI into Nigeria's defence and security enterprise networks.

Understanding the Concept of AI

AI is a branch of computer science that aims to create machines capable of performing tasks that typically require human intelligence. These tasks include reasoning, learning, problem-solving, perception and understanding natural language. The concept of AI is rooted in the idea that machines can be programmed to simulate human cognitive processes, enabling them to perform complex functions autonomously or with minimal human intervention. The concept of AI has evolved significantly since its inception. The term 'artificial intelligence' was first coined by John McCarthy in 1956 during the Dartmouth Conference, which is widely regarded as the birth of AI as a field of study (McCarthy et al., 1956). Early AI research focused on symbolic AI, which involves programming computers to manipulate symbols and solve problems based on a set of predefined rules. This approach led to the development of early AI systems such as expert systems, which were designed to mimic the decision-making abilities of human experts in specific domains (Russell and Norvig, 2016).

In the 1980s and 1990s, AI research shifted towards machine learning, a subset of AI that focuses on the development of algorithms that allow machines to learn from data and improve their performance over time. This paradigm shift was driven by the realization that many real-world problems are too complex to be solved by rule-based systems alone. Machine learning, particularly through the use of neural networks, has enabled significant advancements in AI, leading to the development of systems capable of recognizing patterns, making predictions and adapting to new situations (Goodfellow et al., 2016).

Core Components of AI

AI encompasses several key components, each contributing to its ability to perform intelligent tasks. These components include:

Machine Learning (ML): ML is a core component of AI that involves the development of algorithms that enable machines to learn from and make decisions based on data. ML techniques include supervised learning, unsupervised learning and reinforcement learning, each of which has applications in various domains, including image recognition, natural language processing, and autonomous systems (Goodfellow et al., 2016).

Natural Language Processing (NLP): NLP enables machines to understand and generate human language. This component of AI is crucial for applications such as speech recognition, language translation and sentiment analysis. NLP techniques are used in virtual assistants like Siri and Alexa, which can interpret and respond to user queries in natural language (Jurafsky and Martin, 2021).

Computer Vision: Computer vision involves the development of algorithms that allow machines to interpret and analyse visual information from the world, such as images and videos. This component is essential for applications like facial recognition, object detection, and autonomous vehicles (Szeliski, 2010).

Robotics: Robotics is an interdisciplinary field that integrates AI with mechanical engineering, electronics and computer science to create machines that can perform tasks in the physical world. AI enables robots to navigate, manipulate objects and interact with their environment autonomously (Siciliano and Khatib, 2016).

Expert Systems: These are AI systems designed to mimic the decision-making abilities of human experts. Expert systems use knowledge bases and inference engines to solve specific problems within domains like medical diagnosis, financial planning and engineering (Russell and Norvig, 2016).

Applications of AI

AI has found applications in various fields, ranging from healthcare and finance to transportation and entertainment. In healthcare, AI is used for diagnosing diseases, predicting patient outcomes and personalizing treatment plans. In finance, AI algorithms are employed for fraud detection, algorithmic trading and risk assessment.

Autonomous vehicles, powered by AI, are transforming the transportation industry by enabling self-driving cars that can navigate and make decisions without human input (Brynjolfsson and McAfee, 2014).

In the defence and security sector, AI is increasingly being used to enhance cybersecurity, automate surveillance and support decision-making in military operations. AI-driven systems can analyse vast amounts of data in real-time, identify potential threats and recommend appropriate responses. This has led to the development of autonomous drones, AI-based threat detection systems, and intelligent command and control systems that improve the efficiency and effectiveness of military operations (Taddeo and Floridi, 2018).

Ethical and Societal Implications

While AI offers numerous benefits, it also raises ethical and societal concerns. One major concern is the potential for AI systems to make biased decisions, particularly if they are trained on data that reflects existing social inequalities. This has led to calls for greater transparency and accountability in AI development, as well as the implementation of ethical guidelines to ensure that AI is used responsibly (Binns, 2018).

Another concern is the impact of AI on employment. As AI systems become more capable, there is a risk that they could displace human workers in certain industries, leading to job losses and economic disruption. However, some experts argue that AI could also create new opportunities by enabling humans to focus on higher-level tasks that require creativity and emotional intelligence (Brynjolfsson and McAfee, 2014).

AI is a rapidly evolving field that has the potential to transform various aspects of society. From its origins in symbolic reasoning to the modern advancements in ML and robotics, AI continues to push the boundaries of what machines can do. While AI offers significant opportunities for enhancing productivity, improving decision-making and solving complex problems, it also presents challenges that must be carefully managed. As AI continues to develop, it will be crucial to ensure that it is used in ways that are ethical, transparent and beneficial to society.

Understanding the Concept of Defence and Security Enterprise

The concept of a defence and security enterprise (DSE) encompasses the integrated systems, policies and structures employed by a state or organization to safeguard its national security interests. These enterprises are designed to protect against a broad range of threats, including military aggression, terrorism, cyberattacks and other forms of destabilization. The concept of DSE reflects a holistic approach to national security, incorporating both traditional defence mechanisms and modern technological advancements to address evolving security challenges. Historically, the concept of defence and security was primarily centred on the military's role in protecting a nation's sovereignty and territorial integrity. Traditional defence structures were heavily reliant on armed forces, physical fortifications and conventional warfare strategies. However, the changing nature of threats in the twentieth and twenty-first centuries has necessitated a broader approach to national security. The Cold War era, for example, introduced the concept of nuclear deterrence and intelligence-led security operations as essential components of national defence (Gray, 1990).

The end of the Cold War and the rise of asymmetric threats, such as terrorism and cyber warfare, further expanded the scope of DSEs. The 9/11 attacks in the United States marked a significant shift in global security paradigms, leading to the development of more comprehensive and integrated security strategies that address both state and non-state actors (Buzan and Hansen, 2009). This shift underscored the need for a coordinated approach that involves not only the military but also intelligence agencies, law enforcement, cybersecurity experts and other stakeholders.

Core Components of DSE

A DSE typically includes several key components, each playing a crucial role in maintaining national security. These components are integrated to create a cohesive and responsive system capable of addressing various threats.

Military Forces: The military remains the cornerstone of any DSE, responsible for defending the nation against external threats and conducting operations that protect national interests. This includes land, air, sea and, increasingly, space and cyber forces (Gray, 1990). Modern military forces are equipped with advanced technology, including AI-driven systems, drones and cyber defence capabilities, to enhance their operational effectiveness (Singer, 2009).

Intelligence Agencies: Intelligence is a critical component of DSE, providing the information necessary to anticipate, identify and counter threats. Intelligence agencies collect and analyse data from a variety of sources, including human intelligence (HUMINT), signals intelligence (SIGINT), and open-source intelligence (OSINT), to inform decision-making at all levels of government (Lowenthal, 2017). The integration of AI and ML into intelligence analysis has significantly improved the speed and accuracy of threat detection.

Cybersecurity: In the digital age, cybersecurity has become an indispensable element of national security. Cyber threats, including hacking, espionage and cyber-terrorism, can target critical infrastructure, government systems and private sector networks. A robust cybersecurity framework within a DSE is essential to protect sensitive information and ensure the resilience of national infrastructure (Singer and Friedman, 2014). This involves collaboration between government agencies, private sector partners and international allies.

Law Enforcement: Law enforcement agencies play a vital role in maintaining internal security and countering domestic threats such as terrorism, organized crime and civil unrest. Within a DSE, law enforcement works closely with intelligence and military components to address security challenges that cross national borders and involve both state and non-state actors (Bayley, 2006).

Policy and Governance: Effective governance and policy frameworks are crucial to the functioning of a DSE. National security policies define the strategic objectives, roles and responsibilities of various components of the DSE. These policies also ensure that security operations are conducted within the bounds of the law and respect human rights (Buzan and Hansen, 2009). Governance structures coordinate the efforts of different agencies and ensure that resources are allocated efficiently.

Private Sector and Industry: The private sector, particularly industries involved in technology, defence and critical infrastructure, plays an increasingly important role in the DSE. Public-private partnerships are essential for developing advanced defence technologies, securing supply chains and protecting critical infrastructure from cyber threats (Kshetri, 2010). The private sector also contributes to the resilience of the national economy, which is a key aspect of overall security.

Globally, the concept of DSE is implemented in various forms, depending on the specific security needs and resources of each country. For example, the United States has a highly advanced DSE that integrates military, intelligence and cybersecurity capabilities to address global threats (Singer, 2009). In contrast, smaller nations may focus more on regional security concerns and rely on international alliances to bolster their defence capabilities (Buzan and Hansen, 2009).

In the Nigerian context, the DSE is evolving to address the country's unique security challenges, including insurgency, terrorism and piracy. Nigeria's DSE includes the military, which is engaged in counter-insurgency operations against groups like Boko Haram, as well as intelligence and law enforcement agencies working to prevent terrorist attacks and secure the nation's borders (Onuoha, 2013). The Nigerian government is also increasingly focused on cybersecurity, recognizing the growing threat posed by cyberattacks on critical infrastructure and financial systems (Osah, 2020). However, Nigeria's DSE faces challenges related to limited resources, corruption and the need for better coordination among security agencies.

Global Perspectives on AI in Defence and Security

AI has become a critical component of modern defence and security strategies worldwide. AI's ability to process large volumes of data, recognize patterns, and make decisions autonomously has led to its widespread adoption in military and security operations (Singer, 2009). The integration of AI into defence systems is seen as a force multiplier, enhancing the capabilities of traditional defence mechanisms while introducing new operational paradigms.

One significant area of AI application is in autonomous systems, such as drones and unmanned vehicles, which are increasingly used for surveillance, reconnaissance and even combat operations (Scharre, 2018). These systems can operate in environments that are too dangerous for humans, providing real-time data and executing missions with a high degree of precision. AI-driven systems are also employed in cybersecurity to detect and respond to threats more quickly than human operators could, thus safeguarding critical infrastructure and national security assets (Singer and Friedman,

2014). Moreover, AI is transforming the way intelligence is gathered and analysed. ML algorithms are now capable of processing vast amounts of data from various sources, including satellite imagery, social media and intercepted communications. This has significantly improved the ability of intelligence agencies to predict and prevent threats (Lowenthal, 2017). For instance, AI has been used to track the movements of terrorist groups, analyse the likelihood of future attacks and even identify potential insider threats within security agencies (Taddeo and Floridi, 2018).

However, the integration of AI into defence and security also raises ethical and strategic concerns. There are fears that AI could lower the threshold for conflict, as autonomous systems could be deployed without direct human oversight, leading to unintended escalations (Sharkey, 2012). Additionally, the potential for AI systems to be hacked or manipulated by adversaries poses a significant risk, highlighting the need for robust cybersecurity measures and ethical guidelines (Binns, 2018).

AI Applications in Specific Security Domains

Cybersecurity

Cybersecurity is one of the most critical areas where AI has made significant contributions. As cyber threats become more sophisticated, traditional security measures have struggled to keep pace. AI offers advanced solutions by automating threat detection and response processes. AI systems can analyse network traffic, identify patterns indicative of malicious activity and respond in real-time to mitigate the impact of cyberattacks (Singer and Friedman, 2014).

Deep learning techniques, a subset of AI, have been particularly effective in identifying previously unknown threats (zero-day attacks) by analysing anomalies in network behaviour. AI-driven cybersecurity systems are also capable of adapting to new threats by learning from previous incidents, making them more effective over time (Goodfellow et al., 2016).

Surveillance and Reconnaissance

AI plays a pivotal role in enhancing surveillance and reconnaissance operations. AI-powered systems can process vast amounts of visual and sensor data from surveillance cameras, drones and satellites, enabling real-time monitoring and analysis. These systems can detect unusual patterns, track individuals or vehicles, and provide actionable intelligence to security personnel (Szeliski, 2010). For instance, AI has been used in border security to monitor and control illegal crossings by analysing real-time video feeds and automatically alerting authorities to potential breaches (Singer, 2009). In urban environments, AI-driven facial recognition systems are employed to identify suspects and track their movements across multiple locations, assisting law enforcement agencies in preventing crimes and apprehending criminals (Garvie et al., 2016).

Autonomous Weapon Systems

The development of autonomous weapon systems (AWS) represents one of the most controversial applications of AI in defence. AWS are capable of selecting and engaging targets without human intervention, raising significant ethical and legal questions about their use in combat (Scharre, 2018). Proponents argue that AWS can reduce the risk to human soldiers and increase the precision of military operations, thereby minimizing collateral damage. However, critics warn of the potential for these systems to malfunction or be used inappropriately, leading to unintended casualties and escalating conflicts (Sharkey, 2012).

The debate over AWS has led to calls for international regulations and treaties to govern its development and deployment. The United Nations and various non-governmental organizations have been actively discussing the implications of AI in warfare, advocating for a ban on fully autonomous weapons that operate without meaningful human control (Russell et al., 2015).

Challenges and Opportunities in the Nigerian Context

Nigeria, like many developing countries, faces unique challenges in integrating AI into its DSE networks. These challenges include limited technological infrastructure, insufficient funding and a lack of skilled personnel to develop and maintain AI systems (Osah, 2020). Additionally, corruption and bureaucratic inefficiencies within the security sector further hinder the effective implementation of AI-driven solutions (Onuoha, 2013).

Despite these challenges, there are significant opportunities for AI to enhance Nigeria's defence and security capabilities. For instance, AI can be used to improve intelligence gathering and analysis, particularly in the fight against insurgency in the northeastern region of the country. AI systems can analyse data from various sources, including satellite imagery and intercepted communications, to provide actionable intelligence that can help military and law enforcement agencies combat terrorist groups like Boko Haram (Campbell and Harwood, 2018).

Furthermore, AI can play a crucial role in addressing Nigeria's cybersecurity challenges. With the increasing digitization of the economy and the rise of cybercrime, there is a pressing need for advanced cybersecurity measures. AI-driven systems can help protect critical infrastructure, such as power grids and financial institutions, from cyberattacks, thereby enhancing national security (Osah, 2020).

The successful integration of AI into Nigeria's DSE will require concerted efforts from the government, private sector and international partners. Investment in technological infrastructure, capacity building and public-private partnerships will be essential to harness the full potential of AI in enhancing national security (Kshetri, 2010).

Theoretical Framework

Socio-technical systems (STS) theory, developed in the mid-twentieth century by Eric Trist and colleagues from the Tavistock Institute of Human Relations, offers a holistic approach to understanding the interplay between social and technical aspects within organizations. The theory is based on the premise that any organization comprises two intertwined subsystems: the social system, which includes the people, roles, relationships and culture, and the technical system, which encompasses the tools, technologies and processes used to achieve organizational goals (Trist, 1981).

The core idea behind STS theory is that optimal organizational performance is achieved when there is a balance and alignment between these two subsystems. Disruptions in this balance, whether due to technological changes, organizational restructuring or external pressures, can lead to inefficiencies, reduced productivity and even failure to achieve organizational objectives. STS theory emphasizes that technological innovations should be designed and implemented with careful consideration of their impact on the social structures within the organization and vice versa.

In the context of this study, which examines the role of AI in enhancing DSE networks, STS theory provides a robust theoretical framework for understanding the integration of AI technologies into these critical systems. Defence and security organizations are complex STS where the successful deployment of AI depends not only on the technological capabilities of AI but also on the alignment with the human and organizational aspects of the system.

The integration of AI into DSE networks must be approached with a clear understanding of the existing social structures and the potential impact of AI on these structures. For instance, AI technologies such as autonomous systems, surveillance tools and cybersecurity solutions have the potential to transform traditional roles and responsibilities within security organizations. STS theory suggests that these changes must be managed in a way that preserves the coherence and effectiveness of the social system. For example, AI-driven autonomous systems may reduce the need for human involvement in certain operational tasks, leading to changes in job roles, decision-making processes and even organizational hierarchies. If these changes are not carefully managed, they could lead to resistance from personnel, a breakdown in communication or a loss of trust in the new systems. STS theory underscores the importance of designing AI systems that complement and enhance the human roles within the organization, rather than disrupting them.

STS theory also highlights the potential for technology to act as a force multiplier when effectively integrated into the social system. In defence and security contexts, AI has the potential to enhance human capabilities, allowing security personnel to process more information, make faster decisions and respond more effectively to threats. However, for AI to serve as a force multiplier, it must be designed and implemented in a way that aligns with the social dynamics of the organization. For instance, AI systems used in cybersecurity must be designed to work seamlessly with human analysts, providing them with actionable insights and supporting their decision-making processes. Similarly, AI-driven surveillance systems must be integrated into the broader security infrastructure in a way that enhances, rather than replaces, the capabilities of human operators. STS theory suggests that the most effective AI implementations are those that augment human skills and enable personnel to achieve higher levels of performance.

A key principle of STS theory is the concept of co-evolution, where the social and technical subsystems must adapt and evolve together to respond to changing circumstances. In the fast-paced and dynamic environment of defence and security, the introduction of AI technologies requires ongoing adaptation from both the technical and social sides of the system. This includes continuous training and development for personnel to effectively use AI tools, as well as iterative updates and improvements to the AI systems themselves to meet the evolving needs of the organization. For example, as AI technologies become more sophisticated, security organizations may need to develop new training programmes to ensure that personnel can effectively interact with and control these systems. Similarly, the AI systems themselves must be regularly updated to reflect new threats, changes in the operational environment and feedback from users. STS theory supports the idea that successful AI integration requires a continuous process of learning, adaptation and co-evolution between the social and technical subsystems.

Addressing Ethical and Organizational Challenges

STS theory also provides a framework for addressing the ethical and organizational challenges associated with the use of AI in defence and security. The introduction of AI raises important questions about autonomy, accountability and the potential for unintended consequences. STS theory suggests that these challenges can be mitigated by ensuring that the social and technical subsystems are aligned in a way that promotes ethical decision-making and organizational accountability.

For instance, AI systems that are designed to operate autonomously, such as drones or automated threat detection systems, must be implemented with clear guidelines on human oversight and accountability. This includes defining the roles and responsibilities of personnel in monitoring and controlling these systems, as well as establishing protocols for responding to ethical dilemmas or system failures. STS theory emphasizes the importance of designing AI systems that support, rather than undermine, the ethical and organizational standards of the security enterprise.

STS theory provides a comprehensive framework for understanding the integration of AI into DSE networks. By emphasizing the importance of balancing and aligning the social and technical subsystems, STS theory offers valuable insights into how AI can be effectively and responsibly integrated into these complex systems. The theory highlights the need for careful management of the social implications of AI, the potential for technology to enhance human capabilities, the importance of continuous adaptation and the necessity of addressing ethical and organizational challenges. As such, STS theory serves as a critical foundation for this study, guiding the analysis of how AI can be used to enhance defence and security while maintaining the integrity and effectiveness of the organizational systems involved.

AI, Threat Detection and Response Capabilities Within Nigeria's Defence and Security Networks

AI is increasingly becoming a vital component in enhancing threat detection and response capabilities within defence and security networks globally. In Nigeria, where security challenges are diverse and complex, the integration of AI presents significant opportunities to improve national security. This section discusses the role of AI in threat detection and response, focusing on its applications within Nigeria's defence and security networks, the associated benefits and the challenges that need to be addressed.

AI and Threat Detection: AI enhances threat detection capabilities by leveraging advanced algorithms to analyse vast amounts of data from various sources. In the context of Nigeria's defence and security networks, AI can be applied to several critical areas:

Surveillance Systems

AI-powered surveillance systems can process and analyse video feeds from cameras installed in sensitive areas such as borders, airports and urban centres. ML algorithms can detect unusual patterns or behaviours indicative of potential threats, such as unauthorized access or suspicious activities (Zhao et al., 2020). For example, AI can identify individuals of interest from surveillance footage or detect anomalies in real-time, providing security personnel with actionable intelligence.

Cybersecurity

Nigeria faces significant cybersecurity threats, including cyberattacks targeting critical infrastructure and financial systems (Osah, 2020). AI can improve cybersecurity by identifying and responding to threats more rapidly than traditional methods. AI systems can analyse network traffic for signs of malicious activity, detect anomalies that could indicate a cyberattack, and automate responses to mitigate the impact of breaches (Goodfellow et al., 2016). For instance, AI-driven intrusion detection systems can recognize patterns associated with cyberattacks and alert security teams to potential breaches.

Predictive Analytics

Predictive analytics, powered by AI, can anticipate potential threats before they materialize. By analysing historical data, AI systems can identify trends and patterns that suggest possible future threats. In Nigeria, this capability can be used to predict and prevent insurgent activities or terrorist attacks by analysing data from social media, communications, and previous incidents (Campbell and Harwood, 2018). AI can enhance situational awareness and enable proactive measures to address emerging threats.

AI and Response Capabilities: AI not only improves threat detection but also enhances the response capabilities of defence and security networks. The following are key areas where AI contributes to more effective responses:

Automated Decision-Making

AI systems can support automated decision-making processes by providing real-time analysis and recommendations based on data inputs. In high-pressure situations, such as responding to security incidents or managing emergencies, AI can assist decision-makers by offering data-driven insights and suggesting optimal courses of action (Russell and Norvig, 2021). This capability is crucial for Nigeria's security forces, enabling them to respond quickly and effectively to threats.

Robust Command and Control

AI can enhance command and control systems by integrating data from various sources into a unified platform. This integration allows for more coherent and coordinated responses to security incidents. For example, AI systems can consolidate information from surveillance, intelligence and communications to provide a comprehensive view of a situation, facilitating better coordination among different security agencies (Alberts et al., 2000).

Crisis Management

In crisis management scenarios, AI can assist in optimizing resource allocation and logistics. For example, AI algorithms can analyse real-time data to allocate resources such as personnel and equipment where they are most needed during an emergency. This capability can improve the efficiency and effectiveness of response efforts, ensuring that resources are used strategically to address the crisis (Stoneburner et al., 2002).

The Challenges and Opportunities Associated with Integrating AI into Nigeria's DSE Networks

The integration of AI into Nigeria's DSE networks holds significant promise for enhancing national security. However, this integration comes with a set of challenges and opportunities that must be carefully managed. This section explores these challenges and opportunities, providing a comprehensive analysis of the factors influencing the successful implementation of AI in Nigeria's defence and security sectors.

The challenges associated with integrating AI into Nigeria's DSE networks include the following:

Infrastructure Limitations

Technological Infrastructure

Nigeria's technological infrastructure presents a major challenge for the deployment of advanced AI systems. Many areas in Nigeria suffer from inadequate internet connectivity, unreliable power supplies, and limited access to modern computing resources (Osah, 2020). These infrastructural deficits can hinder the effective operation of AI systems, which often require high-speed internet and stable power for real-time data processing and analysis.

Data Storage and Management

Efficient AI systems require substantial data storage and management capabilities. In Nigeria, issues related to data storage infrastructure and management practices can impact the quality and accessibility of data needed for AI applications. Improving data management systems and investing in robust storage solutions are essential for supporting AI technologies (Onuoha, 2013).

Data Quality and Privacy

Data Collection and Quality

AI systems rely on large volumes of high-quality data for training and operation. In Nigeria, challenges in data collection, data quality and data integration can affect the performance of AI systems. Inaccurate or incomplete data can lead to poor decision-making and reduced effectiveness of AI applications (Binns, 2018).

Privacy Concerns

The use of AI in surveillance and security raises significant privacy concerns. Ensuring that AI systems are implemented in ways that respect individuals' privacy and comply with legal standards is crucial. Balancing the need for security with the protection of civil liberties is a key challenge in deploying AI technologies (Asaro, 2008).

Skilled Personnel

Talent Shortage

The successful integration of AI requires skilled personnel who can develop, manage and maintain AI systems. In Nigeria, there is a shortage of professionals with expertise in AI and ML. Building a skilled workforce through education and training programmes is necessary for the effective deployment and operation of AI technologies (Onuoha, 2013).

Training and Development

Existing personnel in the defence and security sectors need to be trained to work with AI systems. Developing training programmes that equip security personnel with the necessary skills to operate and manage AI technologies is a significant challenge (Stoneburner et al., 2002).

Ethical and Legal Issues

Ethical Considerations

The deployment of AI in defence and security raises ethical issues related to autonomous systems, decision-making and the potential for unintended consequences. Ensuring that AI systems are designed and used ethically is crucial for maintaining public trust and ensuring the responsible use of technology (Floridi and Cowls, 2019).

Legal Frameworks

The legal frameworks governing the use of AI in defence and security need to be well-defined and updated to address the unique challenges posed by AI technologies. Developing comprehensive regulations and guidelines that address issues such as accountability, transparency and human rights is essential (Asaro, 2008).

The opportunities associated with integrating AI into Nigeria's DSE networks include:

Enhanced Threat Detection and Response

Improved Surveillance

AI technologies can significantly enhance surveillance capabilities by enabling real-time analysis of video feeds and identifying potential threats more accurately. AI-powered systems can detect suspicious activities, recognize patterns and provide actionable intelligence to security personnel (Zhao et al., 2020).

Advanced Cybersecurity

AI can strengthen cybersecurity by identifying and responding to cyber threats more effectively. ML algorithms can analyse network traffic for signs of malicious activity, detect anomalies, and automate responses to mitigate the impact of cyberattacks (Goodfellow et al., 2016). This capability is crucial for protecting Nigeria's critical infrastructure from cyber threats.

Operational Efficiency

Automated Decision-Making

AI can support automated decision-making processes, allowing for quicker and more informed responses to security incidents. AI systems can analyse data and provide recommendations for action, improving the efficiency and effectiveness of response efforts (Russell and Norvig, 2021).

Resource Optimization

AI can optimize resource allocation and logistics during security operations. By analysing real-time data, AI systems can help allocate personnel and equipment more effectively, ensuring that resources are used where they are most needed (Stoneburner et al., 2002).

Predictive Analytics

Proactive Threat Management

Predictive analytics powered by AI can help anticipate and manage potential threats before they materialize. By analysing historical data and identifying patterns, AI systems can provide early warnings of potential security incidents, allowing for proactive measures to be taken (Campbell and Harwood, 2018).

Strategic Planning

AI can support strategic planning and decision-making by providing insights into trends and future scenarios. This capability can enhance the ability of Nigeria's defence and security agencies to plan and prepare for emerging threats and challenges (Alberts et al., 2000).

International Collaboration

Knowledge Sharing

Integrating AI into Nigeria's defence and security networks offers opportunities for international collaboration and knowledge sharing. Engaging with global partners and experts can provide access to advanced technologies, best practices and training resources (Singer and Friedman, 2014).

Capacity Building

International cooperation can also support capacity building by providing technical assistance and resources to strengthen Nigeria's AI capabilities. Collaborating with international organizations and partners can enhance Nigeria's ability to deploy and manage AI technologies effectively (Goodfellow et al., 2016).

The integration of AI into Nigeria's DSE networks presents both significant challenges and opportunities. Addressing infrastructure limitations, data quality issues and ethical considerations is crucial for successful AI deployment. At the same time, leveraging AI's capabilities in threat detection, response and operational efficiency offers valuable opportunities for enhancing national security. By addressing these challenges and capitalizing on the opportunities, Nigeria can effectively harness the potential of AI to strengthen its defence and security networks.

Conclusion

This study has explored the integration of AI into Nigeria's DSE networks, focusing on the associated challenges and opportunities. The findings emphasize the transformative potential of AI in enhancing threat detection and response capabilities while also highlighting significant obstacles that need to be addressed to maximize its effectiveness. AI offers substantial benefits for Nigeria's defence and security networks. AI technologies can significantly improve threat detection through advanced surveillance, enhanced cybersecurity measures and predictive analytics. These capabilities enable more effective identification and response to potential security threats, providing actionable intelligence that enhances national security efforts. AI contributes to operational efficiency by supporting automated decision-making, optimizing resource allocation and streamlining crisis management. The integration of AI systems can enhance the coordination and effectiveness of response efforts, allowing security personnel to act more swiftly and decisively during emergencies. The integration of AI in Nigeria's defence and security networks faces several challenges. Infrastructure limitations, such as inadequate internet connectivity and power supply, impact the deployment and effectiveness of AI systems. Data quality and privacy concerns, along with a shortage of skilled personnel, further complicate the implementation of AI technologies. Additionally, ethical and legal considerations must be addressed to ensure the responsible and effective use of AI.

Despite these challenges, there are significant opportunities associated with AI integration. AI presents the potential for improved threat detection and response, proactive threat management through predictive analytics and enhanced international collaboration. By addressing the existing challenges and capitalizing on these opportunities, Nigeria can strengthen its defence and security networks and better respond to evolving threats.

In conclusion, the integration of AI into Nigeria's DSE networks holds significant potential for enhancing national security. By leveraging AI's capabilities in threat detection, response and operational efficiency, Nigeria can address complex security challenges more effectively. However, realizing these benefits requires overcoming infrastructure, data management, personnel and ethical challenges. Strategic investments and a collaborative approach will be crucial in harnessing the full potential of AI and strengthening Nigeria's defence and security systems.

References

African Cybersecurity Report (2021). *Cybersecurity Threats and Responses in Africa*. Cybersecurity Africa. Available at: https://www.interpol.int/en/News-and-Events/News/2021/INTERPOL-report-identifies-top-cyberthreats-in-Africa

African Union (AU) (2020). *Artificial Intelligence and Security in Africa*. African Union. Available at: https://www.au.int/publications.

Alberts, D.S., J.J. Garstka and F.P. Stein (2000). *Network Centric Warfare: Developing and Leveraging Information Superiority*. Washington, DC: CCRP Publication Series.

Anderson, C., and L. Rainie (2022). *The Future of Artificial Intelligence in National Security and Defence*. Washington, DC: Pew Research Centre.

Asaro, P. (2008). *How Just Could a Robot War Be?* Proceedings of the Ethics of Autonomous Military Systems Conference, University of Sheffield.

Bayley, D.H. (2006). *Changing the Guard: Developing Democratic Police Abroad*. Oxford: Oxford University Press.

Binns, R. (2018). *Fairness in Machine Learning: Lessons from Political Philosophy*. Proceedings of the 2018 Conference on Fairness, Accountability, and Transparency, 149–59.

Bostrom, N., and E. Yudkowsky (2014). 'The Ethics of Artificial Intelligence', in K. Frankish and W. Ramsey (eds), *The Cambridge Handbook of Artificial Intelligence*. Cambridge: Cambridge University Press, 316–34.

Brynjolfsson, E., and A. McAfee (2014). *The Second Machine Age: Work, Progress, and Prosperity in a Time of Brilliant Technologies*. New York: W.W. Norton & Company.

Buzan, B., and L. Hansen (2009). *The Evolution of International Security Studies*. Cambridge: Cambridge University Press.

Campbell, J., and A. Harwood (2018). *Boko Haram's Deadly Impact*. Council on Foreign Relations. Available at: https://www.cfr.org/boko-haram

Cebrowski, A.K., and J.J. Garstka (1998). 'Network-Centric Warfare: Its Origin and Future', *Proceedings*, 124(1): 28–35.

Floridi, L., and J. Cowls (2019). 'A Unified Framework of Five Principles for AI in Society', *Harvard Data Science Review*, 1(1): 1–10. Available at: https://doi.org/10.1162/99608f92.8cd550d1

Garvie, C., A. Bedoya and J. Frankle (2016). *The Perpetual Line-Up: Unregulated Police Face Recognition in America*. Washington, DC: Georgetown Law, Centre on Privacy & Technology.

Goodfellow, I., Y. Bengio and A. Courville (2016). *Deep Learning*. Cambridge, MA: MIT Press.

Gray, C.S. (1990). 'The Revolution in Military Affairs: How America's Military Might Decline', *International Security*, 15(1): 14–33.

International Institute for Strategic Studies (IISS) (2020). *The Impact of AI on Military Operations*. International Institute for Strategic Studies. Available at: https://www.iiss.org/publications

Jurafsky, D., and J.H. Martin (2021). *Speech and Language Processing* (3rd ed.). Boston, MA: Pearson.

Korzak, E. (2021). 'AI and Military Decision-Making: Ethical and Operational Challenges', *Journal of Military Ethics*, 20(1): 45–62.

Kshetri, N. (2010). *The Global Cybercrime Industry: Economic, Institutional and Strategic Perspectives*. Berlin: Springer.

Lowenthal, M.M. (2017). *Intelligence: From Secrets to Policy* (7th ed.). Thousand Oaks, CA: Sage.

McCarthy, J., M.L. Minsky, N. Rochester and C.E. Shannon (1956). A Proposal for the Dartmouth Summer Research Project on Artificial Intelligence. Available at: http://www-formal.stanford.edu/jmc/history/dartmouth/dartmouth.html

Mitchell, T.M. (1997). *Machine Learning*. New York: McGraw Hill.

National Information Technology Development Agency (NITDA) (2022). *AI for National Security in Nigeria*. National Information Technology Development Agency. Available at: https://www.nitda.gov.ng/publications

NATO (2021). *Artificial Intelligence and the Future of Cybersecurity*. NATO. Available at: https://www.research.aqmen.ac.uk/wp-content/uploads/sites/38/2021/11/NATO-Summary-of-the-NATO-Artificial-Intelligence-Strategy-22-Oct.-2021.pdf

Nigerian Communications Commission (NCC) (2021). *Cybersecurity and AI: Protecting Nigeria's Digital Infrastructure*. Nigerian Communications Commission. Available at: https://www.ncc.gov.ng/publications

Onuoha, F. (2013). 'The Boko Haram Insurgency in Nigeria', *The RUSI Journal*, 158(4): 62–8.

Osah, G.A. (2020). 'Cybersecurity Challenges in Nigeria: The Way Forward', *International Journal of Computer Applications*, 175(34): 25–32.

Russell, S., and P. Norvig (2016). *Artificial Intelligence: A Modern Approach* (3rd ed.). Harlow, UK: Pearson.

Russell, S.J., and P. Norvig (2021). *Artificial Intelligence: A Modern Approach* (4th ed.). Boston, MA: Pearson.

Russell, S., D. Dewey and M. Tegmark (2015). 'Research Priorities for Robust and Beneficial Artificial Intelligence', *AI Magazine*, 36(4): 105–14.

Scharre, P. (2018). *Army of None: Autonomous Weapons and the Future of War*. New York: W.W. Norton & Company.

Sharkey, N. (2012). 'The Evitability of Autonomous Robot Warfare', *International Review of the Red Cross*, 94(886): 787–99.

Siciliano, B., and O. Khatib (2016). *Springer Handbook of Robotics* (2nd ed.). Berlin: Springer.

Singer, P.W. (2009). *Wired for War: The Robotics Revolution and Conflict in the 21st Century*. New York: Penguin Books.

Singer, P.W., and A. Friedman (2014). *Cybersecurity and Cyberwar: What Everyone Needs to Know*? Oxford: Oxford University Press.

Stoneburner, G., A. Goguen and A. Feringa (2002). *Risk Management Guide for Information Technology Systems*. Gaithersburg, MD: National Institute of Standards and Technology.

Szeliski, R. (2010). *Computer Vision: Algorithms and Applications*. Heidelberg: Springer.

Taddeo, M., and L. Floridi (2018). 'How AI Can Enhance Cyber Defence', *Communications of the ACM*, 61(9): 28–30.

Trist, E. (1981). 'The Evolution of Socio-Technical Systems', in A.H. Van de Ven and W. Joyce (eds), *Perspectives on Organisation Design and Behaviour*. Chichester: Wiley, 19–75.

U.S. Department of Defence (DoD) (2019). *AI in Network Management and Communication Systems*. U.S. Department of Defence. Available at: https://apps.dtic.mil/sti/pdfs/AD1079707.pdf.

Zhao, Q., Li, J., and H. Wang (2020). 'A Survey of Deep Learning Techniques for Image Analysis in Video Surveillance', *Journal of Computer Vision*, 128(5): 789–804.

5

Robotics and Artificial Intelligence in Military Entrepreneurship: A Case Study of the Armed Forces of Nigeria

Abubakar Surajo Imam and Bishir Sirajo

The integration of robotics and artificial intelligence (AI) in military entrepreneurship presents a significant opportunity for the Armed Forces of Nigeria (AFN) to enhance operational effectiveness, self-reliance and economic sustainability. This chapter explores how robotics and AI-driven solutions are being deployed within the AFN for various military and non-military applications, fostering indigenous technological advancements and defence entrepreneurship. Case studies highlight ongoing initiatives, challenges and prospects. Additionally, this paper provides a thorough review of military entrepreneurship, focusing on defence innovation, economic implications and technological advancements.

The modern battlefield is increasingly shaped by technological advancements, with robotics and AI emerging as transformative tools in military strategy, defence logistics, intelligence and combat operations. In recent decades, leading military powers have extensively incorporated AI-driven robotics to improve operational efficiency, enhance decision-making and reduce human exposure to dangerous combat scenarios (Singer, 2009). The United States, China, Russia, Israel and other technologically advanced nations have developed and deployed autonomous systems that contribute to surveillance, reconnaissance, cyber warfare and autonomous weapons systems. These innovations have changed the nature of warfare, allowing for faster decision cycles, precision targeting and reduced operational costs.

Robotics and AI applications in defence encompass a wide range of areas, including unmanned aerial vehicles (UAVs), autonomous ground vehicles (UGVs), AI-powered cybersecurity solutions, robotic surgical assistants, and AI-driven command and control systems (Nadibaidze, 2024). Military forces leverage these technologies for tasks such as real-time data analysis, logistics automation, battlefield medical assistance and counterterrorism operations. The ability of AI to process vast amounts of data and identify patterns makes it invaluable for military intelligence, threat assessment and predictive analytics in combat scenarios (Singer, 2009).

The AFN faces numerous security challenges, including insurgency, terrorism, cross-border crimes and cyber threats. The integration of robotics and AI into Nigeria's defence framework presents a strategic opportunity to enhance national security while also promoting military entrepreneurship. The Nigerian military, through institutions such as the Defence Industries Corporation of Nigeria (DICON) and the Nigerian Defence Space Administration (DSA), has begun embracing robotics and AI technologies in various capacities (Imam, 2025). These initiatives aim to develop indigenous capabilities in defence technology, reduce reliance on foreign military hardware and foster economic growth through local production and innovation.

Military entrepreneurship is a crucial aspect of national defence strategy, as it enables the armed forces to develop self-sufficiency in weapon systems, surveillance tools and cybersecurity infrastructure. By investing in AI-driven robotics, Nigeria can achieve a dual objective: strengthening national security while creating economic opportunities for local industries. AI-powered drones for surveillance, robotic systems for explosive ordnance disposal (EOD) and AI-driven cybersecurity solutions are some of the areas where the AFN has made progress in recent years (Nkala, 2017). These innovations not only improve military efficiency but also have potential commercial applications in law enforcement, border security and disaster management.

One of the key drivers of military entrepreneurship in Nigeria is the collaboration between defence institutions and private sector players. The establishment of research partnerships between the Defence Research and Development Bureau (DRDB), Nigerian Defence Academy (NDA), universities and technology hubs such as Innov8, ICE Hub Technology, among others, has facilitated the development of AI and robotics solutions tailored to the country's security needs. Additionally, the government has prioritized local manufacturing in the defence sector, as evidenced by the expansion of DICON's capabilities and the increasing involvement of indigenous technology firms in military projects (DICON Report, 2022).

However, despite these advancements, challenges persist. Nigeria's defence sector faces funding constraints, technological gaps and limited expertise in AI and robotics. The country still relies on foreign technology for critical defence equipment, and the development of fully autonomous military systems remains in its early stages. Addressing these challenges requires sustained investment in research and development, capacity building and policy support for military innovation (Osahor, 2024).

This paper examines the impact of robotics and AI on military entrepreneurship in Nigeria, focusing on innovation, economic benefits and operational effectiveness. The role of indigenous development and public-private partnerships (PPPs) is highlighted as a means of fostering sustainable technological advancement in the country's defence sector. By leveraging AI and robotics, Nigeria can not only enhance its military capabilities but also stimulate economic growth through defence innovation and local manufacturing. The paper also presents case studies of how robotics and AI are currently being utilized by the AFN and explores prospects for these technologies in Nigeria's defence strategy.

Concept of Military Entrepreneurship

Military entrepreneurship refers to the innovative application of military skills, resources and technologies to create economic opportunities while enhancing self-reliance and national security (Ojo, 2021). This concept encompasses the strategic use of defence infrastructure, personnel expertise and technological innovation to develop products and services that benefit both military and civilian sectors. Military entrepreneurship plays a crucial role in reducing dependency on foreign military technology, promoting indigenous defence industries and driving national economic development.

Core Areas of Military Entrepreneurship

The core areas of military entrepreneurship include:

Research and Development

Research and Development (R&D) is fundamental to the advancement of military technology, providing innovative solutions for modern warfare. Investments in R&D focus on AI-powered robotics, autonomous systems, cybersecurity solutions and next-generation weapons technology. A strong R&D base enables the military to stay ahead of emerging threats, enhance operational effectiveness and strengthen strategic capabilities. For example, the Nigerian Air Force's Tsaigumi UAV was developed through extensive R&D collaborations, resulting in an indigenous surveillance drone tailored to Nigeria's security needs. Additionally, AI-driven cybersecurity programmes developed by the Nigerian Army Cyber Warfare Command help counter cyber threats and prevent data breaches in defence networks.

Defence Manufacturing

Defence manufacturing plays a critical role in enhancing self-reliance and reducing dependence on foreign military imports. This includes the production of military hardware such as drones, armoured vehicles, surveillance systems and small arms. Local manufacturing ensures cost-effective and mission-specific solutions tailored to Nigeria's defence needs. For example, DICON has successfully produced small arms and ammunition, reducing reliance on imported weaponry. Additionally, the Command Engineering Depot (CED) of the Nigerian Army has developed indigenous Mine-Resistant Ambush Protected (MRAP) vehicles, which provide enhanced protection for troops during counterterrorism operations.

Dual-Use Technology Development

Many military innovations have applications beyond defence, contributing to economic growth and civilian industries. AI-powered surveillance systems, UAVs and robotics initially developed for military use are now being adapted for agriculture, disaster management, border security and healthcare. For instance, UAVs developed for battlefield reconnaissance are also used for precision agriculture, wildlife monitoring and search-and-rescue operations. Similarly, AI-powered predictive analytics, originally designed for military threat assessment, is now being employed in financial fraud detection and healthcare diagnostics. By fostering dual-use technology development, Nigeria can expand the commercial viability of military innovations, creating new industries and job opportunities.

Public–Private Partnerships

Collaboration between the military, private sector and academic institutions fosters innovation, technology transfer and commercialization of defence products. Public-private partnerships (PPPs) facilitate the development of indigenous military technology, joint research initiatives and defence industry growth. For example, Nigeria's partnership with local technology firms and research institutions has led to the development of AI-powered surveillance drones, cybersecurity software and autonomous robotic systems. The Nigerian DSA has also partnered with private satellite companies to enhance intelligence gathering, border security and military communication systems. Strengthening PPPs will accelerate technological advancements in Nigeria's defence sector while driving economic diversification and industrial development.

Capacity Building and Skill Transfer

Military entrepreneurship also involves the development of human capital, ensuring that military personnel and local engineers acquire expertise in emerging technologies such as AI, robotics and cyber warfare. Establishing specialized training programmes in AI-driven military applications will equip defence personnel with the technical skills necessary for operating and maintaining autonomous military systems. For example, the NDA Centre for Innovation and Creativity (CINOCRE) is developing training modules on AI-enhanced cybersecurity, drone technology and robotic engineering. Additionally, the Nigerian Army Cyber Warfare Command conducts regular capacity-building workshops to train officers on AI-driven digital defence strategies. By prioritizing capacity building and skill transfer, Nigeria can cultivate a highly skilled defence workforce, ensuring long-term sustainability and innovation in military entrepreneurship.

The Role of Robotics and AI in Military Entrepreneurship

Robotics and AI have become pivotal drivers of military entrepreneurship, providing high-value innovations that enhance national security and economic growth. The adoption of these technologies within the AFN is transforming key defence sectors, leading to the development of AI-powered weapons systems, smart surveillance technologies and autonomous military vehicles. The ability to manufacture and maintain such technologies locally not only strengthens national security but also reduces the costs associated with procuring foreign defence systems.

The impact of AI and robotics on military entrepreneurship can be observed in the following areas:

Autonomous Systems for National Defence

The AFN has made significant investments in UAVs and UGVs to enhance border security, counterterrorism operations and intelligence gathering. These autonomous systems act as force multipliers, reducing human exposure to combat risks while providing real-time surveillance, reconnaissance and precision strike capabilities. The Nigerian Air Force (NAF) has developed indigenous UAVs such as the Tsaigumi and Gulma drones, deployed for intelligence and reconnaissance missions to track insurgent movements, secure borders and support counterterrorism operations, particularly in the northeast. Additionally, the acquisition of CH-3 Rainbow UAVs from China has provided armed reconnaissance capabilities, allowing precision airstrikes against terrorist hideouts. On land, the Nigerian Army has deployed UGVs for EOD, logistics automation and battlefield reconnaissance. These robotic systems, equipped with AI-driven sensors and manipulator arms, can neutralize improvised explosive devices (IEDs), deliver supplies to remote conflict zones and operate autonomously in hazardous environments. The integration of AI-powered navigation, target identification and decision support systems in UAVs and UGVs demonstrates the growing reliance on autonomous technologies in modern warfare. The continued development of indigenous AI-driven defence solutions will enhance Nigeria's ability to address emerging security threats, ensuring self-reliance in military technology and greater operational efficiency.

AI-Powered Cybersecurity Solutions

With increasing cyber threats, AI-driven cybersecurity tools are being developed within Nigeria's military institutions to protect sensitive national data and infrastructure. The Nigerian Army Cyber Warfare Command has implemented AI-powered intrusion detection systems (IDS) and real-time threat analysis tools to detect and mitigate cyberattacks before they compromise military operations. These AI-driven solutions use machine learning algorithms and predictive analytics to identify abnormal network activities, neutralize malware and prevent cyber espionage. AI also enhances automated incident response, allowing the military to react to cyber threats instantly without human intervention. As cyber warfare becomes a growing concern, Nigeria's adoption of AI-powered cyber defence will strengthen the security of classified databases, encrypted communications and defence intelligence systems, ensuring that critical infrastructure remains protected against evolving digital threats.

AI and Robotics in Logistics and Supply Chain Management

The deployment of AI-powered predictive maintenance and automated logistics solutions ensures the efficiency of military operations. AI-based supply chain optimization tools are being used to predict equipment failures, automate inventory management and streamline the transportation of resources to troops in the field. For example, automated warehouse robots and AI-driven fleet management systems help track military assets, reducing operational costs and preventing supply shortages during missions. Additionally, AGVs are being tested for unmanned resupply missions, ensuring that food, medical supplies and ammunition reach combat units safely. AI-powered logistics solutions enable the AFN to anticipate supply chain disruptions, improve operational readiness and enhance efficiency in battlefield resupply, ensuring that troops receive essential resources precisely when needed.

AI-Enabled Predictive Analytics

AI is enhancing decision-making in military operations by providing commanders with real-time data analysis, improving response time in critical missions. AI-powered predictive analytics tools process vast amounts of battlefield data, helping military strategists anticipate enemy movements, assess risks and optimize troop deployment. By analysing satellite imagery, reconnaissance data and historical combat patterns, AI-driven decision support systems offer automated threat forecasting, enabling proactive responses to security threats. Additionally, AI-driven mission simulation software allows commanders to test multiple operational scenarios before execution, improving the success rate of military engagements. The integration of AI-powered predictive models in military intelligence ensures faster and more accurate decision-making, enhancing Nigeria's ability to respond effectively to both conventional and asymmetric threats.

Nigeria's Efforts in Military Entrepreneurship

Nigeria's drive towards military entrepreneurship is evident in various defence initiatives that focus on self-reliance and indigenous production. Notable examples include:

Defence Research and Development Bureau

The Defence Research and Development Bureau (DRDB) is a key institution responsible for coordinating military research, innovation and technological advancements in Nigeria. It serves as a bridge between the AFN, academia and private defence contractors to foster indigenous military technology development. The DRDB facilitates collaborative defence R&D projects, supports military-industrial growth and promotes AI and robotics applications in national security. The bureau oversees research in autonomous systems, AI-driven surveillance, cyber warfare and smart military logistics, ensuring that Nigeria advances its self-reliance in defence technology.

DICON

Established to reduce Nigeria's dependence on foreign arms imports, DICON has made significant progress in manufacturing small arms, ammunition and military equipment. The organization plays a vital role in the localization of defence production by working closely with military engineers and private firms to develop AI-powered surveillance systems, UAV technology, and combat robotics (DICON Report, 2022). Recent advancements include the integration of AI into defence manufacturing, enabling smart weapons development, automated assembly lines and real-time equipment monitoring to improve efficiency and quality. DICON's expansion into AI-enhanced security solutions and battlefield technology is a crucial step toward strengthening Nigeria's defence-industrial base.

Indigenous UAV Production

The NAF, in collaboration with research institutions and local engineering firms, has developed indigenous surveillance drones such as the Tsaigumi UAV. These UAVs are designed to provide real-time intelligence, reconnaissance and surveillance (ISR) capabilities, significantly enhancing border security, counterterrorism efforts and military operations (Laghari et al., 2020). Beyond military applications, these UAVs are being adapted for civilian uses, such as agriculture, disaster response, environmental monitoring and border patrol. The development of locally produced UAVs strengthens Nigeria's self-sufficiency in drone technology, reducing reliance on imports and promoting national security.

Cyber Warfare and AI Development

The Nigerian Army Cyber Warfare Command has adopted AI-driven cybersecurity measures to counter cyber threats and protect sensitive military data, critical infrastructure and classified communications. AI-powered IDS, threat intelligence platforms and predictive analytics are being deployed to monitor, detect and neutralize cyberattacks before they compromise national security (Gilbert and Gilbert, 2024). AI's ability to automate incident response, analyse vast amounts of cyber threat data and identify vulnerabilities in real-time has enhanced Nigeria's ability to mitigate cyber warfare threats from adversaries, hackers and insurgent groups. The AFN is also developing indigenous cybersecurity software and AI-powered encryption tools, reducing reliance on foreign cybersecurity solutions.

Local Robotics Development

Nigerian defence institutions have begun collaborating with universities, research centres and private technology firms to develop robotic systems for EOD. These

AI-powered robots, equipped with autonomous navigation, robotic arms, and real-time threat detection sensors, are being used to neutralize landmines, IEDs, and hazardous explosives in counterterrorism operations (Tunwannarux, 2008). The deployment of EOD robots in conflict zones has reduced casualties among military personnel and increased the efficiency of bomb disposal operations. The success of these robotics initiatives has encouraged further research into autonomous robotic infantry support units, battlefield medical evacuation robots and AI-assisted combat drones.

Public–Private Partnerships

Nigeria has encouraged collaboration between the military, private technology firms and research institutions to drive innovation in AI-driven defence systems, robotics applications and cybersecurity solutions. PPPs have facilitated joint research projects, technology transfer agreements and the establishment of AI and robotics incubation hubs. Several Nigerian defence startups and universities are partnering with global AI firms to co-develop next-generation military technologies, including smart surveillance drones, AI-powered battlefield analytics and autonomous combat robots. PPPs also enable local defence manufacturers to gain access to funding, expertise and high-tech equipment, accelerating Nigeria's military-industrial development. These collaborations position Nigeria as a regional leader in AI-driven defence innovation and autonomous military technology.

Challenges in Military Entrepreneurship in Nigeria

Despite progress in military entrepreneurship, several challenges persist:

Limited Funding and Investment

Defence R&D is capital-intensive, requiring substantial financial investments in advanced equipment, high-tech laboratories and skilled personnel. However, Nigeria's defence budget remains inadequate to support large-scale AI and robotics projects, limiting the country's ability to fully develop indigenous military technologies. Unlike developed nations that allocate billions of dollars annually to military innovation, Nigeria's budgetary constraints hinder progress in AI-driven defence solutions, local drone production and autonomous warfare systems. The lack of consistent government funding slows down research initiatives, making it difficult for Nigerian defence institutions to compete with global military powers in AI-enhanced surveillance, cybersecurity and robotic warfare technologies. To bridge this gap, Nigeria must increase financial allocations for defence R&D, explore alternative funding sources such as PPPs and leverage international defence collaborations to secure investment in AI-driven military innovation.

Dependence on Foreign Technology

While efforts are being made towards self-reliance, Nigeria still relies heavily on foreign expertise, software and components for advanced defence technologies, including AI-driven cybersecurity systems, UAVs and robotic combat units. The importation of critical AI hardware such as high-performance processors, LiDAR sensors and autonomous navigation systems increases costs and exposes Nigeria to supply chain vulnerabilities during geopolitical conflicts or economic sanctions. Additionally, many military AI software applications, including autonomous targeting systems and AI-powered surveillance platforms, are sourced from foreign defence contractors, limiting Nigeria's control over data security, system updates and operational independence. To reduce foreign dependency, Nigeria must strengthen indigenous R&D, invest in AI and robotics training programmes and establish domestic production facilities for critical defence components. Encouraging technology transfer agreements with global AI firms and fostering local defence startups will accelerate the country's transition toward self-sufficient military AI innovation.

Infrastructure and Skilled Workforce Shortages

The absence of specialized infrastructure and a shortage of skilled personnel remain major challenges to the full development of indigenous AI and robotics capabilities. Nigeria currently lacks high-tech AI research centres, robotics testing facilities and dedicated defence AI simulation environments, limiting the ability of researchers to design, test and deploy autonomous military systems. Without proper infrastructure, local AI and robotics experts struggle to build and refine advanced UAVs, UGVs and AI-enhanced cybersecurity solutions. Furthermore, the shortage of AI engineers, data scientists and robotics specialists in Nigeria's defence sector slows down innovation and implementation. Many trained professionals seek better opportunities abroad, leading to a brain drain that negatively impacts local defence technology development. To address this, Nigeria must prioritize investment in AI and robotics education, integrate AI-focused military training into the curriculum of defence academies and establish collaborative AI research hubs with universities and private technology firms. Additionally, incentivizing Nigerian AI professionals in the diaspora to contribute to local defence projects will enhance national expertise in AI-powered military applications.

Regulatory and Ethical Concerns

The deployment of AI and autonomous systems in warfare raises serious ethical, legal and regulatory concerns, particularly regarding accountability, human oversight and compliance with international humanitarian laws. AI-powered autonomous weapons, including drones, robotic combat units and AI-driven missile systems, have the potential to operate without direct human intervention, raising concerns about targeting errors, collateral damage and unintended escalations in conflict zones. Additionally, AI-powered surveillance technologies must be regulated to prevent unlawful data collection, privacy violations and excessive military surveillance on civilians. The absence of clear military AI policies in Nigeria further complicates the deployment of autonomous systems, as it remains unclear who is responsible in the event of an AI-driven military failure – the system developer, the commanding officer or the military institution itself. To address these concerns, Nigeria must develop comprehensive AI governance frameworks, establish ethical guidelines for AI deployment in military operations, and align its AI warfare policies with international conventions such as the UN's Group of Governmental Experts on Lethal Autonomous Weapons Systems. Additionally, AI in military applications should be subject to human oversight, ensuring that autonomous weapons operate within the legal and ethical boundaries of warfare.

Opportunities for Growth in Military Entrepreneurship

To overcome these challenges and further develop military entrepreneurship, Nigeria can leverage the following opportunities:

Strengthening Defence R&D Through Increased Funding

More investment in military innovation will enable Nigeria to develop competitive defence technologies, enhance national security and reduce dependency on imports. Expanding R&D funding will support advancements in AI-powered surveillance systems, autonomous drones, cybersecurity solutions and robotic warfare systems. Increased funding would also enable the establishment of advanced defence technology laboratories, testing facilities and AI simulation environments to facilitate local innovations. To achieve this, Nigeria must prioritize defence R&D in national budget allocations, seek PPPs for research financing and encourage venture capital investments in defence technology startups. A well-funded defence innovation ecosystem will accelerate Nigeria's transition to self-sufficiency in AI-driven military technologies.

Expanding AI and Robotics Training Programmes

Military personnel and local engineers should receive specialized training in emerging AI and robotics technologies to build national expertise and close the skill gap in defence technology development. Integrating AI and robotics courses into the curriculum of military academies and engineering institutions will ensure that Nigeria's armed forces stay ahead of modern warfare advancements. Additionally, establishing defence technology training centres will provide hands-on experience with autonomous UAVs, robotic ground vehicles, AI-driven cybersecurity systems and predictive analytics tools. Collaborative training programmes with global AI research institutions and defence firms will further expose Nigerian engineers and military personnel to cutting-edge AI applications in warfare. Incentivizing scholarships, fellowships and skill development initiatives in AI and robotics will ensure that Nigeria produces a technologically adept military workforce capable of innovating home-grown defence solutions.

Enhancing Collaboration with Global Defence Firms

Nigeria can accelerate technology transfer and skill development through strategic partnerships with leading defence firms, AI research labs and international military institutions. Collaboration with global AI-driven defence companies will allow Nigeria to access advanced robotics technologies, gain expertise in AI-based warfare applications and enhance cybersecurity infrastructure. Joint ventures and co-development agreements will facilitate the local production of AI-powered UAVs, autonomous robotic systems and cyber defence tools. Additionally, participating in international defence expos, AI military conferences and technology-sharing programmes will expose Nigeria to best practices in AI-driven military entrepreneurship. Engaging in bilateral defence technology partnerships with advanced military nations will bolster Nigeria's capacity to develop next-generation AI warfare technologies while reducing reliance on foreign procurement.

Commercialization of Military Technologies

Defence innovations, such as AI-driven surveillance systems, autonomous UAVs and robotic security solutions, can be adapted for civilian applications in agriculture, policing, disaster management and infrastructure security. Military-grade AI technologies can be commercialized for smart city surveillance, industrial security, border control and automated law enforcement. For example, UAVs developed for battlefield reconnaissance can be repurposed for precision agriculture, search-and-rescue operations and environmental monitoring. AI-powered cyber defence tools can be adapted for financial security, telecommunications data protection and government digital infrastructure monitoring. Additionally, robotic systems initially designed for military logistics and EOD can be repurposed for hazardous industrial operations and emergency response missions. Encouraging technology spin-offs from military R&D initiatives will create new economic opportunities, drive job creation and strengthen Nigeria's defence-industrial base. Establishing innovation hubs and defence technology incubators will further support the commercial adaptation of AI-powered military technologies for civilian use.

Thus, military entrepreneurship provides an avenue for Nigeria to strengthen national security while fostering economic growth. The integration of robotics and AI in defence manufacturing, cybersecurity, logistics and surveillance enhances the country's self-reliance and technological advancement. While challenges persist, strategic investments, policy support and capacity-building initiatives will position Nigeria as a leader in military entrepreneurship and innovation. Through sustained commitment and collaboration, the AFN can leverage emerging technologies to not only improve defence capabilities but also contribute to national economic development.

Role of Robotics and AI in Military Entrepreneurship

The integration of robotics and AI in military entrepreneurship has revolutionized defence strategies, logistics, combat operations and decision-making processes. These emerging technologies provide numerous advantages, including improved operational efficiency, enhanced situational awareness, minimized human casualties and cost reductions in military operations. The AFN have recognized the value of robotics and AI in addressing contemporary security threats, leading to advancements in unmanned systems, cybersecurity, medical support and strategic decision-making.

UAVs for Surveillance Applications

UAVs play a vital role in modern military operations, providing real-time ISR and precision strikes without endangering human personnel. UAVs are highly effective in border security, counterterrorism and intelligence-gathering missions. The NAF, through collaborations with indigenous engineers and research institutions, has developed UAVs such as the Tsaigumi drone for surveillance and counterterrorism operations (Defence Watch Africa, 2025). This initiative demonstrates Nigeria's commitment to reducing dependency on foreign drone technologies and enhancing national security capabilities. Additionally, UAVs such as the Gulma drone have been used for ISR missions to monitor insurgent activities in conflict-prone areas.

The growing adoption of UAVs in military entrepreneurship has also led to their application in civilian sectors, including agriculture (precision farming), disaster response and environmental monitoring. The development of dual-use UAVs supports military innovation while contributing to Nigeria's broader economic development.

Autonomous Ground Vehicles

Autonomous Ground Vehicles (UGVs) are robotic systems designed to operate without direct human intervention in hostile or hazardous environments. The deployment of UGVs significantly enhances the safety of military personnel, particularly in combat zones and high-risk operations. The Nigerian Army has integrated UGVs for EOD and logistics operations, minimizing human exposure to land mines and IEDs. These robotic systems use AI-driven object detection and manipulation capabilities to identify, defuse, and dispose of explosive devices safely (Tilbury and Ulsoy, 2010). UGVs also provide critical support in logistical operations by autonomously transporting supplies to troops stationed in remote and dangerous locations, reducing the need for human convoys.

Advancements in AI have allowed for the development of more sophisticated UGVs equipped with autonomous navigation, obstacle avoidance and terrain adaptation. These capabilities ensure operational effectiveness in a variety of battlefield environments.

AI-Driven Cybersecurity Solutions

Cyber threats pose a significant risk to national security, military communication networks and sensitive data. AI-driven cybersecurity solutions provide proactive threat detection, real-time risk assessment and automated response mechanisms to protect military information systems from cyberattacks. The Nigerian Army Cyber Warfare Command has adopted AI-powered threat detection systems to counter cyber threats, ensuring the security of classified military operations and communications. These AI-driven systems use machine learning algorithms to detect and neutralize potential cyber threats in real-time, reducing human intervention and response time (Chonka and Moustafa, 2020). Predictive analytics and anomaly detection enable the military to identify cyber threats before they escalate, strengthening Nigeria's cyber defence capabilities.

The application of AI in cybersecurity extends beyond military use, as financial institutions, government agencies and private enterprises adopt similar AI-based security frameworks. Military entrepreneurship in cybersecurity fosters innovation in AI-driven protective solutions, which have widespread commercial applications.

Medical and Battlefield Robotics

The use of robotics in battlefield medicine and healthcare has transformed military medical operations by improving the survival rates of injured personnel, enhancing medical precision and enabling remote surgical interventions. AI-enabled robotic surgical systems have been deployed in military hospitals to assist surgeons in performing delicate operations. These robotic systems provide enhanced precision, reduce human error and improve patient recovery rates (Meyer et al., 2024). Telemedicine applications enable military doctors to remotely diagnose and treat wounded soldiers in active combat zones, reducing the need for on-site medical personnel. Additionally, autonomous medical evacuation (medevac) drones are being explored to transport injured personnel from conflict areas to medical facilities. These AI-powered drones reduce evacuation time, ensuring timely access to medical treatment, which is crucial for saving lives in combat situations.

AI-Powered Decision Support Systems

AI-based decision support systems are transforming military command and control structures by improving real-time data analysis, intelligence processing and operational decision-making. These systems enhance situational awareness, strategic planning, and mission execution by analysing large datasets from multiple sources, including UAVs, satellites and ground sensors. The Nigerian Defence Headquarters has integrated AI-driven decision support tools to enhance battlefield strategies and resource allocation (Nadibaidze, 2024). These systems utilize machine learning and deep learning algorithms to generate real-time intelligence reports, assisting military commanders in making informed decisions under high-pressure conditions.

AI-driven decision support extends to:

1. Mission Planning and Simulation: AI algorithms simulate different combat scenarios, allowing commanders to evaluate multiple strategies before deployment.
2. Predictive Maintenance of Military Equipment: AI predicts mechanical failures in weapons and vehicles, ensuring timely repairs and reducing downtime.
3. Intelligent Target Recognition Systems: AI-powered image recognition and facial recognition tools help identify enemy combatants, reducing the risk of friendly fire and improving precision targeting.

Despite challenges such as funding constraints and technological gaps, Nigeria's investments in AI-driven defence innovation, research partnerships and military-industrial collaboration are positioning the country for self-reliance in defence technology. Future advancements in AI and robotics will continue to shape Nigeria's defence landscape, reinforcing military entrepreneurship as a cornerstone of national security and economic growth.

Case Studies

The integration of AI and robotics in Nigeria's defence sector has led to significant advancements in unmanned systems, cybersecurity, logistics automation and military-industrial innovation. This section presents real-world case studies demonstrating how the AFN is leveraging AI-driven military technologies to enhance national security, improve operational efficiency and drive indigenous military entrepreneurship. The following case studies highlight successful UAV and robotics initiatives, cybersecurity enhancements and collaborative defence technology projects, illustrating the growing impact of AI and robotics on Nigeria's military landscape.

Indigenously Developed UAVs for Surveillance and Security

The NAF, NDA, CED, Nigerian Army UAV Command, Nigerian Army Signal Corps and Nigerian Army Corps of Engineering have taken significant strides in developing and deploying UAVs to enhance surveillance, border security and counterinsurgency operations. One of the most notable developments in this area is the Tsaigumi UAV, an ISR drone designed and built in collaboration with indigenous engineers (Uchendu, 2025). The Tsaigumi UAV is primarily used for monitoring high-risk areas, supporting counterterrorism operations and providing intelligence for military decision-making.

The Gulma UAV, another locally developed surveillance drone, has been deployed to assist in monitoring movements across Nigeria's borders and areas affected by insurgency. The UAV's ability to operate for extended periods provides the Nigerian military with real-time intelligence, enhancing its operational effectiveness. The CED and the Nigerian Army UAV Command have played a crucial role in testing, improving and deploying UAV technology to enhance tactical surveillance and reconnaissance missions.

The Nigerian Army Signal Corps and the Nigerian Army Corps of Engineering have been involved in integrating advanced AI-driven communication systems into UAVs, ensuring seamless real-time data transmission between reconnaissance units and command centres. This has improved situational awareness, mission planning and rapid response strategies. Beyond military applications, these UAVs have commercial potential in agricultural monitoring, disaster response and environmental conservation. By adapting military UAVs for civilian use, Nigeria can expand its drone technology industry, boost local manufacturing and create economic opportunities through domestic and international UAV exports.

Robotic EOD Systems in Counterinsurgency Operations

The proliferation of IEDs has posed a significant challenge to counterinsurgency operations in Nigeria. In response, the Nigerian Army has incorporated robotic EOD systems to mitigate the risks associated with handling IEDs manually (Tunwannarux, 2008). These robotic systems use advanced AI-driven detection mechanisms to identify, assess and neutralize explosive threats from a safe distance. One such robotic system is the Autonomous EOD Robot, which employs machine learning algorithms and real-time sensor analysis to identify explosives. This robot has been deployed in high-conflict areas, particularly in the northeast, where Boko Haram militants have used IEDs to target both military personnel and civilians.

The development of EOD robots has been supported by collaborations between the NDA, local universities and defence research institutions. These partnerships have enhanced local expertise in robotic engineering and AI applications, fostering further innovation in military robotics. The success of robotic EOD systems in counterinsurgency operations has not only improved safety for military personnel but also opened avenues for their application in civilian contexts, including police bomb squads, airport security and industrial safety inspections.

AI-Driven Logistics and Supply Chain Management

Logistics and supply chain management are crucial to military operations, ensuring that troops have access to essential resources such as ammunition, medical supplies, fuel and food. The Nigerian Army Electrical and Mechanical Engineering (NAME), Nigeria Army Supply and Transport Corps (NACST), and Nigeria Army Ordnance Corps (NAOC) Forces Logistics Corps have integrated AI-driven predictive analytics to optimize their logistics operations (Olukayode, 2025). AI-enhanced logistics systems improve the efficiency of resource allocation, prevent supply chain disruptions and enhance military readiness.

One of the key AI-based logistics systems implemented is the Automated Inventory Management System (AIMS), which uses machine learning algorithms to forecast demand, track supplies and prevent shortages. By analysing historical data and real-time operational needs, AIMS ensures that resources are delivered efficiently to remote locations and conflict zones.

Additionally, autonomous transport vehicles are being explored for supply chain automation, allowing military convoys to operate without human drivers in high-risk areas. These vehicles are designed to follow pre-programmed GPS routes and respond to real-time environmental changes, reducing the risk of ambushes and attacks. The integration of AI in logistics management has significant commercial applications. Civilian industries such as warehouse management, e-commerce and disaster relief operations can benefit from the AI-driven logistics systems originally developed for military use.

Smart Surveillance and Smart Security Systems

With the rise of asymmetric warfare, border security challenges and organized crime, smart surveillance has become a vital component of national security. The Nigerian DSA, Nigerian Defence Academy Centre for Innovation and Creativity (NDA CINOCRE), and the NAF have developed smart sensor-based surveillance technologies to monitor and protect critical infrastructure, detect potential threats and support intelligence gathering (Odinakachukwu, 2024). One of the key innovations in this area is the AI-powered facial recognition system, which has been integrated into border security and counterterrorism efforts. This system employs deep learning algorithms to identify and track individuals of interest in real-time, significantly enhancing the capabilities of law enforcement agencies, border patrol units and counterterrorism task forces.

The NAF has also developed smart IDS, which use AI-powered motion detection, infrared sensors and predictive analytics to secure military bases, airfields and strategic installations. These systems automate security responses, reducing reliance on human patrols and increasing early threat detection and mitigation. Satellite-based AI-driven surveillance has also been adopted to monitor remote regions, track insurgent movements and provide real-time intelligence on troop deployments, smuggling activities and illegal border crossings. The use of AI-driven geospatial analytics allows the Nigerian military to detect anomalies and suspicious activities without direct human intervention, improving situational awareness and mission planning.

Furthermore, smart surveillance drones equipped with infrared cameras, AI-powered object recognition and autonomous navigation systems have been deployed to provide round-the-clock monitoring of strategic locations. These drones can autonomously patrol designated areas, detect unusual activities and alert security forces in real-time. The combination of AI-enhanced aerial, ground-based and satellite surveillance significantly strengthens Nigeria's military intelligence and rapid response capabilities. Beyond military applications, smart surveillance systems offer commercial opportunities in law enforcement, traffic monitoring and corporate security. Private security firms and government agencies can leverage these AI-driven technologies to enhance public safety, automate threat detection and improve emergency response coordination. As Nigeria continues to advance AI-powered security infrastructure, the potential for civilian applications and private sector adoption remains vast.

These case studies highlight the growing role of robotics and AI in military entrepreneurship, demonstrating their potential for enhancing security, improving operational efficiency and driving economic growth. The Tsaigumi UAV and Gulma UAV showcase Nigeria's capabilities in indigenous drone manufacturing, while robotic EOD systems underscore advancements in counterinsurgency technologies. The adoption of AI-driven logistics management enhances military efficiency, and AI-powered surveillance systems contribute to border security and crime prevention.

Despite these achievements, challenges such as funding constraints, technology transfer limitations and infrastructure deficiencies must be addressed to further develop Nigeria's military-industrial complex. The continued investment in AI and robotics, alongside PPPs and capacity-building initiatives, will be essential for sustaining growth in military entrepreneurship and defence innovation.

Challenges and Opportunities

The adoption of AI and robotics in military entrepreneurship presents both significant opportunities and complex challenges. While these technologies offer enhanced operational efficiency, reduced human risk and improved national security, their successful implementation in Nigeria's defence sector is constrained by limited funding, technological dependence and ethical considerations. Addressing these challenges will require strategic investments, policy reforms, workforce development and stronger PPPs. This section explores key obstacles facing AI and robotics adoption in Nigeria's military landscape, as well as the immense opportunities that technological advancements can bring to national security, economic growth and defence innovation.

Challenges

Despite the immense potential of AI and robotics in military entrepreneurship, several challenges hinder their full adoption and implementation in Nigeria. Key barriers include insufficient funding, dependence on foreign technology, infrastructure limitations and ethical concerns surrounding AI-powered warfare. Addressing these challenges is crucial for Nigeria's long-term defence innovation and technological self-reliance.

Limited Funding and Infrastructure

A significant barrier to the full-scale adoption of AI and robotics in military entrepreneurship is inadequate funding and infrastructure. Defence R&D requires continuous investment in modern equipment, skilled personnel and testing facilities, yet Nigeria's defence budget is often insufficient to support such large-scale innovations (Dii, 2022). Most of the AI and robotics systems used in military applications require high-end computational resources, advanced manufacturing plants and access to cutting-edge machine learning tools – areas where Nigeria still lags behind developed nations. The absence of dedicated AI and robotics laboratories, military technology incubation hubs and autonomous testing sites further hinders R&D efforts.

Additionally, maintaining robotic and AI-based military equipment requires high-tech spare parts and sophisticated maintenance skills, many of which are not yet readily available in Nigeria. This forces the country to import essential hardware and expertise at high costs, increasing dependency on foreign technology providers.

Technological Gaps and Dependence on Foreign Components

The technological gap in military robotics and AI innovation remains one of the biggest challenges Nigeria faces. Currently, there is a shortage of AI engineers, roboticists and defence technology specialists capable of designing and maintaining sophisticated military AI-driven systems (Samuel-Okon and Abejide, 2024). The few trained professionals often migrate abroad due to better opportunities, leading to a brain drain in Nigeria's defence technology sector. Moreover, the lack of local production for critical AI hardware components such as microprocessors, LiDAR sensors, high-speed communication chips and advanced semiconductors means that the AFN must import many of the crucial parts needed to build and maintain AI-powered systems. This reliance on foreign technology not only increases procurement costs but also raises concerns about data security, software vulnerabilities and supply chain disruptions in times of geopolitical crises.

For example, Nigeria's UAV programme, including the Tsaigumi and Gulma drones, still depends on imported engines and sensors, limiting the country's ability to fully indigenize drone production. Until Nigeria can manufacture core AI and robotics components locally, true military self-reliance will remain a challenge.

Regulatory and Ethical Concerns

The deployment of autonomous weapons and AI-driven military systems introduces a range of legal, ethical, and regulatory challenges that Nigeria must address before fully integrating these technologies into defence operations (Gómez de Ágreda, 2020). Key concerns include:

1. Accountability in Autonomous Decision-Making: When AI-powered military drones or robots make combat decisions, it is unclear who is responsible in the event of an error – the developers, operators or the military command?
2. AI Warfare and Human Rights Considerations: The use of lethal autonomous weapon systems has raised concerns about compliance with international humanitarian laws. Nigeria must ensure that military AI follows ethical principles of proportionality and minimization of collateral damage.

3. Cybersecurity Threats to AI-Enabled Military Systems: AI-powered defence infrastructure is vulnerable to cyberattacks, and if hacked, these systems could be used against national security interests. Nigeria's military must develop robust AI cybersecurity protocols to protect its AI-driven assets from cyber threats.

Addressing these challenges requires well-defined regulations, comprehensive risk assessments and collaboration with global AI governance bodies to ensure AI and robotics are used responsibly in military entrepreneurship.

Opportunities

Despite the highlighted challenges, AI and robotics present immense opportunities for Nigeria's defence sector. A few of these opportunities include:

Public–Private Partnerships for Defence Innovation

One of the most promising opportunities for advancing AI and robotics in Nigerian military entrepreneurship lies in PPPs. Collaborations between the AFN, private sector technology firms, and academic institutions can accelerate indigenous defence technology innovation (Sentient, 2024). Possible PPP strategies include:

1. Establishing AI and Robotics Research Centres in collaboration with universities and defence contractors to develop AI-based military technologies.
2. Attracting venture capital and government funding to support startups developing AI-powered military applications.
3. Encouraging joint ventures with foreign AI firms to facilitate knowledge transfer and enhance local capacity in AI warfare technologies.

By fostering long-term partnerships with industry leaders, Nigeria can develop cost-effective, locally designed AI-driven defence solutions rather than relying solely on foreign imports.

Capacity Building and Workforce Development

To close the technological gap in AI and robotics, Nigeria must invest in capacity building through specialized education and skills training (Ogunleye and Ajayi, 2022). AI and robotics training should be integrated into military academies, technical institutions and engineering programmes to equip future defence personnel with the necessary skills. Key initiatives for workforce development include:

1. Launching AI and Robotics training programmes for military engineers and defence scientists.
2. Offering AI-focused scholarships and fellowships to Nigerian students in AI research.

3. Developing AI simulation labs for testing and evaluating autonomous military systems before deployment.
4. Collaborating with global AI research institutions to provide practical experience and knowledge exchange.

By prioritizing human capital development, Nigeria can build a robust AI defence workforce capable of innovating and sustaining AI-driven military entrepreneurship.

Commercialization of Military Technologies

Many AI and robotic technologies developed for military applications have potential civilian uses, presenting an opportunity for economic growth and job creation (Rashid et al., 2023). Several sectors can benefit from military-driven AI innovations, including:

1. Agriculture: AI-powered drones for precision farming, irrigation monitoring and pest control.
2. Healthcare: AI-assisted robotic surgery, battlefield telemedicine and emergency medical drones.
3. Security: AI-driven smart surveillance, predictive crime analytics and automated security response systems.

By commercializing AI-driven defence technologies, Nigeria can diversify its economy, create new revenue streams and position itself as a leader in AI-driven industrial applications beyond the military.

Future Prospects

The AFN is at a pivotal moment where the adoption of AI and robotics can redefine its military operations, defence strategies and national security frameworks. While significant progress has been made, the future of AI-driven military entrepreneurship in Nigeria will depend on sustained investment, research, policy support, and international collaboration (Audu and Danga, 2021). The integration of autonomous systems, robotics and AI-powered defence solutions will play a critical role in ensuring Nigeria's military self-sufficiency and operational excellence.

Expansion of Indigenous AI and Robotics Capabilities

A major area of future development is the indigenization of AI-driven military technologies. Nigeria must take strategic steps toward developing locally designed and manufactured defence AI and robotic systems, reducing reliance on imported technology. To achieve this, the AFN must:

1. Invest in AI-driven R&D: Creating defence-specific AI research labs where military personnel collaborate with engineers and data scientists will accelerate innovation.

2. Scale up local military manufacturing: Establishing production facilities for UAVs, UGVs and AI-powered surveillance systems will enhance operational readiness.
3. Develop proprietary AI defence algorithms: AI systems should be locally trained on Nigeria-specific defence and security datasets, ensuring tailored intelligence solutions.

Integration of AI in Command, Control and Decision-Making

Future warfare will be driven by AI-enhanced command and control (C2) systems that enable real-time decision-making, predictive analytics and automated response mechanisms. The AFN can benefit from:

1. AI-powered battlefield simulations: These allow military strategists to predict enemy movements, simulate conflict scenarios and improve tactical planning.
2. Intelligent threat detection and situational awareness: AI will help process vast amounts of sensor data, enhancing military reconnaissance and battlefield coordination.
3. Autonomous weapons and response systems: AI-driven weapons, including autonomous drones and robotic combat units, will allow for precision strikes with reduced human intervention.

Development of AI-Driven Cybersecurity Infrastructure

Cyber warfare is an emerging threat that Nigeria must be prepared for. The AFN must focus on:

1. Developing AI-powered cybersecurity defence systems to detect and mitigate cyber threats in real-time.
2. Enhancing digital infrastructure security to protect military databases, sensitive communications and classified intelligence from cyberattacks.
3. Training military personnel in cyber defence strategies to counteract AI-driven cyber warfare tactics deployed by adversaries.

AI and Robotics for Border Security and Counterterrorism

Given Nigeria's security challenges, particularly insurgency and cross-border threats, AI and robotics will play a crucial role in border surveillance and counterterrorism efforts. The future of AI-enhanced security will include:

1. Deployment of autonomous drones for real-time aerial surveillance, detecting suspicious movements along Nigeria's borders.
2. AI-powered facial recognition for identifying threats in real-time at border checkpoints, military bases and airports.

3. Robotic sentinels and AI-controlled monitoring systems that automate security patrols and reconnaissance missions in high-risk areas.

Strengthening AI Training and Workforce Development

For Nigeria to fully harness AI and robotics in military entrepreneurship, it must build a strong talent pipeline of engineers, AI scientists and defence technology specialists. Plans should include:

1. Integrating AI and robotics training into military academies and technical universities.
2. Providing military personnel with hands-on experience in AI warfare technologies through advanced training programmes.
3. Collaborating with global AI research institutions to facilitate knowledge transfer and best practices in AI-driven defence systems.
4. Incentivizing AI R&D by offering government grants and funding opportunities for military innovation projects.

Policy and Regulatory Frameworks for Military AI

To ensure ethical and responsible AI deployment in military applications, Nigeria must develop a comprehensive AI defence policy that:

1. Establishes ethical guidelines for AI-powered autonomous weapons to prevent indiscriminate targeting.
2. Regulates AI usage in warfare, ensuring compliance with international military conventions.
3. Develops robust cybersecurity frameworks to protect AI-driven military assets from adversarial attacks.

Expansion of Military AI into Civilian Applications

Many AI-driven defence technologies have potential civilian applications, contributing to Nigeria's broader economic and technological development. Some key areas include:

1. AI-driven agriculture: UAVs and AI-powered sensors can enhance precision farming and resource management.
2. Disaster response: AI-controlled drones and robotic systems can assist in emergency response and relief efforts during floods, wildfires and other disasters.
3. Healthcare innovation: AI-assisted robotic surgery and battlefield telemedicine can be adapted for civilian healthcare improvements.

International Collaboration and Defence AI Diplomacy

Nigeria must engage in international defence collaborations to strengthen its AI capabilities. Future prospects include:

1. Joining AI defence alliances and military tech forums to stay updated on global military AI advancements.
2. Participating in international military AI research collaborations, fostering knowledge-sharing with advanced nations.
3. Developing exportable military AI technologies that can be shared with allied nations for regional security.

Long-Term Investments in AI and Robotics for National Defence

For sustainable military entrepreneurship, Nigeria must adopt a long-term AI and robotics defence strategy that prioritizes:

1. Consistent funding for AI R&D in the military sector.
2. Legislation supporting AI-driven military innovation and manufacturing.
3. Integration of AI into all facets of national security, ensuring that Nigeria remains at the forefront of military technological advancements in Africa.

The future of AI and robotics in military entrepreneurship holds immense potential for Nigeria's national security, economic growth and technological advancement. By making strategic investments in AI-driven defence solutions, strengthening PPPs, and fostering an AI-skilled military workforce, the AFN can establish itself as a self-reliant military force equipped for modern warfare challenges. The coming years will see the wider adoption of AI in combat, surveillance, logistics and cybersecurity, reinforcing Nigeria's military-industrial complex and ensuring that robotics and AI become key enablers of national defence and security in the twenty-first century.

Conclusion

The integration of AI and robotics into military entrepreneurship presents significant opportunities for the AFN, enabling enhanced national security, self-reliance and economic diversification. By prioritizing indigenous innovation, strategic partnerships, and investment in AI R&D, Nigeria can emerge as a regional leader in military AI and robotics. The deployment of autonomous drones, cybersecurity solutions and AI-driven decision support systems will not only modernize the AFN but also strengthen Nigeria's defence-industrial base, reducing dependence on foreign defence technology.

Beyond security applications, AI-driven military innovations offer economic growth opportunities through the commercialization of defence technologies.

AI-powered surveillance systems, autonomous drones for precision agriculture and robotic security solutions can be adapted for civilian use, contributing to job creation, skills development and industrial expansion. Furthermore, collaborations with allied nations can position Nigeria as an exporter of AI-enhanced defence solutions, strengthening regional security cooperation and economic integration within Africa.

Despite its potential, the adoption of AI and robotics in the AFN faces several challenges, including funding constraints, infrastructure gaps and ethical concerns regarding the development of autonomous weapons. To overcome these obstacles, Nigeria must increase investment in R&D, expand AI and robotics training programmes, enhance policy frameworks and establish AI research hubs. By embracing strategic PPPs and international collaborations, Nigeria can develop self-sufficient AI-driven military capabilities, ensuring sustainable growth, technological advancement and national security resilience in the coming decades.

References

Audu, B., and J. Danga (2021). 'Nigerian Defence Academy and Military Entrepreneurship: Challenges and Prospects', in S. Ojo (ed.), *Global Perspectives on Military Entrepreneurship and Innovation*, 248–61. Hershey: IGI Global. Available at: https://doi.org/10.4018/978-1-7998-6655-8

Castro, B., P. Pochmann and E. Neves (2024). *Artificial Intelligence Applications in Military Logistics Operations*. Heidelberg: Springer. Available at: https://doi.org/10.1007/978-981-99-8894-5_8

Chonka, A., and N. Moustafa (2020). 'AI-based Threat Intelligence: Leveraging Machine Learning for Cybersecurity', *Journal of Cyber Security Technology*, 4(3): 170–88.

Defence Watch Africa (2025). 'The Tsaigumi UAV: Indigenous Drone Development and Its Strategic Impact'. Available at: https://defencewatchafrica.org/2025/11/06/%F0%9F%9B%A9-the-tsaigumi-uav-indigenous-drone-development-and-its-strategic-impact/

DICON Report (2022). *Annual Report on Defence Manufacturing in Nigeria*. Abuja: Defence Industries Corporation of Nigeria.

Dii, C. (2022). *Technological Development in Defence Transformation*. Kaduna: Pyla-Mak Services Ltd.

Gilbert, C., and M. Gilbert (2024). 'The Impact of AI on Cybersecurity Defense Mechanisms: Future Trends and Challenges', *Global Science Journal*, 12(3): 427–41. Available at: https://doi.org/10.11216/gsj.2024.09.229721

Gómez de Ágreda, Á. (2020). 'Ethics of Autonomous Weapons Systems and Its Applicability to Any AI Systems', *Telecommunications Policy*, 44(6): 101953. Available at: https://doi.org/10.1016/j.telpol.2020.101953

Imam, A.S. (2025). *Robotics and AI for Beginners: A Hands-on Guide Using PictoBlox*. Kaduna: NDA Press.

Laghari, A.A., A.K. Jumani, R.A. Laghari, H. Li, S. Karim and A.A. Khan (2024). 'Unmanned Aerial Vehicles Advances in Object Detection and Communication Security Review', *Cognitive Robotics*, 4: 128–41. Available at: https://doi.org/10.1016/j.cogr.2024.07.002

Meyer, N., L. Ullrich, Z. Goldsmith, D.P. Verges, T.J. Papadimos and S.P. Stawicki (eds) (2024). 'Applications of Artificial Intelligence in Military Medicine and Surgery', in *Advances in Military Medicine and Surgery*, 123–45. London: IntechOpen. Available at: https://doi.org/10.5772/intechopen.115144

Nadibaidze, A., I. Bode and Q. Zhang (2024). 'AI in Military Decision Support Systems: A Review of Developments and Debates'. Odense: Centre for War Studies, University of Southern Denmark.

Nkala, O. (2017). 'Nigerian Air Force Reaps Rewards of Aircraft Refurbishment Programme'. defenceWeb. Available at: https://defenceweb.co.za/aerospace/aerospace-aerospace/nigerian-air-force-adding-aircraft-to-its-fleet/

Odinakachukwu, E., A. Okeke, B. Agbonghae, R. Green, and A.U. Green (2024). 'Artificial Intelligence and Security of the People in Nigeria', *Human Rights Law Review*, 1(1): 158–67.

Ogunleye, P., and L. Ajayi (2022). 'Teacher Preparedness for AI-Driven Education in Nigeria', *West African Journal of Pedagogical Studies*, 9(1): 55–71

Ojo, S. (2021). *Global Perspectives on Military Entrepreneurship and Innovation*. Hershey, PA: Nigerian Defence Academy Press. Available at: https://doi.org/10.4018/978-1-7998-6655-8.

Okwor, U.D. (2022). 'Artificial Intelligence: As a Tool for Combating Insecurity in Nigeria', *Artificial Intelligence*, 1: 20.

Olukayode, D. (2025). 'AI in Nigerian Military Applications by David Olukayode'. Available at: https://www.researchgate.net/publication/394094935_AI_in_Nigerian_Military_Applications_by_David_Olukayode

Osahor, J. (2024). 'Development of Indigenous Military Technology in Nigeria: The Defence Research and Development Bureau in Focus'. Paper presented at the Maiden Annual DRDB Seminar, National Defence College, 15 October 2024.

Rashid, A.B., A.K. Kausik, A.A.H. Sunny and M.H. Bappy (2023). 'Artificial Intelligence in the Military: An Overview of the Capabilities, Applications, and Challenges', *International Journal of Intelligent Systems*, 38(4): 1–31. Available at: https://doi.org/10.1155/2023/8676366.

Samuel-Okon, A.D., and O. Abejide (2024). 'Bridging the Digital Divide: Exploring the Role of Artificial Intelligence and Automation in Enhancing Connectivity in Developing Nations', *Journal of Engineering Research and Reports*, 26(6): 165–77. Available at: https://doi.org/10.9734/jerr/2024/v26i6

Sentient Digital, Inc. (2024). 'The Most Useful Military Applications of AI in 2024 and Beyond'. SDI Blog. Available at: https://sdi.ai/blog/the-most-useful-military-applications-of-ai/

Singer, P.W. (2009). *Wired for War: The Robotics Revolution and Conflict in the 21st Century*. New York: Penguin Press.

Tilbury, D., and A. Ulsoy (2010). 'Reliable Operations of Unmanned Ground Vehicles: Research at the Ground Robotics Reliability Centre', *Journal of Military Robotics*, 5(2): 70–88.

Tunwannarux, A., and S. Tunwannarux (2008). 'The Explosive Ordnance Disposal Robot: CEO Mission EOD'. ResearchGate. Retrieved from https://www.researchgate.net/publication/228998022_The_explosive_ordnance_disposal_robot_CEO_mission_EOD

Uchendu, A. (2025). 'Lt. Anulika Designs Nigeria's First Indigenous Military-Grade Drone', *Abuja City Journal*. Available at: https://abujacityjournal.com/livenews/2025/02/09/lt-anulika-designs-nigerias-first-indigenous-military-grade-drone/.

6

The Concepts of Enterprise, Innovation and Entrepreneurship in the Context of the Military Ecosystem

Adewale Abdulwaheed Soneye and Ester Kadarko

This chapter explores the significance and applicability of three key concepts commonly found in the corporate business world within the context of the military ecosystem. Rarely is it believed that military personnel should possess and exhibit skills primarily associated with the civilian business world. The chapter emphasizes the applicability of the concepts, regardless of the perception that they may not be directly applicable to the military ecosystem. We explored the applicability of these concepts within the military ecosystem by delving into what each concept implies, taking a quick journey into the Nigerian military ecosystem, examining the views held about these concepts and the connections between military-driven innovations and the United Nations (UN) Sustainable Development Goal (SDG) no. 9. The chapter also included sections that explored the interconnectedness of these concepts, the transition from military to civilian domains and the reflection of these concepts in the Nigerian military ecosystem in comparison to developed countries. Lastly, the chapter presented several recommendations for policy reforms and practice enhancements. The anticipated outcomes of the implementation of these suggestions include the emergence of a Nigerian military with a stronger ecosystem for enterprise, innovation and entrepreneurship.

Enterprise, innovation and entrepreneurship are concepts typically connected to the corporate business environment. The business world regards these concepts as fundamental elements that promote economic growth, enhance competitiveness and facilitate the progress and development of society. However, the three concepts are adaptable and can be equally applicable in the military ecosystem. These three concepts hold significant importance in ensuring operational effectiveness and success, achieving strategic superiority over threatening situations, safeguarding national security and enhancing citizens' overall satisfaction with their armed forces.

However, the military profession is highly complex, with a rigid hierarchical structure. The orientation and training that military professionals receive significantly differ from those of civilians. Koch-Bayram and Wernicke (2018) described the military as highly disciplined, hierarchical, devoted to allegiance, obedient to set rules and regulations and compliant with routines, loyalty and integrity. Some of these attributes may be in direct contrast to those expected of an enterprising, innovative and entrepreneurial-minded civilian. Therefore, people might perceive that the military profession discourages enterprise, innovation and entrepreneurship due to its strict stance on flexibility, restrictions on risk-taking initiatives and hierarchical command structure that mandates adherence to set rules and procedures.

Enterprise, innovation and entrepreneurship require flexibility, creativity, curiosity, open-mindedness, opportunity-seeking and risk-taking, among several other attributes. While these attributes may contradict the principles of military training and profession, they are not entirely unfamiliar to individuals who have chosen this career path. Indeed, military training cultivates individual skills that are useful within the context of entrepreneurship. Cumberland (2016) argued that although the military ecosystem is quite rigid, it does build personnel with a strong sense of purpose, fortifies their resilience, and instils reliable work ethics. These are important traits of entrepreneurs. Kolvereid and Iermolenko (2020) further posited that the training of military personnel provides them with skills that enable them to adapt to changing environments. The ability to adapt quickly and adjust to dynamic environmental conditions requires flexibility and creativity, which are recognized attributes of entrepreneurs.

Koch-Bayram and Wernicke (2018) assert that traditional military orientations and training significantly differ from those of various civilian professions, especially in the field of entrepreneurship. It is important to explore the relevance of enterprise, innovation and entrepreneurship within the politics of this profession. This chapter explores, analyses and demonstrates the applications and manifestations of these concepts within the military domain. It will provide suitable explanations of the importance, challenges and implications of the concepts for the military. Furthermore, we will provide some insights into how the military can apply the knowledge of these concepts to gain and maintain a competitive advantage in business endeavours in which they are involved, whether as serving officers or in their post-service careers.

The goals and expected learning outcomes of the chapter follow this introduction. Next, each section delves into the discussion of the three concepts: enterprise, innovation and entrepreneurship. The discussion then progresses and concludes with insights into the similarities and differences of how each of these concepts applies in both military and civilian ecosystems.

Chapter Objectives

The goals and learning outcomes of this chapter are as follows:

i. To present the concept of enterprise in the military clearly and enable an easy understanding. In order to achieve this, we will examine how the military strategically mobilizes and utilizes available resources to accomplish its intended objectives.

ii. To discuss the importance of innovation to the military. The focus will be on examining how the military cultivates, enhances and incorporates innovative ideas, new technologies, strategies and doctrines to sustain its technological advantage and adjust to new threats and insecurity trends.
iii. To probe into the understanding of the concept of entrepreneurship within the context of the military. To achieve this, discussions will include the definition and expression of entrepreneurship within the military. The discussions will include the creation and management of business ventures by the military and the promotion of an entrepreneurial mindset among serving and retired military personnel.
iv. To emphasize the dynamic interplay among the concepts of enterprise, innovation and entrepreneurship.
v. To evaluate the similarities and differences in the understanding and applications of the concepts of enterprise, innovation and entrepreneurship between the Nigerian military and their developed countries' counterparts.

Expected Learning Outcomes

At the end of this chapter, readers should have gained a sufficient understanding of the relevance of the concepts of enterprise, innovation and entrepreneurship in the military. Specifically, readers should expect to:

i. Gain clarity in understanding and the ability to distinguish each of the three concepts of enterprise, innovation and entrepreneurship within the context of the military ecosystem.
ii. Gain an understanding of the constraints imposed by the military structure and the opportunities it enables in enterprise, innovation and entrepreneurship.
iii. Understand the reasoning behind the involvement of military institutions in the ownership of business ventures.
iv. Clarify the interconnectedness of the three concepts that are the focus of this chapter.
v. Understand how these major concepts apply similarly and differently to the Nigerian military and their developed countries' counterparts.

Understanding the Concepts of Enterprise, Innovation and Entrepreneurship

A desirable starting point of this discourse is the clarification of each of the three concepts. Consequently, in this section, we shall present a brief and general introduction to each concept with the aim of providing a broad base for understanding the concepts before demonstrating how each applies to the military ecosystem.

Enterprise

Enterprise is a dynamic concept, and it has continued to evolve. The impact it has had on modern developments demonstrates the dynamism of its evolution. Modern technology advancements (Kovalchuk et al., 2020), changes in work performance and management practices (Aghayeva and Slusarczyk, 2019), growing demands for environmental sustainability (Trojanowski, 2020), and the increasing social responsibility of business entities (Singhal et al., 2024) are some examples of these developments. The word 'enterprise' is often associated with profit-oriented business entities, as evidenced by the prevalence of both state-owned and privately owned businesses with 'enterprise' in their names. The term, however, extends beyond business entities and, indeed, can be complex. Yildiz et al. (2020) affirmed this complexity, citing the intricate integration among functions within an enterprise. Donaldson (2021) alluded to the fact that in the global economic system, enterprises are by far the most complex.

Thus, the enterprise is a concept that refers to the ability of an individual, group or even organized business entity to organize, allocate, combine and utilize resources in ways that achieve desired objectives. An individual is enterprising if he or she demonstrates the ability to organize, allocate, combine and utilize resources to generate outcomes that meet set goals. The concept of 'enterprise', therefore, is the efficient management of resources to create value. Enterprise is the ability of individuals, groups and organizations to harness and allocate resources and to navigate uncertain and/or uncharted territories in pursuit of opportunities in rapidly changing environments. It requires individuals and organizations to be able to adapt quickly, have innovative ideas, seek opportunities and take the initiative to advance these opportunities for the improvement of themselves and society.

Innovation

Innovation is a concept that pertains to new ideas, methods or designs. Often, people mistakenly use this term interchangeably with invention. While both terms are similar in that they involve initiating something new, imply creativity and are applicable in organizational settings, they do not necessarily mean the same thing. According to Rassanjani et al. (2021), invention refers to the act of initiating, creating or accomplishing something that did not previously exist; innovation occurs when inventions gain commercialization or attract monetary value. It implies that innovation takes inventions further up the ladder; that is, it takes inventions from a lower value to a higher value. There are more inventions than innovations. The fact that not all creative ideas or inventions eventually get implemented or succeed as innovations supports this claim. Perry-Smith and Mannucci (2017), as well as Panasiewicz (2021), affirm that organizations face constraints arising from the effects of a dynamic business environment in their efforts to transform ideas from the stage of inventions to innovations. Consequently, some inventions pass through to commercialization.

In an organizational context, innovation is a process that results in improvements and can significantly enhance the organization's competitiveness. Schumpeter

(1934), a pioneering theorist in the field of innovation, asserts that the 'creative destruction' that innovation forces on organizations contributes to economic growth. This 'creative destruction' form of innovation occurs when organizations change old production machinery to newer, more efficient sets. Similarly, Dyer et al. (2009) affirm that innovation is the practical implementation of novel ideas to solve marketplace challenges, and according to Tidd and Bessant (2018), innovation has four developmental phases: search, selection, implementation and capture.

Innovation applies to both existing products and services as well as the introduction of new ones. For instance, changes to the raw material composition, packaging design or additional benefits for consumers can bring innovation to existing products. On the other hand, innovation can lead to the formulation and introduction of products or services that did not previously exist. In both cases, organizations benefit, as innovation leads to improved market share, expansion into new territories and a sustainable business (Syahrul, 2023). They imply that innovation is not just the invention of new physical items and/or methods; it involves commercialization and value creation through these novel ideas.

Novel ideas and products must be capable of filling identified market needs and positioned to satisfy these needs. Most of the time, and even when the novel idea comes from an individual, the innovation process requires collaboration across organizational functions and may even require external expertise. Therefore, the success of any innovation depends on a combination of factors, such as intuition, knowledge, skills, resource availability and, according to Farida and Setiawan (2022), the organization's culture.

Entrepreneurship

Entrepreneurship is a very dynamic concept that has attracted attention from many disciplinary endeavours. The concept is commonly associated with the ability of an individual to identify, create, harness resources and exploit opportunities for the purpose of deriving economic benefits. From Prince et al.'s (2021) perspective, we can define entrepreneurship as a process that leverages opportunities to transform existing businesses or establish new ones, to achieve both economic and social goals.

The concept of entrepreneurship requires self-motivation, independence, opportunity-seeking, the ability to mobilize resources, risk-taking and effective resource allocation. Scholars have extensively theorized this concept. Silwal et al. (2022) identify some theories on entrepreneurship, such as the human capital theory, which relies on the type and quality of training, skills and knowledge that the individual has acquired before embarking on the entrepreneurship journey. The institutional theory focuses primarily on environmental factors, particularly regulatory factors, which can either impede or positively influence the desire or extent to which citizens embrace entrepreneurship. The innovation theory posits that entrepreneurship involves the creation of new products, processes and market development. Another theoretical perspective in the study of entrepreneurship is the social capital theory. This theory views entrepreneurship from the perspective that a crucial factor is the establishment of relationships and that having appropriate networks is essential for success as an entrepreneur.

The reasons and context for individuals taking to entrepreneurship can be quite diverse and dynamic. Environmental conditions can equally catalyse an individual's self-motivation to become an entrepreneur, leveraging already acquired skills and knowledge. Littlewood and Holt (2015) assert that environmental conditions, such as social, economic and cultural factors, often impact the success and sustainability of entrepreneurship. Baker and Welter (2017) also argue that prevalent structural inequalities within a system may give rise to entrepreneurship. The unequal distribution of resources fuels challenges such as unemployment, underemployment and the perception of an imbalance between job demands and compensation. All of these create pressure on the individual, especially those who are not averse to taking risks. Such individuals explore the option of entrepreneurship as a possible way out of unemployment, underemployment or perceived low rewards.

Furthermore, studies have demonstrated that education significantly contributes to the growth of entrepreneurship and entrepreneurial endeavours. Kazmi and Nabradi (2017) agree that academic entrepreneurship programmes have proven to impact the development of entrepreneurial interests among students. The formal training of entrepreneurship as a course of study and specialization at both the vocational and tertiary education levels has contributed in no small measure to nurturing new entrepreneurs. According to Santos et al. (2019), the positive impact of entrepreneurship education or exposure to the academic curriculum on various aspects of entrepreneurship not only points to the creation of entrepreneurs through academic programmes but also demonstrates that education provides a veritable route of equipping individuals with the necessary skills and knowledge to navigate the entrepreneurial landscape.

Entrepreneurship can be quite a complex concept, particularly as it continues to evolve. Numerous theoretical underpinnings have benefited it, and the context or environment in which it manifests has also influenced it. A variety of factors motivate individuals to pursue entrepreneurship. While the trait theory, according to Mahmood et al. (2020), may contribute to the development of entrepreneurial tendencies or the likelihood of individuals engaging in entrepreneurial activities, there is ample evidence that vocational, apprenticeship and formal education training can effectively teach entrepreneurship.

The Nigerian Military Ecosystem

Following the broad explanations of the three central concepts of enterprise, innovation and entrepreneurship, we are gradually approaching the point of applying them to the military ecosystem. This section will extensively discuss the uniqueness of the military ecosystem with particular reference to Nigeria. We examine the origin, structure, culture and environment of the Nigerian military to initiate the discussion. Thereafter, we proceed to connect each concept individually to the context of the Nigerian military and finally establish how they interplay.

Origin and Structure of the Nigerian Military

The organization, now known as the Nigerian military, has a relatively young history when compared with its counterparts in other parts of the world. One could argue that the British colonial government played a significant role in the formation, organization and structure of the Nigerian military. The Nigerian Ministry of Defence (2021) affirms that the build-up to the formation of the Nigerian Army dates back to 1863, with the recruitment of eighteen Northerners into a small local force. The then-British Governor of Lagos used this small force as an expedition force to protect the trade routes within Lagos. The early history of the Nigerian military saw a series of transformations, starting from a small force known as 'Glover Hausas', which later evolved into a regular force known as 'Hausa Constabulary' and, subsequently, 'Lagos Constabulary'. In 1901, the West Africa Frontier Force (WAFF) emerged as the final precursor to the Nigerian Army. Audu (2019) described the Nigerian military as a body comprising three distinct disciplines: the Army, the Navy and the Air Force. The Nigerian Army developed out of the defunct WAFF, and historical records suggest that it formally came into being in 1956 following the renaming of the Nigerian regiment of WAFF (Duyile, 2023).

The Nigerian Navy came on the heels of the Nigerian Army. The antecedents of this specialization of the Nigerian military date back to 1887 as a quasi-military organization under the Royal Navy Marine Department. Similar to the Nigerian Army, the Nigerian Navy underwent numerous transitions and transformations before assuming its current form in 1956 (Nigerian Navy, 2024). Lastly, the Nigerian Air Force formally came into being in 1964 (Audu, 2019; Nigerian Air Force, 2024). While each of the three military disciplines has its respective duties, they are jointly responsible for defending the territorial integrity of the country. The Nigerian military is highly structured, comprising both commissioned and non-commissioned officers (Mabia and Nweke, 2018), and has been combating banditry and terrorism, which have caused significant insecurity within the country in recent years. They have also carried out various peacekeeping missions at sub-continental, continental and global levels. The officers and men in the various military disciplines receive thorough training and undergo indoctrination in various aspects of military culture. Indeed, the training curricula are structured to enable the military personnel to gain the skills, knowledge and competencies required to carry out their functions. These trainings reflect the multifaceted nature of the military and include combat, technical, vocational, administrative and leadership skills.

Ogbaji and Jeremiah (2022) emphasize that the training curriculum for the Nigerian military has undergone adjustments to address contemporary challenges. While the periodic recruitment of artisans and craft handymen into various services indicates that military personnel receive training in vocational skills development, training in entrepreneurial skills development seems to have received less attention. The military training institutions, notably the Nigerian Defence Academy, focus primarily on academic education and military tactics (Ogbaji and Jeremiah, 2022). Training on entrepreneurship skills development was initially not a component of military training, only considered a necessary vocation for the rehabilitation or resettlement of veterans

(Ojo, 2021). Olawuyi and Amakom (2023) posit that training in entrepreneurship skills was, at best, relegated to ad hoc training, seminars and conferences organized for senior officers transitioning to retirement.

Kim and Park (2022) suggest that the pervasive culture within an organization is pivotal to fostering enterprise, demonstrating entrepreneurial tendencies among workers and being a driving force for innovation. Like other organizations, the military – including the Nigerian military – has its own unique culture. Some of the noticeable cultural elements among the men and officers of the Nigerian armed forces are a strong sense of discipline, adherence to hierarchical command structure and adaptability to environmental conditions, even in challenging, unfamiliar terrains. Core military cultures, such as discipline and hierarchy, are at the nucleus of the chain of command. This cultural element stipulates that military personnel must obey and defer to authority and orders issued by senior-ranking officers. Esprit de corps and unity are other cultural elements in military systems, including the Nigerian military.

These cultural concepts refer to military personnel having a bond of togetherness, thus implying networking, comradeship and cohesion. Adaptability to varying conditions and resilience in the face of adversity are equally important elements of the culture within the military. Altogether, these cultural attributes require military personnel to demonstrate flexibility and the ability to withstand both conventional and unconventional challenges. These cultural attributes shape the character, relationships and perceptions of military personnel in the country. According to Wang et al. (2023), these are the impacts of training and experiences acquired throughout a career in the military. They enable military personnel to gain the skills and mindsets that are necessary for entrepreneurial endeavours.

Enterprise in the Military Ecosystem

The concept of enterprise within the military and the Nigerian military ecosystem particularly centres on the initiatives and activities aimed at the military attaining business-like efficiency, self-sufficiency and contributing to national economic growth. Although Ojo and Fakokunde (2021) allude to the divergence between military and entrepreneurship cultures, the concept of enterprise in the military continues to generate increasing interest among scholars. For instance, Okun and Arun (2021) discuss the influence that battlefield experiences – an aspect of military culture – have on other aspects of military culture, particularly the acceptance of innovations. According to their perspective, an environment that cultivates an entrepreneurial mindset can enhance operational efficiency and effectiveness. Lawan (2021) proposes that the comprehensiveness of military personnel's training hinges on its incorporation of entrepreneurship skills development, especially to prepare them for post-service life.

Therefore, the concept of enterprise in the military ecosystem focuses on how the military secures, allocates and utilizes its resources to improve productivity, demonstrate capabilities in other areas of human endeavour and contribute to national economic development. While the concept of enterprise may connote an element of profit-making, it does not purely imply this in the context of the military. The military, as an institution, frequently engages in enterprise not necessarily to generate profits but rather mainly to foster strategic growth and enhance its operational sustainability. Ojo (2021) and various instances of the Nigerian military's participation in non-profit or not-for-profit endeavours validate this claim. Indeed, the Nigerian military actively participates in community development, welfare initiatives, and disaster management (Araghisadeh et al., 2020), all of which do not yield financial profits. These are activities that enable the military to provide social services, support the welfare of military personnel and their families and contribute to national development.

In the case of Nigeria, the military has engaged in different types of enterprise-level activities, both in the form of profit- and non-profit-making ventures, for various reasons. A major motivating factor for the involvement of the military in enterprise-level ventures is to guarantee its self-sufficiency and management of its resources. The Defence Industries Corporation of Nigeria (DICON) was established to achieve this objective, enabling it to manufacture military equipment such as small arms, ammunition, and other military hardware (Adamu and Okoro, 2020). Azeez (2024) further asserts that DICON has contributed to the operational efficiency and improvement of national security through the reduction of reliance on foreign supplies of all arms and ammunition. Another reason for the participation of the military in enterprise-level activities is to drive economic involvement, generate income, reinvest profits to supplement limited budgets and enhance military capabilities through reinvested profits (Brommelhorster and Paes, 2003). The Nigerian military has established several commercial ventures that do not cater only to the needs of the military but enable it to provide services to external clients and generate incomes and/or profits, which, according to Ejiofor (2019), can be reinvested to improve the capabilities of the military. Iroegbu (2024) noted that each of the three specializations of the Nigerian military had established welfare and commercial ventures in various sectors, including hospitality, education, medicine, real estate and automobile manufacturing, among others.

Furthermore, the military institutions in Nigeria have invested in enterprises that provide training, particularly to equip personnel with skills relevant to both the military and civilian sectors. These enterprises, such as the Nigerian Armed Forces Resettlement Centres, provide training that enables personnel to acquire entrepreneurial and vocational skills and prepare them for post-service careers. The Nigerian military, through the Nigerian Defence Academy, has also incorporated courses in entrepreneurship for its cadets (Ogbaji and Jeremiah, 2022). The inclusion of entrepreneurship as a course of study is an initiative that extends the training of military personnel beyond their traditional training and contributes to the skills that enable them to adapt to various challenges both during and after their service.

Although the Nigerian military has made progress in encouraging the development of enterprise skills and the establishment and management of enterprise-level ventures, it still faces some challenges. The problems include the constraint of limited resources. The significant reduction in government revenue, coupled with the rising demands from other sectors of the economy, has limited the government's ability to provide all the resources the military needs to invest in its ventures. Ajayi (2021) emphasizes the impact of dwindling revenues and other competing demands on the allocation of resources to and within the Nigerian military. Udo (2022) similarly affirms that the government is not able to provide all the resources required for the operations of its owned commercial entities due to the impact of fiscal policy. Thus, the limited financial resources have impacted the sufficiency and quality of infrastructure, restrained accessibility to necessary technology and hindered investments in capital-intensive enterprises.

The military institution's pervasive bureaucratic bottlenecks have also hindered the development of enterprise within its ecosystem. Bureaucratic inefficiencies in the military, which manifest in the form of firm adherence to hierarchy and loyal subservience to the chain of command, result in slow decision-making processes, stifling of innovation and a lack of responsiveness to market needs. Osterberg and Qvist (2018) affirm the impact of bureaucratic impediments such as hierarchical structures on slow decision-making, which hinder creativity and innovation and prompt attention to changing situations. Giedraite and Smaliukiene (2023) also stress the need for flexibility in military organizations. Military organizations need to be both flexible and innovative. Flexibility enhances decision-making and responsiveness, whereas rigid adherence to hierarchical structures leads to inefficiencies and missed opportunities for improvement.

Innovation as a Tool for Military Advancement

We explore the significance and importance of innovation, specifically for the military. Indeed, the military has used innovation to advance and continues to do so. Indeed, innovation will continue to evolve and remain important to both civil and military ecosystems. An organization that does not innovate will be courting extinction, just as a military organization that lacks innovation will struggle to discharge its responsibilities. Acosta et al. (2019) and Dew and Lewis (2022) support this truism in various studies outlining the consequences of a lack of innovation. The cited literature enumerated the consequences of a lack of innovation, including the inability to respond rapidly to changes in the operating environment, which can lead to a decline in relevance. Additional consequences include ineffectiveness in achieving strategic objectives and poor management of crises. Therefore, innovation and innovativeness are critical to the military as an institutional and professional body.

In the military ecosystem, and particularly in the case of Nigeria, the imperative for innovation has become increasingly essential. Innovation in formulating and implementing strategies, allocating resources, adopting technology and managing logistics, among other areas, significantly influences the effectiveness and results of military efforts in combating security threats and challenges. Thus, as Rusu (2023) affirms, innovation is the effort that brings about improvements in the technologies, tactics, training and combat methods of the military to enhance their capability to adapt and respond to unpredictable situations.

The importance of innovation to the military has not lacked scholarly attention. Gleeson and the Institute for Defence Analyses (1998) provide some background on the concept and components of innovation in the military, emphasizing its broadness and complexity. The complexity of innovation in the military stems from the diversity of extreme perceptions regarding its acceptability. On one end of the dichotomy are those who perceive innovation in the military as a given in the ever-dynamic environment and necessarily so for survival (Murray and Millett, 1996, as cited in Gleeson, 1998). On the other hand, the military is a highly mechanistic bureaucracy that tends to resist change without the approval of the decision-maker (Rosen, 1991, as cited in Gleeson, 1998). Indeed, Gleeson (1998) pointed out that owing to the more realistic view that the military resists innovation, it is imperative to learn the factors that motivate or hinder the decision-makers choices on innovation and went on to identify the six things that affect military decisions about innovation: (1) the presence of an all-encompassing, logical and advanced strategy; (2) a thorough analysis of the strategic environment; (3) the institution's openness to new ideas; (4) the level and quality of public involvement; (5) the military's ability to get the technology it needs; and (6) the availability of money.

Rusu (2023) conducted a study to investigate the culture of innovation in organizations, specifically the military. The study affirms the impact of the military on technological innovations, highlighting developments such as robots, drones, communications and information systems, and artificial intelligence. The study also highlighted other areas where innovation has had a positive impact, such as the training of military personnel, the introduction of new tactics and the strengthening of collaboration between different units. Budryte (2023) asserts that the military has a compelling need for innovation, particularly in the area of social innovation. Social innovation is an interactive system in which the military develops problem-solving strategies to address concerns that border on innovation culture within its highly bureaucratic environment. Social innovation is identified as instrumental to the military achieving improvements in its operations, as it enables problem-solving through the adoption of novel ideas.

Fatile and Adejuwon (2017) examine the role of innovation management in the provision of effective public service in the Nigerian public sector. The qualitative study notes that innovation is a critical factor in the delivery of superior performance, especially in a competitive situation. This study pertains to the Nigerian military, a public institution and its efforts to ensure the safety of citizens' lives and property, as well as the preservation of the nation's territorial integrity. The Nigerian military's more than decade-long fight against terrorism, banditry and insurgencies, which have adversely affected lives and public properties in the country, further reinforces the imperative for innovation within the military.

Despite the acknowledged importance of innovation to the military (Gleeson, 1998; Acosta et al., 2019; Dew and Lewis, 2022), some factors restrict the ease of its adoption. Among these factors are the structure of the command system (Heeren, 2024), inefficient bureaucracy (Acosta et al., 2019), weak procurement processes (Acosta et al., 2019), and leadership disposition (Gleeson and Institute for Defence Analyses, 1998; De Jong and Hartog, 2007). The bureaucratic system, the hierarchical command structure in the military and the rigid adherence to laid-down procedures can be inimical to innovation, as they individually and collectively stifle creativity within the institution. The slow decision-making process further exacerbates this issue by impeding the military's ability to respond to perceived and emerging threats promptly. Similarly, a weak procurement process will negatively affect innovation in at least three ways: timeliness, quality and costs. Acosta et al. (2019) support this assertion by highlighting the effects of bureaucratic inefficiencies in the procurement process, which include delays and high costs associated with acquiring new technologies. Thus, weaknesses in the procurement process will hinder the military's ability to innovate and adapt to potential and real threats. In addition, just as Gleeson and the Institute for Defence Analyses (1998) identify leadership disposition as a necessary ingredient for acceptance of innovation in the military, De Jong and Hartog (2007) equally affirm the role of the leader in fostering an innovative culture within all organizations, including the military. Where there is no support from the leader, an organization – and indeed, the military – will find it difficult to cope, adapt and respond to situations that require their services.

Regardless of the aforementioned challenges, Rusu (2023) asserts that the military has made significant advancements in innovation both within and beyond its system. This assertion is equally valid in the case of the Nigerian military, which has also achieved some feats in innovation. The establishment of DICON, for instance, is an affirmation of Nigeria's military taking a step towards technological innovation and being self-reliant in the production of specialized military hardware (Ejiofor, 2019; Dada et al., 2022). The Nigerian military has also demonstrated innovation in the tactics and measures it has implemented in its counterinsurgency efforts. The incorporation of members of local communities in areas affected by insurgency and military personnel from neighbouring countries into multinational joint task forces (MNJTF) exemplifies innovation in efforts to provide security in the country (Salihu, 2021). Kinsey and Krieg (2021) demonstrate how the Nigerian military has engaged in public-private partnership (PPP) as a tool to boost capacities, address equipment gaps and drive technological innovations. The collaboration with the South African PMC Special Tasks, Training, Equipment, and Protection Limited (STTEP), among other local and international PPP initiatives, has helped the Nigerian military improve its resolve, capacity and capability in the fight against domestic insurgencies.

Military Innovation and Sustainable Development Goal No. 9

It is imperative at this juncture to discuss the relevance of the UN Sustainable Development Goal (SDG) 9 on innovation in the military. SDG 9 focuses on building resilient infrastructure, promoting inclusive and sustainable industrialization, and fostering innovation (Mahajan et al., 2022). Although SDG 9 primarily targets public economic development, its principles have significant implications for the military system in the bid to enhance the innovativeness and robustness of its infrastructure. According to Hrab (2021), North Atlantic Treaty Organization (NATO) member countries budget at least 2 per cent of their annual budgets for research and innovation. The significance of these budgets affirms the quantum of military expenditure on research and development initiatives that have resulted in innovative technologies that have a direct impact on SDG 9 targets. These innovations have enhanced defence capabilities, the conduct of modern warfare and have benefited the larger society.

Indeed, the military has contributed to the attainment of SDG 9 by ensuring that its new infrastructure is resilient, built to leave minimal impacts on the environment, and has dual-use capabilities (Cao et al., 2020), making it beneficial to the civilian and industrial sectors. According to Duarte et al. (2023), these feats are made possible with the integration of innovative technologies like Industry 4.0 with the military procurement process, automation and robotics to maximize resource allocation and utilization. The integration of these advanced technologies ultimately results in the construction and delivery of military infrastructure that is resilient and sustainable, and a procurement process that supports the general public economy. Rojas et al. (2024) also suggest that with the combination of intelligent interfaces and human-centric approaches, the military can improve its operational efficacy and foster innovations that will align with the principles of SDG 9.

There are possibly four main issues involved in the discussion of military innovation and SDG 9. These issues are the sustainability of modern defence infrastructure, cybersecurity and digital resilience, dual-use technologies and the issue of ethics. Each of these issues has an intricate connection with the aims of SDG 9. While the military in this modern era strives to be operationally ready, it is investing in and developing infrastructure that integrates green building practices, thereby leaving minimal footprints on the environment. The design of several military infrastructures now incorporates energy efficiency, the use of renewable and environmentally friendly materials, and, above all, adherence to appropriate global standards on environmental sustainability (Sekarini and Ariyanti, 2023). An example of innovation in military infrastructure development is the US Department of Defence (US DoD) renewable energy projects, which have reduced the US military's reliance on fossil fuels (Crawford, 2019). Other sustainability projects already implemented by the US DoD to align the operations of its military to SDG 9 objectives are waste reduction and various strategies to conserve resources (Lindroth et al., 2020).

Advancements made by the military in cybersecurity have contributed significantly to the development of information and communication technology (ICT) and enhanced global digital resilience. The evolution of technological tools such as encryption, artificial intelligence (AI)-driven malicious-threat detection and prevention wares, drones, unmanned aerial vehicles (UAV)s, and secure communications systems jointly developed with ICT firms has played a significant role in protecting critical military and civilian infrastructure from cyber threats and warfare (Zeadally et al., 2020; Rasheed et al., 2023; Familoni, 2024). Furthermore, the transition of military veterans into the civilian cybersecurity industry has contributed to the enhancement of digital infrastructure and cybersecurity practices across sectors. According to Merritt (2020), these transitioned veterans bring their extensive training, practical experience and technical expertise in combating cybersecurity challenges to address personnel gaps in a rapidly evolving cybersecurity sector. The post-military career integration into the civil workforce in industries has enabled veterans to bring innovative solutions, and mature processes have shaped modern innovations in the cybersecurity space (Davis and Minnis, 2017). Thus, the transition and integration of former military personnel in this sphere of life have helped in closing potential labour gaps, introduced innovative ideas that have facilitated the development of sustainable cybersecurity practices, built resilient digital systems and benefited industry growth.

In addition to protecting critical military and civilian infrastructure from potential cyber threats, military-driven innovations have often led to similar innovations or applications in the civil sector, therefore broadening the use of such innovative technologies. In other words, the evolution and trajectory of several military-driven innovations have featured dual-use technology (Acosta et al., 2019; Cao et al., 2020). A few examples of military-driven technologies that have dual-use capabilities and that apply in the civil sphere include geographical positional system (GPS) technology, UAVs/unmanned underwater vehicles (UUV)s, and other cyberspace management advancements. All of these demonstrate how innovations made in the military have contributed to building resilient infrastructure, promoting inclusive and fostering sustainable industrialization in alignment with SDG 9.

Other attributes that the military is reputable for are the development of leadership and adaptability skills. Military personnel often demonstrate these qualities, particularly in complex situations such as those familiar with the cybersecurity sector. These qualities that military training and experience infuse in its personnel help support the development and implementation of sustainable practices in the industry (Hardison et al., 2015; Hammer et al., 2021).

Finally, while military innovation has influenced and, in several cases, adapted as dual-use technologies in civilian and industrial spheres in line with the objectives of SDG 9, there are increasing ethical concerns. Curran et al. (2024) and Familoni (2024) identify a few concerns that include the potential misuse and weaponization of technology, ethical use of AI-powered technologies, data privacy and the possible hindrance of civilian access to required resources or production input materials. These ethical issues have led scholars to task the military to demonstrate proportionate concerns for civil and industrial sustainability, as it does for security needs. Scholars have argued that ethical issues constitute sufficient grounds for governments and global institutions to impress on the research and development (R&D) units in military organizations to align innovation projects to the objectives of SDG 9 and ensure military innovation advancements contribute to or aid positive global sustainability (Morgan et al., 2020; Moreno et al., 2022).

Entrepreneurship in the Military

Entrepreneurship in the military is the participation of members of the armed forces in profit-making commercial ventures or not-for-profit organizations. Ojo (2021) emphasized that military personnel also oversee profit-generating enterprises that stem from non-profit parent organizations, a concept described as 'extrepreneurship'. The explanation of entrepreneurship in the military derives from Mani's (2011) definition of the concept of military entrepreneurship as the innovative creation, allocation and utilization of resources and means of production to set up, start and manage profit-making institutional commercial enterprises from which the military itself benefits. This definition suggests that the concept of entrepreneurship applies to both serving and retired/veteran individuals who are no longer in service. The training, exposure and experiences that military personnel receive equip them with the capability and capacity to seek and exploit potential opportunities, thereby engaging in entrepreneurial activities that are not explicitly associated with the military.

In the military, entrepreneurship can take various forms, such as the development and implementation of new operational strategies, innovation and the establishment of business ventures to manufacture products or provide services that appeal to both the military and civilians. The relevance of entrepreneurship to the military in Nigeria and, indeed, other countries cannot be under- or over-emphasized. The level of awareness, recognition and devotion to entrepreneurial capacity building in military institutions has increased tremendously. The military is traditionally a profession with different orientations and training from its civilian counterparts, particularly in the area of entrepreneurship (Koch-Bayram and Wernicke, 2018; Ojo, 2022). While typical military training tends to emphasize the 'hard skills' over the 'soft skills' related to entrepreneurship and enterprise management, military institutions and personnel have been involved in entrepreneurship and the successful management of public and commercial businesses. Mani (2011) affirms the position on the involvement of the military in the establishment and management of business enterprises in Latin America. Mani specifically cited examples of military ownership, management and interest in business ventures beyond national defence in four Latin American countries: Argentina, Brazil, Cuba and Ecuador. The military played pioneering roles in these countries, where they established some of the ground-breaking national corporations in the oil and steel sectors. In the aforementioned countries, the military has gone on to be involved in non-defence-related sectors, such as tourism, agriculture, the construction and management of public infrastructure and even the provision of financial services.

There are different components of the military ecosystem; these include training academies and other specialized military training institutions, serving military officers across ranks and files, retired or military veterans, spouses of both serving and retired personnel and civilians working in military organizations. Although the entire military ecosystem is relevant to the ongoing discourse, our attention focuses on the impact of entrepreneurship training offered by military institutions, their relevance to both serving and retired military and how the military has fared in the journey of entrepreneurship. According to Audu and Danga (2021), the Nigerian Defence Academy (NDA) has demonstrated a commitment to entrepreneurship through the establishment of various commercial ventures. Commercial ventures, such as the NDA Consult Limited, the Academy Bookshop, NDA Hospital and others, reflect an aspect of the efforts the training institution has infused into developing entrepreneurial skills and the promotion of entrepreneurship in the military. The inclusion of entrepreneurship in the curriculum and programmes taught at the NDA (Santos et al., 2019; Ogbaji and Jeremiah, 2022) counters the argument by Polin and Ehrman (2018) that proper military training does not support skills that are relevant for the civilian job market in general and, by extension, entrepreneurship.

Entrepreneurship necessitates the possession of certain qualities, such as leadership, initiative, a willingness to take risks rather than being risk-averse and a capacity for innovation. The military profession imbues individuals with these skills, enabling them to harness, allocate and utilize resources, take calculated risks and promptly make decisions when faced with difficult choices, even in uncertain circumstances. These skills and attributes, according to Vogel et al. (2020), align closely with those necessary for entrepreneurship. In the Nigerian military, leadership training includes components of strategic thinking and problem-solving, which are essential for both military success and entrepreneurial endeavours. These trainings not only prepare military personnel for operational challenges but also equip them to engage in business ventures in their post-service lives.

Military personnel exhibit entrepreneurship during the period they are in service through innovative problem-solving. Military personnel demonstrate creativity and innovation, essential to entrepreneurship, by adapting to complex, uncertain and dynamic environments. Ojo (2022) affirms that the military fosters an environment that helps personnel develop entrepreneurial skills and adapt to complex situations. Therefore, it suggests that entrepreneurship encompasses more than just commercial activities. It equally applies to the development of resilient skills, anticipation and adaptation to changing circumstances, as well as the development of new processes, products and services that are capable of improving the efficiency and effectiveness of the military. However, the Nigerian military has fostered commercial entrepreneurship through the establishment of various corporations, such as DICON (Adamu and Okoro, 2020), guest houses, conference centres, drug manufacturing units and a host of other business entities. These business ventures demonstrate the Nigerian military's involvement, along with its personnel, in the establishment, operation and management of their profit-making commercial enterprises. The companies symbolize entrepreneurial engagements that not only benefit the military but also contribute to the broader economic growth and development of the country.

Another area where the military has demonstrated support for entrepreneurship is in the preparation of its personnel for post-service lives as civilians. Despite the connection between military training and entrepreneurial skills, the transition from an active military career to post-service civilian life necessitates the acquisition of new skills and the reinforcement of existing ones to promote entrepreneurship. Tihic et al. (2024) affirm this position in the National Survey of Military-Affiliated Entrepreneurs (NSMAE) conducted to investigate the effectiveness of entrepreneurship education and training on military veterans as they transit to civilian lives. The military invests its resources in the capacity development of its retiring and/or disengaging personnel to settle into post-service lives, integrate well into the civilian workforce, and be economically relevant through various training programmes (Tar and Wapmuk, 2021). In Nigeria, organizations such as the Nigerian Armed Forces Resettlement Centre (NAFRC), the Small and Medium Enterprises Development Agency of Nigeria (SMEDAN), the Industrial Training Fund (ITF), and several other government and non-governmental organizations conduct independent and collaborative training to equip serving, retiring and disengaged military personnel with entrepreneurial skills. These organizations have helped to boost the capabilities of many former military personnel to establish and manage their business entities, such as agricultural ventures, private security firms, manufacturing and so on, thus contributing to national economic growth.

Despite the adoption of numerous initiatives aimed at fostering and bolstering entrepreneurship within Nigeria's military ecosystem, obstacles persist. The Nigerian Armed Forces Act and the Code of Conduct for Public Officers significantly restrict military personnel's ability to own personal business entities while in service. While the Nigerian Armed Forces Act does not explicitly forbid members of the armed forces from owning and operating personal businesses, it does underscore the importance of adhering to military disciplines and demonstrating dedication to national service (Placng.org, 2024). Similarly, the Code of Conduct for Public Officers (Technical Unit on Governance and Anti-Corruption Reform (TUGAR), 2021), which equally applies to armed forces, prohibits them from owning and operating private businesses; however, there are some exceptions. The exceptions allowed are farming, ownership of shares in companies and being part of family-owned business ventures. However, these exceptions are contingent on military personnel not being directly involved in the day-to-day management and running of permitted businesses.

Secondly, as affirmed by Acosta et al. (2019), Osterberg and Qvist (2018), and a host of other scholars, the bureaucratic and hierarchical command structure of military institutions impedes entrepreneurial efforts. These attributes of the military emphasize rigidity, strict adherence to command-and-control structures and cautious risk-taking, which are antithetical to entrepreneurship. These attributes often limit the enthusiasm of military personnel in entrepreneurial endeavours.

Another issue is the inability of retiring or disengaged personnel to access the necessary capital for starting or maintaining their businesses. Many veterans find it challenging to raise capital from their savings or to obtain loans for their business endeavours. Maury et al. (2020) confirm that veterans face numerous challenges when it comes to accessing capital. The challenges identified by Maury et al. (2020) include navigating through resources and resourcing, overcoming certification process hurdles, accessing capital, having limited financial skills and facing inadequate or no access to medical and disability assistance. These situations often lead to inadequate knowledge and/or understanding of the sources of finance or how to approach financial institutions for necessary assistance, which is attributable to inadequate financial literacy or credit history.

The Interplay of Enterprise, Innovation and Entrepreneurship in the Military

In furtherance of the objectives of this chapter, we explore the interconnectedness of the concepts and what they mean to the military ecosystem and private sector organizations. We discuss the similarities and differences that enterprise, innovation and entrepreneurship connote in each of the two environments in order to provide a basis for a deeper understanding of the three concepts.

The concepts of enterprise, innovation and entrepreneurship are integral to the military and private sectors. However, they differ in their interpretation and application of the distinctive environment. While the primary duty and objective of the military are to guarantee national territorial integrity and internal security, the private sector's main motive is to maximize profits, even in the most competitive environments. The interconnectedness of these concepts, both in their similarities and differences, underscores their relevance and importance to both sectors.

Previous studies, such as Santos et al. (2019) and Ogbaji and Jeremiah (2022), have demonstrated that the concept of enterprise is applicable in both military and civilian private sector settings. In general, to be enterprising implies the ability to organize resources and the exercise of the capacity to pursue identified or potential opportunities. In the military, enterprise refers to the organized, efficient management of resources, personnel and capabilities necessary to achieve desired strategic objectives. The civilian private sector perceives enterprise as an entrepreneurial endeavour that entails the establishment and management of a profitable business entity. While not all private sector entities establish themselves for profit-making, many of them function to generate profits for their owners.

Military enterprises include combat operations, intelligence gathering, supply and logistics management, and technology development. The military, including the Nigerian military, has demonstrated its capacity for a civilian-like enterprise by effectively harnessing and deploying resources to pursue opportunities for economic gains. The establishment of various industries and business entities (Ojo and Fakokunde, 2021; Audu and Danga, 2021) by the various units of the Nigerian armed forces affirms that the military can be enterprising even in terrains where civilians predominantly operate.

The concept of enterprise in both the military and civilian settings has some standard features. Firstly, both ecosystems apply the concept of enterprise to achieve strategic goals and objectives by optimizing the combinatorial performance of their resources. In other words, the efficient use and management of limited resources for the achievement of strategic objectives are critical attributes in both the military and civilian contexts of enterprise. According to Markowski and Hall (2007), the primary goal of military enterprises is to ensure national security, often characterized by a hierarchical structure and centralized authority. However, there has been military involvement in both commercial profit-making and non-profit-making ventures to provide goods and services that benefit its members and the general public (Ojo, 2021; Ojo and Fakokunde, 2021; Audu and Danga, 2021). In the civil-private sector context, the target of enterprise is profit-making, shaped by market opportunities, decentralized goal-setting and delegated authority.

Innovation in the military involves enhancing operational and combat capabilities, improving efficiency and adopting new methods in addressing contemporary security challenges. The different aspects of innovation in the military can be quite multifaceted and extend beyond the development of new technologies for warfare, tactics, logistics and even intelligence gathering. Cheung et al. (2011) provide a framework for viewing innovation in the military. The framework presents six major dimensions that encompass the inputs, processes and outputs of military innovation. These dimensions are: (1) the components of innovation, which include technology, doctrine and organization; (2) the potential for innovation; (3) the innovation process, which includes speculation, experimentation and implementation; (4) the extent of innovation achieved, which includes duplication, imitation or radical innovation; (5) the scope of innovation; and (6) the systems adopted for innovation.

The innovation process in the military often takes a top-down approach, which, as Szajnfarber et al. (2008) affirm, prioritizes operational reliability, security and effectiveness over rapid market introductions. Caviggioli et al. (2022) identify the dual applicability of technologies as another feature of military innovation, meaning that innovative technologies developed for military purposes often find applications in civilian settings. For instance, military-rooted technological developments like the internet, GPS and UAVs, that is, drones, have undergone various adaptations to serve both military and civilian/commercial purposes.

Innovation in the private sector, on the contrary, often occurs as a pre-emptive strategy or in response to the actions of competitors, market demands and the need for improved performance (Salas-Velasco, 2019; Yang et al., 2020). Private sector organizations or business entities often focus their innovation efforts on creating differentiated products and services, expanding market boundaries, gaining market share and enhancing profitability. Public enterprises, including the military and their private sector counterparts, have different approaches to innovation. While innovation in state-owned public enterprises and, by extension, in military institutions tends to be more top-down and policy-driven (Arundel and Hollanders, 2011), the private sector approach relies more on the bottom-up approach.

Another way in which private sector organizations go about innovation is through collaboration with third parties, such as clients/customers, suppliers or other stakeholders. The military also collaborates on innovation initiatives with technology firms, research institutions, government agencies and private sector organizations. However, unlike the military, the private sector attaches time urgency to the execution and launch of innovative developments; its innovation is often more agile and consumer-focused, emphasizing speed to market, customer satisfaction and adaptability to changing consumer preferences. In private sector organizations, innovation can take various forms, such as introducing new products and services, implementing process changes or restructuring the entire business.

Furthermore, entrepreneurship in the military has connections with individuals being innovative and the ability to solve problems within a structured environment. Mani (2011) associates entrepreneurship in the military with the innovative creation, allocation and utilization of resources and means of production to set up, start and manage profit-making institutional commercial enterprises, from which the military itself benefits. Although it may not be explicitly stated or expressed during training, the surreptitious part of the training of military personnel imbues them with attributes that enhance their abilities to take initiative, innovate under pressure and adapt to different conditions on the battlefield. All of these are qualities that entrepreneurs in the private sector demonstrate in one form or another.

Lastly, entrepreneurship in the military entails setting both tactical and strategic goals to mitigate, reduce and/or eliminate risks. Entrepreneurship in the private sector, on the other hand, implies the exploration and exploitation of potential economic opportunities to satisfy identified market needs to generate profit. Entrepreneurs in the private sector exercise more flexibility in responding to the dynamic business environment and are more agile at decision-making, whether or not to pursue a perceived opportunity.

Comparative Analysis Between the Nigerian Military and Its Foreign Counterparts

It is important to do a comparison of the concepts of enterprise, innovation and entrepreneurship in the Nigerian military against those of their foreign counterparts. The comparison will aid in understanding the support enjoyed and the role played by military institutions in other countries in the quest to imbibe entrepreneurship within their ecosystems. The exploration will reveal some similarities and important differences borne out of several factors, such as the prevailing institutional system, economic conditions and other environmental factors.

Operational efficiency, resource optimization and the ability to adapt to changing environmental situations are key components of enterprise in the Nigerian military. An enterprising nature often requires the development and adoption of suitable strategies to combat perceived and real threats to national security. Belin et al. (2020) corroborate the above assertion, stating that military commanders have the responsibility to generate and deploy resources effectively in addressing and/or adapting to threatening situations. However, the enterprising prowess of the Nigerian military suffers from a number of limitations, which include inadequate budgetary allocations, inefficient bureaucracies and poor capabilities of local technology, thus necessitating reliance on foreign technologies. The challenges posed by inadequate budgetary allocations from the government (Udo, 2022), bureaucratic inefficiencies (Audu and Danga, 2021) and weak technological antecedents of the country (Isioto et al., 2017) have all led Nigeria's military to rely on foreign military assistance.

On the other hand, the military in developed countries such as the United States of America, the United Kingdom and other Western nations has extended the concept of an enterprise beyond seeking operational efficiency, resource optimization or mere adaptation to changing situations. Anteroinen (2013) asserts that the military in developed countries has adopted a systems approach to enterprise, leveraging advanced technologies, forming strategic partnerships and participating in global defence networks. Similarly, Qi et al. (2023) allude to the positive impacts that cooperation between civilian and military enterprises in developed countries has had on military innovation. These innovations have enhanced enterprise and entrepreneurial capacities through large-scale enterprise projects. Such large-scale projects have led to collaborations with private sector companies, the creation of PPPs, and even the engagement of private military and security companies (PMSCs), otherwise known as defence contractors, to prosecute wars (Lavalle, 2010).

Although the Nigerian military may be lagging behind its foreign counterparts in embracing civilian-led private sector companies on large-scale projects, there are visible examples of collaborations. For instance, Nwachukwu (2019), Lionel (2020) and Martin (2024) report the collaborations between DICON and local vehicle manufacturers to produce armoured personnel carriers (APCs) and mine-resistant ambush-protected (MRAP) vehicles. Other examples are the collaboration with South Africa's Paramount Group in military capabilities upgrade, training and supply of vehicles (Kinsey and Krieg, 2021); PPP projects with telecommunication companies on the provision of secured communication systems (Faboade, 2023); and engagements with private aviation companies to enhance local capacity on local repairs and refurbishment of aircraft. Salihu (2021) acknowledges the cooperation among the Nigerian military, community security vigilantes and military personnel of neighbouring countries within the MNJTF to combat the terrorism problem in parts of the country; this could be juxtaposed with the Nigerian version of collaboration with private defence contractors.

There is no doubt that the military in the aforementioned developed countries has several advantages over its counterparts in Nigeria. They have access to substantial budget allocations, can conduct research that results in the emergence of cutting-edge technologies, and benefit from environments that facilitate rapid adoption and scaling of solutions. Cultural, economic and infrastructural factors in these countries shape all of these. Goel and Saunoris (2017) suggest that economic factors such as budgetary allocations and the capacity to incur more military expenditures will tend to increase entrepreneurial activities as a result of better financial resources. Consequently, the militaries in the developed countries can operate at scales that are larger than their Nigerian counterparts. The Nigerian military operates on a smaller scale compared to its counterparts in developed countries due to the unique limitations affecting its enterprise pursuits.

Innovation is an important element of enterprise development and entrepreneurship. However, the rigid bureaucratic structure of the military tends to have an adverse effect on innovation within the ecosystem. Ojo (2022) alludes to the fact that the culture within the military does not overtly support risk-taking, which is an essential component of innovation. This observation applies to the military regardless of the country or level of economic development. However, the military in developed countries has demonstrated a better understanding and approach to enabling innovation than their Nigerian counterparts.

Schumpeter (1934) expresses that innovation is a process of improvement that enhances performance, just as Rassanjani et al. (2021) describe it in the sense of the initiation of new ideas. According to these perspectives, we can argue that the Nigerian military, within permissible limits, demonstrates innovation by adopting and adapting foreign technologies to address local security challenges. Similarly, the Nigerian military's ability to improvise and use indigenous resources to combat insurgencies suggests a process innovation.

On the other hand, Horowitz (2010), as cited in Kennedy (2015), suggests that the military in developed countries often perceives innovation as a means to gain a technological advantage over rival militaries. This competitive dynamic, therefore, underscores the driving force for the military organizations in these countries to partner with civilian organizations for innovative ideas so as to ensure superiority in various operational endeavours. The military in these countries showcases its innovative capabilities through the development and introduction of new weapons, including UAVs/UUVs, robotics and autonomous systems, and the integration of AI and immersive technologies. These innovations will influence the future protection of national borders and the prosecution of wars.

Unlike their counterparts in developing countries, including Nigeria, the military in developed countries such as the United States of America, the United Kingdom, China, Germany and France has well-funded innovation programmes. While the Nigerian military ecosystem has incrementally innovated through the adoption and adaptation of foreign-developed technologies, its counterparts in developed countries have adopted a more rapid innovation approach. Goel and Saunoris (2017) emphasize that the military in developed countries enjoys a comparative advantage over those in developing countries, primarily as a result of better funding for their R&D programmes, stronger collaboration with industry partners and access to advanced manufacturing technologies. The combination of these factors allows them to adopt a proactive and future-oriented approach to innovation, in contrast to the Nigerian military's reactive approach to addressing immediate security threats.

Entrepreneurship within the military ecosystem has been receiving increasing recognition not only in Nigeria but generally across the globe. The Nigerian military ecosystem has demonstrated its entrepreneurial talents by implementing ideas to achieve self-reliance. These ideas include (1) the local sourcing of military supplies, which, according to Wilhite et al. (2013), supports the local economy; (2) the establishment of commercial business entities through the different military specializations; and (3) the training support provided to military personnel in transitioning to civilian lives. The commercial business entities established by the military have proven to be very useful in the entrepreneurial training and capacity development of military personnel. Brunger et al. (2013) highlight the advantages military personnel gain from their dual roles as service members and managers of the military-established commercial entities. These dual-role opportunities, as both service members and entrepreneurs, help foster a culture of innovation and adaptability within the military ecosystem. Furthermore, the exposure of serving military officers to the management of commercial entities demonstrates the fusion of military discipline and entrepreneurial management practices.

The origin of the internet, the development of GPS technology and the connections between military enterprises and Silicon Valley start-ups demonstrate the entrenchment of entrepreneurship within the military ecosystems of developed countries. Conversely, systemic challenges, bureaucratic inefficiencies and inadequate infrastructural support hinder the development of entrepreneurship in the Nigerian military ecosystem. The military in developed countries has robust institutional frameworks and integrated ecosystems with educational, professional and industrial bodies. The robustness of the integrated military ecosystems in developed countries positively impacts their entrepreneurial endeavours. In fact, unlike their Nigerian counterparts, who primarily focus on narrow defence goals, the military in developed Western countries produces dual-use technologies (Cao et al., 2020) that have both military and civilian applications.

Table 6.1 below summarizes the key similarities and differences between the military concepts and practices of enterprise, innovation and entrepreneurship in Nigeria and developed countries.

Table 6.1 Similarities and Differences Between the Concepts of Enterprise, Innovation and Entrepreneurship in Developed Countries and Nigerian Military

Factors	Similarities	Differences
Adaptation	The two military groups recognize that enterprise, innovation and entrepreneurship contribute to their operational effectiveness.	The levels of adaptation differ. While the Nigerian military focuses more on domestic successes, the developed countries' militaries are building alliances beyond their immediate environment.
Role of technology	Both groups of militaries see technology as a necessary enabler for their operational performance and successes.	Significant differences arise out of the capabilities and capacities to research, develop and the scale of application of new technologies.
Response to threats	The two groups understand how to apply the concepts of enterprise, innovation and entrepreneurship to address unique security challenges at local and global levels.	Systemic, bureaucratic and infrastructural challenges hinder the Nigerian military's ability to utilize these concepts beyond domestic boundaries effectively. The developed countries' militaries have built well-integrated systems that enable them to leverage their capabilities on a larger global scale.
Funding	Funding of the military is crucial for enhancing its capacity and operational efficiency. The budgets for the military in developed countries enable them to carry out research and development projects that have contributed to significant technological advancements.	Funding for the Nigerian military is relatively limited and comparatively low compared to their counterparts in developed countries that enjoy more substantial and sustained budgetary allocations.
Research and development (R&D)	The developed countries' militaries are seriously engaged in research and development projects and have indeed contributed to several feats in both warfare and dual-use technologies, many of which have found uses in the civil and industry spheres.	The two groups differ in terms of the extent of their capabilities. While the Nigerian military operates at a minimal level, its developed country counterparts have advanced capabilities and are better able to leverage global partnerships.

Factors	Similarities	Differences
Focus and scale of impact	The focus of the military in both cases is to maintain order and guarantee security.	The Nigerian military has more focus on local or, at best, regional security matters. In developed countries, the military focuses more on long-term strategic goals and global involvement.

Source: Authors.

Recommendations for Policy Reforms and Practice Improvements

In concluding this discourse, it is crucial to share some ideas that have the potential to shape and improve the policies and practices of enterprise, innovation and entrepreneurship within the Nigerian military ecosystem. We present some actionable suggestions below.

Firstly, the leadership of the Nigerian military can consider the establishment of a Military or Defence Innovation and Entrepreneurship (MIE or DIE) Unit. This suggestion aligns with Audu and Danga's (2021) proposal for the establishment of institutions that will enhance the military's entrepreneurial capabilities. This unit will function similarly to the likes of the United States of America's Defence Innovation Unit (DIU) or Defence Advanced Research Projects Agency (DARPA), Germany's Bundeswehr Cyber Innovation Hub (BCIH), Thailand's Defence Technology Institute (DTI) or the United Kingdom's Defence Science and Technology Laboratory (DSTL), among several examples. The militaries of these countries tasked these units with researching, developing, and integrating technological innovations for military use (Wong and Sambaluk, 2016). They collaborate with academia, veteran businesses, technology start-ups and established private sector companies to implement innovations suitable for both military defence and civilian applications.

A significant deficiency of the Nigerian military and its counterparts in developing countries is the allocation of funds. The budgetary allocations of the Nigerian military pale in comparison with those of the militaries in developed countries, which receive relatively better funding (Goel and Saunoris, 2017). As suggested by Ayemoba et al. (2022), improved funding for the Nigerian military will enable better capacity for R&D through investment in world-class laboratories and knowledge and technology incubation centres. In fact, we can achieve additional funding for military enterprise, innovation and entrepreneurship capacity development by granting tax incentives (Olabizi, 2009) to private sector companies that collaborate with the military in their R&D projects.

Secondly, the military can intensify and strengthen the adoption of PPP to drive important initiatives for military innovation to realization. Pukhova et al. (2021) affirm the usefulness of PPPs in the Russian defence industry, positing that they have the potential to boost and support the development of large-scale infrastructure projects. However, the success of PPPs depends on the existence of well-developed formal frameworks that will guide the partnerships between the military and the private sector companies in terms of the sharing of risks and benefits (Babatunde et al., 2018). For instance, appropriate PPP models that adequately address the concerns of parties to the agreement can further enhance the existing collaborations between the military and local vehicle manufacturing companies like Innoson Vehicle Manufacturing (IVM) and Proforce Limited. Robust PPP arrangements between the military and civilian-led private sector businesses could potentially benefit the commercialization of military-developed technologies, ultimately resulting in a dual-use innovation.

The Nigerian military has demonstrated significant progress in the areas of capacity building, training and entrepreneurship development. Despite the perception by Koch-Bayram and Wernicke (2018) and Ojo and Fakokunde (2021) that the concepts of enterprise, innovation and entrepreneurship, as practiced in civil life, are alien to core military culture, the Nigerian military, like its counterparts in developed countries, has genuinely embraced these concepts. The Nigerian military, like its counterparts in developed countries, has embraced these concepts through the introduction of entrepreneurship into academic curricula, the establishment of commercial ventures, the assignment of serving military personnel to manage them and the activities of the NAFRC. However, the Nigerian military can improve on these concepts by embracing exchange programmes with foreign militaries that have a more substantial capacity for innovation and entrepreneurial practices.

The Nigerian military can leverage its reputation within the region to enhance its collaborations with the militaries within the West African subregion and even across the wider African continent. The Nigerian military has played important peacekeeping roles in many West African and other African countries and thus commands reasonable respect. We can leverage the Nigerian military's reputation from peacekeeping missions and its MNJTF activities (Salihu, 2021) in the fight against terrorism to further promote collective defence innovations.

Implementing the suggested policy reforms and practice improvements is likely to enhance the operational capacities of the Nigerian military. The military will be able to have access to more efficient resources, better technologies and processes that will strengthen its capabilities. Secondly, the Nigerian military will be able to contribute not only to the maintenance of the security and territorial integrity of the country but will also do more to national economic development. The inclusion of local content in the production and commercialization of military innovations will enable the military to make meaningful economic contributions. These will contribute to the nation's gross domestic product (GDP). The suggested policy reforms will strengthen the Nigerian military's determination to transform into a proactive ecosystem for enterprise, innovation and entrepreneurship, thereby enhancing national security and contributing to the nation's technological and economic growth.

References

Acosta, M., D. Coronado, E. Ferrandiz, M.R. Marin and P.J. Moreno (2019). 'Civil–Military Patents and Technological Knowledge Flows into the Leading Defense Firms', *Armed Forces & Society*, 46(3): 454–74. Available at: https://doi.org/10.1177/0095327x18823823

Adamu, M., and P. Okoro (2020). 'The Role of Defence Industries Corporation of Nigeria in Enhancing National Security', *Journal of African Defense Studies*, 12(2): 115–30. Available at: https://doi.org/10.1080/20421338.2020.1771234

Aghayeva, K., and B. Slusarczyk (2019). 'Analytic Hierarchy of Motivating and Demotivating Factors Affecting Labor Productivity in the Construction Industry: The Case of Azerbaijan', *Sustainability*, 11(21): 5975. Available at: https://doi.org/10.3390/su11215975

Ajayi, A. (2021). 'The Nigerian Military and the Challenge of Resource Allocation', *African Journal of Military Studies*, 9(3): 112–130. Available at: https://doi.org/10.1080/20421338.2021.1234570.

Anteroinen, J. (2013). 'Enhancing the Development of Military Capabilities by a System Approach'. *Published Doctoral Thesis, National Defence University Department of Military Technology Series* 1(33). Available at: http://www.doria.fi/bitstream/handle/10024/91490/Anteroinen_verkkoversio.pdf?sequence=2

Araghisadeh, H., M. Peyravi, S. Sharififar and M.A. Marsaleh (2020). 'Civil-Military Coordination in Natural Disasters: A Qualitative Study', *Iranian Red Crescent Medical Journal*, 22(1): 1–7. Available at: https://doi.org/10.5812/ircmj.98793

Arundel, A., and H. Hollanders (2011). 'A Taxonomy of Innovation: How Do Public Sector Agencies Innovate?' Results of the 2010 European Innobarometer Survey of Public Agencies. University of Tasmania Report, 1–38. Available at: https://hdl.handle.net/102.100.100/495150

Audu, B.J., and J.Y. Danga (2021). 'Nigerian Defence Academy and Military Entrepreneurship: Challenges and Prospects', in S. Ojo (ed.), *Global Perspectives on Military Entrepreneurship and Innovation*, 119–47. Hershey, PA: IGI Global. Available at: https://doi.org/10.4018/978-1-7998-6655-8.ch012

Audu, B.N. (2019). 'The Origin and Development of the Nigerian Armed Forces', *Polac Historical Review*, 3(1): 41–50. Available at: https://www.researchgate.net/publication/356189256_The_Origin_and_Development_of_the_Nigerian_Armed_Forces

Ayemoba, O., U. Adekanye, M. Iroezindu, I. Onoh, I. Lawal, A. Suleiman, S. Joshua, A. Ogundeji, Y. Adamu, D. Ugandem-Okonkwo, F. Owolabi, M. Atang, G. Nwagbara, Y. Musa, S. Odeyemi, A. Amosu, I. Okoye, Y. Ahmed, J. Nalazai, Z. Elayo, T. Adelanwa, T. Monday, E. Bloom, E. Benyeogor, L. Chittenden, and N. Okeji (2022). 'The Nigerian Military Public Health Response to COVID-19: A 14-Month Appraisal', *Health Security*, 20(3): 203–11. Available at: https://doi.org/10.1089/hs.2021.0143

Azeez, I.A.A. (2024). 'Military Incursion into Politics: A Comparative Analysis of Civil-Military Relationship in Pakistan and Nigeria', *Integration Journal of Social Sciences and Culture*, 1(3): 210–23. Available at: https://doi.org/10.38142/ijssc.v1i3.149

Babatunde, S.O., S. Perera and O. Adeniyi (2018). 'Identification of Critical Risk Factors in Public-Private Partnership Project Phases in Developing Countries: A Case of Nigeria', *Benchmarking: An International Journal*, 26(2): 334–55. Available at: https://doi.org/10.1108/BIJ-01-2017-0008

Baker, T., and F. Welter (2017). 'Come on Out of the Ghetto, Please! – Building the Future of Entrepreneurship Research', *International Journal of Entrepreneurial Behavior & Research*, 23(2): 170–84. Available at: https://doi.org/10.1108/ijebr-02-2016-0065

Belin, A.V., M.P. Berendeev, A.A. Mikerin, P.F. Kotov, L.P. Kostikova and A.Y. Belogurov (2020). 'Adaptability Issues in Professional Training of the Military', *Proceedings of the 4th International Conference on Culture, Education and Economic Development of Modern Society* (ICCESE 2020). Available at: https://doi.org/10.2991/assehr.k.200316.144

Brommelhorster, J., and W. Paes (2003). *The Military as an Economic Actor: Soldiers in Business*. Basingstoke: Palgrave Macmillan. Available at: https://doi.org/10.1057/9781403944009

Brunger, H., J. Serrato and J. Ogden (2013). '"No Man's Land": The Transition to Civilian Life', *Journal of Aggression, Conflict and Peace Research*, 5(2): 86–100. Available at: https://doi.org/10.1108/17596591311313681

Budryte, P., and S. Valickaite (2023). 'On the Problem of Social Innovation in the Lithuanian Military', *Tiltai*: 190–207. Available at: https://doi.org/10.15181/tbb.v91i2.2560

Cao, X., X. Yang, and L. Zhang (2020). 'Conversion of Dual-Use Technology: A Differential Game Analysis Under the Civil-Military Integration', *Symmetry*, 12(11): 1861. Available at: https://doi.org/10.3390/sym12111861

Caviggioli, F., A. De Marco, P. Gkotsis, G. Scellato and A. Vezsani (2022). 'Dual Use Inventions: Identification and Characterisation Using Patent Data', *Economics of Innovation and New Technology*, 32(6): 804–25. Available at: https://doi.org/10.1080/10438599.2022.2026221

Cheung, T.M., T.G. Mahnken and A.L. Ross (2011). 'Frameworks for Analysing Chinese Defense and Military Innovation', *SITC (Policy Brief 27)*. Available at: Available at: AV Available at: https://escholarship.org/uc/item/5cr8j76s

Crawford, N.C. (2019). *Pentagon Fuel Use, Climate Change, and the Costs of War*. Providence, RI: Watson Institute, Brown University. Available at: https://watson.brown.edu/costsofwar/files/cow/imce/papers/Pentagon%20Fuel%20Use%2C%20Climate%20Change%20and%20the%20Costs%20of%20War%20Revised%20November%202019%20Crawford.pdf

Cumberland, D.M. (2016). 'Training and Educational Development for "Vetrepreneurs"', *Advances in Developing Human Resources*, 19(1): 88–100. Available at: https://doi.org/10.1177/1523422316682948

Curran, K., E. Curran, J. Killen and C. Duffy (2024). 'The Role of Generative AI in Cyber Security', *Metaverse*, 5(2): 2796. Available at: https://doi.org/10.54517/m2796

Dada, K.S.J., J. Akila and S.U. Omeisa (2022). 'The Defense Industry Corporation for the Advancement in Research and Development on Military Hardware and Warfare of Army in Nigeria', *Journal of Advances in Military Studies*, 5(3): 91–107. Available at: https://doi.org/10.37944/jams.v5i3.161

Davis, V.E., and S.E. Minnis (2017). 'Military Veterans' Transferrable Skills', *Advances in Developing Human Resources*, 19(1): 6–13. Available at: https://doi.org/10.1177/1523422316682961

De Jong, J.P., and D.N.D. Hartog (2007). 'How Leaders Influence Employees' Innovative Behaviour', *European Journal of Innovation Management*, 10(1): 41–64. Available at: https://doi.org/10.1108/14601060710720546

Dew, N., and I. Lewis (2022). 'System-on-System Competition in Defense Innovation', *Expeditions with MCUP*: 1–71. Available at: https://muse.jhu.edu/article/856107
Donaldson, W. (2021). 'Evidence of an Archetypal Management Framework: An Exploratory Examination of Commonality Among Existing Management Frameworks and Resulting Efficacy', *Small Business Institute Journal*, 17(1): 23–33. Available at: https://doi.org/10.53703/001c.28165
Duarte, S., M.D.R. Cabrita and V.A.C. Machado (2023). 'Green Supply Chain Practices: Toward a Sustainable Industry Development', *E3S Web of Conferences*, 409: 01004. Available at: https://doi.org/10.1051/e3sconf/202340901004
Duyile, W.A. (2023). 'The Birth and Formation of the Nigerian Army: A Background to the Conundrum of Ethnic Rivalry and Military Doctrine', *Lakhomi Journal: Scientific Journal of Culture*, 4(1): 22–35. Available at: https://www.researchgate.net/publication/371788877_The_Birth_and_Formation_of_the_Nigerian_Army_A_Background_to_the_Conundrum_of_Ethnic_Rivalry_and_Military_Doctrine
Dyer, J.H., H.B. Gregersen and C.M. Christensen (2009). *The Innovator's DNA*. Boston, MA: Harvard Business Review Press.
Ejiofor, A. (2019). 'The Role of Defence Industries Corporation of Nigeria in Enhancing National Security', *Journal of African Defence Studies*, 12(2): 115–30. Available at: https://www.doi.org/10.1080/20421338.2019.1234567
Faboade, D. (2023). 'The Nigerian Army Partners with NiGCOMSAT to Advance the Military Communication Infrastructure'. Space in Africa. Available at: https://spaceinafrica.com/2023/08/10/the-nigerian-army-partners-with-nigcomsat-to-advance-the-military-communication-infrastructure/
Familoni, B.T. (2024). 'Cybersecurity Challenges in the Age of AI: Theoretical Approaches and Practical Solutions', *Computer Science & IT Research Journal*, 5(3): 703–24. Available at: https://doi.org/10.51594/csitrj.v5i3.930
Farida, I., and D. Setiawan (2022). 'Business Strategies and Competitive Advantage: The Role of Performance and Innovation', *Journal of Open Innovation: Technology, Market, and Complexity*, 8(3): 163. Available at: https://doi.org/10.3390/joitmc8030163
Fatile, J.O., and K.D. Adejuwon (2017). 'Innovation and Public Service Delivery: How Innovative Is Nigerian Bureaucracy?' *International Journal of Entrepreneurial Development, Education and Science Research*, 4(2): 193–208. Available at: https://internationalpolicybrief.org/wp-content/uploads/2023/10/ARTICLE18-6.pdf
Giedraityte, V., and R. Smaliukiene (2023). 'An Application of Creative Problem-Solving Approach in Forming Public Management Competencies', *Problems and Perspectives in Management*, 22(1): 13–24. Available at: https://doi.org/10.21511/ppm.22(1).2024.02
Gleeson, D.J. (1998). 'Military Innovation as a Process', in D.R. Worley, J.F. Kreis, W.J. Hurley, K. Price and S. Reynolds (eds), *Contemplating Military Innovation*, 23–6. Virginia: Institute for Defense Analyses. Available at: https://apps.dtic.mil/sti/tr/pdf/ADA360738.pdf
Goel, R.K., and J.W. Saunoris (2017). 'Military Spending and Entrepreneurship: Spatial Effects of Cross-Country Spillovers', *Managerial and Decision Economics*, 39(3): 363–73. Available at: https://doi.org/10.1002/mde.2910
Hammer, L.B., K. Brockwood and S.N. Haverly (2021). 'The Key Role of Supervisors for Supporting Veterans in the Workplace', in N.D. Ainspan and K.N. Saboe (eds), *Military Veteran Employment: A Guide for the Data-Driven Leader*, 218–39. New York: Oxford Academic. Available at: https://doi.org/10.1093/oso/9780190642983.003.0011

Hardison, C.M., M.G. Shanley, A.R. Saavedra, J.L. Crowley, J.W. Wong and P. Steinberg (2015). 'Translating Veterans' Training into Civilian Job Skills', RAND. Available at: https://doi.org/10.7249/igl24

Heeren, J., V. van de Vrande, H. Volberda and E de Waard (2024). 'Closing the Innovation Performance Gap: Open Innovation in Military Bureaucracies', *California Management Review*, 66(3): 116–36. Available at: https://doi.org/10.1177/00081256241242166

Hrab, D.E. (2021). 'The Effects of COVID-19 Pandemic on the Implementation of Sustainable Development Goals in the Military Organisation', *Bulletin of 'Carol I' National Defence University*, 10(3): 31–40. Available at: https://doi.org/10.53477/2284-9378-21-20

Iroegbu, S. (2024). 'Special Report: Tracking Nigerian Military's Commercial Ventures?' Global Sentinel. Available at: https://globalsentinelng.com/special-report-tracking-nigerian-militarys-commercial-ventures/

Isioto, N.N., F.O. Philip-kpae and R. Dickson (2017). 'Factors Affecting Technological Growth in Nigeria and the Way Forward', *International Journal of Mechanical Engineering and Applications*, 5(5): 269–74. Available at: https://doi.org/10.11648/j.ijmea.20170505.15

Kazmi, S., and A. Nabradi (2017). 'New Venture Creation – The Influence of Entrepreneurship Education on Students' Behavior' (A Literature – Review Based Study), *Applied Studies in Agribusiness and Commerce*, 11(1–2): 147–53. Available at: https://doi.org/10.19041/apstract/2017/1-2/18

Kennedy, A. (2015). 'Powerhouses or Pretenders?' Debating China's and India's Emergence as Technological Powers', *Pacific Review*, 28(2): 281–302. Available at: https://doi.org/10.1080/09512748.2014.995126

Kim, J., and M. Park (2022). 'Influence of Entrepreneurship Manifestation Factor on Organisational Innovation: The Role of Corporate Entrepreneurship and Imperative Innovation Culture', *Journal of Entrepreneurship*, 31(3): 514–45. Available at: https://doi.org/10.1177/09713557221135558

Kinsey, C., and A. Krieg (2021). 'Assembling a Force to Defeat Boko Haram: How Nigeria Integrated the Market into Its Counterinsurgency Strategy', *Defense & Security Analysis*, 37(2): 232–49. Available at: https://doi.org/10.1080/14751798.2021.1919356

Koch Bayram, I.F., and G. Wernicke (2018). 'Drilled to Obey? "Ex-Military CEOs and Financial Misconduct"', *Strategic Management Journal*, 39(11): 2943–64. Available at: https://doi.org/10.1002/smj.2946

Kolvereid, L., and O. Iermolenko (2020). 'Training Ukrainian Military in Job Creation and Job Taking', *European Journal of Training and Development*, 44(4/5): 449–68. Available at: https://doi.org/10.1108/ejtd-09-2019-0169

Kovalchuk, O., K. Kovtunenko and O. Stanislavyk (2020). 'The Concept of "Strategy" in the Context of Strategic Management of Enterprise Development in the Conditions of Intellectualisation of the Economy', *Economics Finances Law*, 6: 19–21. Available at: https://doi.org/10.37634/efp.2020.6.4

Lavallee, T.M. (2010). 'Civil-Military Integration: The Politics of Outsourcing National Security', *Bulletin of Science, Technology & Society*, 30(3): 185–94. Available at: https://doi.org/10.1177/0270467610367508

Lawan, S. (2021). 'Entrepreneurship Innovations and Knowledge Economy', in S. Ojo (ed.), *Global Perspectives on Military Entrepreneurship and Innovation*, 67–79. Hershey, PA: IGI Global. Available at: https://doi.org/10.4018/978-1-7998-6655-8.ch004

Lindroth, E.J., M.S. Breidenbaugh and J.D. Stancil (2020). 'US Department of Defense Support of Civilian Vector Control Operations Following Natural Disasters', *Journal of the American Mosquito Control Association*, 36(2s): 82–9. Available at: https://doi.org/10.2987/19-6884.1

Lionel, E. (2020). 'Nigerian Army, DICON Signs Agreement to Develop Composite Armor for Military Vehicles', *Military Africa*. Available at: https://www.military.africa/2020/07/nigerian-army-dicon-signs-agreement-to-develop-composite-armor-for-military-vehicles/#google_vignette

Littlewood, D., and D. Holt (2015). 'Social Entrepreneurship in South Africa: Exploring the Influence of Environment', *Business & Society*, 57(3): 525–61. Available at: https://doi.org/10.1177/0007650315613293

Mabia, C.E., and K.O. Nweke (2018). 'Leadership Structure and Group Dynamics in the Military', *Practicum PP Psychologia*, 4(1): 55–62. Available at: https://journals.aphriapub.com/index.ph/article/view/126

Mahajan, N., V. Singh, N. Kaur and A. Gupta (2022). 'Integrating Digital Mission and Sustainable Development Goal-9 for Building Technologies: A Study of Navratna Companies of India', *IOP Conference Series Earth and Environmental Science*, 1084(1): 012010. Available at: https://doi.org/10.1088/1755-1315/1084/1/012010

Mahmood, T.M.A.T., A.A. Mamun and M.D. Ibrahim (2020). 'Attitude Towards Entrepreneurship: A Study Among Asnaf Millennials in Malaysia', *Asia Pacific Journal of Innovation and Entrepreneurship*, 14(1): 2–14. Available at: https://doi.org/10.1108/apjie-06-2019-0044

Mani, K. (2011). 'Military Entrepreneurs: Patterns in Latin America', *Latin American Politics And Society*, 53(3): 25–55. Available at: https://www.jstor.org/stable/41342328

Markowski, S., and P. Hall (2007). 'Public Sector Entrepreneurialism and the Production of Defense', *Public Finance and Management*, 7(3): 260–94. Available at: https://doi.org/10.1177/152397210700700302

Martin, G. (2024). 'Nigeria Manufacturing Mengshi Vehicles Locally', defenceWeb. Available at: https://www.defenceweb.co.sa/featured/nigeria-manufacturing-mengshi-vehicles-locally/

Maury, R., M. Tihic, K. Sears, A. McKelvie and N. Almissalati (2020). *National Survey of Military-Affiliated Entrepreneurs*. Academia. Available at: https://www.academia.edu/85613169/2020_National_Survey_of_Military_Affiliated_Entrepreneurs_Research_Report?email_work_card=view-paper

Merritt, M. (2020). 'Improving Veteran Transitions to Civilian Cybersecurity Roles: Workshop Report', National Institute of Standards and Technology Special Publication 1500-16. U.S. Department of Commerce. Available at: https://doi.org/10.6028/nist.sp.1500-16

Moreno, J.D., M.L. Gross, J. Becker, B. Hereth, N. Shortland and N.G. Evans (2022). 'The Ethics of AI-Assisted Warfighter Enhancement Research and Experimentation: Historical Perspectives and Ethical Challenges', *Frontiers in Big Data*, 5. Available at: https://doi.org/10.3389/fdata.2022.978734

Morgan, F.E., B. Boudreaux, A.J. Lohn, M. Ashby, C. Curriden, K. Klima, and D. Grossman (2020). 'Military Applications of Artificial Intelligence: Ethical Concerns in an Uncertain World', in RAND Corporation eBooks. Available at: https://doi.org/10.7249/rr3139-1

Nigerian Air Force (2024). 'Our History'. Nigerian Air Force. Available at: https://Air-force.mil.ng/history

Nigerian Ministry of Defence (2021). 'Nigerian Army: Founding of the Nigerian Army'. Nigerian Ministry of Defence. Available at: https://defence.gov.ng/nigerian-army/
Nigerian Navy (2024). 'History: Nigerian Navy'. Nigerian Navy. Available at: https://navy.mil.ng/history/
Nwachukwu, J.O. (2019). 'Nigerian Army Begins Local Production of Tactical Vehicles'. *Daily Post Nigeria*. Available at: https://dailypost.ng/2019/06/20/nigerian-army-begins-local-production-tactical-vehicles/
Ogbaji, J., and J. Jeremiah (2022). 'Leadership Training in the Nigerian Army: An Assessment of the Performance of Platoon Commanders', *NIU Journal Of Social Sciences*, 8(1): 141–7. Available at: https://doi.org/10.58709/niujss.v8i1.1417
Ojo, S. (2021). 'Investigating Entrepreneurship Among Nigerian Retired Military Veterans', in S. Ojo (ed.), *Global Perspectives on Military Entrepreneurship and Innovation*, 119–47. Hershey, PA: IGI Global. Available at: https://doi.org/10.4018/978-1-7998-6655-8.ch007
Ojo, S. (2022). 'Exploring Veteran Entrepreneurship in Nigeria', *Journal of Enterprising Communities: People and Places in the Global Economy*, 17(3): 644–63. Available at: https://doi.org/10.1108/jec-10-2021-0148
Ojo, S., and M.O. Fakokunde (2021). 'Military Enterprise and Entrepreneurship: A Case Study of the Nigerian Armed Forces Resettlement Centre', in S. Ojo (ed.), *Global Perspectives on Military Entrepreneurship and Innovation*, 216–47. Hershey, PA: IGI Global. Available at: https://doi.org/10.4018/978-1-7998-6655-8.ch011
Okun, O., and K. Arun (2021). 'Entrepreneurship and Intrapreneurship as Innovation Source in the Defense Industry and Military', in S. Ojo (ed.), *Global Perspectives on Military Entrepreneurship and Innovation*, 190–215. Hershey, PA: IGI Global. Available at: https://doi.org/10.4018/978-1-7998-6655-8.ch010
Olabisi, J. (2009). 'Tax Incentive as a Catalyst for Economic Development in Nigeria', *Journal of Research in National Development*, 7(2): 95–100. Available at: https://doi.org/10.4314/jorind.v7i2.50962
Olawuyi, I.B., and U. Amakom (2023). 'Pre-Retirement Entrepreneurship Training and Veterans' Occupation: A Tracer Study of Nigerian Armed Forces Resettlement Centre (2002–2023)', *International Journal of Economics, Environmental Development and Society*, 4(4): 468–91. Available at: https://www.ijeeds.com.ng/assets/vol.%2C-4(4)-idowu-benjamin-olawuyi-(2023).pdf
Osterberg, E.E., and M. Qvist (2018). 'Public Sector Innovation as Governance Reform: A Comparative Analysis of Competitive and Collaborative Strategies in the Swedish Transport Sector', *Administration & Society*, 52(2): 292–318. Available at: https://doi.org/10.1177/0095399718789077
Panasiewicz, L. (2021). 'Informative and Affective Determinants of Pro-Innovative Behaviours', *European Research Studies Journal*, XXIV(Special Issue 2): 763–72. Available at: https://doi.org/10.35808/ersj/2310
Perry-Smith, J., and P.V. Mannucci (2017). 'From Creativity to Innovation: The Social Network Drivers of the Four Phases of the Idea Journey', *Academy of Management Review*, 42(1): 53–79. Available at: https://doi.org/10.5465/amr.2014.0462
Placng.org (2024). *Armed Forces Act*. Policy and Legal Advocacy Centre, Nigeria. Available at: https://lawsofnigeria.placng.org/print.php?sn=35

Polin, B.A., and C.M. Ehrman (2018). 'The Curious Relationship Between Military Service and Entrepreneurial Intentions in Israel', *Armed Forces & Society*, 46(3): 438–53. Available at: https://doi.org/10.1177/0095327x18789074

Prince, S.D., S. Chapman and P. Cassey (2021). 'The Definition of Entrepreneurship: Is it Less Complex than We Think?' *International Journal of Entrepreneurial Behavior & Research*, 27(9): 26–47. Available at: https://doi.org/10.1108/ijebr-11-2019-0634

Pukhova, M.M., I.A. Merkulina and D.Y. Bashkov (2021). 'Developing Public–Private Partnership Projects to Enhance Innovation Capability in the Defence Industry', *Economies*, 9(4): 147. Available at: https://doi.org/10.3390/economies9040147

Qi, N., A. Zhang and Q. Zhu (2023). 'Evolutionary Game of Vertical Cooperation and Innovation Between Civilian and Military Enterprises: A Civilian-Military Integration Supply Chain System with Chinese Characteristics', *Complexity*: 1–23. Available at: https://doi.org/10.1155/2023/9963809

Rasheed, H.M.W., Y. Chen, H.M.U. Khizar, and A.A. Safeer (2023). 'Understanding the Factors Affecting AI Services Adoption in Hospitality: The Role of Behavioral Reasons and Emotional Intelligence', *Heliyon*, 9(6): E16968. Available at: https://doi.org/10.1016/j.heliyon.2023.e16968

Rashid, A.B., A.K. Kausik, A.A.H. Sunny and M.H. Bappy (2023). 'Artificial Intelligence in the Military: An Overview of the Capabilities, Applications, and Challenges', *International Journal of Intelligent Systems*, 2023(4): 1–31. Available at: https://doi.org/10.1155/2023/8676366

Rassanjani, S., H. Herisal, M. Mukhrijal, W. Alqarni and B. Usman (2021). 'Managing Creativity and Innovation in the 4th Industrial Revolution: Learning from Giants', *Journal of Innovation in Business and Economics*, 5(1): 15–22. Available at: https://doi.org/10.22219/jibe.v5i01.15390

Rojas, M., J. Maldonado-Romo, J.I. Mendez, P. Ponce and A. Molina (2024). 'Smart Interfaces to Assist the Operator in the Context of Industry 4.0 with a 5S Human-Centric Approach'. *Wearable Technologies*, 5e24. Available at: https://doi.org/10.1017/wtc.2024.17

Rusu, M.L. (2023). 'The Military Organisation – A Culture of Innovation', *Land Forces Academy Review*, 28: 126–35. Available at: https://doi.org/10.2478/raft-2023-0016

Salas-Velasco, M. (2019). 'Competitiveness and Production Efficiency Across OECD Countries', *Competitiveness Review: An International Business Journal Incorporating Journal of Global Competitiveness*, 29(2): 160–80. Available at: https://doi.org/10.1108/cr-07-2017-0043

Salihu, M. (2021). 'The Relevance of Community Involvement in Military Counter-Insurgency Operations in North Eastern Nigeria', *African Journal of Social Sciences and Humanities Research*, 4(3): 14–32. Available at: hHttps://doi.org/10.52589/ajsshr-ex7cbpbi

Santos, S.C., X. Neumeyer and M.H. Morris (2019). 'Entrepreneurship Education in a Poverty Context: An Empowerment Perspective', *Journal of Small Business Management*, 57(sup1): 6–32. Available at: https://doi.org/10.1111/jsbm.12485

Schumpeter, J.A. (1934). *The Theory of Economic Development*. Cambridge, MA: Harvard University Press.

Sekarini, A., and D. Ariyanti (2023). 'Integrating Heavy Metal Adsorption on Organic Waste Materials into Defense and Security Studies: A Sustainable Approach', *Jurnal Pertahanan Media Informasi Tentang Kajian Dan Strategi Pertahanan Yang Mengedepankan Identity Nasionalism Dan Integrity*, 9(3): 427–42. Available at: https://doi.org/10.33172/jp.v9i3.17011

Silwal, Y.B., S.K. Poudel, K. Dahal, S. Thapaliya and B.K. Sah (2022). 'Theoretical Foundations for Entrepreneurship Development Program', *Nepal Journal of Multidisciplinary Research*, 5(5): 109–18. Available at: https://doi.org/10.3126/njmr.v5i5.51809

Singhal, N., P. Paul, S. Giri and S. Taneja (2024). 'Corporate Social Responsibility: Impact on Firm Performance for an Emerging Economy', *Journal of Risk and Financial Management*, 17(4): 171. Available at: https://doi.org/10.3390/jrfm17040171

Syahrul, A.R., S.E. Saputra, H. Mulyadi and C. Furqon (2023). 'Innovation Capability Strategy: How Does the Culinary Industry Deal with Business Sustainability Case Study on Culinary SMEs in Padang', Proceedings of the 7th Global Conference on Business, Management, and Entrepreneurship (GCBME 2022), Advances in Economics, Business and Management Research, 1676–81. Available at: https://doi.org/10.2991/978-94-6463-234-7_176

Szajnfarber, Z., M. Richards and A. Weigel (2008). 'Implications of DoD Acquisition Policy for Innovation: The Case of Operationally Responsive Space', AIAA SPACE Conference & Exposition, 9–11 September, San Diego, California. Available at: https://doi.org/10.2514/6.2008-7650

Tar, U., and S. Wapmuk (2021). 'Entrepreneurial Training for the Nigerian Armed Forces and Its Significance in Post-Retirement Era: Opportunities and Challenges for Self Reliance', in S. Ojo (ed.), *Global Perspectives on Military Entrepreneurship and Innovation*, 45–66. Hershey, PA: IGI Global. Available at: https://doi.org/10.4018/978-1-7998-6655-8.ch003

Technical Unit on Governance and Anti-Corruption Reform (TUGAR) (2021). *Explanatory Manual on: The Code of Conduct for Public Officers (CCPO)*. Technical Unit on Governance and Anti-Corruption Reform. Available at: https://tugar.org.ng/wp-content/uploads/2021/09/Manual-for-CCC-latest.pdf

Tidd, J., and J.R. Bessant (2018). *Managing Innovation: Integrating Technological, Market and Organisational Change*. Hoboken, NJ: Wiley.

Tihic, M., A.J. Pritchard, A. McKelvie and R.V. Maury (2024). 'Entrepreneurship Education and Its Role in Transitional Entrepreneurship as Veterans Transition from Military to Civilian Life', *Entrepreneurship Education and Pedagogy*, 8(3): 424–51. Available at: https://doi.org/10.1177/25151274241232357

Trojanowski, T. (2020). 'Sustainable Management of Production Activities in Polish Enterprises of the Food Industry', *Management Theory and Studies for Rural Business and Infrastructure Development*, 41(4): 80–8. Available at: https://doi.org/10.15544/mts.2020.08

Udo, A. (2022). 'The Role of Fiscal Policy in Military Funding: A Study of Nigeria', *Nigerian Journal of Defence Studies*, 5(1): 55–70. Available at: https://doi.org/10.1080/20421338.2022.1234569

Vogel, R., J. Smith and L. Johnson (2020). 'Entrepreneurial Leadership and Its Role in Promoting Innovation Within the Military', *Journal of Military Leadership Studies*, 7(3): 58–73.

Wang, H., Y. Wang, B. Lyu, Y. Yang and H. Huang (2023). 'Military Experience and Individual Entrepreneurship – Imprinting Theory Perspective: Empirical Evidence from China', *Sage Open*, 13(1). Available at: https://doi.org/10.1177/21582440231159866

Wilhite, A., L. Burns, R. Patnayakuni and F. Tseng (2013). 'Military Supply Chains and Closed-Loop Systems: Resource Allocation and Incentives in Supply Sourcing and

Supply Chain Design', *International Journal of Production Research*, 52(7): 1926–39. Available at: https://doi.org/10.1080/00207543.2013.787173

Wong, E.Y., and N.M. Sambaluk (2016). 'Disruptive Innovations to Help Protect Against Future Threats', International Conference on Cyber Conflict (CyCon U.S.), 1–5. Washington, DC. Available at: https://doi.org/10.1109/CYCONUS.2016.7836629

Yang, H., H.K. Steensma and T. Ren (2020). 'State Ownership, Firm Innovation and the Moderating Role of Private-Sector Competition: The Case of China', *Competitiveness Review*, 31(4): 729–46. Available at: https://doi.org/10.1108/CR-02-2019-0024

Yildiz, E., C. Moller and A. Bilberg (2020). 'Virtual Factory: Competence-Based Adaptive Modelling and Simulation Approach for Manufacturing Enterprise', in J. Grabis and D. Bork (eds), The Practice of Enterprise Modeling. PoEM 2020. *Lecture Notes in Business Information Processing*, vol. 400, 197–207. Cham: Springer. Available at: https://doi.org/10.1007/978-3-030-63479-7_14

Zeadally, S., E. Adi, Z. Baig and I.A. Khan (2020). 'Harnessing Artificial Intelligence Capabilities to Improve Cybersecurity', *IEEE Access*, 8: 23817–37. Available at: https://doi.org/10.1109/access.2020.2968045

Part III

The Social Capital of Military Entrepreneurship

7

The Role of Religion and Faith in Military Entrepreneurship

Anthony Onyemaechi Chukwu

This chapter presents a unique perspective on how religion influences military entrepreneurship, particularly in Africa. It highlights the deeply rooted religious beliefs held by Africans, including those within the military, which significantly shape their actions. Religion is a vital part of the military environment, covering military tradition, warfare, the defence community and military entrepreneurship. Although there is no established theory of religious military entrepreneurship, this chapter, based entirely on secondary literature and interviews, demonstrates that religious values such as ethics, social networks, hard work, perseverance and social responsibility can greatly encourage and influence entrepreneurial behaviour and mindsets - even within the structured setting of the military. This is not only because military organizations support the religious practices and beliefs of service members, but also because they view religious freedom as a fundamental right. The military's accommodation of religious practices also enables personal faith to continue influencing how service members approach their duties, which may, in turn, promote innovative thinking and entrepreneurial initiatives in various forms. This chapter explores the relationship between faith and military entrepreneurship, highlighting its complexity.

The wide aperture for viewing the military ecosystem includes religion and entrepreneurship. As a risk-taking behaviour, entrepreneurship is buoyed by faith and religion as mitigating measures. Whether creating new business organizations or generating new entrepreneurial endeavours, entrepreneurship is subject to many unknowns. Moreover, as a wager, African military personnel have been known to deploy religious beliefs and faith to attenuate or avoid potential losses in any entrepreneurial flow. Religion and faith may not be unique to Africans; nevertheless, to a high degree, Africans have been known to incorporate their faith and religion into their daily activities. This is because they have a transcendental sense of connection to a greater being than themselves, which individuals may seek to find and express meaning and purpose in life for themselves, others and nature. In other words, the connection to the greater being typically involves a sacred spiritual experience and a deep sense of interconnectedness with the being, nature and the whole community. 'Spirituality is a broad concept that is often confused with religion. While spirituality can be part of a particular religion, it can also be independent of religion. Spirituality is the part of us that connects us to our state of mind, being and place, and gives us a sense of purpose' (Torchinsky, 2014). I use both terms interchangeably in this chapter because, in African cosmology, African values intersect with animate beings, inanimate beings and spiritual beings.

This spirituality, which goes way back, is rooted in Africa's traditional beliefs before Christianity and Islam made inroads into Africa on the coattails of colonialism. So, for many Africans, religion/spirituality is a way of life that can never be separated from life's daily activities in both public and private spheres. In other words, religion and spirituality permeate every aspect of life, from governance and marriage to health, dress, morality, economics, childbirth and death. Unlike the Yoruba and a few others, spirituality in traditional African society does not entail a sort of theocracy with a Supreme Being that exercises ecclesiastical authority. Instead, spirituality in the traditional African setting recognizes the existence of deities, beliefs and practices that suffuse every facet of human life. Thus, unlike the strict separation between church and state in Western societies, the notion of spirituality in traditional African societies is all-encompassing. Ergo, in modern African states, spirituality remains holistic and suffuses everything. Notwithstanding that modern Africa – i.e. post-colonial Africa – has passed through colonization by Islam and Christianity, which extensively and successfully proselytized Africans, African devotees of these religions continue with their deep-rooted African worldview that spirituality permeates everything, mundane or otherwise. Behind this belief lies the idea that maintaining good standing with ancestors, spirit beings, and, in some cases, the Yoruba's Supreme Being, Olodumare, assisted by deities known as Orishas, guarantees blessings and forestalls misfortunes. So, Africans, no matter what they do, especially to earn a living, not only invoke religion and faith for protection, but they also employ their spirituality to enhance their materiality. This idea is succinctly captured by Ojo and Nwankwo (2020) as 'God in the marketplace'. The authors in this work demonstrate how religious values underpin market spaces, being ingrained in market-based operations. It is a work in a long line of literature exploring the intersectionality of religion and entrepreneurship, such as Dana (2010), Rafiq (1992), Dodd and Seaman (1998), Witham (2010), Dana (2007) and Meagher (2009).

This chapter examines the new genre that explores the intersection of religious values and enterprise culture. It specifically explores the interface of faith, religious beliefs and entrepreneurship within Nigeria's military. The focus is primarily on how faith and religion influence entrepreneurial activity in the military. This discourse will examine the complexities of the intersection between faith and religion in the military, the defence community and military entrepreneurship.

Although African military personnel possess an 'agentic' mindset and thinking (Bandura, 1986), they still believe that the help of a higher being is essential in navigating the uncertain terrain of entrepreneurship. This is not surprising given that military entrepreneurship is not exclusive to serving military personnel but engages all groups within the military ecosystem, i.e. serving personnel, veterans, military families and others (see Steyaert and Hjorth, 2003; Steyaert and Hjorth, 2006; Hjorth and Steyaert, 2009). There are several reasons why an agentic being would require the help of a higher being in entrepreneurial activity – the main reason cited by Schneider and Dornbusch (1958) is the influence of the 'prosperity religion', which they argue promotes breakthrough and success in any endeavour to ensure wealth and wellness even in these modern times. Unlike this, this chapter presents a more profound spiritual reason why agentic beings require the help of a transcendental being in their entrepreneurial activity. This is found in the Yoruba saying rooted in the metaphysical history of the Yoruba, '"*ise o kan oriire*," exertion is not connected to success...' (Agwuele, 2021). This saying, which to a large extent has a near-universal African, if not human, application – something that touches us all – indicates that there is a perplexing mismatch between *ise* (hard work) and *oriire* (success) due to the machinations of an invisible hand of the gods that cracks the kernel of their favourite. The saying captures a humbling reality that people face daily, whether indolent or industrious. While the former appreciates their modest estate, the latter becomes unassuming in estimating someone's ability. What the Yoruba ancestors who distilled their observations into their sayings, pithy proverbs, and anecdotes transmitted intergenerationally to their progeny seem to imply with '*ise o kan oriire*' is that grit and grind are not enough to occasion success, which inevitably lies externally with the gods. It is not a coping mechanism to tamp down angst when 'two people, equally endowed, driven and committed to their professions, end up with starkly different results – one wealthy and the other poor' (p. 91). It illustrates, leaning on their metaphysical history, the ephemeral and transient connection between '*ise*' and '*oriire*'. Thus, to achieve success, the help of the gods is fundamentally required. Moreover, to gain their support, religion and spirituality are essential. This is why, as we shall see in this chapter, the role of religion is inevitable in military entrepreneurship.

The chapter does not assert that the African military has allegiance to religion. Quite the opposite. It is evident that most militaries, like the American military, operate under what is specifically known as a balance of 'non-establishment' and 'free exercise' First Amendment clauses. This means the military cannot establish a religion but must also protect the religious freedoms of its personnel. Therefore, while religious beliefs are permitted, there are limits in place to prevent coercion or proselytization. The chapter has five main sections that include (1) the history of religion and faith in the Nigerian military, (2) entrepreneurship and the nature of the military organization, (3) the role of religion and faith in entrepreneurship, (4) a critical evaluation of the intersectionality of religion and faith on military tradition, the defence community and entrepreneurship, and (5) a summary and conclusion.

The History of Religion and Faith in the Nigerian Military

Since this chapter seeks to examine the role of religion in military entrepreneurship, the right place to start, albeit briefly, is the history of religion in the Nigerian military. The Nigerian Armed Forces is an offshoot of the Royal West African Frontier Force (RWAFF), formed in 1900 (Gorges, 2004). With the amalgamation of Nigeria in

1914, the West African Frontier Force (RWAFF) and various sub-units distributed throughout Nigeria came together to form the Nigerian Regiment. In 1956, as a sequel to the force's participation in the First and Second World Wars, it was renamed West African Command. A couple of years later, in 1959, it was known again as the Queen's Regiment in Nigeria. In 1960, at Nigeria's independence, it was rechristened yet again as the Nigerian Military Command or the Royal Nigerian Army. It took its final name, Nigerian Army, in 1963, when Nigeria became a republic.

The Nigerian Army originated from the British Army, which explains why the religious structure within the Nigerian military mirrors that of the British military. The British Army Chaplaincy was established by an Act of Parliament in 1796, creating the Royal Army Chaplain Department to cater to the spiritual needs of British soldiers. The role of the Chaplain includes preaching the Word of God, administering sacraments, providing counselling and serving as a spiritual advisor to military commanders. Additionally, the Chaplain was tasked with organizing Christian education and promoting moral integrity among soldiers and their families.

The Chaplaincy of the Nigerian Army is a vital religious institution that delivers essential spiritual, moral and psychological support to military personnel engaged in the defence of Nigeria's homeland. It consists of three definitive units representing various religious identities: Catholic, Protestant and Islamic Affairs. Since the army's inception, the presence of clergy has been indispensable, providing crucial services to soldiers in both barracks and combat situations, as well as to their families. This support is not merely beneficial; it is fundamental to maintaining the resilience and well-being of the military community and enhancing the army's overall effectiveness. The concept was initially informal, but the urgent need for a structured religious institution became evident as a means to support and serve the spiritual needs of the military more effectively. Once established, the Nigerian Army's chaplaincy, akin to any other military force worldwide, greatly enhanced military personnel's religious, psychological, and social lives (Miners, 1992; Crosby, 1994; Bergen, 2004).

Military service is not for the faint of heart; it demands exceptional physical fitness, unwavering dedication, steadfast perseverance and remarkable resilience. Acknowledging this reality, the chaplaincy prioritizes fully prepared soldiers – physically, cognitively, emotionally and psychologically – to confront the demanding challenges of military training and the realities of combat (Bergen, 2004). This commitment is grounded in a longstanding tradition, as the church has historically sent clergy to accompany soldiers into battle, ensuring that a spiritual presence is felt amid the chaos of war (Hassner, 2013; 2016). This support not only nurtures the soldiers' spiritual well-being but also bolsters their strength to endure and overcome.

In *Religion in the Ranks* (2011), the virtues of chaplains are highlighted as impartial listeners who can significantly help those who have PTSD. They are also recognized as religious experts who comprehend the complex beliefs present in conflict zones, serving as advisors to both commanders and soldiers. Overall, it is clear that chaplains provide valuable services and can act as knowledgeable interpreters of religious contexts in foreign environments.

During the First and Second World Wars, the brutal realities of combat necessitated the establishment of the Queen's regulations governing military conduct and operations. This clearly demonstrated the Chaplaincy's imperative role in providing soldiers with essential spiritual guidance. Wherever the British Army was deployed, the Chaplaincy's influence was undeniable. As a result, when the Nigerian Army was formed, it decisively adopted the British Army Chaplaincy model. Although many of the colonial founders of the Nigerian military were Christians, it is crucial to note that the training and orientation of the soldiers were not fundamentally rooted in Christian ideologies. Instead, they incorporated specific Christian practices, such as military weddings and funerals, while maintaining an inclusive and diverse approach. This framework ensured that the spiritual needs of all soldiers were acknowledged and addressed effectively.

During the Nigerian Civil War from 1967 to 1970, the increasing demand for soldiers also created a significant need for more chaplains to provide spiritual support to troops in both front-line and rear formations. To address this need, civilian priests were seconded to the army and literate soldiers were drafted as catechists to offer ministry and prayer during the conflict.

After the war ended in 1970, many soldiers found themselves without places to worship, making it difficult for them to obtain the spiritual support necessary for healing from their experiences. Additionally, there was a shortage of catechists to guide them. To tackle these challenges, Generals David Ejoor and TY Danjuma intervened, playing a key role in appointing Major (Canon) RA Uhumuavbi as the first Indigenous Director of Army Chaplaincy in Nigeria. This appointment was a significant step forward in providing much-needed support for our soldiers (Sgt Isa Mohammed).

Before this, the Nigerian Army had employed foreign chaplains, starting with the first senior chaplain, a British national named Rev. Colton, in 1951. The period from 1960 to 1970, which included a civil war in Nigeria, coincided with a rising demand for more places of worship and officiating chaplains. Therefore, as more civilians were drafted into the army, some were commissioned into the chaplaincy to meet the exigency. The roles of the chaplains, whether in war or peace times, include but are not limited to the following: evacuating wounded military members, informing the family of a deceased soldier, counselling, praying, conducting the funerals of deceased soldiers, serving as spiritual advisers to commanders, organizing regular religious services, visiting and encouraging troops and families, visiting troops in mission and peacekeeping operation areas, organizing workshops and seminars and providing leadership on socio-religious activities such as weddings, sacraments, funerals, crusades and conferences, etc.

Considering the significant role of chaplains, which demonstrates how religion influences every aspect of a soldier's life, it is unsurprising that spirituality may also impact military entrepreneurship. This raises the question: Why does religion permeate entrepreneurship? Before we delve into this topic and thereafter explore the nature of military organizations about entrepreneurship, let us take a cursory look at how religion is fundamental to military readiness.

Religion and Readiness

In a military context, readiness refers to a nation's armed forces' capability to conduct combat operations. It encompasses the force's equipment, personnel and training preparedness. More specifically, combat readiness refers to the military's ability to increase its capacity to fight an opposing force and complete missions. In other words, combat readiness defines the essential strength of armed forces, encompassing their units, warships, aircraft and weapon systems.

While it is one thing for the military to be combat-ready, it is another for individual soldiers to be combat-ready or ready to deploy. One factor that makes a soldier combat-ready, especially a soldier who is a person of faith, is spiritual readiness. Spiritual readiness is at the core of the domain of military readiness. It ensures that the readiness of logistics, equipment, personnel, plans and other elements is complete and holistic. Spirituality centres on sacred emotions and convictions rather than the physical aspects of life (Maringira et al., 2019). Military spirituality examines how religiosity and a sense of the transcendent influence military operations. Although armed forces operate within physical territories during battles, their spirituality greatly enhances their efforts. It broadens the mind beyond limitations and nurtures a belief in something larger than oneself, imparting meaning and purpose to life, as there is more to existence than what is seen or heard (Simmons et al., 2018).

Spiritual readiness prepares soldiers for their ongoing and upcoming operational assignments and any other potential outcomes. It is a fundamental resource that helps develop the innate aspects of a soldier's worldview into tools for dealing with stress, hardship and tragic outcomes. 'The spiritual dimension draws on an individual's core religious, philosophical, or human values to develop an individual's sense of motivation, character, and integrity' (Department of the Army, 2020: 3–5). As it were, 'Spiritual readiness supports individual and collective readiness as soldiers negotiate challenging moral and ethical situations in training or operational environments' (Department of the Army, 2020: 1–2).

Spiritual readiness is crucial as it enhances soldiers' resilience, enabling them to be more effective in their roles. Spiritually prepared soldiers engage in meditation, reflection, processing experiences, making ethical decisions and overcoming the adversities and challenges that arise during their duties. This readiness is essential not only for soldiers but for all members of the force.

Therefore, not only are spiritually prepared soldiers ready for combat and points of conflict, but more importantly, they are determined to handle any incident intact and be prepared for the next challenge. Thus, regardless of how things turn out or how they are affected, they can manage trauma with minimal risk of suicide; after all, they have trained through hardship and stress.

The spiritually prepared soldiers help their organizations become more resilient, cohesive and maintain high morale. Such soldiers are firmly anchored in their beliefs and values, similar to the Stoics. Moreover, just as the Stoics did, they evade moral injury by steadfastly adhering to their beliefs and values. How do the Stoics achieve this? Gordon (2020) explains that they protect themselves against moral injury through 'a system that enabled them to reconcile good and evil to ensure their actions aligned with their beliefs' (p. 81) and by working to align their lives with some greater good. The Stoic philosopher Epictetus stated, 'Another person will not hurt you without your cooperation; you are hurt the moment you believe yourself to be' (Epictetus, *ca.* 125 CE/2008: 234). Therefore, a spiritually prepared soldier lives their values authentically, is free from bad faith and avoids moral injury.

According to Gordon (2020), the Stoics argue that moral injury occurs when individuals create conflict by straying from their values. This personal struggle, often stemming from a lack of spiritual readiness, can also hurt the larger organizational context. Having determined the central role of religion in readiness, let us examine entrepreneurship and the military institution.

Entrepreneurship and the Nature of Military Organization

Entrepreneurship is a venture that involves taking risks and requires, among other things, the abilities and skills of an individual known as an entrepreneur to establish, coordinate and manage a business. This often involves facing uncertainties in the pursuit of profit. Risk-taking behaviour in entrepreneurship occurs on two levels: the micro level, which concentrates on individual traits and their networks while they work diligently, and the macro level, which includes group or institutional activities that support or hinder entrepreneurial behaviour within the broader context ecosystem.

Military entrepreneurship presents challenges at both levels, but particularly at the macro level. As a result, considerable attention has been paid to this macro perspective, specifically the role of institutions. When discussing military entrepreneurship, it is crucial to assess the military institution's influence as an institutional actor in promoting entrepreneurship and the behaviours that drive it. A critical question arises: Does the military institution encourage, stimulate or even foster entrepreneurial behaviour? In other words, is the military capable of creating an environment that allows for the development of new business organizations? More fundamentally, can the military institution generate new organizational paradigms and processes that facilitate entrepreneurial ventures?

This question is important because entrepreneurial activity is often influenced by existing institutions, which shape and alter behaviours to develop new organizational forms. Institutions experience dynamic changes in their environments, creating opportunities to reshape existing behaviours. Hwang and Powell (2006) noted that an institutional view of entrepreneurship is more 'constructivist' than 'agentic'. From this, it can be understood that although entrepreneurial activities may appear purposeful, they are not always deliberately planned from the start. Hwang and Powell also point out that as organizational goals and missions are discussed and redefined, participants naturally identify their interests as strategies and goals evolve.

Because of the foregoing, an entrepreneurial culture exists within the military institution, even though the design of military culture and traditions – such as command structure and strict bureaucracy – may appear to conflict with the norms of entrepreneurial practice. So, what kind of entrepreneurship does the military demonstrate when, in terms of character and implications, both the military and entrepreneurship seem to differ from each other? Moreover, there is a divergence among the activities and groups within the military – serving personnel, veterans, military families and others – who engage in entrepreneurship. The tradition of critical entrepreneurship scholarship explores this heterogeneity (see Steyaert and Hjorth, 2003; Steyaert and Hjorth, 2006; Hjorth and Steyaert, 2009). Due to this apparent discrepancy between military and entrepreneurship, let us examine the concept of military entrepreneurship in the remainder of this section to understand the nature and organization of entrepreneurship within the military, and to determine whether military entrepreneurship aligns with the types of entrepreneurships anticipated by civil society.

The term 'military entrepreneurship' might initially seem contradictory. The military operates under a seniority structure with a culture and tradition that emphasize a top-down command model, which contrasts with the independent judgment associated with entrepreneurship. This raises the question of whether military and entrepreneurship can coexist. However, it is important to consider the nuances.

Despite the military's rigid, rule-following and bureaucratic nature, there is evidence of creative and innovative entrepreneurial practices within military organizations worldwide. A military system cannot thrive without an element of business orientation. As Leipold (2014) observes, military formations must adopt 'world-class' business practices. This apparent contradiction suggests that entrepreneurship within a military context is not a settled concept, prompting ongoing scholarly exploration.

Anderson (1998) articulates that the essence of entrepreneurship lies in the ability to generate and extract value from various situations. Mani (2011: 29) defines military entrepreneurship as 'the innovative creation of resources and new means of production by commissioned military officers who act in an institutional capacity as formal owners, managers and stakeholders of enterprises that generate financial resources or goods directly benefiting the military'.

Knight (1961) characterizes it as a speculative endeavour, while Schumpeter (1934) views it as an innovative technical ability. Cole (1959) approaches it as the theory of enterprise creation, and Kirzner (1973) sees it as a heightened awareness of opportunity. Sharma and Chrisman (1999) define it as enhancing growth and creating value. Due to the absence of a singular definition of entrepreneurship, it is often regarded as a nebulous concept. Ojo (2013) reflects this complexity, noting the challenges in defining entrepreneurship within a coherent framework.

Some definitions of entrepreneurship focus on personality traits, while others emphasize the act of starting a small business. No single perspective is considered superior to the others. The selection of any particular definition as a framework for analysing and explaining aspects of the entrepreneurial process depends on the researcher's judgment and the specific information they wish to highlight (Cunningham and Lischeron, 1991). Military entrepreneurship is not exclusive to active-duty personnel; it is accessible to all groups within the military ecosystem, including veterans, military families, and others (see Steyaert and Hjorth, 2003; Steyaert and Hjorth, 2006; Hjorth and Steyaert, 2009). Ross (2015) argues that this type of entrepreneurship is viable for veterans, as they can leverage their military skills, such as resilience, ambition and leadership.

Ross (2015) overlooks several important issues in discussing military entrepreneurship. First, veteran entrepreneurs come from diverse backgrounds and possess unique lived experiences that shape how they address the challenges they face in their business ventures. Success in entrepreneurship often requires making quick, effective and agile decisions in chaotic environments, along with traits such as confidence, independence, high self-efficacy, and a strong drive for achievement (Boldon et al., 2017). Veteran entrepreneurs encounter various challenges related to financial resources, social networks, and decision-making (Boldon et al., 2017). According to Sankaran and Battisto (2018), these entrepreneurs often struggle more than their non-veteran peers to secure capital. This difficulty primarily arises because veterans typically seek smaller loans – usually $100,000 or less – that larger banks are less willing to approve. Furthermore, many veterans have limited credit histories due to their military lifestyle, hindering their ability to obtain bank loans.

Veterans encounter considerable challenges in entrepreneurship, often finding it difficult to adjust to a less structured lifestyle after their military service. The daily routines and regimented schedules they are used to can complicate this transition. Consequently, military entrepreneurship is mainly regarded as successful in academic studies rather than real-world practice (Chukwu, 2021). Ultimately, military entrepreneurship may not be as promising as some scholars claim (Chukwu, 2021).

The Role of Religion and Faith in Entrepreneurship

This section examines the connection between religion, faith and entrepreneurship. The sections 'The History of Religion and Faith in the Nigerian Military' and 'Religion and Readiness' discuss how religion influences the military. The military seeks spiritual guidance, counselling and the presence of a minister for conducting military weddings and funerals, among other religious activities. Essentially, soldiers rely on their faith to find meaning in their work and are free to practice their religion wherever they choose. Since soldiers do not only depend on their faith during critical moments related to their duties, it is natural for them to also invoke their beliefs in the competitive environment of entrepreneurship. They recognize that hard work alone does not guarantee success, so they often seek the favour of spiritual powers to secure business achievements.

Soldiers in Nigeria recognize that grit and determination are crucial to achieving success in their endeavours, especially in entrepreneurial ventures. While they acknowledge the meritocracy's requirement for hard work, they also know life's inevitabilities. They are acquainted with lived experience that someone may work tirelessly and invest everything in their venture, and yet fail, while another individual, who, though laissez-faire, nonetheless stumbled upon success by chance. They are clear about the disparity between hard work and success. They are also rational enough to understand that the former is necessary to achieve the latter. However, these two realities – an indolent fellow being fortunate while the diligent worker struggles to attain success – lead them to attribute fortune to an external force.

We will briefly draw on one of Yoruba's ruminations to explain the incommensurability between hard work and success, and to illustrate why religion is involved in military entrepreneurship. For the Yoruba, '*ise o kan oriire*', exertion does not pertain to good fortune or success (Agwuele, 2021: 810), explains the melodramatic nature of life. On the one hand, it shows why an indolent person may stumble upon success while a hard worker's efforts may end in futility. On the other hand, it illustrates why 'two people, equally endowed, driven, and committed to their professions, end up with starkly different results – one wealthy and the other poor' (p. 810). It demonstrates that while one individual may achieve success through effort, another may find it elusive despite making similar or even greater efforts. Furthermore, for the Yoruba, it is not solely about efforts or lack thereof; it ultimately depends on the assistance of an external force – one's predestination to success. Alternatively, 'the fate of a person was sealed at the outset' (p. 810). Another scenario depicted by '*ise o kan oriire*' involves an indolent individual who succeeds effortlessly. Overall, the metaphysical representation of this idea is that the uneven playing fields among individuals arise when the gods intervene on behalf of certain people, granting them an undue advantage and victory. For further understanding of the Yoruba concept of human personality and critical expositions on Yoruba beliefs, see (Abimbola, 1971; Abiodun, 1981; 1987; Akin-Makinde, 1984; Hallen and Sodipo, 1986; Abimbola, 2006; Makinde, 1985; Oladipupo, 1992; Oduwole, 1996; Gbadegesin, 2003).

Having observed how one can be industrious without achieving success while another, with little or no effort, does, the Yoruba 'conclude that there is no link between work and success/good fortune' (p. 810). Furthermore, they argue that if such a link exists, 'it is tenuous and fleeting' (p. 810). This implies that: 'One's kernel is either cracked or not by the gods' (p. 810). In other words, the disconnection between *ise* (work) and *oriire* (success) remains mysterious. Success is regarded as fatalistic and inevitable, akin to a flute that 'echoes what was blown into it' (p. 810). The Yoruba's contemplation of the incommensurability of effort and outcome, i.e. '*ise okan oriire*', does not imply that they do not value hard work. To suggest that would be to overlook J.F. Odunjo's well-known poem titled *Ise l'ogun Ise*, which celebrates hard work. At its essence, the poem champions diligence. It illustrates that the Yoruba regard *ise* (hard work) as the only remedy for poverty (*ise*), the sole path to prosperity and comfort, asserting that the only things that endure and grow are those that an individual rightfully acquires, 'through their own labour and sweat – whatever the occupation' (p. 817).

The two views can be asserted without contradiction. In other words, both '*ise okan oriire*' and '*Ise l'ogun ise*' can coexist without any inconsistency within the culture, except when viewed through the lens of globalization or the rapid social changes of modern lifestyles. In Yoruba culture, the concept of '*ori*' can signify destiny, meaning that everything is preordained or predetermined. Thus, when the Yoruba assert '*ise okan oriire*', they imply that no amount of hard work can guarantee success if one is outside their preordained area. Similarly, when they say '*Ise l'ogun ise*', they praise the virtue of effort, even within one's calling area. They sternly warn that idleness in one's calling area is a warranty for poverty.

One of the major points highlighted in the preceding text is the significance and role of religion in people's lives and endeavours. Religion enables individuals to tap into their spiritual capital and achieve success. Exploring the relationship between religious values and entrepreneurial culture further, scholars such as Rafiq (1992), Dodd and Seaman (1998), Dana (2007), and Meagher (2009) assert that this connection allows individuals to exercise their entrepreneurial agency and marketing by integrating their religious values and faith. They do this to transform their economic realities and achieve success. More specifically, the appropriation of religion to transform social and economic realities has led to the evolution of what Schneider and Dornbusch (1958) termed 'prosperity religion'.

As we can see so far, Africans are religious and incorporate their faith into all their activities. This is where the role of religion in military entrepreneurship stems. Just as military personnel must prepare spiritually for military tasks, they must also prepare spiritually for military entrepreneurship and other engagements. The role of religion in military entrepreneurship is essentially to help them endure and navigate challenging business situations, overcome adversity and thrive. It gives them hope that providence will guide them through the treacherous path of business and support them when they fall short. The following section critically evaluates how the intersectionality of religion and faith impacts military tradition, the defence community and entrepreneurship.

The Issues Surrounding the Intersection of Religion and Faith in Military Tradition, the Defence Community and Entrepreneurship

The last two sections demonstrate that religion plays a vital role in the military ecosystem, enhancing readiness, overcoming the fear of the unknown, and facilitating survival and thriving in uncharted territory, such as entrepreneurship. However, the intersection of religion and faith within the military ecosystem is not without its challenges. This section critically examines the intersectionality and the associated issues that arise from it.

Military tradition encompasses the practices associated with the military. These include military uniforms, drills, the military band, the chain of command and other related aspects. Given the holistic view of religion for a religious individual – i.e. everything is religion, and religion impacts everything, including military, finance, politics, etc.

The Intersection of Religion and Military Tradition

A conflict of ideas may arise for a soldier who prioritizes their religion and sees everything holistically through their religious lens. In the near term, for such a soldier, there will be more tenseness than tranquillity as military tradition or culture and profession meet the religious culture or tradition. Undoubtedly, such a soldier will not be a natural fit for their unit, which is essential for ensuring cohesion and the success of any mission or operation. Moreover, they may jettison *esprit de corps* and disregard the chain of command when the mission is against a group or people of the same religion as them. The latter takes precedence when military tradition collides with religious imperatives for soldiers who are deeply immersed in their faith.

The precedence of religion over military traditions, also known as the primacy of religion, can pose significant challenges for the military. This issue can manifest in various ways. One such form is the threat posed by an individual within the ranks – a soldier who, due to religious or occult affiliations, plans to sabotage his unit or fellow service members or countrymen. A notable example is Ethan Melzer, a 22-year-old US soldier in 2020. He was associated with the Order of Nine Angles – also known as the ONA, or O9A – an 'occult-based neo-Nazi and racially motivated violent extremist group' (BBC, 2020). Melzer sent an encrypted message to the group disclosing sensitive information about his unit's locations, movements and security plans. His intention was for this information to be passed on to jihadist groups to facilitate an attack on his unit.

A tragic form of terror can also arise from an enemy within – i.e. a traitor-soldier driven by religious radicalism, turning against their comrades. An example of this is Nidal Malik Hasan, an army major who, on 5 November 2009, killed thirteen of his fellow servicemembers at Fort Hood in Texas, USA. In addition to those killed, thirty-two others were injured, and 'countless other lives were forever changed' (Poppe, 2018).

The Intersection of Religion and the Defence Community

A defence community comprises any city, county or region that hosts military installations, along with the homes of service members and their families. It also offers support to ensure the well-being of these families and installations. This community stands out as a place where non-military residents actively welcome and fully embrace the service members. They celebrate the return of troops from their tours, support Golden Star families during their sacrifices and provide essential educational opportunities for military spouses and children. Additionally, service members are consistently recognized and appreciated for their unwavering dedication and service to their country. In sum, these communities strive to incorporate service members and their families, ensuring they experience a high quality of life.

Religion can pose challenges within the defence community, particularly when a Roman Catholic or Protestant chaplain is the only available counsellor. The specific principles of their faith may not adequately address the diverse needs of the multi-religious and non-religious individuals in modern armed forces. For instance, how can a Catholic or Protestant chaplain effectively minister to a Muslim or a Pagan? Additionally, how can they provide counsel and support to a homosexual person, an atheist or an unmarried woman contemplating abortion, as well as to a married woman who is pregnant by someone else and also considering abortion? (Benham Rennick, 2011).

In *Gender Identity in the Military*, Alan Okros and Denise Scott (2013) assert that there is a fundamental conflict between the beliefs held by chaplains and issues related to transgender individuals. They emphatically explain that the policy created to direct Canadian Armed Forces (CAF) personnel in managing transgender members must confront and address these challenges head-on. They further note that it was essential to avoid any phrasing that could be interpreted as mandating chaplain participation in providing support to transgender personnel. These issues can fray any defence community.

The Intersection of Religion and Military Entrepreneurship

Important scholarly investigations and work on religion and entrepreneurship have provided essential insights into how institutional, cultural, social, political and even economic forces shape human experience. A special issue on religion and entrepreneurship shows this (Janssen et al., 2021). The concept of military entrepreneurship can be broadened to encompass ventures that are primarily operated by the military for profit. This includes the involvement of armed forces personnel or the personal financial interests of members of the defence establishment. Such ventures form a significant aspect of the political economy but have not received the attention they warrant (Siddiqa, 2007). Besides the involvement of the military as an institution in commercial activities for profit, military entrepreneurship also includes military members such as active personnel, retired personnel or veterans, and their family members in business ventures to generate income, create jobs and contribute to development.

As such, military entrepreneurship highlights the significant potential and unique contributions of individuals with military experience or affiliations to the economic landscape. These individuals often possess distinct skills such as leadership, discipline, strategic planning and resilience, which they apply to their business ventures. By leveraging their training and experiences gained in the armed forces, military entrepreneurs can drive innovation, create jobs and promote economic growth, thereby enriching both their communities and the broader economy. In many countries, military establishments are taking on active roles in commercial and profit-making ventures, presenting an opportunity to broaden their operational focus beyond just defence. Military-run enterprises can be military-controlled industries that engage in diverse businesses, many of which can also fulfil civilian needs and contribute to economic growth, or those that specialize in developing and producing goods and services primarily for military use. This dual engagement enhances national security and promotes economic innovation and job creation (Siddiqa, 2007).

Religion plays a vital role in shaping the entrepreneurial mindset of military entrepreneurs, as religious values often influence their drive and ethical outlook. Additionally, traits like honesty, work ethic, thrift, discipline and a sense of purpose are frequently reinforced and supported by religious beliefs, which are unquestionably beneficial for entrepreneurial success. Moreover, religion can foster qualities such as risk-taking and perseverance, essential for achieving business success. Some religious beliefs might also encourage informal learning and persistence in entrepreneurial efforts. Furthermore, spirituality and religiosity can nurture a sense of social responsibility, motivating military entrepreneurs to prioritize societal betterment alongside their financial goals. Military entrepreneurship may arise from a quest for purpose and meaning in life. In this context, religious beliefs can provide a strong sense of purpose or calling, inspiring individuals to pursue entrepreneurial ventures as an extension of their faith. Although religion can foster entrepreneurship, some beliefs may hinder it by imposing strict rules or prioritizing spiritual pursuits over economic activity.

The intersection of religion and entrepreneurship, ditto military entrepreneurship, can be problematic. First, bridging religion and entrepreneurship undermines the strength and integrity of religious beliefs and practices (Sigalow, 2016) or infuses commercial practices with superfluous moral concerns (Joas, 2014). Concerns about the relationship between religion and entrepreneurship have been expressed while emphasizing the importance of decentralizing entrepreneurship as a form of secular work (Patel and Wolfe, 2022; Hunt and Ortiz-Hunt, 2017). Furthermore, the intersection of religion and entrepreneurship, by extension, military entrepreneurship, is a potent source of 'meaningful heterodoxy' (Pidduck and Tucker, 2022). The authors contend that 'entrepreneurial actors are the embodiment of heterodoxy – deviation from accepted or orthodox standards or beliefs'. In other words, the relationship between religion and entrepreneurship is highly contextual and nuanced. It all boils down to the specific tenets of a religion, the level of an individual's religiosity and the broader socio-political environment, all of which play a role. Put simply, at worst, the intersection of religion, entrepreneurship and the military is a reductive absurdity and a source of meaningful heterodoxy in entrepreneurship research and practice. At best, it is to 'generate novel and valuable ways of solving problems' (Pidduck and Tucker, 2022: 1). These critiques highlight the issues surrounding the intersection of religion, entrepreneurship or military entrepreneurship, significantly undermining it.

Conclusion

This chapter examines the role of religion in military entrepreneurship and argues that religious values, ethical principles, social connections and personal motivations play a key role in shaping entrepreneurial behaviour, even within the structured environment of the military. The military's strong dedication to religious accommodation not only supports the faith of service members but also improves their professional duties.

It is organized into five sections. The first section discusses the history of religion and faith within the Nigerian military. The second section explores the concept of entrepreneurship and the nature of military organizations. The third section analyses the role of religion and faith in entrepreneurship, focusing on how these elements intersect with military traditions and the defence community. The chapter emphasizes that Africans' deeply rooted religious beliefs, including those of military personnel, significantly shape their actions and decisions. As spiritual individuals, soldiers prepare themselves for various aspects of military life – including traditions, warfare and entrepreneurship – through spiritual readiness. This notion extends beyond just combat preparedness; it encompasses the overall capabilities of the armed forces, including equipment, personnel, training and entrepreneurial initiatives. Another key point is the critical role of chaplains, who provide spiritual support by preaching, administering sacraments, offering counselling and advising military commanders. Ultimately, this chapter highlights the intricate relationship between faith and military entrepreneurship, underscoring the complexities of integrating these two aspects.

References

Abimbola, K. (2006). *Yoruba Culture: A Philosophical Account*. Birmingham: Iroko Academic Publishers.

Abimbola, W. (1971). 'The Yoruba Concept of Human Personality', in G. Dieterlen (ed.), *La Notion de Personne en Afrique Noire. Collogues Internationaux de Centre National de la Recherche Scientifique*. Paris: Centre National de la Recherche Scientifique, pp. 73–89.

Abiodun, R. (1981). 'Ori Divinity: Its Worship, Symbolism and Artistic Manifestation', in *Proceedings of the World Conference on Orisa Tradition*. Ife: Department of African Languages and Literatures, University of Ife.

Abiodun, R. (1987). 'Verbal and Visual Metaphors: Mythical Allusions in Yoruba Ritualistic Art of Ori', *Word and Image*, 3(3): 252–70.

Agwuele, A. (2021). '"Exertion Is Not Connected to Success": Everyday Yoruba Discourse of Work and Success', *Africa*, 91(5): 810–31.

Akin-Makinde, M. (1984). 'An African Concept of Human Personality: The Yoruba Example', *Ultimate Reality and Meaning*, 7(3): 189–200.

Anderson, A.R. (1998). 'Cultivating the Garden of Eden: Environmental Entrepreneuring', *Journal of Organisational Change Management*, 11(2): 135–44.

Bandura, A. (1986). *Social Foundations of Thought and Action: A Social Cognitive Theory*. Englewood Cliffs, NJ: Prentice-Hall.

BBC (2020). 'US Soldier Ethan Melzer Accused of Planning Attack on Own Unit'. BBC News. Available at: https://www.bbc.co.uk/news/world-us-canada-53145806

Benham Rennick, J. (2011). *Religion in the Ranks: Belief and Religious Experience in the Canadian Forces*. Toronto: University of Toronto Press.

Bergen, Doris L., ed. (2004). *The Sword of the Lord: Military Chaplains from the First to the Twenty-First Century*. South Bend, IN: University of Notre Dame Press.

Boldon, N.Y., R.V. Maury, N. Armstrong and R.V. Slyke (2017). 'The State of Veteran Entrepreneurship Research: What We Know and Next Steps', Institute for Veterans and Military Families, 50. Available at: https://surface.syr.edu/ivmf/50

Chukwu, A. (2021). 'The Fallacy of the Idea Military Entrepreneurship', in S. Ojo (ed.), *Global Perspectives on Military Entrepreneurship and Innovation*, 1–16. Hershey, PA: IGI Global.

Cole, A.H. (1959). *Business Enterprise in a Social Setting*. Cambridge, MA: Harvard University Press

Crosby, D.F. (1994). *Battlefield Chaplains: Catholic Priests in World War II*. Lawrence: University Press of Kansas.

Cunningham, J.B., and J. Lischeron (1991). 'Defining Entrepreneurship', *Journal of Small Business Management*, 29: 45–61.
Dana, L.P. (2007). 'A Humility-Based Enterprising Community: The Amish People in Lancaster County', *Journal of Enterprising Communities: People and Places in the Global Economy*, 33(2): 142–54.
Dana, L.P. (2010). *Entrepreneurship and Religion*. Cheltenham: Edward Elgar.
Department of the Army. (2020). 'Holistic Health and Fitness (FM 7-22)'. Army Publishing Directorate, USA. Available at: https://armypubs.army.mil/epubs/DR_pubs/DR_a/ARN30964-FM_7-22-001-WEB-4.pdf
Dodd, S.D., and Seaman, P. (1998). 'Religion and Enterprise: An Introductory Exploration', *Entrepreneurship Theory and Practice*, 23(1): 71–86.
Epictetus, *ca.* 125 CE/2008.
Gbadegesin, S. (2003). 'Ènìyàn: The Yoruba Concept of a Person', in P.H. Coetzee and A.P.J. Roux (eds), *The African Philosophy Reader* (2nd ed.), 149–68. London: Oxford University Press.
Gordon, T. (2020). 'The Invincible Man: Teaching resilience'. Marine Corps Association. Available at: https://www.mca-marines.org/wp-content/uploads/The-Invincible-Man.pdf
Gorges, E.H. (1930/2004). *The Great War in West Africa*. 1930, London: Hutchinson & Co. Ltd.; 2004, Uckfield: Naval & Military Press.
Hallen, B., and J.O. Sodipo (1986). *Knowledge, Belief, and Witchcraft: Analytic Experiments in African Philosophy*. London: Ethnographica.
Hassner, R.E. (2013). *Religion in the Military Worldwide*. New York: Cambridge University Press.
Hassner, R.E. (2016). *Religion on the Battlefield*. Ithaca, NY: Cornell University Press.
Hjorth, D., and C. Steyaert (eds) (2009). *The Politics and Aesthetics of Entrepreneurship*. Cheltenham: Edward Elgar.
Hunt, R., and L. Ortiz-Hunt (2017). 'Entrepreneurial Round-Tripping: The Benefits of Newness and Smallness in Multi-Directional Value Creation', *Manag. Decis.*, 55: 491–511.
Hwang, H., and W.W. Powell (2006). 'Institutions and Entrepreneurship', in H. Hwang and W.W. Powell (eds.), *The Handbook of Entrepreneurship* (1st ed.), 179–210. California: Springer Publishing.
Janssen, F., B. Hoogendoorn, N. Rietveld, E. van Burg and M. Dejardin (2021). 'Call for Papers: Special Issue on Religion and Entrepreneurship', *Small Bus. Econ.*
Joas, H. (2014). *Faith as an Option: Possible Futures for Christianity*. Redwood City, CA: Stanford University Press.
Kirzner, I.M. (1973). *Competition and Entrepreneurship*. Chicago, IL: University of Chicago Press.
Knight, F.H. (1961). *Risk Uncertainty and Profit* (2nd ed.). New York: Kelley.
Leipold, J.D. (2014). 'Is The Army a Business?' U.S. Army. Available at: https://www.army.mil/article/126882/is_the_army_a_business
Lillington, M.C. (2012). *Christian and Canadian Forces College. Mental Injuries Sustained by Veterans of the Afghanistan Campaign: A Comprehensive Issue*. Master's Thesis (Canadian Forces College). Vol. JCSP/PCEMI 38-16. Toronto: Canadian Forces College, 2012.
Makinde, M.A. (1985). 'A Philosophical Analysis of the Yoruba Concept of Ori and Human Destiny', *International Studies in Philosophy*, 17(1): 54–69.
Mani, K. (2011). 'Military Entrepreneurship: Patterns in Latin America', *Latin American Politics and Society*, 53(3): 25–55.

Maringira, G., R. Woodward and S. Bulmer (2019). 'Spirituality and War: Soldier Practices in Deployment in African International Peacekeeping Operations', *Religion, State & Society*, 47(1): 78–91.
Meagher, K. (2009). 'Trading on Faith: Religious Movements and Informal Economic Governance in Nigeria', *Journal of Modern African Studies*, 47(3): 397–423.
Miners, N.J. (1992). *History of the Nigerian Army 1963–1992*. Abuja: Nigerian Army Education Corps Schools (NAECS).
Oduwole, E. (1996). 'The Concepts of Ori and Human Destiny', *Journal of Philosophy and Development*, 1(1–2): 40–52.
Ojo, S. (2013). 'Diaspora Entrepreneurship: A Study of Nigerian Entrepreneurs in London', PhD thesis, University of East London. Available at: https://chrome-extension://efaidnbmnnnibpcajpcglclefindmkaj/https://repository.uel.ac.uk/download/ab11e8a166fccda061112c317dce9fcffd07f2c4e29a6441027d3cff526403ad/2154641/2013_PhD_Ojo.pdf (accessed 17 February 2025)
Ojo, S., and S. Nwankwo. (2020). 'God in the Marketplace: Pentecostalism and Marketing Ritualization Among Black Africans in the UK', *Journal of Enterprising Communities: People and Places in the Global Economy*, 14(3): 349–72. Available at: https://doi.org/10.1108/JEC-12-2019-0126
Okros, A., and D. Scott (2013). *Gender Identity in the Military: Perspectives on Trans Members of the Canadian Forces*. Report Provided to the Directorate of Human Rights and Diversity, Department of National Defence.
Oladipo, S. (1992). 'Predestination in Yoruba Thought: Philosopher's Interpretation', *Orita: Journal of Religion*, 24(1–2): 34–51.
Patel, P.C., and M.T. Wolfe (2022). 'Of Free Markets and a Secular Mind: The Value of Economic Decentralization and Individual Secular Values in Entrepreneurship', *Small Bus Econ*, 58: 93–119. Available at: https://doi.org/10.1007/s11187-020-00401-4
Pidduck, R., and R. Tucker (2022). 'Meaningful Heterodoxies: Advancing Entrepreneurship Through Engagement with Unorthodox Phenomena', *Journal of Business Venturing Insights*, 18: e00319. Available at: https://www.elsevier.com/locate/jbvi
Poppe, K. (2018). *Nidal Hasan: A Case Study in Lone-Actor Terrorism*. Washington, DC: Washington University.
Rafiq, M. (1992). 'Ethnicity and Enterprise: A Comparison of Muslim and Non-Muslim Owned Asian Businesses in Britain', *New Community*, 19(1): 43–60.
Ross, E. (2015). 'Life After War: Veterans Turned Successful Entrepreneurs'. *Guardian*. Available at: https://www.theguardian.com/small-business-network/2015/mar/03/war-veterans-successful-entrepreneurs-military
Sankaran, S., and J. Battisto (2018). *Financing Their Future: Veteran Entrepreneurs and Capital Access*. Federal Reserve Bank of New York and U.S. Small Business Administration. Available at: https://www.fedsmallbusiness.org/analysis/2018/financing-their-future-veteran-entrepreneurs-and-capital-access
Schneider, L., and S.M. Dornbusch (1958). *Popular Religion: Inspirational Books in America*. Chicago, IL: The University of Chicago Press.
Schumpeter, J.A. (1934). *The Theory of Economic Development*. Cambridge, MA: Harvard University Press.
Sharma, P., and J. Chrisman (1999). 'Toward a Reconciliation of the Definitional Issues in the Field of Corporate Entrepreneurship', *Entrepreneurship Theory and Practice*, 23(3): 11–27.
Siddiqa, A. (2007). *Military Inc.: Inside Pakistan's Military Economy*. London: Pluto Press.

Sigalow, E. (2016). 'Towards a Sociological Framework of Religious Syncretism in the United States.' *J. Am. Acad. Relig.*, 84: 1029–55.

Simmons, A.M., F. Rivers, S. Gordon and L.H. Yoder. (2018). 'The Role of Spirituality Among Military En Route Care Nurses: Source of Strength or Moral Injury?' *Critical Care Nurse*, 38(2): 61–7. Available at: https://doi.org/10.4037/ccn2018674

Steyaert, C., and D. Hjorth (eds) (2003). *New Movements in Entrepreneurship*. Cheltenham: Edward Elgar.

Steyaert, C., and D. Hjorth (eds) (2006). *Entrepreneurship as Social Change*. Cheltenham: Edward Elgar.

Torchinsky, M.S. (2014). *Strengthening the Military by Way of the Soul: The Role of Spirituality in the Canadian Armed Forces*. Joint Command and Staff Programme Paper, Canadian Forces College,12.

Witham, L. (2010). *Marketplace of the Gods: How Economics Explains Religion*. New York: Oxford University Press.

8

Conceptualizing the Warrior Ethos in Military Entrepreneurship

Yusuf Ali

This chapter explores the concept of the warrior ethos in military entrepreneurship through the lens of Clausewitz's trinity of society, state and soldier. It emphasizes the soldier's role in using coercive power to protect the state from external threats, in line with McNamara's security model for state modernization. The chapter argues that the warrior ethos, rooted in the readiness to sacrifice for public security, intersects with entrepreneurial endeavours often driven by profit maximization. It contends that the mental, physical and psychological traits soldiers develop, such as tolerance, selflessness, compassion and courage, are crucial for successful entrepreneurship, particularly in high-risk and uncertain environments.

People often discuss the concepts of warrior ethos and entrepreneurship in society, the state and the military, as both involve themes of survival and prosperity. The need to overcome obstacles in pursuit of individual or collective goals, such as career development, social responsibilities and financial stability, provides some basis for these concepts. The warrior ethos includes virtues such as courage, selflessness, loyalty, patience, compassion and endurance, which reflect the values and customs of most societies (Pressfield, 2011). Cultural influences, education and personal experiences instil these traits, which are essential for achieving societal goals. According to Rico et al. (cited in Ojo, 2021), military personnel develop these traits during their training and service, often integrating them into their identities. This integration can facilitate their transition into civilian life and entrepreneurship.

Entrepreneurship significantly promotes economic growth, innovation and development, especially in countries where micro and macro enterprises contribute to employment and prosperity. However, starting and sustaining an enterprise involves significant risks and sacrifices (Fleming, 2005). Like the warrior ethos, entrepreneurship necessitates perseverance and the capacity to surmount obstacles, shaped by factors like personal capital, talent, social networks, government regulations and experience (Bruhn, 2011). An individual's background, including military service, often shapes their decision to embark on entrepreneurship, with the warrior ethos serving as a strong foundation for navigating the uncertainties of business ventures.

Before exploring the decision to transition into entrepreneurship, it is important to consider the imprinting theory. This theory suggests that significant life experiences can shape an individual's future path. For military personnel transitioning to entrepreneurship, their collective experiences in the military are a critical factor (Benmelech and Friedman, 2015). Despite this, the impact of military experiences on entrepreneurship still requires much study. Moreover, ethical concerns in the entrepreneurial world, such as the promotion of selflessness and sacrifice in business practices, remain significant. This paper argues that the warrior ethos provides soldiers with the attitude and mindset to succeed in entrepreneurship, as its core values align with the creation of business environments that serve both individual and societal interests, ultimately promoting the common good for individuals and the broader community.

Conceptualization

The key concepts in this paper are warrior ethos and military, and entrepreneurship. Subsequent paragraphs will clarify these concepts for better understanding.

Warrior

The concept of a warrior can be interpreted in various ways. In French, the terms 'guerrier' and 'guerroyer', which loosely translate to 'making war', are used to describe individuals who specialize in the conduct of war. The English word 'warrior' is derived from the Old French word 'worrier' and the Latin word 'bellum' (*Oxford English Dictionary*, 2025). Warriors are often viewed as disciplined individuals, typically associated with military personnel who engage in armed conflict. They exhibit traits such as loyalty, commitment, aggression, audacity, and at times, arrogance. Warriors are characterized by their readiness to serve others, even at the cost of personal sacrifice. They possess the ability to discipline both their minds and bodies to pursue a greater purpose beyond self-interest and pleasure (Cook, 2004). Huntington (1957) highlights the unique values of warriors and suggests that professional soldiers' commitment to service, acceptance of hardship and willingness to make sacrifices for a greater purpose or goal achievement distinguish them from other professionals and laypeople. Broadly speaking, warriors can be defined as military personnel who possess unique identities and sets of beliefs that set them apart and shape their actions and decisions.

Ethos

This refers to an individual's belief system and moral framework, influencing their actions, values, attitudes and practices. It shapes the behaviour of individuals, groups and societies by determining their moral constitution and guiding decision-making. In this context, ethos provides a historical framework for understanding how cultural norms, values and beliefs are formed, practiced and sustained. A warrior ethos, therefore, represents a set of beliefs and values that develop through training, constant practice and experiences, influencing military personnel's decisions and behaviour.

This ethos emphasizes traits such as honour, commitment, courage, compassion and sacrifice, shaping the moral foundation of military conduct (Nagl, 2002).

Military Entrepreneurship

This encompasses the actions and mindset of individuals or groups within the military who actively work to enhance organizational effectiveness by managing and utilizing various resources at their disposal (West, 1990). These resources may include financial, material and human elements available to the personnel at various levels of command. The concept is closely associated with the ability to think creatively and strategically, focusing on how military entrepreneurs contribute to improving resource management and the organization's overall impact (Williams, 2008). Military entrepreneurship emphasizes innovation, creativity, sustainability and adaptability, with individuals often required to identify challenges and develop solutions to address them.

In a broader context, military entrepreneurship involves a proactive approach to overcoming constant challenges by fostering creative solutions and actions. Military entrepreneurs must exhibit versatility, with a well-rounded skill set that includes critical thinking, emotional control, resilience and intellectual attentiveness. These qualities align with the warrior ethos, reflecting a mindset centred on strategic foresight, risk-taking and excellence. Military entrepreneurship, therefore, is a crucial element of innovative activities within the military, facilitating actions that enhance strategic outcomes and support long-term success (Guillot, 2004).

Furthermore, military entrepreneurship refers to the engagement of military personnel or organizations in business ventures beyond their official duties. This can include activities by serving members, veterans or their families. According to Ojo (2021), military entrepreneurship involves commercial activities outside the military's statutory functions. This view is restrictive when considered against the backdrop of its reconstruction to encompass a broader range of actors and roles that continuously redefine its meaning and role in the modern world. Sharon et al. (2014) emphasize that military entrepreneurship reflects innovative business practices undertaken by former military personnel or defence-related organizations. These ventures often leverage the unique skills, discipline and experiences gained during military service, particularly in sectors like technology, logistics and security services.

Kivirist (2020) highlights that military entrepreneurship stems from the ability of military personnel to apply leadership, risk management and strategic thinking skills developed in the armed forces to drive business success. The discipline and resilience learned in the military often translate into effective entrepreneurial practices. Similarly, Bachmann (2018) views military entrepreneurship as a mindset shaped by high-pressure military experiences that foster problem-solving and adaptability – traits crucial for navigating the uncertainties of the business world.

Military entrepreneurship blends acquired military skills with civilian business models, leading to a distinct approach to innovation and enterprise development. While this integration offers significant potential for entrepreneurial success, it also presents challenges, particularly in transitioning to the evolving military culture-based and civilian business environment. This unique intersection allows military personnel and organizations to contribute meaningfully to the frequently evolving entrepreneurial ecosystem.

Evolution of Warrior Ethos and Military Entrepreneurship

Warrior ethos and military entrepreneurship have evolved significantly over time, shaped by the nature of warfare, societal contexts and political ideologies, among other factors. Traditionally, the warrior ethos represented values such as honour, bravery, compassion, loyalty, love for their country and discipline. In ancient Greece, warriors were expected to serve their comrades and communities with pride, as emphasized by Hanson (2000). Greek and Roman cultures regarded the warrior ethos as the pinnacle of human endeavour, encouraging self-sacrifice for collective ideals. Pressfield (2011) also believed that warriors were ideal 'brother warriors' who fought for the greater good, ensuring justice and protecting the state's territorial integrity. These classical values still resonate in modern military codes, such as the Soldier's Creed, which stresses national service and ethical conduct (Pressfield, 2011).

In contemporary contexts, the warrior ethos has adapted to the complexities of modern warfare, characterized by asymmetric conflicts and technological advancements. This has led to discussions on the need for a code of conduct that transcends cultural boundaries, incorporating broader notions of patriotism, entrepreneurship and social responsibility. Reflecting on the aftermath of the September 11 attacks, Faludi (2007) noted how the soldier's role shifted from being a combatant to a protector of societal values, influencing public perceptions of military service.

Military entrepreneurship intersects with military strategy, economics and organizational behaviour. In ancient civilizations, military leaders, especially Roman generals, used war successes to gain economic and political power, leveraging victories for land and wealth. During the medieval period, military figures controlled significant resources and land, establishing local economies. Similarly, knights and mercenaries shaped the terms of their service, embodying early forms of military entrepreneurship (Heather, 2006).

The Enlightenment and the Industrial Revolution introduced new governance, economic and military structures. As capitalism emerged, veterans adapted their military experience to emerging industries, contributing to economic growth in a post-industrial society (McNeill, 1984). This period arguably marked the beginning of military entrepreneurship as veterans applied their organizational skills to business ventures, paving the way for future developments in the field. After the World Wars, military entrepreneurship surged as veterans turned their experiences into business ventures. As Brokaw (1998) highlighted, returning soldiers capitalized on military skills to start businesses, supported by initiatives like the GI Bill in America, which provided them with education and capital.

In Europe, veterans contributed to post-war economic recovery by forming cooperatives and leveraging government assistance. Today, military entrepreneurship has further evolved with the rise of veteran-focused organizations, networking and incubators. The late twentieth century saw a significant increase in veterans entering entrepreneurship, supported by tailored initiatives that provide resources and opportunities for veteran-run businesses (Lauterbach and Schmid, 2020). Thus, the warrior ethos and military entrepreneurship have been shaped by historical, cultural, technological and economic factors, reflecting the changing roles of military leaders and professionals over time.

Theoretical Frameworks

The analysis of the warrior ethos in military entrepreneurship underscores the importance of understanding how various frameworks shape these concepts, their cultivation and their operationalization, due to their implications for both military culture and civilian sectors. Many theories that seek to provide insights into the subject include the social identity theory, ethical theory and cultural psychology, among others. However, the enterprising genius theory and the imprinting theory are used in this paper to examine the concept of the warrior ethos in military entrepreneurship. The two theories provide the conceptual frameworks for understanding the characteristics, behaviours and cultural influences that shape entrepreneurial activities within military contexts.

The Theory of Enterprising Genius

This concept was propounded by Clausewitz (1984) in his seminal work *On War* as a crucial component of military leadership. He posits that successful commanders demonstrate a blend of creativity, decisiveness and the ability to adapt swiftly to the chaos of battle. This notion was elaborated on by Keegan (1993) as not just a personal attribute of military leadership but a necessary response to the unpredictability and fluidity inherent in warfare. He argues that the effective commander must possess an innate creativity and a profound understanding of the art of war, allowing them to exploit opportunities as they arise.

Keegan (1993) opines further that it is the ability to adapt that sets great military leaders apart from their contemporaries, enabling them to navigate the complexities of battle with innovative strategies rather than relying on formal training or rigid tactics. Thus, the intersection of Clausewitz's theory of enterprising genius and Keegan's interpretation underscores the essential role of innovative leadership and strategy in military success, whether in the boardroom or on the battlefield.

The Imprinting Theory

The imprinting theory, rooted in sociology and organizational theory, highlights the critical role of formative experiences in shaping individual and organizational behaviours, particularly in entrepreneurship (Pieper et al., 2015). This theory suggests that early experiences during a sensitive developmental period have a lasting impact on cognitive concepts and behaviour patterns, which persist even after the individual leaves that sensitive period (Milanov and Fernhaber, 2009). This supports the idea that military veterans often exhibit strengths in entrepreneurship, attributed to their imprinting experience (Cohen, 2020).

Similarly, Kaffka and Krueger (2018) argues that the values of loyalty and service learned in the military can lead to socially responsible business practices among military entrepreneurs. Hence, their commitment to serving others can manifest in businesses that prioritize community impact, aligning with contemporary consumer expectations for ethical entrepreneurship. Prakash further highlights how institutional legacy, shaped by historical conflicts and military traditions, serves as an imprint guiding ethical decision-making and risk-taking in military and entrepreneurial contexts (Prakash, 2017).

Relationship Between the Enterprising Genius Theory, Imprinting Theory and Warrior Ethos in Military Entrepreneurship

The enterprising genius theory focuses on individual traits such as innovation, creativity and resourcefulness that drive entrepreneurial success. These qualities align closely with the warrior ethos, which embodies the values of courage, adaptability, discipline, perseverance and initiative in a challenging environment. According to Baron (2007), military entrepreneurs frequently display these traits when confronted with unique operational problems or when leveraging their experiences to develop civilian applications.

The imprinting theory seeks to explain the relationship between what people do at certain times of their lives and how such experiences influence their behaviour and, to a larger extent, how they make their decisions. It follows, therefore, that the military, being a socialized institution that emphasizes the core values of loyalty and a sense of responsibility, could provide an environment for the formation of soldiers' imprinting values, which will significantly affect their risk preference, thinking mode and personality traits (Elder, 1986; Wansink et al., 2008).

From the perspectives of the enterprising genius and imprinting theory, there is still a need for in-depth research on the influence of the warrior ethos in military entrepreneurship on the entrepreneurial landscape, especially within the context of developing economies such as Nigeria. Hence, exploring the warrior ethos through the lens of the enterprising genius theory and imprint theory can help us understand how military entrepreneurs navigate challenges, overcome obstacles and drive business ventures towards success.

The Importance of the Warrior Ethos to Military Entrepreneurship and States' Survival

The importance of instilling key traits characterized by warrior ethos, such as resilience, determination and selfless service, in the citizenry in order to promote national survival and prosperity cannot be overemphasized. This ethos, when embodied by leaders, can inspire subordinates to develop effective decision-making capabilities, especially in challenging environments. Although entrepreneurship in business and warfare has traditionally been separated from management theory, the strategic insights of most military leaders offer valuable lessons for entrepreneurs. Military strategy and business share common ground, particularly in the ability of leaders to influence outcomes under uncertainty, as captured in Clausewitz's concept of 'enterprising genius' (Keegan, 1976).

This ability to make decisions under pressure, seize opportunities and shape events parallels the skills needed in entrepreneurship. Hence, the role of entrepreneurs in shaping the success of their enterprises by responding appropriately to market challenges continues to dominate scholarly discourse. Entrepreneurs, like military strategists, use defined strategies to mitigate unforeseen circumstances and capitalize on opportunities (Mintzberg et al., 2005) by drawing lessons from varied evolutionary epochs. Thus, the warrior ethos draws from a blend of cultural, historical, political, religious and socio-economic factors. In the United States, the warrior ethos helps soldiers believe they can accomplish tasks under extreme conditions in furtherance of national objectives, regardless of the risks. This aligns with Aristotle's framework for success, which stresses wisdom, integrity, courage and discipline for the collective good, rather than self-glorification (Smith and Thompson, 2020).

In its psychological element, the warrior ethos enables the discipline to prioritize a larger purpose over personal pleasure and provide a model for citizens to aspire to virtues that contribute to a good life and an appropriate response to life's complexities. Smith (2007) connects this ethos to loyalty to the state, noting that the psychological dimension extends beyond battlefield behaviour to strengthen collective identity and align personal values with national objectives, thereby reinforcing loyalty to the state. This understanding highlights the importance of the warrior ethos in cultivating a sense of purpose and responsibility among citizens. Morley expands the relationship between military culture, from which the warrior ethos is derived, to broader socio-political contexts, noting that the warrior ethos creates a subculture that sometimes clashes with civilian norms, complicating the reintegration of veterans (Morley, 2019). However, he suggests that military personnel can leverage their skills and networks to become leaders in various sectors, such as business, technology and even private military companies. This reflects military entrepreneurship's pragmatism, where military values like discipline and strategic planning are adapted to market-oriented contexts. Thus, this highlights the need for the state to provide frameworks that integrate military entrepreneurship into national policies, especially in terms of supporting veteran reintegration.

In a wider sense, the concept of the warrior ethos has evolved beyond the military to include anyone striving to live by a code of behaviour in their daily lives. It applies not only to soldiers but also to individuals in workplaces, families and communities who defend a sense of purpose and personal values (Pressfield, 2011). Therefore, the warrior ethos is about physical and mental states that empower individuals to serve others, even at personal sacrifice. It represents the values and convictions shared by a nation's people, underscoring the importance of this ethos in fostering commitment to service in various endeavours.

Critique of the Warrior Ethos in Military Entrepreneurship

The concepts of warrior ethos and military entrepreneurship have garnered significant attention in both practical and academic discussions. The concepts raise questions about their implications for individuals, groups, organizations and society at large. Coker (2007) critiques the warrior ethos over its lack of flexibility and the impact on motivation and adaptability required in modern warfare. French (2003) expresses concern over the influence of mercenaries and the potential erosion of core values like valour, courage and honour. Avant (2015) explores how the commodification of military values through private military companies challenges the flexibility and ethical foundations of the warrior ethos, with implications for society. Other critiques of the warrior ethos in military entrepreneurship are discussed in subsequent paragraphs.

One of the central tenets of the warrior ethos is the criticality of leadership, which requires courage, boldness and the act of leading from the front. However, the rise of modern technology, such as drones, has changed the perception of the warrior as a brute force figure. Technologies that detach soldiers from the immediate impacts of warfare, like drone operators who control combat from thousands of miles away, seem to diminish the significance of traditional military values such as valour and courage. Singer (2009) asserts that this disconnection reduces the visceral and moral responsibility inherent in warfare, highlighting the shift from traditional to post-modern military ethos in a globalized world of advanced technology.

Edgerton (1999) critiques the warrior ethos, arguing that its focus on ideals like bravery, honour, sacrifice and loyalty creates a narrow and oversimplified definition of military service. He suggests that the glorification of these traits often overshadows the moral complexities and ambiguities of real combat. Edgerton also critiques military entrepreneurship, which involves service members or veterans using their military experiences to engage in business ventures. He argues that this commodification of military values dilutes the core principles of service, transforming them into marketable products rather than lived ideals. The interplay between individualism and collectivism in military culture is another perspective on warrior ethos and military entrepreneurship that has attracted the attention of critics. Military entrepreneurship focuses on individual opportunities for profit, which contrasts with the collectivist nature of the warrior ethos, where service is rooted in shared goals and public duty. This tension raises challenges in balancing individual entrepreneurial pursuits with the collective values that underpin military service, which could lead to conflicts between personal ambition and the sense of duty to the public cause.

Furthermore, Schilling and O'Reilly (2010) suggest that military entrepreneurs use their initiative, unique experiences and creativity to solve problems for the public good. However, while the cohesion fostered by collectivism is essential in high-stress environments, it can also promote resistance to change and hinder innovation, creating tension between military tradition and the flexibility required for entrepreneurial activities. As the conversations about warrior ethos in military entrepreneurship continue to generate diverse interests, the warrior ethos remains a broad philosophical concept that is deeply rooted in military traditions and cultures, and which can be applied to varied contexts.

Tenets of Warrior Ethos and Their Relevance to Military Entrepreneurship

The concept of warrior ethos embodies several key tenets that guide military personnel in their duties, many of which apply to military entrepreneurship. The first and foundational tenet is the commitment to duty and responsibility, often summarized as 'mission first', which emphasizes the prioritization of tasks. This principle is crucial both on the battlefield and in business, as it enables individuals to rank and address tasks effectively. Successful military entrepreneurs leverage this philosophy to create a strong mission and vision for their ventures, serving as guiding principles to motivate their teams and stakeholders (Kotter, 1996).

Additionally, Behn explores how military duty and responsibility shape entrepreneurial ventures by instilling a deep commitment to service, ethical conduct, and organizational goals (Behn, 2003). The 'mission first' tenet also extends beyond the military, applying to the broader goals of society and entrepreneurship. Military entrepreneurs often align their business goals with the broader mission of service, similar to how soldiers adhere to the principles of protecting the Constitution and their nation. Steele (2020) emphasizes that military entrepreneurs apply the 'mission first' philosophy by focusing on the fundamental objectives of their businesses, akin to leading troops towards a common goal. This focus ensures clarity and cohesion in business operations, aligning entrepreneurial efforts with a clear sense of purpose and mission (Steele, 2020).

The second tenet of the warrior ethos is the principle of 'never accept defeat'. This tenet encourages soldiers to resist surrender and view defeat as a temporary setback, presenting opportunities for continued resistance and eventual victory (Carter, 2011). In military entrepreneurship, this mindset mirrors persistence and resilience, emphasizing the importance of overcoming challenges despite setbacks. This tenet fosters courage and resilience, teaching individuals to embrace challenges rather than fear them, which leads to growth and learning from failures (Brown, 2012). Similarly, resilience helps entrepreneurs build strong teams, much like soldiers rely on each other to overcome adversity and achieve success (Junger, 2016).

The third tenet is 'never quit', which is also vital in both military and entrepreneurial settings. It demands physical toughness, mental acuity, and spiritual resilience to continue pursuing goals despite overwhelming odds (Goleman, 2013). In business, this mindset encourages leaders to persevere through obstacles, fostering a culture of innovation and overcoming adversity. Pressfield argues that 'never quit' cultivates military discipline and entrepreneurial spirit, empowering entrepreneurs to push through setbacks and maintain their vision (Pressfield, 2011). This resolve is essential when navigating the uncertainties of starting and running a business, much like soldiers' commitment to their mission and their peers (Baker et al., 2019).

The final tenet is the 'never leave a fallen comrade' principle, which highlights the importance of trust and support within a team, both in the military and in business. Soldiers trust that they will not be abandoned, and this provides them with the confidence to pursue their mission. This sense of camaraderie ensures that soldiers continue their fight, knowing that they are supported by their society and peers

(Wong et al., 2003a). In the entrepreneurial realm, this tenet underscores the value of loyalty, teamwork and support, which entrepreneurs often translate into strong ethical business practices. The emotional bonds formed in military units inspire veterans to create businesses that emphasize collective achievement, loyalty and mutual support, leading to innovative collaboration and strong customer relationships (McClelland, 1987; Lichtenfeld, 2013; Bank, 2015).

Collectively, the four tenets of the warrior ethos – 'mission first', 'never accept defeat', 'never quit', and 'never leave a fallen comrade' – also promote ethical considerations that influence military entrepreneurship. These principles encourage entrepreneurs to maintain a strong moral compass, drive business success and foster values that could contribute to the common good of society. By emphasizing resilience, perseverance and trust, military entrepreneurs create businesses that reflect the discipline and values ingrained in the warrior ethos, ultimately benefiting their teams, customers and communities.

Nexus Between Military Culture and Entrepreneurship

The intersection of military culture and entrepreneurship has continued to provoke interest among practitioners and scholars. This could be attributed to the recognition of the military as an institution that has made a significant impact on innovation and invention in many societies. Entrepreneurial processes for the development of new weapons technology have often been induced by the necessity of warfare. There are also perspectives that contemporary military institutions are culture-driven and, in a sense, provide mechanisms for interaction with the economic sector.

Therefore, this section aims to interrogate how the values and principles of military service translate into entrepreneurial practices. It will assess the leadership and command dimension of military culture and the mindset of resilience, adaptability, innovation, risk-taking and decision-making in uncertain and chaotic environments associated with both warfare and entrepreneurship. Some examples of adaptability that are relevant to responding to market changes and decision-making will be explored.

Leadership and Command: Leadership and command in military culture provide the foundation for the transition chain from an individual follower to a leader and a decision-maker. Military leadership often demonstrates strict discipline and a strong sense of duty, imbued with setting and leading by example as a key component of organizational design. Relatedly, command exposes the military personnel to key components of leadership styles and the human element of military organization. It is characterized by a structured process of decision-making under pressure tied to effective communication with clear, consistent and fair direction aimed at inspiring teams.

Accordingly, military leadership and command can be considered as a unit function where leaders direct and control a group of people towards a common task. Intrinsic to military command and leadership is a structured environment that instils discipline, strong work ethics and the ability to lead teams effectively, which Naylor (2011) argues are critical skills that are advantageous to entrepreneurs. These skills are easily transferable to entrepreneurship, where leaders must navigate uncertainty, motivate employees and make strategic decisions that can affect the success of their ventures.

Resilience, Perseverance and Adaptability: The military setting is often described as a stressful environment where individuals are required to build resilience and the ability to adapt to changing circumstances, to the point where they no longer see strenuous tasks in civilian organizations as challenging. During training, soldiers and officers are conditioned to stressful levels remaining undeterred by the expectation of risk to their lives, enabling them to cope with complex and uncertain futures with relative ease. The military hones crisis management skills, which could enable military entrepreneurs to deal with overwhelming decisions that would unsettle the average CEO. Hence, Zhang and Chan (2016) emphasize that entrepreneurs frequently face setbacks and must pivot their strategies in response to market demands or unexpected failures and other challenges.

The ability to remain calm, composed and resourceful amid chaos and adversity is a critical trait that the military cultivates and practices through realistic training exercises, which develop individual confidence and permeate the team. The resilience and adaptability fostered through military experiences can lead to more perseverant business leaders.

Risk Management and Decision-Making: Military decision-making and risk management play critical roles in warfighting and are also relevant to military entrepreneurship. Essentially, military entrepreneurship entails innovative and risk-taking behaviours exhibited by military leaders and organizations in pursuing new strategies, technologies and operational methods to enhance effectiveness and efficiency. As such, military personnel are trained to assess risks and make strategic decisions in high-pressure situations. Hence, veterans are adept at managing their risk assessment skills in business settings, enabling them to navigate uncertainties inherent in entrepreneurship (Morris et al., 2016). Thus, this helps them to make decisions under conditions of certainty, uncertainty and high risk.

Effective military decision-making involves a structured approach called the Military Decision-Making Process (MDMP), which emphasizes data analysis, brainstorming, and contingency planning (NATO Allied Command Transformation, 2017). Also, the OODA Loop (Observe, Orient, Decide, and Act), which is a concept developed by the military strategist John Boyd, is critical to the understanding of military decision-making in uncertain environments. This aligns with the work of Garvin (1993) in organizational learning, where he emphasizes the importance of creating a culture that encourages experimentation and learning from failure. This is pivotal to military entrepreneurship, where leaders must make decisions in uncertain environments and manage risks associated with them. This view is further buttressed by McNamara and Aveni (2007), who emphasize that the skills that military leaders are trained in to make quick decisions in high-stress environments are transferable to the fast-paced entrepreneurial landscape.

Innovation: In military entrepreneurship, innovation is rooted in veterans' ability to leverage their training to approach problems strategically, often employing creative solutions developed from their problem-solving experiences. Military entrepreneurs, particularly in resource-constrained environments, demonstrate critical thinking, resilience and risk-taking traits integral to entrepreneurial success (McGrane, 2017). McGrane further explores how the entrepreneurial mindset of veterans is shaped by their training and ethos, emphasizing how these qualities drive them to create innovative solutions for underserved markets.

Schmidt et al. highlight the importance of agility, shared mission, and resilience in leadership, arguing that these traits help entrepreneurs adapt, iterate and innovate, akin to military operations requiring rapid response (Schmidt and Rosenberg, 2014). Stavridis (2018) draws parallels between military strategy and business innovation, noting how the warrior ethos fosters a culture of risk-taking, adaptability and learning from failure, which are key to thriving in entrepreneurial contexts. Extending this view further, McChrystal (2015) suggests that the commitment to teamwork and shared purpose within the warrior ethos enhances innovation by encouraging diverse teams and iterative processes that mirror battlefield decision-making.

Challenges Faced by Military Entrepreneurs

The contributions of military personnel, serving and retired, who leverage their training and experiences to provide innovative and strategic initiatives to the society in which they live are generally recognized. This is not without some obstacles, as it is commonly acknowledged that military personnel face some challenges in transitioning from their military environment into the civil domain in the pursuit of entrepreneurship to establish and grow businesses. Some of these challenges relate to earning potential and career advancement (Loughran and Klerman, 2008). Others include adaptation, lack of funds, inadequate knowledge of market dynamics and inadequate networks and support systems, among others (Kauffman Foundation, 2016).

Transitioning Skills: Generally, military personnel possess skills such as leadership, discipline and strategic planning that are highly transferable to civilian life. But the problem lies in their ability to transfer these skills into a business concept. This is because some of the skills and experience they acquire from the military may not necessarily translate into direct jobs in the civilian market setting (Katz and Green, 2017). Moreover, most of the newly retired military personnel struggle to adapt to civilian life after service. Accordingly, Smith posits that difficulties often faced by military personnel in securing jobs in the civilian market after their retirement can hinder their entrepreneurial efforts (Smith, 2009). Considering that the transition experience is comparable to a 'reverse culture shock', Westwood averred that it is unclear how a veteran, even with military retirement training programmes on entrepreneurship, can be in the right frame of mind to acquire the skill of entrepreneurship (Westwood, 1999).

Access to Capital: Most entrepreneurs face the hurdle of securing funding for their projects and business ventures. While this is a common problem for all investors, retired service personnel experience this barrier more due to a lack of access to traditional options, such as credit history or collateral for financing military entrepreneurial ventures (Kauffman Foundation, 2016). To surmount this problem, Umar and colleagues advocate for the establishment of special funds or grants aimed explicitly at retired military personnel (Umar et al., 2020). Also, veterans frequently have difficulty connecting with business leaders and investors who can provide the required resources for a business venture due to their lack of familiarity with the entrepreneurial landscape (Hsu et al., 2017).

Networking and Geographic Mobility: The lack of sustained contact or a limited civilian network can limit veteran exposure to civilian business networks. Having spent most of their time in the military environment, the lack of connection can hinder access to resources, mentorship and potential partnerships that are crucial to entrepreneurial success (Kealley et al., 2011). Also, the frequent relocation of veterans after service often disrupts their ability to build and maintain a professional network. Such frequent movement can lead to a lack of continuity in relationships that are vital for business growth (Baker et al., 2019).

Cultural Difference: The military culture is very different from the civilian business culture. Veterans often struggle to navigate the nuances of civilian networking, which can lead to misunderstanding or miscommunication (Katz et al., 2016). This cultural gap can create barriers to forming relationships that are essential for business development. There are also concerns about the feeling of uncertainty that life after retirement presents to the veteran, bordering on loss of professional identity and perceived deprivation of military solidarity, which could reduce life satisfaction and increase the likelihood of depression among veterans (Pranger et al., 2009).

Social Stigma and Support System: There can be a social stigma associated with veterans, which can deter potential partners, investors, and customers from engaging with veteran-owned businesses (Eisenberg et al., 2016). Such concerns could result from the perception that the veteran may have post-traumatic stress disorder (PTSD), which, if internalized, could lead to decreased confidence in their entrepreneurial ability. Some veterans live in isolation and find it difficult to replicate the sense of support and camaraderie found in the military (Sullivan et al., 2015). This makes it difficult for veterans to seek out support, as some may not be aware of existing support systems and resources, or they sometimes discover that available programmes do not adequately address their specific needs (Bates, 2014). This makes it necessary for the military to create the necessary awareness for veterans before their retirement, while governments make deliberate efforts to provide an inclusive environment and resources tailored to the unique experiences of veterans in order to facilitate their successful transition into entrepreneurship.

Case Studies on Successful Adaptation of Warrior Ethos in Military Entrepreneurship in Nigeria

The engagement of military personnel in business ventures, often leveraging their leadership skills, experiences, networks, strategic thinking and discipline gained from military training and practice, has remained a topical issue in scholarly discourse. In Nigeria, this phenomenon gained prominence in the post–Civil War era, particularly during the military rule, which created a conducive environment for some officers to venture into entrepreneurship. Some scholars argue that most officers in the post–Civil War era have exploited their positions and influence to foster business opportunities in their favour (Ogundipe and Ogundipe, n.d.).

Some prominent retired military officers who are engaged in thriving entrepreneurship include Colonel Sani Bello, General Theophilus Danjuma and General Olusegun Obasanjo, among others. Individually, they have made significant contributions to military entrepreneurship in Nigeria and influenced many sectors, such as communication, real estate, manufacturing, transportation, oil and gas, and agriculture, thereby enhancing security and development in Nigeria.

This segment provides examples of successful military entrepreneurs and analyses the impacts of the warrior ethos on their achievements. It also discusses different sectors where these military veterans have made significant entrepreneurial contributions and shows how retired servicemen/veterans leveraged their skills, training and experiences in the military to navigate the uncertain terrain of entrepreneurship as individuals. The military values of discipline, resilience, leadership and commitment to service form the intersection of military values and business practices in most of the cases under study.

Colonel Sani Bello: He is a former military officer turned politician, businessman and diplomat. He served as an ambassador to Zimbabwe after retirement, but he is mostly known for his contributions to farming and agricultural development in Nigeria. He significantly invested in agribusiness, recognizing Nigeria's vast agricultural potential and emphasizing the importance of agriculture in achieving national food security and economic revitalization that has not been sufficiently realized to date in Nigeria. He is also involved in advocacy for policies that support small-scale farmers. Apart from agriculture, he has leveraged his wide network to invest in other critical sectors of the economy with interests covering insurance, banking, construction, oil, gas and telecommunications.

By leveraging logistics and discipline, he is reputed to have created a model for entrepreneurial ventures that emphasizes organization, efficiency, and strategic planning as reflected in the activities of most former military personnel, who often bring a unique perspective to entrepreneurship that includes risk assessment and management strategies honed during service. Bello is also a renowned philanthropist who has been active in mentoring younger military officers and civilian youths in entrepreneurship.

His philanthropic programmes also cover medical support for the sick and wounded, as well as humanitarian assistance to the needy, thus promoting rural development initiatives and poverty alleviation (Stan, 2020). Bello also runs an NGO that supports youth empowerment in the areas of education and vocational skills acquisition programmes as part of his contribution to national development and security.

Lieutenant General Theophilus Danjuma: The next retired service personnel who has continued to thrive in entrepreneurship is Lieutenant General Theophilus Danjuma.

He was a former Chief of Army Staff and later Minister of Defence, who played a critical role during Nigeria's civil war, an astute businessman and philanthropist. The entrepreneurial journey of Theophilus Danjuma is traceable to his establishment of the Nigerian American Line, which is a marine trading company, in 1979. The company, which was used for trading between Lagos and South America, later expanded after he formed the COMET shipping agency in 1984.

Theophilus Danjuma's investment covers real estate, communication, oil, gas, petrochemicals and port management, among others. As a prominent figure in the oil and gas sector, Danjuma established South African Petroleum (SAPETRO), which has been deeply engaged in the exploration and production of oil and gas in Nigeria. His contribution to national security extends beyond entrepreneurship, as he has been involved in philanthropic efforts aimed at improving health care and education in Nigeria. The impact of his contribution to national security and development is largely felt through the TY Danjuma Foundation, where he has so far donated more than USD 500,000 to NGOs working to provide basic health and educational services for children and youths, including victims of terrorism. Furthermore, Danjuma has written on the need to promote responsible management in both military and business practices in his advocacy for integrity and transparency in governance (Danjuma, 2024).

General Olusegun Obasanjo: The last military entrepreneur in Nigeria to be discussed in this segment is General Olusegun Obasanjo, who served as Nigeria's military ruler from 1976 to 1979 and later as civilian president from 1999 to 2007. As a military head of state and president under military and civilian dispensation, his entrepreneurial engagement represents a significant discourse in post-colonial studies and analysis of African political transitions. After his release from prison in the late 1990s, Obasanjo returned to rule as a civilian, emphasizing the significance of military personalities in shaping political transition in Africa. Olukoshi argues that former military leaders often have unique capacities to leverage their experience in governance when moving to civilian roles, navigating political landscapes with a blend of authoritative and populist appeal (Olukoshi, 1998).

After serving as president from 1999 to 2007, Obasanjo became active in various ventures, particularly in agriculture, energy and consultancy. He expanded the Obasanjo Farms and engaged in many agricultural projects aimed at enhancing food security and economic development in Nigeria. This transition emphasizes a broader trend where former military leaders engage in entrepreneurship as a means of sustaining influence and promoting military entrepreneurship. Obasanjo has been actively involved in agriculture with a strong emphasis on sustainable practices and food security. Obasanjo's involvement in various business ventures after retirement is closely linked to what has so far been illustrated in this work as military entrepreneurship.

Falola and Heaton (2008) highlight this phenomenon when they posit that military-turned-entrepreneurs often possess unique advantages of their network resources that enable them to navigate complex business environments. In this case, Obasanjo's background as a military commander and leader in post-civil-war Nigeria afforded him the necessary political connections and a public profile that aided his entrepreneurial pursuits. As elucidated by Iliffe (2011), military entrepreneurs often draw upon their statecraft and political acumen to establish business ventures.

The Linkage Between the State, Society, Military and the Warrior Ethos in Military Entrepreneurship

In analysing the tenets of the warrior ethos, it becomes evident that they both reinforce classical and contemporary military culture and contribute to military entrepreneurship. These elements evolve in response to historical, cultural, technological, economic and social systems, which shape how states and societies influence or are influenced by the warrior ethos in military entrepreneurship. Consequently, the final section of this chapter aims to explore the connection between Clausewitz's concept of the state, society, military and the warrior ethos in military entrepreneurship, which also aligns with McNamara's model of security and development, as discussed in subsequent paragraphs.

Clausewitz's seminal work *On War* delves into the intricate relationship between war, politics and society, establishing a foundational framework for understanding warfare dynamics and national security. According to Clausewitz (1832), the state is the primary actor in war, which he describes as the continuation of politics by other means. The state must protect its citizens and maintain order, necessitating a robust military. The military, as an instrument of the state, executes its will through force. Moreover, Clausewitz emphasizes that society plays a critical role in war, acknowledging that military effectiveness requires state support, particularly as public opinion influences political decisions and military strategies. Further, Clausewitz stresses that a strong warrior ethos is essential for enhancing military effectiveness. This ethos instils discipline, loyalty and purpose in soldiers, which are necessary to fulfil the military's role in supporting the state's political objectives (Howard, 1976).

Keegan (1993) argues that war is deeply embedded in the social fabric, with the warrior ethos reflecting societal values that influence military conduct and public support for military actions. Reinforcing this idea, Galula suggests that a warrior ethos, characterized by values like honour, courage and commitment, is crucial for military personnel engaging with local populations and achieving strategic objectives, particularly in counterinsurgency operations (Galula, 2006).

Military entrepreneurship further illustrates how the warrior ethos intertwines with national stability and economic development. The proactive initiatives taken by military personnel, leveraging their skills and experiences, have contributed to fostering stability and economic growth in many societies. This aligns with Clausewitz's view of the military as an extension of the state. Lynn (2003) supports this point of view, noting that military leaders can transition into entrepreneurial roles, applying their leadership skills to create businesses that support national security objectives. The integration of the warrior ethos with military entrepreneurship reflects Clausewitz's belief in the interconnectedness of the state, society and military. A strong warrior ethos inspires military personnel. First, as a citizen and a professional, to engage in entrepreneurial activities that contribute to both national security and societal development.

Conclusion

This paper sets out to prove that there is a relationship between Clausewitz's concept of the state, society and military and the concept of military ethos in military entrepreneurship. This informs the attempt to define and conceptualize the concepts of warrior ethos and military entrepreneurship, highlighting their interconnection. A discussion of the views of some critics of the two concepts was also included. Therefore, Clausewitz's concept of the state, society and military provides a valuable framework for understanding the relationship between the warrior ethos in military entrepreneurship.

The warrior ethos, which, among other benefits, fosters a sense of duty and commitment among military personnel, proves essential for effective military operations conducted mainly to preserve sovereignty and territorial integrity, cohesion and public peace. Fundamentally, military entrepreneurship, which in itself reflects excellence in military planning and execution of strategies, enables those individuals imbued with such values to leverage the skills acquired in the service of the state in ways that contribute to national security and societal development while in service or retirement.

Together, these elements reflect Clausewitz's assertion that war is a complex interplay of political, social, economic and military factors, emphasizing the need for a cohesive approach to security and development as buttressed by Robert McNamara. In the main, this paper highlights how Clausewitz's theories can be applied to contemporary discussions about military culture, the role of the military in society and the importance of military entrepreneurship in promoting national security and development.

Recommendations

The dialectic construction and reconstruction of the warrior ethos and military entrepreneurship have resulted in the interplay of ideas, experiences and societal contexts aimed at analysing and redefining the concepts over time. This process reflects how the concepts have evolved as they are challenged and critiqued. Hence, it is recommended that further studies be conducted to interrogate how military entrepreneurship differs from normative entrepreneurship (whilst being sensitive to its different inflections). This could require a deeper dive into contemporary configurations of entrepreneurial orientation to see whether military entrepreneurship translates into leveraging opportunity structures, adaptability to environmental jolts, etc. This could provide the opportunity to see the duality in approach: professionalization interfaces with professional (military) ethos embedded or distilled from prior training and professional growth and personalization idiosyncratic and rent-seeking values among other possible inflections.

References

Avant, D. (2015). *The Market Force: The Consequences of Privatizing Security*. Cambridge: Cambridge University Press.

Bachmann, S. (2018). *Military Entrepreneurship: The Mindset of Military Retirees in Entrepreneurship*. Saarbrücken: Lambert Academic Publishing.

Baker, D.C., J. Smith and A.R. Johnson (2019). *The Resolve of a Fighter: Principles of Military Strategy in Entrepreneurship*. Oxford: Oxford University Press.

Bank, S. (2015). *Warrior Ethos and Entrepreneurship: Lessons from the Battlefield to the Boardroom*. New York: Business Leadership Press.

Baron, R.A. (2007). 'Behavioural and Cognitive Factors in Entrepreneurship: Entrepreneurs as the Active Element in New Venture Creation', *Strategic Entrepreneurship Journal*, 1(1–2): 167–82. Available at: https://doi.org/10.1002/sej.12.

Bates, T. (2014). 'The Role of Veterans in the US Economy: A Review of Literature', *Journal of Business Venturing*, 29(3): 357–72.

Behn, M. (2003). 'Duty and Responsibility: The Role of Military Values in Entrepreneurship', *Journal of Military and Strategic Studies*, 2(6): 101–15.

Benmelech, E., and E. Friedman (2015). 'The Effect of Military Service on Psychological Traits: Evidence from the Israel Defense Forces', *Journal of Human Resources*, 4(50): 941–65.

Brokaw, T. (1998). *The Greatest Generation*. New York: Random House.

Brown, B. (2012). *Daring Greatly: How the Courage to Be Vulnerable Transforms the Way We Live, Love, Parent, and Lead*. Sheridan, WY: Gotham Books.

Bruhn, M. (2011). 'Licensing, Regulation, and Economic Opportunities', *World Bank Economic Review*, 25(3): 443–7. Available at: https://doi.org/10.1093/wber/lhr017

Carter, D. (2011). *The Warrior Ethos: An Analysis of the Enduring Soldier's Creed*. Fort Leavenworth, KS: US Army Command and General Staff College.

Chukwu, A. (2021). 'The Fallacy of the Idea of Military Entrepreneurship', in S. Ojo (ed.), *Global Perspective on Military Entrepreneurship and Innovation*, 1–16. Henshey, PA: IGI Global.

Clausewitz, C. (1984/1832). *On War*. M. Howard and P. Paret (eds. and trans.). Princeton, NJ: Princeton University Press.

Cohen, A. (2020). 'The Impact of Military Service on Entrepreneurial Behaviour: An Examination of Imprinting Theory', *Journal of Business Venturing*, 35(2): 123–34. Available at: https://doi.org/10.1016/j.jbusvent.2020.01.002.

Coker, C. (2007). *The Warrior Ethos: Military Culture and War on Terror*. London: Routledge.

Cook, M. (2004). *The Moral Warrior: Ethics and Service in the U.S. Military*. Albany: State University of New York Press.

Danjuma, T. (2024). *Theophilus Danjuma: A Life of Service and Entrepreneurship*. TY Danjuma Foundation. Available at: https://www.tydanjumafoundation.org.

Driver, M. (2020). 'Entrepreneurship in the Military Context: An Examination of Innovation Through the Warrior Ethos', *Journal of Business Venturing Insights*, 15: 100126.

Edgerton, R. (1999). 'Warriors and War: The Warrior Ethos and Its Implications for Military Culture', *Journal of Military Ethics*, 1(1): 18–31.

Eisenberg, D., J. Hunt and N. Speer (2016). 'Mental Health in the Military and Entrepreneurial Challenges: Social Stigmas and Veteran Well-Being', *Journal of Veteran Studies*, 3(2): 45–60.

Elder, G.H. (1986). 'Military Times and Life Course: A Developmental Perspective on Military Socialization', *Journal of Social Issues*, 43(3): 65–85.

Falola, T., and M.M. Heaton (2008). *A History of Nigeria*. Cambridge: Cambridge University Press.

Faludi, S. (2007). 'The Terrorist and the Warrior: A Story of the Two Cultures', *The New Yorker*, 83(1): 44–53.

Fleming, R. (2005). *The Warrior Ethos: Military Lessons for Leadership and Management*. Lanham, MD: University Press of America.

French, S.E. (2003). *The Code of the Warrior: Exploring Warrior Values Past and Present*. Lanham, MD: Rowman & Littlefield Publishers.

Galula, D. (2006). *Counterinsurgency warfare: Theory and practice*. Westport, CT: Praeger Security International.

Garvin, D. (1993). 'Building a Learning Organisation', *Harvard Business Review*, 4(71): 78–91.

George, L.K. (1993). 'Sociological Perspectives on Life Transitions: Implications for Mental Health', *Annual Review of Sociology*, 19: 353–73.

Goleman, D. (2013). *Focus: The Hidden Driver of Excellence*. New York: Harper Collins.

Guillot, W. (2004). 'Critical Thinking for the Military Professional', *Air & Space Power Chronicles*, 17(4): 1–12.

Hamilton, R. (2021). 'The Fist of Virtue: The Virtue-Skill Analogy and Traditional Martial Arts', *J Value Inquiry*, 55: 371–85. Available at: https://doi.org/10.1007/s10790-021-09821-1

Hanson, D. (2000). *The Western Way of War: Infantry Battle in Classical Greece*. Oakland: University of California Press.

Heather, P. (2006). *The Fall of the Roman Empire: A New History*. Oxford: Oxford University Press.

Hirshson, S. (2002). *General Patton: A Soldier's Life*. New York: Harper Collins.

Howard, M. (1976). *The Causes of War*. Cambridge, MA: Harvard University Press.

Huntington, S.P. (1957). *The Soldier and the State: The Theory and Politics of Civil-Military Relations*. Cambridge, MA: Harvard University Press.

Hsu, D.K., J. Wiklund and R.D. Cotton (2017). 'Success Factors in Entrepreneurial Ventures: Lessons from Military Transitions', *Journal of Small Business Management*, 1(55): 1–14.

Iliffe, J. (2011). *Obasanjo, Nigeria, and the World*. Woodbridge: Boydell & Brewer.

James, C., and S. Junger (2016). *The Tribe: On Homecoming and Belonging*. Hoboken: Wiley.

Junger, S. (2016). *Tribe: On Homecoming and Belonging*. Boston: Houghton Mifflin Harcourt.

Kaffka, G., and N. Krueger (2018). The Entrepreneurial 'Mindset': Entrepreneurial Intentions from the Entrepreneurial Event to Neuroentrepreneurship, *Foundational Research in Entrepreneurship Studies: Insightful Contributions and Future Pathways*, 203–224. Available at: https://doi.org/10.1007/978-3-319-73528-3_10.

Katz, J.A., and R.P. Green (2017). *Entrepreneurial Small Business*. New York: McGraw-Hill Education.

Katz, J., R.G. Liles and N.J. Armstrong (2016). *Beyond 'Thank You for Your Service': The Need to Assist Veterans Transitioning to the Civilian Workforce*. Syracuse, NY: Syracuse University Institute for Veterans and Military Families.

Kauffman Foundation (2016). *The State of Entrepreneurship 2016: A Big Future for Small Business*. Kansas City, MO: Kauffman Foundation.

Kealley, C., S. Waring, A.H. Roberts and C. Watson (2011). 'Veterans' Transition to Civilian Entrepreneurship: A Review of Influencing Factors and Outcomes', *Journal of Veterans Studies*, 2(3): 25–39.

Keegan, J. (1976). *The Face of Battle: A study of Agincourt, Waterloo, and the Somme*. London: Penguin Books.

Keegan, J. (1993). *A History of Warfare*. New York: Vintage Books.

Kivirist, K. (2020). 'Military Entrepreneurship: Leadership, Risk Management, and Strategic Thinking in Business', *Journal of Military and Entrepreneurial Studies*, 12(3): 45–58.

Koch-Bayram, B., and G. Wernicke (2018). 'How Military Experience Shapes Executives' Career Paths and Decision-Making Behaviours', *Journal of Organisational Behaviour*, 39(5): 622–40.

Kotter, J. (1996). *Leading Change*. Boston, MA: Harvard Business Review Press.

Lauterbach, K., and M. Schmid (2020). 'Veterans' Cooperatives and Entrepreneurship in Post-War Economic Recovery', *European Journal of Military Affairs*, 25(4): 56–72.

Lichtenfeld, M. (2013). *Leadership in the Military: The Principles of Teamwork, Solidarity, and Ethical Conduct*. San Diego, CA: Military Press.

Loughran, D.S., and J.A. Klerman (2008). 'How do Earnings Change When Reservists Are Activated? A Military-Civilian Comparison', *Journal of Labor Economics*, 26(2): 299–321.

Lynn, J. (2003). *The Art of Military Innovation: Clausewitz's Theory and Its Application to Modern Military Entrepreneurship*. San Diego, CA: Military Press.

Martin, A. (2020). 'The Evolution of the Warrior Ethos in Military Culture', *Journal of Military History*, 45(2): 150–175.

Mathias, B.D., D.W. Williams and J.L. Hunsicker (2015). 'Personality Traits and Entrepreneurial Cognition: The Role of Early Experiences in Entrepreneurial Development', *Journal of Business Venturing*, 30(5): 729–40.

McChrystal, S. (2015). *Teams of Teams: New Rules for Engagement for a Complex World*. New York: Penguin Press.

McClelland, D. (1987). *Human Motivation*. Cambridge: Cambridge University Press.

McGrane, J. (2017). 'Military Entrepreneurship and Innovation: Leveraging Military Training for Strategic Problem-Solving in Business', *Journal of Military Entrepreneurship*, 3(12): 45–56.

McNamara, R.K., and R.A. Aveni (2007). 'Adaptive Leadership: Responding to Turbulence in the Global Business Environment', in J. Kouzes and B. Posner (Eds), *In The Leadership Challenge*. Hoboken: Wiley, 234–46.

McNeill, W. (1984). *The Pursuit of Power: Technology, Armed Force, and Society Since A.D. 1000*. Chicago: University of Chicago Press.

Milanov, M., and S.A. Fernhaber (2009). 'The Impact of Early Developmental Experiences on Behavioural Characteristics and Their Long-Term Effects', *Journal of Developmental Psychology*, 34(2): 115–30.

Millen, R., and S. Potter (2003). *The Nature of Military Leadership and Its Implications for Soldier Performance*. Carlisle, PA: U.S. Army War College.

Mintzberg, H., B. Ahlstrand and J. Lampel (2005). *Strategy Safari: A Guided Tour Through the Wilds of Strategic Management* (2nd ed.). New York: Free Press.

Morley, E. (2019). 'The Warrior Ethos and Its Impact on Military-Civilian Reintegration: Opportunities and Challenges for Veterans', *Journal of Military Sociology*, 2(34): 123–45.

Morris, M.H., J.W. Webb, J.R. Fu and M. Singham (2016). 'Entrepreneurship and Veterans: A Review of the Literature', *Journal of Small Business Management*, 54(4): 1320–35.
Nagl, J. (2002). *Learning to Eat Soup with a Knife: Counterinsurgency Lessons from Malaya and Vietnam*. Chicago: University of Chicago Press.
NATO Allied Command Transformation (2017). *Military Decision-Making Process* (MDMP). Brussels: NATO Communications and Information Agency.
Naylor, T. (2011). 'Leadership and Command in Military Culture: From Follower to Entrepreneur', *Military Leadership Journal*, 2(8): 56–72.
Northouse, P.G. (2018). *Leadership: Theory and Practice*. Thousand Oaks, CA: Sage.
Ogundipe, A., and O.O. Ogundipe (n.d.). 'The Entrepreneurial Evolution of Military Officers in Post-Civil War Nigeria: Leadership, Influence, and Transition', *Journal of African Studies*, 4(35): 45–62.
Ojo, S. (2021). 'Military Enterprises and Entrepreneurship: A Critical Perspective', in *Global Perspectives on Military Entrepreneurship and Innovation*. Hershey, PA: IGI Global.
Olukoshi, A. (1998). *The Military, Politics, and Development in Africa: A Comparative Perspective*. Dakar: Codesria.
Oxford English Dictionary (2025). 'worry (n.)'. Available at: https://doi.org/10.1093/OED/2796917862.
Pieper, T.M., T. Kautonen and A. Sillanpää (2015). 'Imprinting and Entrepreneurial Behaviour: A Critical Review of the Literature', *International Journal of Entrepreneurial Behaviour & Research*, 21(16): 878–900.
Prakash, G. (2017). 'Institutional Legacy and Military Entrepreneurship: A Framework for Understanding Behaviours in Military and Entrepreneurial Contexts', *Military Review*, 97(2): 45–55.
Pranger, T., K. Murphy and J.M. Thompson (2009). 'Reintegration Challenges After Military Service: Understanding Identity and Social Support', *Military Medicine*, 5(174): 514–20.
Pressfield, S. (2011). *The Warrior Ethos*. New York: Black Irish Entertainment LLC.
Regan, H.B., and R.L. Oaxaca (2008). 'Human Capital, Military Experience, and Wages: A Model of Veteran Labor Market Outcomes', *Industrial Relations Research Journal*, 29(3): 235–54.
Schilling, J.M., and K.A.P. O'Reilly (2010). *Entrepreneurship and Innovation: An Introduction*. London: Pearson Education.
Schmidt, E., and J. Rosenberg (2014). *How Google Works: The Rules for Success in the Digital World*. New York: Grand Central Publishing.
Sharon, A.K., C. Denise, C.N. Megan and K. Bruce (2014). 'Military Veterans Marching Towards Entrepreneurship: An Exploratory Mixed Methods Study', *International Journal of Management Education*, 12(3): 1–10.
Singer, P. (2009). *Wired for War: The Robotics Revolution and Conflict in the 21st Century*. New York: Penguin Press.
Smith, B.J.B. (2009). *The Transition from Military to Civilian Life*. London: Taylor & Francis.
Smith, J.R., and M.L. Thompson (2020). 'Warrior Ethos and Military Entrepreneurship: A Critical Analysis of Values and Discipline in the Modern Military', *Journal of Military Ethics*, 2(19): 145–62.
Smith, W. (2007). 'The Warrior Ethos: A Psychological Construct and Its Implications for Loyalty to the State', *Journal of Military Psychology*, 12: 345–58.

Stan, E. (2020). *Start up Tips Daily Media. The 40th Richest Man in Africa in 2013: A Closer Look at His Philanthropy and Contributions to Rural Development*. Lagos: Start Up Tips Daily Media.

Stavridis, J. (2018). 'The Agile Warrior: Military Strategy and Business Innovation', *Harvard Business Review*, 4(96): 52–60.

Steele, D. (2020). *The Military Entrepreneur: Leadership Lessons on Entrepreneurship from the Battlefield*. Austin, TX: Greenleaf Book Group Press.

Sullivan, K.P., G. Voelker and J. Reinberg (2015). 'The Post-Military Adjustment: Social Isolation and Entrepreneurial Confidence Among Veterans', *Military Behavioural Health*, 2(3): 97–110.

Umar, S., A.A. Musa and T. Ali (2020). 'Entrepreneurship and Economic Integration of Retired Military Personnel in Nigeria: The Role of Special Grants', *Journal of Military Studies*, 3(45): 112–27.

Wansink, B., M.M. Cheney and L. Chan (2008). 'Exploring the Relationship Between Military Service and Food Risk Perception', *International Journal of Military Psychology*, 20(2): 136–45.

West, M.R. (1990). *The Army Organisational Effectiveness Program: A Historical Perspective*. Fort Leavenworth, KS: U.S. Army Command and General Staff.

Westwood, M. (1999). *Career Transition Program for Canadian Peacekeeping Veterans*. Veterans Affairs, Canada.

Williams, A.P.O. (2008). 'Strategic Thinking in Emerging Economies', *International Journal of Business and Management Science*, 1(1): 1–16.

Wong, L., T.A. Kolditz, R.A. Millen and T. Potter (2003a). *Why They Fight: Combat Motivation in the Iraq War*. Carlisle, PA: U.S. Army War College.

Wong, L., T.A. Kolditz, R.M. Millen and T. Potter (2003b). *Conversations with Soldiers: The Warrior Ethos and Its Implications for Military Leadership*. Camberley: Centre for Army Leadership.

Zhang, X., and K.W. Chan (2016). 'Military Training and Resilience: How Military Experience Fosters Entrepreneurship Skills and Leadership', *Journal of Business and Psychology*, 4(31): 543–56.

Zhang, Y., and X. Zhao (2017). 'Military Experience and Investment Decisions: Empirical Evidence from Corporate Boards', *International Review of Economics & Finance*, 51: 1–13.

Part IV

Military Family Entrepreneurship

9

Military Spouses' (Wives) Entrepreneurship

Aisha Yahaya Bambale and Irene Oka Isaac

The chapter looks at the entrepreneurial activities of military spouses, which often result from the ephemeral lifestyle of military life and its demands, leading military spouses, particularly wives, to pursue different entrepreneurial activities and business ventures that serve their various interests, skills and people's needs within the military base. The chapter analyses the entrepreneurial endeavours of military spouses (wives) at the Nigerian Air Force (NAF) Base, Kaduna. Examining the motivations, challenges and support systems that influence and impact their business ventures.

Entrepreneurship is a multi-dimensional concept and a multidisciplinary study and course. It can be found in many disciplines such as medicine, education, agriculture, business and many more. It is an agent of growth that stimulates life in any business or economy where there is deadness (Adeyeye, 2020). As studies emerge, many scholars have found the meaning of entrepreneurship, which involves entrepreneurial innovation, organization creation, value creation, profit or non-profit, growth, uniqueness and owner-manager.

Entrepreneurship involves starting, founding and creating a firm, new business or new venture, innovation, new products and new markets, the pursuit of opportunities, profit-seeking and personal benefit, risk-taking, risk management and uncertainty, new combination of resources and means of production, management, value creation, and the pursuit of growth and creation of change. The military spouse needs to understand these dimensions of entrepreneurship and what needs to be done in order to support their families and households for better results (Vandana and Kulkarni, 2023).

When a military spouse becomes an entrepreneur, it is a bold feat. They seek a purpose where they don't have to quit their job every 2–3 years, but instead, they get to pick up their passion and bring it with them anywhere they go. Entrepreneurship offers a unique flexibility where they can go from constantly having to solve childcare issues to making their schedule and never missing one of their spouse's pinning ceremonies again. They want to free themselves from those ever-missing pieces of community support and build a special camaraderie that can only be found with fellow entrepreneurs in their area. Entrepreneurship is uniquely positioned to benefit military spouses as it presents opportunities to create their own salary, build their community and pursue their own career goals (Hamilton, 2022).

Military spouses, renowned for their resilience, navigate unpredictable circumstances while supporting their loved ones, a testament to their remarkable adaptability. They exemplify unwavering strength and dedication in the face of all challenges. Though many put their own lives on hold to follow their spouses around the world and support their careers, when it comes to pursuing their passions, military spouses may find themselves struggling to navigate the workforce, leading to more entrepreneurial interest (Seymor, 2024).

Military spouses make an incalculable contribution to their community by bearing a unique and heavy burden – a burden that extends far beyond long separations, single parenting and simmering anxiety for the well-being of their deployed spouse, which often leads to feelings of unfulfillment, frustration and resentment among military spouses unable to pursue their own professional goals. Interrupted relationships, social uncertainty or isolation, kids pulled out of schools and away from friends, anxiety and re-adjustment. Perhaps most problematic, a change of duty stations makes holding a job or pursuing a career that matches the education and qualifications of military spouses difficult or even impossible. Fortunately, a powerful solution exists, a pathway that offers economic empowerment, financial remuneration and on terms consistent with the unique needs of military spouses – entrepreneurship. Entrepreneurship provides a pathway to personal and professional fulfilment, the chance to pursue a long-time interest or idea, to create, to build something new from scratch and to become one's own boss and potentially an employer of others. In its inherent flexibility and self-autonomy, entrepreneurship is tailor-made for military spouses. Military spouses make profound sacrifices that a grateful nation can never fully repay. Acknowledging their unique economic needs and providing the business training and support they have earned and deserve is a great start – especially given the importance of their personal satisfaction and economic well-being to the nation's military readiness. (Dearie, 2023).

The purpose of this study is to explore the motivations, challenges and support systems that influence military spouse entrepreneurship, using NAF Base, Kaduna, how they overcome these challenges and recommendations on how to improve their entrepreneurial venture. An increasing body of evidence identifies the inherent characteristics of the military lifestyle: frequent and/or unpredictable relocations, the physical distance of assignments from home brought by deployments for the service member, and the military come first culture (Vuga and Juvan, 2013) have detrimental effects on the military spouses' ability to find and maintain employment within their chosen career fields, earn wages that match their skills and maintain long-term career progression, so the more reason they turn to entrepreneurs (Abdelaal, 2022; Ballard and Borden, 2020; Chrisinger, 2019, 2020, 2021; DaLomba et al., 2020; Hiring our Heroes, 2020; Huffman et al, 2019; Posard et al., 2021; Williams et al., 2020).

Military Spouses' (Wives) Entrepreneurship

An entrepreneur is a person who identifies business opportunities and organizes the required resources to initiate successful business activities. A military spouse (wife) is a person/female, legally married to an active-duty military service member as recognized by the military (Agbisit, 2019; Disque, 2016). Entrepreneurship is characterized by a myriad of essential traits, including unwavering commitment, ingenuity, novelty, autonomy, persistence, receptiveness to new ideas, aspiration for accomplishment, practicality, capacity for handling uncertainty, forward-thinking, willingness to tackle challenges, propensity for risk-taking and intrinsic control (Priyadi and Mulyani, 2024; Shuaibu et al., 2021). This concept is further expounded upon by Rosemaro (2022), who characterizes entrepreneurship as the activities involved in generating innovative and valuable goods or enterprises, embodying qualities such as strong dedication, creativity and persistence. However, for military wives to understand the totality of entrepreneurship, these basic concepts must be the reason for their adventure. These are:

Entrepreneurship Motivations

The motivation for an individual's involvement in entrepreneurship can be perceived in two ways: opportunity-driven and necessity-driven entrepreneurship (Chowdhury et al., 2024). Opportunity-driven entrepreneurship is when military officers' wives go into entrepreneurship as a result of their skills, traits, interests, knowledge or identified opportunity, while necessity-driven entrepreneurship is based on how people must survive and live; this is driven by poverty, hunger, unemployment, pressure to earn a living from families and friends, and social disaster.

Military spouses are drawn to entrepreneurship for different compelling reasons. The flexibility and mobility of owning a business are valuable in the face of frequent relocations, which is a common aspect of military life and the current economic conditions. Unlike military jobs, which become challenging, with moves every few years, a portable business offers a sustainable career that can be adapted to different locations (Hamilton, 2022).

Financial security is another powerful motivator. Entrepreneurship allows military spouses (wives) to contribute an additional income stream, which can be sometimes necessary given the typical modest salaries of military personnel. Many spouses (wives) seek financial independence and stability due to high unemployment rates within this demographic, making entrepreneurship an attractive path (McMahon, 2017).

Beyond financial motivations, personal fulfilment is also important. For many, entrepreneurship offers a sense of purpose and identity beyond the roles of caregiver and supporter, providing an outlet for creativity, skills and ambition. The entrepreneurial venture is a way to achieve a sense of accomplishment and independence that can be deeply rewarding.

Lastly, entrepreneurship fosters community and support among military families. Businesses owned by military spouses (wives) often serve the unique needs of the base community, creating strong networks of mutual support and connection. This sense of shared purpose and understanding further reinforces the appeal of entrepreneurship for military spouses (wives) as they build businesses that not only sustain their families but also enrich their communities.

Phases of Entrepreneurial Activities

These involve:

i. Degree of Entrepreneurship – refers to the extent to which individuals engage in entrepreneurial behaviour. It entails their willingness to take risks, pursue innovative ideas and proactively identify and act on opportunities in the face of uncertainty. This dimension reflects the entrepreneurial mindset and the commitment to drive change and innovation. A high degree of entrepreneurship is characterized by bold decision-making, creativity and a focus on transformation.
ii. Frequency of Entrepreneurship – looks at how often entrepreneurial activities occur within a specific timeframe, the consistency and regularity of initiating new ventures, projects or innovations. This dimension captures the recurrence of entrepreneurial efforts, whether by starting multiple businesses, launching new products or undertaking continuous improvements in existing business ventures.
iii. Intensity of Entrepreneurship – shows the level of effort and resources dedicated to entrepreneurial activities, through measuring the scale and scope of these efforts, such as the amount of capital invested, the complexity of initiatives and the level of commitment required. High intensity often involves large-scale ventures or transformational projects that have a significant impact, requiring substantial energy and resource allocation.

The military spouse needs to understand these phases before jumping into entrepreneurship in order to avoid a loss of interest in business.

Characteristics of Successful Entrepreneurs

i. Personal attributes – such as resilience, adaptability, self-confidence and a strong sense of initiative. They are often highly motivated, disciplined, and persistent, enabling them to overcome challenges and uncertainties. Their creativity and vision help them identify opportunities, while their passion and drive inspire others to share in their goals. It includes:
   - Commitment, determination and perseverance
   - Behaviour, i.e. creativity and innovativeness
   - Mindset, i.e. ability to take Initiative, inquire, evaluate business opportunities, set goals and be driven by the inner pursuit
   - Tolerance of failure and ambiguity, i.e. job security and retirement, does not bother them
   - Teamwork builder
   - Self-mastery or self-management, which involves diligence, discipline and sacrifice
   - Personal vision and objective with a dream list
   - Self-confidence with a high level of enthusiasm
   - Time management
   - Firm, friendly and tactful in relationships

ii. Technical proficiency – is the entrepreneur's expertise and skills in their chosen field. This includes a deep understanding of the products and services they are working with, as well as the ability to leverage technical knowledge for innovation and problem-solving. Entrepreneurs with strong technical skills can design and deliver solutions that meet market needs effectively, providing them with a competitive edge. This includes:
   - Commitment and single-mindedness
   - Knowledge in the area of focus and willingness to learn
   - Result-oriented and necessarily perfect, but acceptable
   - Reality test, i.e. environmental survey
   - Opportunities awareness
   - Skilfulness

iii. Managerial competencies – involves the ability to plan, organize, lead and control resources efficiently. Successful entrepreneurs exhibit strong leadership skills, strategic thinking and decision-making abilities; they are adept at managing teams, finances and operations to achieve business goals. These competencies ensure that they can scale their ventures, adapt to changing market conditions and maintain sustainable growth.
   - Leadership, organizing and directing ability
   - Wisdom in decision-making and sound judgement
   - Stress tolerance and management
   - Sagacious in selecting, motivating and developing people
   - Strategic action competency, i.e. being in the right place at the right time, putting the right thing in the right place
   - Planning and administration competency
   - Communication competency in turning vision into reality
   - Negotiating aptitude and skills

Roles of Entrepreneurial Creativity

Primus (2022) mentioned the following as roles of creativity:

1. Unconsciousness scanning – involves the subconscious processing of information, where an entrepreneur's mind gathers and organizes data from an environment without conscious effort. It allows entrepreneurs to notice patterns, opportunities or problems that may not be immediately apparent. This passive but essential role of creativity often leads to the recognition of entrepreneurial opportunities.
2. Intuition is the ability to make decisions quickly without relying on deliberate reasoning. In entrepreneurship, this role of creativity helps in making swift, often accurate, decisions when time is limited or information is incomplete. Intuition is shaped by experience, expertise and the entrepreneur's ability to trust their instincts.
3. Insight – refers to the moment of clarity when an entrepreneur connects disparate pieces of information to form a novel idea or solution. It is a sudden

realization or understanding that sparks innovative thinking. Insights often lead to breakthrough ideas that set businesses apart from competitors.

4. Logical formulation – this involves structuring and refining creative ideas into practical and actionable plans. Logical formulation ensures that the creative process leads to viable business solutions by aligning insights with strategic goals, resources and market needs. It bridges the gap between abstract ideas and tangible entrepreneurial action.

Problems of Entrepreneurship a Military Spouse Must Watch Out For

The problems of entrepreneurship could be categorized into two: (1) internal factors and (2) external factors:

Internal factors: These are problems that arise from within, perhaps the owner's mistakes

a. Plunging into business without an adequate feasibility study
b. Wrong choice of locations
c. Wrong choice of business with little or no prospects
d. Underestimation of business requirements and incubation period
e. Lack of business connections and poor human relationships
f. Lack of knowledge and inexperience in the business
g. Lack of building up capital and poor financial control/records
h. Lack of entrepreneurial managerial know-how
i. Under-pricing of goods and over-extension of credit facilities to customers
j. Extravagant spending without accountability
k. Poor inventory control.

External factors: George (2021) argues that external problems are environmental problems; these are:

a. Financing problems ranging from inability to secure funds or loans, long-term equity capital and building financial reserves
b. Competition with large companies
c. Inaccessibility to relevant modern technology
d. Inability to procure raw materials, especially when it is imported
e. Unfavourable policy framework by the government, economic and political instability
f. Limitation in available extension services, infrastructural supplies and power supplies
g. Natural disasters like war, drought, trade disruptions

From the perspective of the researcher, military spouses' (wives) entrepreneurship is seen as an entrepreneurial activity and business venture undertaken by the spouses of active-duty military personnel, wives in particular. These entrepreneurial endeavours range from small home-based businesses to larger enterprises, tailored to fit the unique lifestyle and challenges faced by military families. They start and manage their businesses.

Prospects of Entrepreneurship

Mohammed (2021) asserts that the following prospects of entrepreneurship must be keenly considered by military spouses:

a. Exploitation of untapped industrial opportunities
b. Promotion of Indigenous technology
c. Reduction of crimes in urban areas
d. Job opportunities and reduced unemployment
e. Enhanced regional economic balances
f. Preservation of healthy competition in the business world
g. Reduction in human resource wastage
h. Discovery of genius and making of entrepreneurs
i. Planning to facilitate specialization in terms of a particular area for a particular industry
j. Poverty reduction and a better standard of living. The national income per capita will shoot up positively.

Contributions of Entrepreneurs to Nigeria's Economy

A summary of the contributions of entrepreneurs to Nigeria's economy is as follows:

a. Developments of new market
b. Discovery of new sources of materials
c. Mobilization of capital resources
d. Induction of new technologies. New industries and new products
e. Creation of employment (Tscholl et al., 2021).

Military Spouses' (Wives) Entrepreneurship Ventures

Military spouse entrepreneurship often involves: Portable business models that can operate remotely or relocate easily; flexibility to balance work and family responsibilities during deployments or moves; resilience and adaptability developed through military life experiences, leveraging skills gained through volunteering and community involvement. Thus, meeting the needs of consumers and potentially generating income for military spouses (wives), leverage their skills and experiences to create businesses and engage in diverse entrepreneurial activities that cater to various interests, skills and market needs. Military spouses' (wives) entrepreneurial ventures at the NAF base, Kaduna, can be categorized into several types based on the nature of the businesses, the motivations behind starting them and the specific challenges faced by military spouses. Here are the primary types:

Home-Based Businesses

This involves the sale of various items and foodstuffs from home, either raw or processed. Many military spouses (wives) in the NAF base, Kaduna, run home-based businesses, selling a variety of essential goods and foodstuffs directly from their homes. These items include both raw and minimally processed goods like pepper, dried fish, groundnut cake, bean flour, powdered pepper, garlic, millet flour, honey and crayfish, which cater to the community's everyday needs. In addition, some spouses add value through basic food processing, creating items such as youghofura, zobo drink, ginger drink, kunun aya, gullisuwa, tuwon madara, groundnut paste, powdered pepper, dried fish and ground millet or beans. This approach not only adds convenience for NAF base residents but also places these entrepreneurs as a vital part of the local food market chain, filling a niche within the retail sector. Another popular venture among military spouses (wives) is the production and sale of traditional incense (turaren wuta) and body perfume oils (humra). These items are cherished for personal use and special occasions, with the blending and crafting of unique scents that resonate with the base community, thus creating a loyal customer base within their community. Direct sale of some products is also popular among military spouses (wives), who often represent companies such as GHT, Oriflame and other locally made products, to sell beauty, wellness and lifestyle products directly to customers in and beyond the base community through social networks and word of mouth, allowing them to work from home and manage their business according to their schedules.

Online and E-Commerce Businesses

Military spouses (wives) at the NAF base in Kaduna venture into the digital marketplace, establishing online stores that offer a wide variety of products. From fashion items like clothes, veils, shoes, handbags and accessories such as earrings and wristwatches, to skincare and wellness products like body lotions, cleansers and health supplements, these e-commerce businesses meet the various needs of their customers within the NAF base. By leveraging social media platforms and e-commerce sites, military spouses (wives) can reach customers both on and off the NAF base, thus expanding their businesses. This online approach provides flexibility, allowing them to manage sales and marketing from home while balancing family and other responsibilities, and also enabling them to stay competitive in the growing digital economy.

Educational, Coaching and Mentoring Services

Military spouses (wives) at the NAF base in Kaduna actively engage in educational and mentoring roles, offering different services that benefit both children and adults within the NAF base community. Some provide tutoring and create educational content in academic subjects and specialized skills. For young children aged 2–3 who are not yet enrolled in school, some military spouses (wives) run early-learning programmes at home, offering structured lessons that enable working parents, especially mothers, to balance their careers while ensuring their children are cared for and receive foundational education. In addition, military spouses (wives) offer empowerment coaching sessions, helping other women develop confidence and self-reliance. Skill-based training is also common, with classes in baking, knitting, sewing and other crafts for those interested in learning a trade, usually done at home, in shops or at Nigerian Air Force Officers' Wives Association (NAFOWA) vocational centre. For example, baking and pastry classes attract entrepreneurs who have a passion for it, while sewing and knitting allow participants to make products for personal use or sale. Through these educational and coaching services, military spouses (wives) not only contribute to the base community development but also help others gain practical skills, enhancing their potential for economic independence.

Fashion Business

The fashion business has become a popular and vibrant entrepreneurial venture among military spouses (wives) at the NAF base in Kaduna. Many military wives, with their keen eye for style and understanding of the community's preferences, have established successful fashion enterprises, ranging from clothing boutiques to accessories and custom apparel. These entrepreneurs create a diverse range of products, including traditional Nigerian attire, hijabs, gowns, wrappers, contemporary clothing and handmade accessories that appeal to both the military and civilian residents on base. Operating a fashion business on the base provides military spouses (wives) with flexibility, allowing them to manage their businesses around family responsibilities. Some of these businesses operate out of the shops in the Mammy market or from home-based setups, making it easier to balance entrepreneurship with the unique demands of military life. The NAF base community supports these businesses by buying ready-made garments and accessories, reducing the need for residents to go outside the base for some fashion needs, thus fostering a customer base right within the NAF base. By so doing, these fashion entrepreneurs not only generate income but also create an avenue for self-expression and skill development. Their entrepreneurial spirit contributes significantly to the NAF base community, empowering them to be financially independent and actively involved in the base community development.

Event Planning and Coordination Services

This is another entrepreneurial venture for military spouses (wives) at the NAF base, Kaduna. They do so by offering essential rental services for parties and gatherings, providing a variety of event supplies, including decorations, furniture, canopies, entertainment options and party equipment. Organizations like the NAFOWA Air Training Command chapter and the Airmen Wives Association (AWA) support these efforts by renting out items such as chairs, canopies and large cooking pots for events within the base community. These services allow NAF base residents to host well-organized events without needing to purchase costly items, fostering a sense of community and enabling military spouses (wives) to contribute meaningfully to the NAF base's social life. This business not only creates a source of income for military spouses (wives) but also makes event hosting accessible and affordable for base residents.

Baking Business

This involves the production and sale of baked goods, such as bread, cakes, pastries, cookies and other baked items. A bakery can be a physical storefront or a home-based operation, depending on the scale. The business falls under food production because it involves making consumable goods. It also falls into retail because the products are sold directly to customers. Baked goods can be sold to walk-in customers, delivered to events or supplied to other businesses such as cafés or restaurants. The baking business is an entrepreneurial venture among military spouses (wives) at the NAF base, Kaduna, which entails the production and sale of a variety of baked goods, including bread, cakes, pastries, cookies and other speciality items. Depending on the size and scope of production, this business can be in the form of a home-based operation by the military spouse (wives) to a full-scale bakery, such as the NAFOWA ATC chapter bakery located on the base, which produces fresh and tasty bread for consumers. Military spouses (wives) in this venture cater to diverse needs, providing items for walk-in customers, offering delivery services for events and even supplying products to shops in and outside the base. Many also provide customized services for special occasions, including birthdays, weddings and community gatherings both on and off the base. The baking business not only provides a steady income to the NAFOWA ATC chapter in Kaduna but also empowers military spouses (wives) to contribute to the NAF base community and establish a fulfilling, flexible career within the base environment.

Healthcare Business

This usually takes the form of pharmacy services, which play a key role in supporting the well-being of the NAF base Kaduna community. This entrepreneurial venture involves the sale of prescription medications, over-the-counter drugs, medical supplies and various health-related products that cater to the needs of residents. By operating pharmacies within accessible areas such as the Mammy Central Market on the base, military spouses (wives) provide essential health services, ensuring that residents have convenient access to necessary medications and basic healthcare products. These pharmacies not only supply medicines but also offer valuable health guidance, helping NAF base residents understand their prescriptions and offering advice on common health concerns. This business meets a critical demand within the base, reducing the need for residents to go far for their medical needs. For military spouses (wives), operating a pharmacy or healthcare shop represents a stable and meaningful business opportunity, allowing the entrepreneurs to contribute to the NAF base community's health and establish themselves as trusted providers in the local healthcare landscape.

Animal, Poultry and Fishery

This is another growing business opportunity among military spouses (wives) at the NAF base, Kaduna. Animal and poultry farming is a branch of livestock production that entails rearing animals such as rams, cows and chickens, primarily for meat and egg production. Fish farming, which falls under aquaculture, focuses on controlled breeding, rearing and harvesting of fish for sale and consumption within and outside the base community. To support these agricultural ventures, the Base Services Group (BSG) NAF Base, Kaduna, has allocated designated plots within the base for those interested in starting poultry or fish farms. These plots provide enough space to construct facilities, including small caretaker quarters, providing convenience and security for farm management. This provision not only encourages self-sufficiency and economic growth within the base community but also enables military spouses (wives) to engage in food production, supporting community food supply, and food security and creating income streams while at the same time building sustainable, productive businesses.

Tailoring Design Business

Tailoring is a vibrant business within the fashion and textile industry, involving the skilled work of sewing, knitting, designing and altering clothing to meet customers' specific needs. Military spouses (wives) at the NAF base, Kaduna, have embraced tailoring as an entrepreneurial venture, transforming spaces within their homes, such as garages, into mini tailoring shops, shops at the Mammy market or even running home-based operations. These tailoring businesses provide a variety of services, such as custom clothing designs, garment repairs and alterations, catering to the various clothing needs of the base community. This business combines creative flair with technical expertise, as tailors not only produce and design garments but also ensure high-quality finishing and attention to detail. The NAFOWA Vocational Centre on the base further supports this venture by offering training in tailoring skills, including specialized courses like bedsheet-making, to both base residents and outsiders. However, some military spouses (wives) sell tailoring accessories at the Mammy market, such as threads, needles, buttons and fabrics, meeting the demand for sewing supplies within the NAF base. Tailoring businesses run by military spouses (wives) are valuable to the NAF base community, as they foster economic independence, skill development and access to high-quality and customized fashion.

Stationery Supply Business

This is a retail venture that serves the essential educational needs of the NAF base community, Kaduna. This business provides school supplies such as notebooks, pencils, pens, crayons, rulers and other necessary materials that students require for their studies, positioning it firmly within the educational materials sector. This entrepreneurial venture helps students, parents and even schools to fulfil a critical need by offering easy access to academic essentials. Military spouses (wives) operate these stationery businesses in various ways, with some selling within their homes and others establishing small storefronts at the Mammy Central Market on the base. This allows them to serve a consistent customer base of families, teachers and students, ensuring that educational supplies are always readily available without the need to go outside the base. By so doing, military spouses (wives) contribute significantly to the educational support system within the NAF base community while achieving financial independence through a steady, dependable retail business.

Event Hosting/Emceeing Business

This is a business venture that military spouses (wives) have embraced, acting as masters of ceremonies (MCs) at various events within and outside the NAF base community. These include school competitions, weddings, corporate functions, birthdays and other social gatherings. As MCs, they play a vital role in coordinating and guiding the event's flow, making essential announcements, engaging the audience and adding vibes and flow to the overall entertainment. Their responsibilities fall under event planning, as they help manage aspects of the event to ensure it runs smoothly and maintains the desired ambience. They contribute humour, commentary and audience interaction that enhance the experience and bring energy to gatherings and events. These services are in demand both within the base community and beyond, as some MCs travel to other states to host events. This business is particularly flexible, allowing military spouses (wives) to work from home or perform on-site at event venues, based on the event's unique needs. Through emceeing, military spouses (wives) contribute to the social fabric of their communities while pursuing fulfilling, income-generating businesses.

Benefits of Military Spouses' (Wives) Entrepreneurship

1. Flexibility and Portability: Entrepreneurship allows military spouses to maintain a career that can move with them as they relocate. This flexibility helps them manage childcare and family responsibilities while pursuing their professional goals (Hamilton, 2022).
2. Community Building: Starting a business can foster a sense of community among military spouses, providing camaraderie and support that is often lacking due to frequent moves (Hamilton, 2022).
3. Financial Independence: Entrepreneurship enables military spouses to create their income streams, reducing reliance on dual incomes and addressing the unemployment rate among this demographic (USVM, 2024).
4. The socio-economic contributions of these entrepreneurial ventures include job creation, community development and fostering a culture of entrepreneurship within the military environment.

Challenges

Despite its potential benefits, military spouses face several barriers to successful entrepreneurship.

1. Frequent Relocations: The nature of military life often requires spouses to move frequently due to Permanent Change of Station (PCS) orders. This can disrupt business operations and make it difficult to establish a stable customer base or local presence, as businesses may need to be portable and adaptable to new locations.
2. Unemployment: Most military spouses experience unemployment, which highlights the struggle to find stable employment that accommodates their lifestyle. This underemployment can lead to financial insecurity, making it challenging to invest in a new business venture.
3. Limited Access to Capital: Many military spouses may lack the financial resources or credit history needed to secure funding for their businesses. Concerns about initial investments and ongoing financial stability can deter them from pursuing entrepreneurship.
4. Balancing Family Responsibilities: The demands of family life, especially during deployments, often fall disproportionately on military spouses. This can limit the time and energy available for starting and managing a business, leading to stress and burnout.
5. Lack of Local Support Networks: While there are numerous resources available for military spouse entrepreneurs, finding localized support can be challenging. Many spouses may not know where to look for mentorship or networking opportunities specific to their location and business venture.
6. Self-Doubt and Imposter Syndrome: Many military spouses struggle with confidence in their entrepreneurial abilities due to past employment challenges or societal expectations. This self-doubt can hinder their willingness to take the risks necessary for starting a business.

Support System

Recognizing these challenges, various support systems and resources are in place to assist military spouses (wives) in their entrepreneurial endeavours:

1. Base Service Group (BSG) – The BSG of the NAF in Kaduna is an organizational unit within the NAF base located in Kaduna. It provides essential support services for military operations, ensuring the base and its personnel are well-supported to fulfil their roles. It provides essential support for military operations, focusing on logistics, facility management, healthcare, training, security and administration. The BSG ensures smooth base operations by maintaining infrastructure, supporting personnel welfare, enhancing skills and safeguarding the base environment. It acts as a crucial support system for the NAF's mission readiness and daily functions. The BSG actively supports military spouse (wives)

entrepreneurs by providing opportunities for business development within the NAF base. It allocates designated plots of land for farming, poultry and other agricultural ventures, fostering self-reliance and providing a sustainable source of income. Additionally, the BSG rents out shop spaces at the base's Mammy market, allowing military spouses (wives) to set up small businesses, trade goods and provide services to the community. This support system not only empowers military spouses economically but also enhances their overall well-being and stability within the base environment. It also promotes financial independence for military wives, and at the same time, contributes to a close-knit community where spouses feel valued and empowered. By creating access to land, market space and a steady customer base, the NAF base in Kaduna actively contributes to the economic well-being and resilience of military families, fostering a thriving environment for entrepreneurship amidst the demands of military life.

2. Nigerian Air Force Officers' Wives Association (NAFOWA): The NAFOWA, whose motto is 'Service to Humanity', is a philanthropic, non-governmental organization whose membership is voluntary and open to the wives of all serving NAF officers. The association started as an informal tea party, organized to exchange pleasantries and subsequently became a regular meeting with the idea of extending assistance to the sick and the needy and empowering women and the youth. In 1968, it was formally established as a legal entity known as the NAFOWA, whose core values are Transparency, Compassion and Service to Humanity. Traditionally, the wife of the incumbent Chief of the Air Staff is the National President of the Association, while the Headquarters of the Association is located in Abuja. NAFOWA is also very active at all Air Force Command levels and in various Air Force formations throughout the country. The association was established in 1968 with the primary objective of promoting the socio-cultural and educational well-being of the wider Air Force community and the general public, especially the less privileged. NAFOWA has embarked specifically on activities that promote the welfare of the 'Air Force Family' and the public in general. Among its activities is promoting the intellectual capacity of members and assisting them to empower themselves financially. Its mission is to make life easy and meaningful for its members and the general public at large most especially children and women through various charity projects. Vision: NAFOWA's vision is embedded in the Association's motto which is 'Service to Humanity'. NAFOWA ATC chapter, Kaduna, has opened a vocational centre, which provides skills acquisition, career advancement and empowerment programmes to NAF personnel's wives and other women in the communities where NAF bases are located offering training on computer, catering, fashion design, mentoring and networking opportunities tailored to military spouses. NAFOWA children's park is also built on the base where there are shops available for military spouse entrepreneurs to rent for their business and provide leisure to children. There are also online platforms like WhatsApp where members are allowed to advertise their products and services, connect, share experiences and provide mutual support to each other on their business ventures. These programmes are designed

to help women become financially independent and contribute to their families' well-being. Its mission is to make life easy and meaningful to its members and the general public at large, most especially children and women, through various charity projects. Vision: NAFOWA's vision is embedded in the Association's motto, which is 'Service to Humanity'.

3. NAF base, Kaduna, residents – The residents of the NAF base in Kaduna play a vital role in supporting military spouses (wives), in their entrepreneurial ventures. Through a culture of solidarity and patronage, NAF residents help these businesses thrive by actively purchasing goods and services offered within the base community. Whether it's buying fresh produce from local poultry and fish farming ventures, buying goods at home or shopping at stores and stalls run by military wives in the Mammy market, residents foster a dependable customer base. Many residents also encourage new entrepreneurs by offering advice, sharing resources, or helping to promote their businesses through word of mouth and connecting with new and more customers, which helps grow their business ventures. This community-driven support not only enhances the income of military spouse entrepreneurs but also strengthens community bonds, helping them feel a sense of belonging and mutual support in a unique and often challenging environment.
4. Family and friends play an important role in supporting military spouse (wives) entrepreneurs, offering both practical and emotional backing that empowers them to succeed in their business ventures. For military spouses (wives), balancing the demands of family life and business can be quite challenging, especially with the added pressures of the military lifestyle. Family members often step in by helping with childcare or household responsibilities, giving the entrepreneurs the time and focus needed to manage and grow their businesses. Friends, both within and outside the NAF base community, contribute by spreading the word, recommending the military spouse's (wife) products or services, and even becoming loyal customers themselves. In some cases, family members contribute start-up capital and resources to help military spouses (wives) launch their ventures, providing a financial cushion during the initial stages of the business. In addition, the emotional support and encouragement from family and friends build resilience and confidence. This circle of support serves as a strong foundation for military spouses (wives), enabling them to overcome unique challenges, connect with a broader network and establish thriving business ventures that contribute meaningfully to their household and the NAF base community.

Theoretical Framework

For military spouse entrepreneurship, this study applies the Entrepreneurial Intent Theory to understand the motivation challenges and support system to military spouse (wives) entrepreneurship opportunities faced by this demographic.

Entrepreneurial Intent Theory

The Theory of Entrepreneurial Intentionality was developed by Chandra S. Mishra and Ramona K. Zachary, as presented in their 2014 work titled 'The Theory of Entrepreneurial Intentionality', part of the book *The Theory of Entrepreneurship*, published by Palgrave Macmillan. This theory builds on earlier frameworks, particularly the Theory of Planned Behaviour (TPB) by Ajzen (1991), which posits that intentions are a key predictor of behaviour.

The Theory of Entrepreneurial Intentionality focuses on the processes that lead to entrepreneurial intentions, which are seen as critical precursors to entrepreneurial actions. It emphasizes that without intention, potential entrepreneurial opportunities may be overlooked. The theory delineates how various factors, including internal motivations and external stimuli, influence an individual's intention to engage in entrepreneurial activities.

Main Components of the Theory of Entrepreneurial Intentionality

The Theory of Entrepreneurial Intentionality, developed by Chandra S. Mishra and Ramona K. Zachary, identifies several key components that drive entrepreneurial intentions and actions. Here are the main components:

1. Entrepreneurial Intention: Entrepreneurial intention is a crucial input in the entrepreneurial process, acting as a precursor to recognizing and acting upon opportunities. It is characterized as a mindset that directs attention and action towards business creation. Without intention, potential entrepreneurial opportunities may go unnoticed, highlighting its role as a necessary condition for entrepreneurship.
2. Opportunity Recognition: The theory posits that entrepreneurial intentions facilitate the discovery of opportunities. This relationship underscores the significance of being intentional in recognizing viable business prospects.
3. Developmental Processes: The theory explains how entrepreneurial intentions evolve through various developmental processes, emphasizing adaptability in thinking and acting within entrepreneurial contexts. It outlines a structured approach to how intentions are formed, which includes cognitive processes that influence decision-making.
4. Influencing Factors: The formation of entrepreneurial intentions is influenced by both personal motivations (such as individual aspirations and goals) and external factors (such as social norms and economic conditions). The theory integrates concepts from the Theory of Planned Behaviour, which identifies attitudes, subjective norms and perceived behavioural control as critical to shaping intentions.
5. Behavioural Actions: The theory highlights that intentions must translate into actions for successful entrepreneurship. It emphasizes the importance of moving from intention to actual entrepreneurial behaviour (Mishra and Zachary, 2015).

This framework serves to explain not only why individuals become entrepreneurs but also how their intentions evolve, ultimately impacting their entrepreneurial actions and success. This theory can be useful in examining the motivation and challenges that influence military spouses' (wives) intention to engage in entrepreneurial activities. Factors such as perceived behavioural control, subjective norms and personal attitudes are relevant for military spouses considering entrepreneurship. By exploring these intentions, researchers can identify barriers and motivators specific to military spouses (Mishra and Zachary, 2015). The experiences of military spouse entrepreneurs not only illuminate the challenges they face but also enrich existing entrepreneurial theories by providing real-world examples of resilience, adaptability and community engagement. By integrating these insights into theoretical frameworks, researchers can develop a more understanding of entrepreneurship that accounts for diverse backgrounds and life circumstances. This approach fosters a more inclusive perspective on entrepreneurship that recognizes the value of varied experiences in shaping entrepreneurial outcomes for military spouses.

Methodology

Research Design

This study adopts a descriptive survey research design to explore the motivations, challenges and support systems that influence military spouses' entrepreneurship. The focus is on understanding the entrepreneurial activities of military spouses (wives) in Kaduna's NAF base and also examining the impact of these ventures on the NAF community. A questionnaire was employed as the primary data collection tool to gather detailed insights directly from military spouse entrepreneurs.

Population and Sample

The population for this study consists of military spouses (wives) residing at the NAF base, Kaduna, who are involved in entrepreneurship. A sample size of twelve military spouse entrepreneurs was selected using purposive sampling. This sampling technique was chosen to ensure that the participants are not only military spouses but are also actively engaged in entrepreneurial activities, making them well-suited to provide relevant information for the study. The purposive sampling approach is well-suited for this study, as it targets participants who are directly relevant to the research focus, thereby enhancing the quality of the insights gained. Additionally, by engaging only ten participants, this study remains manageable while still yielding valuable data that reflect the entrepreneurial landscape of military spouses at the NAF base in Kaduna.

Data Collection Instrument

A structured questionnaire was designed specifically for this study to capture the necessary information regarding the motivation factors that drive military spouses to start entrepreneurial ventures, such as financial independence, flexibility or personal fulfilment. The challenges they face in their entrepreneurial journey include balancing work and family life, access to capital, mobility issues related to military postings and other socio-economic factors. The formal and informal systems that support their entrepreneurship, such as mentorship programmes, access to training, family or community support and BSG backing.

The questionnaire consists of both closed-ended questions (using Likert scales and multiple-choice options) and open-ended questions to allow for both quantitative analysis and qualitative insights. The closed-ended questions focus on capturing the frequency and intensity of different factors, while the open-ended questions provide room for participants to elaborate on their experiences in their own words. Given the specific nature of the study population and the need for structured responses, the use of a questionnaire was deemed the best approach. This method ensures that participants can provide detailed and reflective responses at their convenience while also allowing for a systematic collection of comparable data across all respondents. The combination of closed and open-ended questions facilitates a comprehensive understanding of the research objectives, offering both breadth and depth in the data collected.

Data Collection Procedure

The questionnaire was distributed to the twelve selected military spouse entrepreneurs residing in the NAF base, Kaduna. Each participant was given clear instructions on how to complete the questionnaire, and they were assured of the confidentiality of their responses. The data collection took place over one month, ensuring that the participants had sufficient time to reflect on their experiences and provide thoughtful responses.

Data Analysis

The data obtained from the questionnaires were analysed using both quantitative and qualitative methods:

- Quantitative Analysis: The closed-ended questions were analysed using descriptive statistics such as frequency counts. This helps in identifying patterns and commonalities in the participants' responses regarding motivations, challenges and support systems.
- Qualitative Analysis: The responses to open-ended questions were subjected to thematic analysis to identify recurring themes, unique perspectives, and in-depth insights related to the military spouse (wives) entrepreneurial experiences and the impact of their ventures on the NAF base community.

Data Presentation and Analysis

The study employed a structured questionnaire to collect data from twelve military spouse entrepreneurs (wives) at the NAF base in Kaduna. A combination of

Table 9.1 Research Dataset

Respondent	Age (Range)	Business
1.	25 – 35	Fashion
2.	35 – 50	Entertainment
3.	35 – 50	Food services
4.	25 – 35	Food services and perfumery
5.	35 – 50	Baking
6.	25 – 35	Knitting
7.	35 – 50	Fragrance crafting and fashion
8.	35 – 50	Fashion
9.	25 – 35	Health (Pharmaceutical)
10.	35 – 50	Fashion (Fabric)
11.	35 – 50	– Animal and Poultry – Culinary enterprise – Interior decoration items – Kitchen items supply – Children and adult wears
12.	35 – 50	– Coaching and mentorship

Source: Authors' Fieldwork (2024).

quantitative and qualitative methods was used to analyse the data, providing insight into their entrepreneurial activities. Quantitative analysis involves descriptive statistics, such as frequency counts, to summarize key demographic and business-related data. Qualitative analysis used thematic analysis to find out themes in their responses, highlighting the experiences of military spouse entrepreneurs and their impact on the community.

The data provides insight into various aspects of the entrepreneurial activities of the military spouses (wives), focusing on their motivations, challenges and support systems within the NAF base in Kaduna. The age range of the respondents spans from 25 to 50 years (see Table 9.1). For those between 25 and 35 years, their primary motivations for entrepreneurship include achieving financial independence and improving personal income. Meanwhile, respondents in the 35–50 age group are driven by passion, a desire for financial independence and a commitment to community service.

The types of businesses these military spouse entrepreneurs operate are diverse, including fashion, food services, coaching, baking and pharmaceutical enterprises. Their motivations often centre on passion, achieving financial independence, contributing to the community and addressing personal challenges, which drive their entrepreneurial endeavours altogether.

However, these entrepreneurs face several notable challenges, with a lack of financing, irregular income and economic instability standing out as common obstacles. Across all age groups, the prevailing economic situation impacts income stability and business growth. Limited access to financing and a lack of experience in business management, particularly in areas like accounting and financial planning, are more pronounced among older military spouse (wives) entrepreneurs.

The support systems for these military spouses (wives) entrepreneurs are primarily drawn from family, friends, and the broader base community, underscoring the essential role of close social networks. Some entrepreneurs also benefit from additional support through organizations like the NAFOWA and the BSG, thus indicating the value of community-based organizations in fostering entrepreneurial resilience and providing resources within specific networks.

Discussion of Findings

The findings reveal that motivations such as financial independence and passion are pivotal drivers for military spouse (wives) entrepreneurs. For younger entrepreneurs, the emphasis on financial stability is particularly strong, likely due to limited opportunities within traditional employment markets. This group of entrepreneurs views entrepreneurship as a viable path to economic self-sufficiency. Meanwhile, older military spouse (wives) entrepreneurs are primarily motivated by passion and a desire to positively impact their community, reflecting a stronger alignment with personal values and long-term aspirations. Their entrepreneurial pursuits are not only financially driven but also deeply rooted in a sense of purpose and community contribution.

The challenges reported by respondents highlight current economic constraints and limited access to financing as primary obstacles. These reflect underlying systemic issues in the broader economic environment that hinder business sustainability and growth. Additionally, concerns about irregular income and fear of failure underscore the high-risk nature of entrepreneurship in this context. Without adequate safety nets, these entrepreneurs face significant uncertainty, making it challenging to maintain stable income streams and secure financial stability over time. Thus, this level of risk may deter potential military spouse (wives) entrepreneurs from launching or expanding their ventures.

The findings highlight the importance of social networks and community organizations in supporting military spouse (wives) entrepreneurs. Organizations such as the NAFOWA and the BSG provide not only networking opportunities but also, in some cases, financial assistance, helping to bridge the resource gaps that many entrepreneurs face. These support systems effectively compensate for the limited access to formal financial institutions, offering a lifeline to entrepreneurs within the base community. The data also shows how personal motivation, combined with social support, helps sustain entrepreneurial efforts despite significant challenges. Together, these support structures enable military spouse (wives) entrepreneurs to persist and adapt in a challenging economic environment.

Implications

1. The reliance on family and community support systems suggests that military spouse (wives) entrepreneurs benefit from targeted support programmes for their business.

2. The findings point out the need for financial literacy and business management training to address the lack of experience in accounting and management, which will help enhance business sustainability.
3. The presence of community organizations like NAFOWA and BSG and the base community shows that organized groups can play a critical role in entrepreneurship support, which will help the military spouse (wives) entrepreneurs strengthen their businesses.

Limitations

1. Sample Diversity: The sample may not be fully representative, as it primarily covers a small community, the NAF base, Kaduna, thus limiting the generalizability of the findings to other military bases.
2. Qualitative Nature: The data is primarily qualitative, which makes it difficult to quantify the impact of certain factors, such as the exact extent of financial challenges or the effectiveness of community support.
3. These limitations suggest that while the findings offer valuable insights, further research with a broader and more diverse sample size could enhance the applicability of the conclusions.

Conclusion

Military spouse (wives) entrepreneurs at the NAF base, Kaduna, exhibit a strong entrepreneurial spirit driven by various motivations, such as passion and the desire for financial independence, that drive their entrepreneurial ventures. However, they face substantial challenges, primarily related to financing, economic instability and a lack of formal business management skills. Family, friends and community organizations provide vital support, helping to mitigate these challenges to some extent.

Recommendations

1. Financial Support Programmes – Introducing financing options tailored to military spouse (wives) entrepreneurs could address the lack of access to capital and irregular income issues.
2. Business Training and Mentorship Programmes – NAFOWA and the BSG could implement training workshops on entrepreneurship, financial management, accounting, and basic business skills to support military spouse (wives) entrepreneurs' operational needs.
3. Encouraging more collaboration between military spouses (wives), entrepreneurs and expanding the scope of NAFOWA and the BSG could offer additional resources and foster a stronger entrepreneurial community.
4. Policy Advocacy – through engaging with the BSG and NAFOWA, policymakers

can create a more supportive economic environment for small businesses, such as grants, which would benefit military spouse (wives) entrepreneurs within the base community.

5. Future research can increase the sample size and incorporate diverse data collection methods, such as interviews, to enhance validity. Additionally, exploring other NAF bases and other military branches (army and navy) could provide a broader understanding of the entrepreneurial landscape among military spouses (wives).

References

Abdelaal, H. (2022). 'White Paper on the Military Spouse Employment Dilemma: The Multi-Dollar Question That No One Is Asking… Until Now', *National Military Spouse Network*. Available at: https://www.nationalmilitaryspousenetwork.org

Adeyeye, M.O. (2020). *Introduction to Entrepreneurship Education*. Nigeria: Ben-sat publishers.

Agbisit, M.D. (2019). 'Exploring the Lived Experiences of Career Oriented Military Spouses Pursuing Education for Career Advancement', PhD dissertation, Old Dominion University: ODU Digital Commons.

Ajzen, I. (1991). 'The Theory of Planned Behavior', *Organizational Behavior and Human Decision Processes*, 50(2): 179–211. Available at: https://doi.org/10.1016/0749-5978(91)90020-T

Ballard, J., and L. Borden (2020). 'A Study on Military Spouse Licensure Portability in Legislation and Practice', *Journal of Financial Counseling and Planning*, 31(2): 209–18.

Bridger, E., and B. Gannaway (2024). *Employee Experience by Design: How to Create an Effective EX for Competitive Advantage*. London: Kogan Page.

Chowdhury, N.T., N.S. Mahdzan and M. Rahman (2024). 'Beyond Intuition: The Role of Financial Knowledge in Navigating Investments in Emerging Markets', *International Journal of Economics and Financial Issues*, 14(4): 267–81.

Chrisinger, D. (2019). 'White Paper on Military Spouse Employment: 5 Recommendations for Removing Barriers to Entrepreneurship', *National Military Spouse Network*. Available at: https://www.nationalmilitaryspousenetwork.org

Chrisinger, D. (2020). 'White Paper on Military Spouse Employment: 3 Recommendations for Supporting Career Portability Overseas', *National Military Spouse Network*. Available at: https://www.nationalmilitaryspousenetwork.org

Chrisinger, D. (2021). 'White Paper on Roadmap to Employment Stability for Military Spouses: Five Recommendations to Build Financial Security Throughout the Military Lifecycle', *National Military Spouse Network*. Available at: https://www.nationalmilitaryspousenetwork.org

DaLomba, E., M.J. Greer, E. Cruz, A. Harris, C. King, L. Laurel, T. McCraig and R. Wilder (2020). 'The Experiences of Active Duty Military Spouses with Advanced Degrees in Maintaining and Advancing Their Careers', *Work*, 6(2): 387–98.

Dearie, J. (2023). 'The Military Spouse Entrepreneurship Act Will Strengthen America's Military Readiness', Centre for American Entrepreneurship, 24 July. Available at: Av Available at: https://businessimpactnw.org/aspire-military-spouse-program/

Disque, A. (2016). 'Exploring the Experiences of Senior Enlisted Military Wives Seeking Higher Education Through Distance Learning', Doctoral dissertation, University of New England. *DUNE*: Digital UNE.

George, A.S. (2021). 'The Evolution of Economic Models: From Knowledge to Intuition and Optimisation', *Partners Universal Multidisciplinary Research Journal*, 1(1): 16–40.

Hamilton, F. (2022). 'How Military Spouses Can Find Success in Their Entrepreneurship', 15 March. Business Impact MW. Available at: https://businessimpactnw.org/military-spouses-entrepreneurship/

Hiring our Heroes (2017). '2017 Military Spouse in the Workplace: Understanding the Impacts Spouse Unemployment on Military Recruitment, Retention, and Readiness', United States Chamber of Commerce. Available at: https://www.hiringourheroes.org/resources/military-spouses-in-the-workplace-2017/

Hiring Our Heroes (2020). 'Hiring Our Heroes Survey: Meaningful Employment Promotes Positive Emotional Wellbeing for Military Spouses', Washington, DC: U.S. Chamber of Commerce Foundation.

Huffman, A.H., N. Dunbar, A.G. Billington and S.S. Howes (2019). 'Soldiers' Perceptions of Military Spouses' Career Experiences', *Military Psychology*, 31(6): 510–22. Available at: http://doi.org/10.1080/08995605.2019.1676601

McMahon, L. (2017). 'Entrepreneurship for Military Spouses', U.S. Small Business Administration, 14 June. Available at: https://www.sba.gov/blog/entrepreneurship-military-spouses

Mishra, C., and R.K. Zachary (2015). 'The Theory of Entrepreneurship', *Entrepreneurship Research Journal, De Gruyter,* 5(4): 251–68.

Mohammed, S.H. (2021). 'The Impact of Regional Institutional Quality on Firm Innovation: Evidence from Africa', *Innovation and Development*, 11(1): 69–90.

Porkodi, S., S.S.K. Al Balushi, M.K.M. Al Balushi, K.O.R. Al Hadi and K.I.H.M. Al Balushi (2023). 'Digital Personal Experience and Organisational Performance: A Study of the Telecommunications Sector in Oman', *Business, Management and Economics Engineering*, 21(2): 248–68.

Posard, M.N., G.C. Gonzalez, L.J. Matthews, K. Christianson, J. Ryan, S.M. Ross and I. Cabreros (2021). 'Evaluation of the Military Spouse Employment Partnership Program: Report on the Second Stage of Analysis', *RAND Corporation*. Available at: https://www.rand.org/pubs/research_reports/RRA531-1.html

Primus, K. (2022). 'Part V of Spinoza's Ethics: Intuitive Knowledge, Contentment of Mind, and Intellectual Love of God', *Philosophy Compass*, 17(6): E2838.

Priyadi, H., and A.S. Mulyani (2024). 'The Concept of Entrepreneurship in a Business Perspective', *Indonesian Journal of Applied and Industrial Sciences (ESA)*, 3: 119–28.

Rosemaro, E. (2022). 'Understanding the Concept of Entrepreneurship Management and Its Contribution in Organisation', *International Journal of New Practices in Management and Engineering*, 11: 24–30.

Seymor, E. (2024). 'ASPIRE Military Spouse Program: Unlocking Potential and Empowering Military Spouses to Entrepreneurship', 21 March. Business Impact NW. Available at: https://businessimpactnw.org/aspire-military-spouse-program/

Shuaibu, H., Y. Bin Kamin, U.M. Isa and A.M. Cledumas (2021). 'The Concept of Entrepreneurship', in S. Waller, L. Waller, V. Mpofu and M. Kurebwa (Eds), *Education at the Intersection of Globalization and Technology*, 1–11. London: NtechOpen Limited.

Trujillo-Diaz, J., F.N. Diaz-Piraquive, M.M. Herrera, J. Gomez, J.A. Rodriguez and H.R. Sarmiento (2019). 'Design of Theoretical Dimensions for a Knowledge Management Model Applied to the Colombian Swine Industry', *Congreso Internacional De*

Innovación Y Tendencias En Ingenieria (CONIITI) Conference Proceedings (1–6). Available at: https://doi.org/10.1109/CONIITI48476.2019.8960785

Tscholl, M., J. Morphew and R. Lindgren (2021). 'Inferences on Enacted Understanding: Using Immersive Technologies to Assess Intuitive Physical Science Knowledge', *Information and Learning Sciences*, 122(7/8): 503–24.

USVM (2024). 'Resources for Military Spouse Entrepreneurship', *US Veterans Magazine*, 20 May. Available at: https://usveteransmagazine.com/usvm/resources-for-military-spouse-entrepreneurship/

Vandana, M., and M.B. Kulkarni (2023). 'Personal Experience – Disruptive Approach to Employee Engagement', *International Journal of Management Concepts and Philosophy*, 16(3): 195–210.

Vuga, J., and J. Juvan (2013). 'Work-Family Conflict Between Two Greedy Institutions – The Family and the Military', *Current Sociology*, 61(1): 1058–77.

Williams, R., J. Mariani, A. Routh, A. Keyal and M. Hill (2020). A Report from The Deloitte Centre for Government Insights: Military Spouse Unemployment. 'Exploring Solutions to a Local Problem of National Importance.' *Deloitte Insights*. Available at: https://www2.deloitte.com/us/en/insights/industry/public-sector/military-spouse-unemployment.html

10

Empowering the Barrack Boys Through Entrepreneurship in Nigeria

Lateef Olumide Mustapha and Ayobami Oluwatoyin Ajepe

This chapter is interested in the experiences of young men residing in barracks, particularly their limited access to education, property and business in Nigeria. Despite entrepreneurship development and financial awareness, most of the youths do not apply theoretical principles to business practice, further deteriorating their economic well-being in the barracks. The purpose of this study is to ascertain the determinants of barrack boy entrepreneurship, with respect specifically to skill development, access to resources and guidance.

People find it necessary to establish business ventures to influence economic change and reduce prejudices in marginalized groups. Everywhere, small business efforts and enterprises have helped individuals and communities rise to financial prosperity, reducing unemployment and promoting local business development (Mandel and Noyes, 2020). In developing communities, where the rate of job deployment might be low, business development contributes to economic independence (Smith, 2019). In such life situations as military barracks, for instance, young people can easily find positive ways to address economic constraints in their lives through entrepreneurship.

In Nigeria, the term 'barrack boys' describes youth raised in military or police compounds who alas have few resources and limited chances of success (Okoye, 2021). But many of these youth are faced with problems such as low educational achievements, low employment opportunities and limited exposure to skills that would in one way or another help them economically. These hurdles may entrench them in poverty and provide few options through which they can reasonably transition to become productively engaged within the economy of their community. However, if those young people could be trained and provided with the necessary entrepreneurial tools, they could be encouraged to establish their own businesses, thus providing for their needs and becoming financially mobile individuals (Adeyemi and Bello, 2022).

Among the most basic bricks that form the initial structure from which the concept of entrepreneurship is cultivated among the barrack boys, skills can be regarded as one of the major ones. Most of these young people have great opportunities to create value, but they do not have the technical and business knowledge to transform them into commercial ventures. In skills development, the skills enhancement project seeks to teach them business management skills, marketing skills, and trade-specific skills (Jenkins and Taylor, 2020). That is why, with such capabilities, they are given the means to manage a business and deal with finances and decision-making that will allow them to build an enterprise that can support them throughout life and develop over the years (Nigerian Entrepreneurship Program, 2021).

Part and parcel of this empowering strategy is resources. Experience reveals that the availability of resources is what young entrepreneurs need to turn their ideas into a business. In response, many barracks communities lack the physical infrastructure, financial backups and equipment that could foster business development. Such small funds, space and primary equipment would bring the barrack boys relief from the common financial and infrastructural constraints that hinder most startups in vulnerable areas (UNDP, 2021).

Financial literacy is also important for the economic empowerment of these young people. Along with technical and business skills, proper financial control and management are essential to having a prosperous business. Financial literacy training entails using materials in budgeting, saving, control of credit management and mastery of profit and loss. Through such knowledge, young entrepreneurs can take responsibility for their businesses' finances, thereby increasing their chances of survival in the industry during any type of market volatility (Brown and Harper, 2022).

However, there are still practical issues that put barrack boys to the test in carrying out their entrepreneurial activities: lack of adequate mentorship and legal expertise, poor access to competitive markets and finally, social and structural barriers that negatively affect youth entrepreneurship in these communities, including social and structural barriers that limit the ability and willingness of youths in such communities to engage in entrepreneurship (Onyema, 2020). Understanding these practicalities within a policy framework, community responsiveness and a comprehensive training paradigm can help facilitate this young population into economically productive agents of change as entrepreneurs.

The next section focuses on the literature review, followed by the methodology adopted in carrying out this study and finally, the conclusion and recommendations.

Literature Review

Barrack boys are children who grow up in military or police barracks, usually the children of personnel staying in these barracks in government-provided living quarters. These young people mostly lack exposure to multiple economic burdens, socially styled barracks life, and rigid schedules (Okoye, 2021). Although this definition underscores the orderly character of military and police-containing ambience, it fails to address typical socio-economic restraints and possible discriminatory negative perceptions of the youths. It also has no accentuation of their ability to be strong and inventive despite these adversities.

Barrack boys are young people who reside within military barracks or police stations, usually for socio-political reasons; they are mostly locked out of the opportunity to gain proper education, financial support and an additional chance for self-development for various reasons. The assertion drawn from this definition offers an understanding of socio-politically defined restrictions that these youths encounter, but opens up the hardship of generalizing barrack youth experience while neglecting to capture the geographical and personal diversity concerning barriers to access opportunities.

Accordingly, barrack boys (also referring to sons and daughters of military/paramilitary personnel raised in barracks) are deeply rooted in the culture of a society that is widely regarded as impoverished and culturally constricted and sheltered from most aspects of civilian life (Nwankwo, 2021). While this definition is illustrative of cultural and economic constraints, it can distort the degree of civilian encumbrance, which may lead to underestimating the flexibility and opportunities that these actors gain in such contexts. Therefore, barrack boys, in this study, refer to the young people living in Nigerian military or police barracks who experience socio-economic problems, low access to entrepreneurship, and inadequate resources to support economic development (Okoye, 2021).

Entrepreneurship involves undertaking the creation, planning and operation of a for-profit business venture, frequently in a novel and high-risk environment and through exploiting opportunities in the marketplace (Mandel and Noyes, 2020). This definition does cover profit-making and innovation, but might exclude simpler local and survival-type entrepreneurship. Entrepreneurship is a process of recognizing a need in society and then creating and introducing an innovation that satisfies that particular need through the formation of small enterprises to serve that demand (Smith, 2019). Although this definition would include local business endeavours, it can be criticized for not capturing the tenacity and nature of strategies that a businessperson in such conditions employs.

Entrepreneurship can also be defined as a means by which people, especially those in attention communities, utilize scarce resources to start and manage firms that provide services in their communities and support self-employment (UNDP, 2021). This definition covers disadvantaged communities, which is useful, but there is a tendency to portray entrepreneurship as an opportunity for everyone without regard to some vices inherent with structures such as barriers and risk-taking, something that is dangerous in environments such as barracks. According to the definition adopted for this study, entrepreneurship refers to the process of establishing and maintaining small business ventures targeting the provision of necessities and improvements in the quality of life for members of society, with a special emphasis on environments characterized by resource scarcity (Mandel and Noyes, 2020).

Skills refer to the knowledge and mastery of respective capacities or competencies, cognitive or psychomotor, that are needed in employment or business (Jenkins and Taylor, 2020). It provides a broad definition of skills, but it may need clarification on which skills students need most. Skills acquisition, on the other hand, involves more specific training for an individual in vocational and financial skills, with the aim of making the trainee more marketable for employment or for managing a business venture (Brown and Harper, 2022). Although components of vocation and finances are stressed, this definition might be enhanced by referring to soft competencies like problem-solving that may be especially relevant in entrepreneurial landscapes.

Training for skills is the systematic acquisition of skills, including academic, leadership, managerial, entrepreneurial, financial and formal technical skills that would support the creation and sustenance of a sustainable business (Nigerian Entrepreneurship Program, 2021). It encompasses many skills, though they are generally outlined and not ordered in terms of benefit, where one is likely to find oneself in a limited environment like barracks. Following Jenkins and Taylor (2020), skills development in this study refers to a type of training aimed at preparing young people at military barracks to find and successfully run small businesses relevant to the local economy.

One of the concepts commonly used in the context of the entrepreneurial process is access to resources, which means acquiring financial, technical and other material and non-material business startup and operation requirements such as funding, equipment and space (Mandel and Noyes, 2020). Although this definition accurately enumerates potential business resources and must not be denied, it may poorly measure contextual resources, like social capital or local community support, which may be most important for youth inhabiting unfavourable environments. Another aspect of resources relates to the provision of instruments of support, like funds in the form of grants or loans, tangible assets and networks that enable the entrepreneur to prepare, finance and run a business (Adeyemi and Bello, 2022). While this definition is useful to emphasize financial and network resources, it still overemphasizes the availability of resources and does not capture the issue of availability and access that the barrack youth and other marginalized groups face.

Resources available to entrepreneurs are the financial, informational and logistical support provided to entitled groups born out of underprivileged backgrounds, helping break the entry barrier into the business world (Smith, 2019). While it defines what is meant by support for the needy, this definition might not encompass all the types of resources required for sustainability and expansion beyond the early stage. In this study, access to resources is operationalized as the financial capital and other tools, equipment and support mechanisms that barrack boys need to set up viable enterprises while bearing in mind the barriers that would make it difficult for them to secure conventional resources (Mandel and Noyes, 2020).

It was agreed that financial literacy means having cognitive skills in managing a personal economy, including making budgets, saving money, using credit and investing (Nigerian Entrepreneurship Program, 2021). However, compared with the above definition, this definition focuses more on financial literacy but lacks operationalization of this knowledge, which is very important for young people, especially young entrepreneurs. There is a disconnect between book knowledge and performance in a business environment where individuals do not use their knowledge to improve their financial behaviour. Financial literacy refers to the knowledge and competency of handling one's individual, as well as business, money by reading, interpreting the documents related to cost and profit, and making financially sustainable decisions (Brown and Harper, 2022). It is quite useful and includes individual as well as business finance management. However, it may not give full credit to social realities such as the lack of creditworthiness or lack of free and easy access to banking systems for those in lower social classes.

Learners can understand and apply financial information to make efficient economic decisions regarding the expenditure of their funds, earnings and investments (Mandel and Noyes, 2020). Although this definition emphasizes decision-making, it might mean that knowledge alone results in good investment without taking into consideration the ability to finance these investments, as those from low-income brackets may not have a chance to access financial resources that may not be easily available to them. Financial literacy in this study will be operationalized as the knowledge and practical proficiencies that enable the barrack boys to conduct business and make financial decisions required to control expenditure, save and manage profits based on the business environments and opportunities within the eastern African region (Nigerian Entrepreneurship Program, 2021).

Access to mentorship means the availability of well-experienced people who offer their knowledge, advice and encouragement to beginners in the business world and help them identify potential challenges and make the right choices (Brown and Harper, 2022). However, this definition emphasizes the importance of guidance from experts; it may not realize the importance of mentors familiar with the defined community problems that are so crucial for barrack boys who encounter certain cultural and economic difficulties. Availability of mentorship includes programmes and engagements in which experienced practitioners provide knowledge and support in one-on-one communication processes (Onyema, 2020). This definition is comprehensive, but from it, one may be given the impression that all forms of mentoring are equally good; this is not true for persons in specialized and/or disadvantaged fields. Barrack boys may benefit from mentors who understand the contexts within which the programme exists and the level of resilience required for such settings.

Mentorship can be conceived of as meaning that there is structured interaction with people who possess business experience, are equipped to guide the mentor and assist the mentee in developing, prospering and gaining insight into business strategies, functioning and finance. While this definition provides a hierarchical approach to express what a mentor does, it is poorly inclusive of emotional and social support, which are critical to helping young people from difficult backgrounds build confidence in places like barracks. This study operationalizes access to mentorship as the ability of barrack boys to receive mentorship from individuals who understand the process of entrepreneurship as well as other socio-economic issues arising out of growing up in barrack settlements (Brown and Harper, 2022).

Skill acquisition is central to the growth of young men from barracks to enable them to acquire skills to run an enterprise. Barracks do not provide opportunities for proper education as well as other structured development activities for many youths who grow up in these environments (Okoye, 2021). To this end, surveys in quantitative designs and workshops have been used to assess the skill deficiency upon entry to the entrepreneurship training programmes and the enhancement in the skill levels after the training programmes (Jenkins and Taylor, 2020). Research evidence suggests positive changes in business-related skills and technological competence after specific training. However, in a similar respect, while participants comprehensively challenged themselves through enhanced development of their practical skills, there was hardly any progressive supporting system to ensure the sustainability of this outcome (Adeyemi and Bello, 2022). This further emphasizes that skill development, although a solution, should be complemented by sustained intervention and reinforcement and sufficient enabling resources.

Another factor that affects the entrepreneurial capabilities of barrack boys is the availability of resources. As used in this article, resource availability is a state of having resource support in the form of finances, materials and infrastructure. Access to these resources still presents some difficult structural socio-economic barriers. Some research methodologies have included case studies that contrast the successful and unsuccessful entrepreneurial careers of barrack boys, whereby those who had access to microloans and grants comprised the success basket (Onyema, 2020). Some focus group studies have also pointed out that extensive paperwork and insufficient knowledge about the sources of funding for ethnography are problematic (Brown and Harper, 2022). Brown and Harper's (2022) study also highlighted the importance of women having access to resources, and this, on its own, is not sufficient if women do not receive financial literacy education and coaching or help on the proper usage of these resources.

Financial literacy refers to the ability to comprehend and apply financial knowledge, which is vital for the survival of the business. Some of the barrack boys have a limited understanding of how to manage basics like budgeting and saving money, not to mention handling investments (Nigerian Entrepreneurship Program, 2021). Some of the approaches used to respond to this problem were the pre- and post-training tests, which showed significant increases in the level of budgeting and savings among the participants after the financial literacy sessions (Mandel and Noyes, 2020). However, while the knowledge levels improved, failure to establish their application outside of the programme hindered the sustainability of these approaches (Adeyemi and Bello, 2022). This study shows that while attaining financial literacy, one must be put through scenarios that facilitate the implementation of the learned skills in the context of sustainable finance and entrepreneurship.

The role of mentoring is valuable, especially for barrack boys, as it offers examples and samples, as well as the encouragement necessary to respond to some business-related issues. Scholarly approaches such as structured mentorship initiatives that involve experienced businesspeople together with youths from barracks backgrounds have been documented to enhance their perception of strategic business management courses, business challenge simulations and the resolution of business puzzles (Jenkins and Taylor, 2020). The post-mentorship programme surveys showed that everyone had benefited from the information and motivation given by mentors again, especially the ones with similar low-resource backgrounds to Okoye (2021). However, there is still a lot to be achieved, and most of the existing mentorship programmes can only last for a short time because of the scarcity of funds, thus offering limited long-term results (Brown and Harper, 2022). This raises the need for creating long-term funding strategies for mentorship as an aspect of development for entrepreneurs.

This research is underpinned by agency theory as its foundation through an analysis of agreements in which barrack boys represent agents, while supportive organizations and training institutions, together with trainers and resource suppliers, act as principals. This theory explains the effects of having other goals and information on the optimality of the empowerment programmes (Jensen and Meckling, 1976). The key tenet of agency theory postulates that the objectives of training institutions and the barrack boys must be aligned to improve the chances of success of the skill development programme. Universities and other training institutions must also be able to ensure that what is taught is applicable and has a close relationship with the youth's employment objectives of becoming entrepreneurs (Okoye, 2021). Sometimes, such programmes do not have long-term benefits when they are not supported constantly (Jenkins and Taylor, 2020).

Furthermore, the agency theory assists in explaining the factors behind the reasons why the barrack boys have difficulties accessing resources. Financial institutions, mainly working as principals, have been known to subordinate themselves, putting the agents to date-time flexible funding (Smith, 2019). This indicates that for access to be effective, programmes must reconcile the goals of the resource providers, barrack boys and other related stakeholders. Financial literacy programmes fill information gaps but have to link their goals with the possibilities for practice among barrack boys (Mandel and Noyes, 2020). When structures do not excite participant applicants to practice newly acquired à la carte knowledge, then the accomplishment gained in any given programme is wanting (Adeyemi and Bello, 2022).

Programmes illustrate agency theory because the barrack boys are agents who have to be supervised and guided by their mentors, the mentors being principals. The effectiveness of mentorship requires an investment of time and effort since the objective of both the mentor and the mentee is growth (Jenkins and Taylor, 2020). Temporary types of mentorships may be problematic if objectives are incompatible (Brown and Harper, 2022). Agency theory helps in the application of organizational goals through the enhancement of agency contractual arrangements to empower barrack boys through entrepreneurship fully.

Review Findings

The review findings reveal that training schools have been instrumental in equipping barrack boys in Nigeria with enhanced vocational skills and improved financial management capabilities. These outcomes indicate that structured training interventions can serve as a strong foundation for entrepreneurship development. However, despite these encouraging results, significant limitations persist – particularly with regard to access to long-term financial and material resources. This constraint continues to hinder the entrepreneurial successes of barrack boys, often restricting their ability to translate acquired skills into sustainable business ventures.

Beyond technical training, the study also highlights the critical importance of one-on-one mentorship. Mentorship provided by individuals who understand the unique socio-economic realities of barrack life not only builds self-confidence but also offers practical, hands-on experience that complements formal training. Such personalized guidance enables barrack boys to navigate the challenges of transitioning from a dependent military community environment to independent economic actors in the wider society.

In essence, the empowerment of barrack boys through entrepreneurship is not a singular intervention but a holistic process. It requires the integration of three key elements: skill formation, access to adequate and sustainable resources and continuous mentorship tailored to their lived experiences. When these elements are combined, they create a supportive ecosystem that can transform barrack boys into self-reliant entrepreneurs, thereby contributing to both personal upliftment and broader socio-economic development.

Conclusion and Recommendations

In conclusion, this chapter establishes that while itinerant skill development programmes have been effective in enhancing the entrepreneurial competencies of barrack boys, the absence of long-term support structures threatens the sustainability of these gains. The most pressing challenge lies in access to critical resources such as microloans, grants and infrastructure. These difficulties are compounded by entrenched socio-economic barriers and a lack of adequate knowledge about existing funding opportunities, which together limit the capacity of barrack boys to transform acquired skills into viable enterprises.

Although financial literacy initiatives have had some success in teaching budgeting and savings, their effectiveness diminishes when applied beyond the structured training environment. Without complementary resource support, financial literacy alone is insufficient to bridge the gap between entrepreneurial intention and successful practice. Equally, mentorship remains an essential component of entrepreneurial development. For barrack boys in particular, mentors who understand the unique socio-economic conditions of barrack life provide indispensable guidance, self-confidence and practical knowledge. However, the impact of mentorship is undermined by the short-lived nature of many modern programmes, which often lack consistent funding and therefore fail to deliver long-term benefits.

Ultimately, the chapter underscores the need for a comprehensive empowerment framework that combines skill development with sustainable resource access and enduring mentorship. Only through the integration of these elements can the entrepreneurial potential of barrack boys be fully harnessed, thereby ensuring both their personal upliftment and wider socio-economic contributions.

This study recommends that:

1. There is an urgent need to create ecosystems and a more viable ownership model, one that leverages being part of entrepreneurship training beyond short-term workshops. Continuous mentoring, a path to resources and continued financial

education can then take place.

2. Programmes should strive to remove socio-economic barriers for individuals in accessing resources while increasing awareness of how new money works, including microanalysis or grants and simplifying the process, beginning with the Memorandum of Understanding as an agreement which states that the Résumé Agency is a temporary agency that can only employ 1099 temporary W2 employees.
3. These financial literacy programmes need to serve not just resources of information but also platforms for practical involvement, such as simulated budgeting or real-life finance management situations, which allow the participants to practice and apply what they know in a business setting.
4. Funding programmes to support long-term mentorships are key when trying to overcome the limitations that come with short-term mentoring, and there are clearer objectives established in common by mentors and mentees around what growth in entrepreneurship should look like.

References

Adeyemi, T., and R. Bello (2022). 'Entrepreneurship and Poverty Alleviation in Nigeria: A Community-Based Approach', *Journal of African Development*, 17(3): 243–59.

Brown, J., and S. Harper (2022). 'Financial Literacy and Youth Empowerment: Building Economic Resilience in Low-Income Communities', *International Journal of Finance and Economics*, 15(4): 356–71.

Jenkins, K., and M. Taylor (2020). 'Skills for Success: Entrepreneurship Training for Disadvantaged Youth', *Youth Employment Journal*, 12(2): 97–115.

Jensen, M.C., and W.H. Meckling (1976). 'Theory of the Firm: Managerial Behavior, Agency Costs and Ownership Structure', *Journal of Financial Economics*, 3(4): 305–60.

Mandel, A., and R. Noyes (2020). 'The Role of Entrepreneurship in Socio-Economic Transformation', *Journal of Global Business Research*, 8(1): 58–72.

Nigerian Entrepreneurship Program (2021). *Empowering Youth Through Entrepreneurship in Nigeria: A Policy Perspective*. Abuja: NEP Publications.

Nwankwo, F. (2021). 'Youth Economic Inclusion: Perspectives from Nigerian Military Barracks', *Journal of Economic Development in Africa*, 20(2): 155–69.

Okoye, I. (2021). 'Understanding the Challenges of Barrack Youth: Economic Empowerment and Community Support', *Nigerian Journal of Social Issues*, 29(1): 134–50.

Onyema, U. (2020). 'Barriers to Youth Entrepreneurship in Nigeria: A Socio-Economic Analysis', *Journal of Development Economics*, 23(3): 145–67.

Smith, L. (2019). 'Entrepreneurship as a Pathway to Economic Independence for Marginalized Communities', *Social Enterprise Journal*, 10(2): 111–23.

United Nations Development Programme (UNDP) (2021). *Supporting Youth Entrepreneurship in Africa: An Impact Assessment*. New York: UNDP Publications.

11

Military Family Lifestyle, Military Spouse Career Progression and Readiness: A Nigerian Perspective

Etham Bwalasom Mijah

The Nigerian military, like most others in the world, has traditionally focused on training, discipline, equipping, doctrine, etc., to achieve the objectives of national defence and security. Very little or no attention is paid to military families, their lifestyle, spouses' careers and career progression as they affect readiness. This chapter examines how military family lifestyle affects military spouse career progression, and also how that can contribute to the state of readiness of the Nigerian armed forces to counter and defeat present and future threats to Nigeria's national security. It relies on secondary data from previous research and published works, but also benefits from discussion and interaction with military families in Kaduna, mainly those who have experienced the problem under discussion. It argues that military spouses, by their affiliation with the military, do face adverse challenges of family and work. It finds that at work, the career progression of military spouses is stunted. Therefore, the military should do all within its power to protect career spouses seeking to secure and retain jobs within the context of the demands of the military profession.

As the complexities of modern society and the growing threat to security in Nigeria increase, one of the top concerns of the national military establishment has been increasing the readiness of the armed forces to effectively counter and contain the threats to national security. The traditional approach in most instances has been with matters of training, discipline, equipping, doctrine, etc. Very little or no attention is paid to military families and the lifestyle which their affiliation with the military has engendered for them on the one hand, and how that, in turn, impacts military readiness on the other hand. Changes in family structure and the roles members have come to play in it have caused spouses of military officers to take up employment in the formal sector. This brings relief to the military family and the active service officer in several ways, including financial savings for post-service life. However, military spouses, by virtue of their affiliation with the military, face extra career challenges occasioned by, for instance, frequent short-duration postings, imposed family separation, disruption in educational and training pursuits, truncated career progression, etc. These all have a socio-psychological and economic impact on the morale of the active service officer, thereby adversely affecting readiness.

This chapter attempts to examine how military family lifestyle affects military spouse career progression, and also how that can contribute to the state of readiness of the Nigerian armed forces to counter and defeat present and future threats to Nigeria's national security. On the part of serving military officers, the employment that military spouses gain and the income accrued from it go a long way to affect their effectiveness on the job, the lifestyle of their families and other experiences during periods soon after retirement. By taking a significant part of the financial and other responsibilities of their spouse from the income they earn from employment, military spouses allow their active service spouses to work with a less crowded mind, thereby allowing them the rightful state of mind to focus and perform optimally on their job as members of the armed forces. This goes a long way in affecting morale and, by extension, the state of readiness of the armed forces. The overarching objective of this study is to contribute to the development of readiness in the Armed Forces of Nigeria (AFN) by leveraging and mainstreaming the capacities of military spouses, most of whom are women.

Despite the intrinsic value of this theme to national security and gender mainstreaming, the issue has received little or no scholarly or policy attention in Nigeria. What receives attention now, albeit scantily, is the issue of transforming the gender combat character of the AFN. Researching military spouses and the impact they make on the state of readiness in Nigeria is a compelling issue, and their contribution to the existing body of knowledge on the broad issue area will be significant.

As members of the AFN dedicate themselves to the service of the nation, they also preoccupy themselves with matters of the family during and especially after active service. Both concerns need to be balanced if the security needs of the nation are to be served without compromising those of the family, which lies at the heart of national security as well. For instance, a steady and predictable stream of income from a military spouse could offer substantial relief to the serving officer on such matters as rent, school fees, medical bills and even a successful retirement plan. This allows serving personnel to perform optimally on the job. However, there is a glaring neglect of the family variable in scholarly and policy discourses on national security calculations in Nigeria. This scenario reveals a wide gap in our knowledge of national security. The need to fill such a gap is in itself compelling and inevitable. This contribution is a modest attempt at that.

There is a mutually reinforcing connection between military spouse, their career progress and the readiness of the AFN to defend Nigeria's national security. In other words, the family lifestyle engendered by the dictates and demands of the military profession affects the effective performance of the AFN.

A typical *family lifestyle* of members of the armed forces is characterized by relatively frequent moves owing to postings, prolonged family separations, disrupted children's education, spouse's career disruption, etc. These, especially frequent spouse career disruptions, add to the burden of the responsibilities the serving military officer shoulders. A disrupted career affects the stream of income the military spouse could contribute to family upkeep and even long-term plans, such as owning a house.

Military readiness is not all about military hardware, organization, command and control efficiency, etc. What determines the effectiveness and ultimately the readiness of the national armed forces is also determined by the state of mind of officers and men (Barnett 2004: 34–7). The heavy burden of family responsibility in the face of limited capacity to meet such responsibilities can weigh on the morale of even the best armed forces, thereby adversely affecting readiness to defend national security. Indeed, the nature of military service, military family lifestyle and military readiness are mutually reinforcing notions that need to be better appreciated in their connectedness.

Although there has been growing interest in gendering the armed forces the world over (see Moskos, Williams and Segal, 2000: 43–7), a preponderance of such interest is devoted to questioning the male-gendered perception of the combat roles of the armed forces. Indeed, in the African context, this is largely a novel area of research as there are only scant, non-scholarly writings on the subject matter. For instance, not even a chapter was devoted to military families in a 41-chapter edited work on the defence policy of Nigeria, by Bassey and Dokubor (2011). Only recently has the theme of women in the armed forces elicited scholarly interest. For instance, Dogo is currently researching the role of women in the regular officer corps of the AFN. On a related plank, Ugwukah and Adam (2023) researched the impact of international peace-keeping engagements on military families in Nigeria. Although the prolonged absence of the military spouse is a recurring theme in the research, its core focus is quite different from the focus of this engagement. What is pertinent to state about these modest efforts is that none of them interrogate the social, economic and security dimensions of military family lifestyle and how that conjuncture affects readiness.

This chapter is structured in five parts. The preceding pages constitute section one. In the next section, we discuss the military family and its place in the career of active service military officers. This is followed by an overview of the trend, character and contributions of the military spouse career, its progression and the challenges it faces owing to the peculiarities of the military family lifestyle. In section four, we engage the interplay between military family lifestyle, military spouse career progression and how these two variables affect the state of readiness of the AFN. The work is concluded with actionable and attainable policy recommendations.

Military Family and Military Family Lifestyle

Conceptualizing the notion of 'family' has been the subject of an age-old debate. The difficulty associated with the subject is compounded by the shifts in the patterns of the distribution of opportunities and material resources between male and female categories in society, especially in this part of the world. Thus, other than the composition of the family as male (husband and often traditionally conceived as head of the family), female (wife/wives and mother(s) of children of the union), children and other direct dependents of the family, a more nuanced conception of the notion defines family along gendered relations in the unit. Whose role contributes more material resources that supply the material and other needs of the unit? It is along this pattern that a hierarchy emerges, which almost automatically confers headship and more powers on the man as head of the family.

Demographic changes in the composition of the AFN, where there has been a growing female population, in both officer and other rank corps and the increasing entry into the services of young single men and women, the highly plural and equally varied social and cultural backgrounds of the members of the AFN, among other factors have come to compound the challenges of defining the military family. As we noted elsewhere (Mijah, 2007: 73–5; Strachan and Scheipers, 2011), the increasing pace and complexities of the changing character of war will continue to bear on the conception of the military family or the peculiar challenges confronting it. Notwithstanding, Cozza and Lerner (2013: 6) submit that a military family could be defined as 'the spouses and dependent children (aged 22 and younger) of men and women on active duty'. This definition gives a good image of what a military family could be, but it is made weak by its cultural specificity. For instance, it does not reflect the social, cultural and other varied nature of Nigerian society, as reflected in the composition of the AFN and the impacts of those factors on the perception of the family. For this study, a military family is defined loosely as the spouse, children and other persons living with the family under some ties or bond they share with the family. This definition attempts to reflect the broad perception of the notion of family in the wider Nigerian and other African contexts. Given the predominantly androgenic character of the military the world over (Kelty and Segal, 2007), particularly here in Nigeria, the military spouse is to an equal extent feminine. Military spouses are up to 92 per cent women.

While the lifestyle of families is typically characterized by some measure of liberty in a more inclusive community, a typical military family lifestyle is not. By their affiliation and or association with the military, military families are exposed to other conditions that place certain demands (often strenuous) on them. Within the context of such peculiarities, military families have, over time, come to display a pattern or style of living that is almost exclusive to the military. Military family lifestyle can be referred to as a regimented life that places on its members and their families unique and extremely intense demands, including frequent deployment, separation and eventual reunions, relocations, risk of injury or death, changing work schedules, isolation from civilian society and an overarching culture that is still heavily masculine (e.g. valuing hierarchy, dominance, power and control of emotions). These demands significantly disrupt family life (Huffman et al., 2001). The realities, combined with isolation from traditional sources of support, such as extended families, close friends and stable community relationships (Black, 1993; Chandler, 1989), are associated with personal and interpersonal stress for some military families.

The lifestyle of the military family can be said to be characterized by uncertainty – uncertainty over issues such as when the next move may come, living together as a family, the quality of education the children may receive or even the possibility of completing an educational programme by the female spouse before the next move. Indeed, the lifestyle of the military family is characterized by the more imminent uncertainty of life, as deployment to a theatre of war could make all the difference between life and death for the active service spouse. Add to this the tendency of the family budget to get slimmer as the size of the family enlarges. Often, this, coupled with other valid reasons such as the desire to impact society, has been a major driver of military spouses to seek formal employment in the formal sectors of society, whether in the private or public sector. It is important to state at this point that the attitude of military spouses to finding formal employment is not homogeneous. Three broad typologies have been identified in this regard. The first category is the spouses who are not employed and do not desire to have a job. To these spouses, family is the top and only priority. Such spouses move with their active service partner with relative ease. A second category is those who are not employed but are seeking employment. This category thinks that work is necessary. The third category is that of those who are working and are still working hard to keep the job! For those in this category, both work and family are important. This study focuses on those who are not working but are looking to be employed, and especially those who are working and working hard to keep their jobs. Because these categories of military spouses attach great importance to the family, they opine that getting a job is good for the family and that they are ready to contribute to the well-being of the family in both the short and long run. Further, it should be noted that for the good of the family, some spouses take to self-employment in such urban agriculture as fish farming, poultry, hair and beauty salons, etc. These job forms allow for work flexibility and the convenience of moving the family as the need arises.

Military Lifestyle and the Career Prospects of Military Spouses

Military spouse employment is important not only to the family but to the military institution itself. It is important to state, for instance, that the pay cheque of the military officer may not be sufficient to conveniently meet the present and future needs of the family. Thus, when military spouses take on paid employment, they supplement the income of the officer by taking care of some basic financial commitments of the family, such as general family upkeep, especially when families are separated by posting or active-duty deployment. In other words, in the absence of the male spouse serving officer, employed spouses contribute significantly to meeting short-term family financial commitments. In some instances, the stream of income from the earnings of the spouse contributes directly to long-term family plans for owning their own house, meeting the educational needs of children post-service and in the transition to civil life.

A cursory look at the pattern of the career of military spouses in Nigeria, particularly among spouses of those in the officer corps, shows that they are mostly literate, to varying extents. Up to 50 per cent of military spouses are said to have attained tertiary education, with another significant number of them in school. Similarly, most of the military spouses in paid employment are employed in military organizations. This trend reflects the growing ratio of civilians to the military in military organizations (Kelty and Segal, 2007). The nature of employment they take up, where they find it, may not be flexible enough to accommodate the frequent short-duration moves occasioned by short-duration postings. Thus, in a lot of instances, military spouses have had to abandon paid employment or move with the family on posting. Failing that, especially considering the contributions the added income from the job makes, some stay back while the active-duty spouse moves on.

Still, even where military spouses stay at a location for a lot of reasons, including the need to keep their jobs, children's education, etc., the progression of military spouses, like that of other women in the larger society, is often stunted due to several factors. For instance, military spouses sampled in military establishments in the Kaduna metropolis revealed that in most instances, their career progression stops because in such military organizations, only serving military officers are statutorily recognized in some positions. For instance, in the Nigerian Defence Academy, the post of Academic Registrar is statutorily the position of a top-ranking Army officer. As a result, military spouses (and their male civilian counterparts also) get to certain positions beyond which they cannot rise – the proverbial glass ceiling.

In another vein, even as military spouses seek to up-scale skills to enhance their upward career mobility through the acquisition of education, often higher education, frequent short-duration moves on posting truncate such efforts, as spouses have had to abandon their educational pursuits to move with the family. As higher educational qualifications and the prospects of enhanced career prospects become or continue to be a mirage, so also does making appreciable progress on the job elude the military spouse. The opportunity cost of that is family separation, with all the possible attendant consequences.

In the desperation to simply get a job and earn a little income before the next move, or as a result of the growing competition in the labour market, military spouses hardly get professional counselling on determining and making a successful career. Thus, spouses take on jobs, the nature of which can hardly, if ever, be reconciled to the realities of military family lifestyle. In such instances, too, military spouses are torn between keeping the family together and making a successful career. The lack of professional counselling or access to one in military establishments, especially as it affects spouses, is a major bane of the career progression of military spouses, despite their valuable contributions to the effectiveness of the active-duty spouse.

Women face certain peculiar challenges in making a successful career in Nigerian society. According to Ackers (2014), 'women were more likely to defer to their partners' career interests, when couples were faced with an international move, whereas men in a similar situation were less likely to do this even when the women's job attracted higher pay'. Women spouses of military officers are in a more challenging context. The challenges they face in choosing and making a career are multiplied by their affiliation with the military. Needless to add, this has immense strategic implications for the state of readiness in the AFN. It is to a discussion of this that we now turn our attention.

Military Family Lifestyle, Military Spouse Career Progression and Readiness in the AFN

There is no doubt that technology plays a determining role in the life of society, especially in the defence sphere of national life. However, just as technology, the human side of the defence enterprise is another core determinant in national defence calculations. The most fungible element in national power determination is the human factor. This factor is often at its optimal best when it is not crowded by worries beyond what it can handle. We are more focused and are also at our best when we have little or no strong feelings of vulnerability. In other words, when our core personal interests and needs are met, we perform better than when we have strong, outstanding core needs. This is one of the factors that makes welfare a central notion in the development of morale in the armed forces. At times, adverse family conditions, for example, basic needs such as shelter and the payment of rent, health care, education (especially children's education) and the uncertainty of what life may be like after a career in the military, could be issues of serious concern that could weigh down the morale of the best soldier or officer. Thus, other than the formal social safety nets such as the post-service housing scheme, Nigerian Army Welfare Insurance Scheme (NAWIS), etc., the stream of income that the spouses of active service officers contribute to keeping the family is always a major contributory factor to the state of mind of the serving spouse.

By being career persons, military spouses make significant sacrifices by picking up some bills, such as minor hospital bills, fixing and keeping the car on the road while the serving spouse is on deployment, far from where the family may be. In the long run, spouses' contribution to transition plans when the family begins to plan for a house of their own, how to generate and sustain a stream of income that could pay school fees of children who may still be in school after the serving spouse might have retired, etc. The contributions which military spouses make help relieve the serving spouse of some of the stress factors that could depress them, thereby allowing the serving spouse to remain focused and committed to the military job.

The financial contributions which military spouses make help develop confidence and integrity in the serving officer. The relief which officers get from the contributions by their spouses helps draw a line between public and private resources. Where pressing and recurring family needs are conveniently met, the temptation to dip one's own hands into public resources in order to supplement their income to meet family and other private personal needs will be diminished. That leaves resources at the disposal of the military authorities for core military duties and the attainment of professionalism. At least in principle, this helps reduce the tendency for corrupt practices in the AFN and could engender more prudence in the use of public resources by the AFN. The often-imposed family separation due to frequent short-duration postings, averaging three years, or due to deployment to a theatre of war has evolved among most military families into a coping mechanism hinged on accepted separation as the way out (Van Vranken et al., 1984). In situations such as this, the spouse, together with the children, remains sedentary at a particular location in the country, while the active service member of the family moves around the country, or even goes overseas alone on posting or deployment. Such accepted separation affects the upbringing of the children who have to grow up without the impact of a father figure to guide or reprimand them when they err. This, in the long run, affects the character development of the military child (Weins and Boss, 2006: 167–8).

The roles which career military spouses play in national defence and security, and the readiness of national armed forces, include their roles as caregivers, especially to officers on rotation from the theatre of active combat duty. In such conditions, the military spouse, in addition to working to supplement the supply to the family, often has to cope with the challenge of monitoring the returnee for any possible abnormal behaviour, such as being violent. Also, military spouses help monitor early signs and symptoms of post-traumatic stress disorder (PTSD). Often, they alert other officers in their neighbourhood to the need for their returnee spouse for close medical attention. This reduces the number or frequency of advanced PTSD cases among the officer corps of the military. By doing this, they help keep the number of active-duty officers up, especially in periods of insurgency when officers to prosecute the war may not be sufficient. According to informed military hospital sources in Kaduna, the role which military spouses play in the management of PTSD is of immense strategic importance to national defence and security because they help keep the number of trained officers high as posted.

A large number of military spouses work in military establishments. In Kaduna alone, for instance, military spouses account for 35–50 per cent of women employed in organizations such as the Defence Industry Corporation of Nigeria (DICON), the Nigerian Defence Academy (NDA), 1 Division Headquarters, etc. This means that by working directly for, or with, the military, military spouses contribute (no matter how insignificant their contributions are) to the overall organizational processes that create the necessary and sufficient atmosphere for thinking through the security challenges confronting the country. Despite the challenges of the military family lifestyle and of building a career, and also the psycho-social and mental stress that military spouses deployed to active combat theatre, and the associated costs and uncertainty regarding the future of the military family, there is still a military community populated by the corps with children, and their mothers and other dependents. By helping to keep the military family and the larger community in place (though not without a few fractured or broken families), military spouses contribute in great measure to the morale of the active service spouse at all times. Officers told us they are often encouraged and do perform better in the knowledge of the fact that their families are well, and their welfare needs are adequately met. This too counts for those spouses who often make personal and other career-related sacrifices to keep the family intact. By working to maintain the very foundation upon which the larger society rests and draws its dynamics, military spouses contribute to the provision of the necessary and sufficient conditions for the development of the defence and security apparatuses of Nigeria.

Conclusion

This chapter attempted to detail the impact of military family lifestyle on the career progression of military spouses on one hand, and how that affects the readiness of the AFN. It argued that military spouses, by virtue of their affiliation to the military, do face adverse challenges of family and work. It found that at work, the career progression of military spouses is stunted. The chapter also argued that how military spouses cope with these challenges goes a long way to affect the state of mind of their active service spouses, thereby affecting the state of their readiness for the defence of national security.

Although empirical data supporting our thesis is not commonly available, we found irrefutable evidence through formal and informal interaction with military families of the rare coping capacity which military spouses deploy to the challenges they face as key to the survival of individual and collective military families. Thus, by working to protect and provide for the needs of military families, military spouses contribute immensely to the strengthening of the foundation of society. Thus, we conclude that military spouses do play great and significant roles in the national defence and security permutations of Nigeria.

References

Ackers, P. (2014). 'Rethinking the Employment Relationship: A Neo-Pluralist Critique of British Industrial Relations Orthodoxy', *The International Journal of Human Resource Management*, 25(18): 2608–25. Available at: https://doi.org/10.1080/09585192.2012.667429

Barnett, P.M.T. (2004). *The Pentagon's New Map: War and Peace in the Twenty First Century*. New York: Penguin.

Bassey, C.O., and Q.D. Charles (eds) (2011). *Defence Policy of Nigeria: Capability and Context-A Reader*. Bloomington: Author House.

Bassey, E.B., and S.D. Dokubor (2011). 'Nigeria's Defence Policy: An Analysis', in N.N.O. Nwosu (ed.), *The Politics and Defense of Nigeria*, 123–64. Lagos: Nigerian Press Ltd.

Black, W. (1993). 'Military-Induced Family Separation: A Stress Reduction Intervention', *Social Work*, 38(3): 258–65.

Chandler, J. (1989). 'Marriage and the Housing Careers of Naval Wives', *Sociological Review*, 37: 253–76.

Cozza, S.J., and R.M. Lerner (2013). 'Military Children and Families: Introducing the Issues', *Future of Children*, 23(2): 1–19.

Huffman, A.H., S.C. Payne, L.M. Koehly, S.S. Culbertson and C.A. Castro (2014). 'Examining Time Demands and Work–Family Conflict on Psychological Distress', *Military Behavioral Health*, 2(1): 26–32. Available at: https://doi.org/10.1080/21635781.2013.844662

Kelty, R., and D.R. Segal (2007). 'The Civilianization of the US Military: Army and Navy Case Studies of the Effects of Civilian Integration on Military Personnel', in T. Jäger and G. Kümmel (eds), *Private Military and Security Companies*, 123–45: VS Verlag für Sozialwissenschaften. Available at: https://doi.org/10.1007/978-3-531-90313-2_14

Mijah, E. (2007). 'Democracy, Internal Security and the Challenges of Policing in Nigeria', paper presented at the Loccum International Conference, Germany, 15–17 June.

Mijah, B.E. (2017). 'The Nature of the Armed Forces, Conflict and Insecurity After the Cold War', in A.M. Ashafa and H. Jibrin (eds), *The Nigerian Army in a Democracy Since 1999: Essays in Honour of General Tukur Yusuf Buratai*, 45–68. Abuja: Directorate of Army Standards and Evaluation.

Moskos, C.C., J.A. Williams and D. Segal (eds) (2000). *The Postmodern Military*. New York: Oxford University Press.

Strachan, H., and S. Scheipers (2011). 'The Changing Character of War', in S. Baylis, S. Smith and P. Owens (eds), *The Globalization of World Politics* (5th ed.). Oxford: Oxford University Press, 1–25.

Ugwukah, A., and E. Adam (2023). 'Nigeria's Military Forces in Peace-Keeping Efforts in Africa and Beyond: An Impact Analysis', *International Affairs and Global Strategy*, 100: 18–29. Available at: https://doi.org/10.7176/IAGS/100-04.

Van Vranken, E., L. Jellen, K. Knudson, D. Marlowe and M. Segal (1984). *The Impact of Deployment Separation on Army Families*'. Washington, DC: Walter Reed Army Institute of Research.

Weins, T.W., and P. Boss (2006). 'Maintaining Family Resiliency Before, During, and After Military Separation', in C.A. Castro, A.B. Adler and C.A. Britt (eds), *Military Life: The Psychology of Serving in Peace and Combat*, 13–38. Bridgeport, CT: Praeger Security International.

Part V

Education and Finance Matters

12

Veteran Entrepreneurship Training in Nigeria: A Review and Future Research Directions

Sanya Ojo and Osogu Nweji Ebe Collins

This chapter provides a review of veteran entrepreneurship as well as entrepreneurship training, job creation and veteran empowerment in the Nigerian military through the lens of the Nigerian Armed Forces Resettlement Centre (NAFRC). From inception, NAFRC was charged with the responsibility of training entrepreneurial skills relevant to the resettlement needs of ex-servicemen (veterans). Military pre-retirement entrepreneurship training equips personnel with business skills and knowledge to facilitate a smooth transition into civilian life and potentially establish viable post-service careers. The Nigerian Army, like other employers of labour, owes soldiers the duty to ensure that they are adequately prepared and equipped for post-retirement life by exposing them to new skills through entrepreneurship training long before they finally take their exit from the service. In this regard, the Nigerian military has shown a growing interest in interventions that promote entrepreneurial success among veterans by making significant investments in entrepreneurial training (Tar and Wapmuk, 2021). As more military personnel return to civilian life, the likelihood that these veterans will pursue entrepreneurship increases. Ensuring that entrepreneurship training provides veterans with the needed skills to launch a successful business is critical (Kerrick et al., 2014).

The impact of entrepreneurial activities and the creation of new businesses on the economic growth of a country and the generation of jobs are recognized worldwide (Sánchez, 2012). Today, entrepreneurship is associated with economic growth, social development and innovation, and its positive impact is beyond question (Wennekers and Thurik, 1999; Murphy et al., 1996). Some studies (e.g. Olokundun et al., 2014; Ojo, 2021) have surmised that entrepreneurship competence is relevant for all areas of working and business life, in both new and established activities and enterprises. Studies have established positive correlations not only between entrepreneurial activity and innovation, but also between entrepreneurship and job creation. Whereas entrepreneurship is deemed to be an efficient tool to fight socio-economic difficulties such as poverty and inequality, researchers recognized that entrepreneurs from marginalized groups (such as veterans) often lack access to resources, capabilities and ecosystems to tackle them. In their review, Chang and Xu (2023) draw attention to the constraints of entrepreneurship among persons at the bottom of the pyramid (BOP).

Trained entrepreneurship offers potential rewards for people across the gamut of socio-economic space, including vulnerable people and workers in the informal sector, for whom it provides potentially more stable income flows, increased profits and more secure employment. The failure of small businesses has been linked to the absence of entrepreneurship training during the initial stages of the establishment (Al-Awlaqi et al., 2021). Veterans have greater capacities to perceive opportunities and a greater perception of fear of failure. The spur of entrepreneurial programmes for veterans enhances self-employment. Sometimes, this entrepreneurial force to start a business is linked to barriers such as lack of technical knowledge, experience and culture or financial infrastructure (Crecente et al., 2021).

Two key questions are of interest in this chapter: First, to what extent do the pre-retirement entrepreneurship and vocational training at NAFRC impact the entrepreneurial knowledge and skills of the veterans in Nigeria? Second is how well is the NAFRC equipped to provide value to veterans in their training programme? The rest of the chapter is arranged into five sections: First is the conceptual background, the second section describes the contextual setting, the third section explains the methodology, the fourth section presents the analysis and discussion and the final section offers the conclusion and recommendations.

Conceptual Background

Entrepreneurship Training

These days, entrepreneurship educators view entrepreneurship as a valid concept in all human activities, not just in business (Gibb, 1993; Kirby, 2004). Accordingly, entrepreneurship is defined broadly, including enterprising behaviours, even outside the business context. But the key question remains: can entrepreneurship be taught? According to some authors (e.g. Low, 2001; Woollard et al., 2007), entrepreneurship can certainly be taught and learned though its success depends on internal (individual) and external (contextual) factors (Davidsson, 2003) and should also be related to the development of entrepreneurial behaviour (Fayolle, 2007; Fayolle and Gailly, 2015; O'Connor, 2012). In this sense, an enterprising person may not necessarily be an entrepreneur, and his/her skills and characteristics may be exercised in different contexts (e.g. in a social context as a family or local community) instead of in the market. The academic training aspect of entrepreneurship is important to expose trainees/students to new ideas and trends in management and business in the process of obtaining entrepreneurship knowledge. In the fast-changing competitive environment, it is no longer enough to know how to perform a specific activity. The ability to create new knowledge is also of crucial importance.

The aims and objectives of entrepreneurship training have been ventilated by several authors. For example, Brown (2011) submits that entrepreneurship training is designed to equip individuals with the ability to generate ideas, start a business venture and establish a sustainable enterprise. Kulmie et al. (2023) assert that entrepreneurship training also involves personal development and enterprise development. Ultimately, entrepreneurship training aims to enrich individuals' attitudes, values, motivations, abilities, and knowledge in the field (Mwasalwiba, 2010). Nevertheless, it should be admitted that the specific objectives may vary depending on factors such as target audience, duration of the programme, resource availability, and perceived effectiveness (Azim, 2013). Essentially, entrepreneurship training and education enhance an entrepreneur's absorptive capacity, thereby further influencing the capability to acquire and create new knowledge and enabling the entrepreneur to better articulate and structure the knowledge-transfer process. In their study, Al-Awlaqi et al. (2021) found that entrepreneurship training has a positive causal effect on entrepreneurial orientation, on innovativeness, on risk-taking and on proactiveness. The theoretical knowledge in entrepreneurship education/training should emphasize skills like critical thinking, creativity, communication, user orientation and teamwork, as well as using domain-specific and linguistic knowledge.

Furthermore, the impact of entrepreneurship training on entrepreneurial intention and how it would help to create the desire to start new businesses has been studied (e.g. Adekiya and Ibrahim, 2016; Afolabi et al., 2017; Elert et al., 2015; Feder and Niţu-Antonie, 2017). Entrepreneurial intention was interpreted in the literature as the desire of individuals to start new businesses and to become self-employed. Entrepreneurial intention consists of six dimensions: Locus of control, need for achievement, the propensity to risk, self-confidence, innovativeness, and tolerance to ambiguity (do Paço et al., 2015). Thus, entrepreneurial intention could be seen as the trigger for starting new businesses. Similarly, entrepreneurship training also has an impact on entrepreneurial orientation, which is a firm-level strategy that consists of three dimensions: Risk-taking, innovativeness, and proactiveness (Bhuian et al., 2012; Morgan et al., 2014). Al-Awlaqi et al. (2021) advocate that entrepreneurial orientation is better measured as a multidimensional construct. As a business strategy, entrepreneurial orientation helps entrepreneurs to be innovative, take the lead in exploring new opportunities and markets and deal with risk differently (Rauch et al., 2007). Hence, entrepreneurial orientation could facilitate business growth and better performance (Buli, 2017; Rezaei and Ortt, 2018). Altogether, entrepreneurial intention should help entrepreneurs to start businesses, while entrepreneurial orientation will help entrepreneurs to continue running their businesses with an entrepreneurial mindset.

Nevertheless, there are several approaches to training/teaching entrepreneurship, as various researchers recommend varied methods in giving entrepreneurial knowledge and skills to trainees/students (Fiet, 2000a; Fiet, 2000b). Some of these approaches extended from conventional methods such as textbooks (Fiet, 2002), examinations (McMullan and Cahoon, 1979) to unconventional methods like a business plan (Audet, 2000), life histories of working entrepreneurs (McKenzie, 2005); guest lectures (Brown, 1999; Klandt and Volkmann, 2006), and field study or visits to business organizations (Cooper et al., 2004). Notwithstanding the differences in curriculum and delivery approaches, the ultimate aim of entrepreneurship training programmes is to kindle entrepreneurship cognizance among trainees/students to increase their interest in entrepreneurship. Taken together, the debate has moved beyond whether entrepreneurship can or should be taught to the focus on how to continuously improve entrepreneurship content and delivery to meet the needs of trainees/students (e.g. Gendron, 2004).

Veteran Entrepreneurship

Quite a lot of scholars (e.g. Maune, 2023; Mani, 2007; Ojo, 2021) argue that military service delivers specific competencies and capabilities that are transferable to entrepreneurship. Competencies such as duty, responsibility, loyalty, selfless service, honour, integrity and personal courage are considered the key components that account for success in entrepreneurship. Likewise, the military is known to possess enhanced problem-solving capacity, better ability to cope with physical difficulties and emotional tensions, enhanced independence, self-confidence and a greater willingness to take responsibility among its cadres (Ojo, 2021). Veterans are usually highly skilled, qualified and adaptable people, making them effective entrepreneurs who are reliable, ambitious, and able to adapt military resources to solve problems (e.g. job creation) in a civilian setting (Ojo and Fakokunde, 2021).

Veteran entrepreneurs, aside from providing jobs for themselves, create employment for others, thus giving back to the society they once served when in the military and are serving again as civilians (out of military service). Veterans are not immune to the challenges of entrepreneurship. Veteran entrepreneurship has certain particularities that underline its attributes, which distinguish it from 'civilian' entrepreneurship. Unarguably, veteran entrepreneurs bring some of the acquired military skills and experiences into their business enterprises, and these have both positive and negative impacts (Ojo, 2021). Military training supports veteran entrepreneurs in their enterprises, but the difference between the highly structured military environment and the less structured civilian environment creates challenges in organizing veteran entrepreneurship in some instances. According to Ojo (2021), the skill sets veterans obtained in the military promote veteran entrepreneurship, yet the same skill sets could also create an impediment for the unguarded veteran entrepreneur. Moreover, veterans could attain technical skills and leadership ability from their military service, but have little information about specific entrepreneurial tasks, such as developing a business plan (Cater and Young, 2020).

The military culture/identity can be argued to be largely an albatross to veteran entrepreneurship, particularly in terms of difficulties around the ability to adapt seamlessly into civil life. Furthermore, the Nigerian business environment could be very problematic for veteran entrepreneurship (like any other enterprise) to flourish due to factors including infrastructural deficit, unsupportive institutions and disalignment between military and civilian structures. Yet, the business environment has its redeeming features (e.g. large market space). Ojo (2017: 601) claimed that '… opportunities and challenges of entrepreneurship are often a function of the environment'.

Operating a business venture could be very challenging in most cases, and it is not surprising that many businesses that start up on a very promising note fail within a very limited time due to a number of reasons. According to Tar and Wapmuk (2021: 58), some of these reasons include:

> limited to poor conceptualization of the business; lack of business plan to guide operations of the business; lack of separation between personal and business account; poor records and accounts keeping; poor management; inadequate funding including working capital; lack of staff commitment and loyalty; lack of knowledge about the market and inability to deal with competitors; and poor customer services (Akinnawo, 2013).

Contextual Rearticulation

The Nigerian Armed Forces Resettlement Centre

The Nigerian Armed Forces Resettlement Centre (NAFRC), Lagos, is mandated to impart enterprise and entrepreneurship skills to able-bodied retiring military personnel who are about to leave active service. Originally, the Centre was founded by the British colonial authorities as the Vocational Resettlement Centre immediately after World War II but was later expanded to include the rehabilitation of disabled soldiers in 1972. A decade later, it became known as the NAFRC to reflect the change in its mandate, viz, from 'rehabilitation' to 'resettlement centre' for demobilized soldiers (Liman, 2019; Usman, 2019). NAFRC has trained over 45,000 personnel since its inception (Liman, 2019) and continues to enhance retiring officers' capacity to productively reintegrate into civil society upon retirement. The centre's mission is to constantly provide quality training, geared towards preparing Nigerian armed forces personnel to face the challenges of re-integrating into civil life.

As one of the agencies under the supervision of the Nigerian Defence Headquarters, the NAFRC is typically commanded by a serving Air Force Officer of Air Vice Marshall (AVM) rank. The centre has five directorates, including (a) administration, (b) training, (c) coordination, (d) logistics and (e) finance, all manned by directors. These directors, plus the commandant and deputy commandant, constitute the top hierarchy of the NAFRC. All workshops and management wings are under the directorate of training. Each wing/department has a military Commanding Officer (CO) and a civilian Head of Department (HOD) running it. The workshops are where trainees receive vocational skill instructions such as automobile, bakery, carpentry, electrical, photography, painting, welding, etc. The departments under the management wing comprise general management, security and safety, entrepreneurship, information technology, waste management and guidance and counselling. Trainees are required to select any vocational skill of their choice from the list of available resources; however, all trainees must attend the entrepreneurship class once a week. In the entrepreneurship class, trainees are taught basic entrepreneurial skills, including the process of starting up a business (e.g. business plan writing, bookkeeping, etc.), business fundraising, business laws and regulations, etc.

Typically, each batch of trainees is trained for a six-month period at the centre. There have been concerted efforts by past and present commandants of NAFRC to bring innovation into the structure of the centre. For instance, the initial mandate of training retiring non-commissioned officers is under review and mid-level and senior officers have started to benefit from entrepreneurship training and skill acquisition provided by the centre (Usman, 2018). Moreover, the training programme is restructured to allow mid-level and senior officer trainees to return to their various units after their training at NAFRC and start some agricultural business whilst still in service (Wada, 2020). Furthermore, NAFRC, in July 2020, started training personnel from the Police, Nigerian Customs Service (NCS), Correctional Services, Immigration, National Environment Management Authority (NEMA) and the Ministry of Finance, Defence, Foreign Affairs, among others (Usman, 2020). According to Wada (2020), the inclusion of other security agencies and civilians is designed to provide a useful forum for the exchange of ideas, networking, as well as improving civil-military relationships. Additionally, in response to the current security challenges (e.g. Boko Haram Terrorism) in Nigeria, NAFRC has expanded its 'training curriculum to accommodate a wide range of contemporary national security issues'. The training regime now includes 'acquisition of skills in intelligence gathering to counter insurgency operations' (Liman, 2019: 58). NAFRC also signed a Memorandum of Understanding (MOU) with the Yaba College of Technology, Lagos, to provide further training on security and enhance trainees' knowledge of the concept of security.

Trainees receive training in some management courses such as entrepreneurship and general studies, general management, security and safety practice, business plan and model, fundamentals of business laws and taxation, as well as human resource/supply chain management and Marketing. Vocational skills training includes shoemaking, barbing, tailoring, laundering and weaving workshops. There are also facilities for training in fine arts and printing, soap and cosmetics, agriculture, woodwork, building and civil works, electrical and electronics, automobile mechanics, fabrication and welding, music, information technology, and food and beverages (Usman, 2018). In addition, trainees undergo a one-month industrial attachment in organizations/firms relevant to their training programme. Consequently, NAFRC collaborates with external partners such as the Alliance Professional Resources Persons Limited, Empretech Nigeria Foundation, Enterprise Development Centre, Administrative Staff College, Yaba College of Technology, and the University of Lagos (Usman, 2018, 2019). Agriculture workshop/course often has the largest number of trainees signing up for it. This is as a result of the low capital input required to start an agriculture business compared to many other vocations that involve high investments in terms of finance, equipment and tools to set up. According to Ojo and Fakokunde (2021), the high enrolment of trainees in agriculture classes is due to the concession given to serving military personnel to engage in agriculture. Serving military personnel are barred from participating in any business venture besides soldiering.

The army trainees are usually the largest, most of the time, among the trainees in NAFRC, possibly due to being the largest in terms of numerical strength in the Nigerian military. For example, in the 2017 batch, the Army had 281, the Nigerian

Navy had 17, and the Nigerian Air Force had 105 (Usman, 2017). In 2018, the Nigerian Army had 262 personnel, the Nigerian Navy had 44, and the Nigerian Air Force had 14 retiring personnel (Usman, 2018). For Course 01/2020, 243 personnel were from the Nigerian Army, 100 from the Navy and 16 from the Nigerian Air Force (Usman, 2020). Yet, this is not always the case; for instance, at the Trainees Course 2/2011, out of a total number of 150 service personnel, 11 were from the Army, 17 from the Air Force and 122 from the Navy (Usman, 2011). NAFRC instructors/trainers are equally given training once a week (i.e. every Thursday of the week) to keep them abreast of contemporary issues that have to do with their specialization. Ojo and Fakokunde (2021) confirm that successive NAFRC commandants tried hard to outperform their predecessors in bringing innovation to the centre. For instance, Air Vice Marshall (AVM) Liman, in 2019, brought in a lot of progressive changes, including the establishment of a cattle ranch, launched an oven auto spraying workshop, inaugurated *Hope* magazine (NAFRC publication), and a series of road and building constructions (Yohana and Ugboaja, 2019). It was during AVM Lar's tenure that the government approved the expansion of the course to include non-military retirees from Ministries, Departments, and Agencies (MDAs).

Methodology

This chapter reviews published articles to examine the significance of entrepreneurship training within the context of military veterans' job creation and empowerment process. The chapter utilizes secondary data gathered from different sources, including journal articles, theses and books that are pertinent to the variables under investigation. Papers and books closely related to the field of study are selected and subsequently categorized by utilizing systematic review procedures to undertake a thorough and methodical analysis. Thereafter, the correlation between entrepreneurial training, job creation and veteran empowerment was explored. In other words, the chapter investigates the nature and characteristics of entrepreneurship education and training as veterans transition from military to civilian life in the Nigerian military through the analysis of the NAFRC's training programme gathered from published journal articles.

Analysis and Discussion

The review of the literature reveals the potency of the entrepreneurship training provided by the NAFRC, such that many veterans who were trained there received valuable training that helped their business ventures. This view is supported by Ojo and Fakokunde (2021: 243): '... NAFRC constantly improve on its service delivery and succeeding NAFRC Commandants have continued to introduce innovative ideas and projects to the Centre to enhance users' experience.' Tar and Wapmuk (2021: 60) also confirm in their assertion: 'The entrepreneurship trainings afford the individual military personnel valuable opportunities to acquire business skills and beneficiaries to adjust to post-retirement life.' The effectiveness of the NAFRC entrepreneurship training is also demonstrated in Yusuf and Minai's (2016: 226) statement: 'The findings show that a significant number of retiring military personnel have chosen the entrepreneurial career upon retirement… There are significant changes in terms of their intention and career paths opted as the result of attending the entrepreneurial and vocational training by the retiring military personnel.' This is in line with the literature that affirms that the provision of entrepreneurship education/training is believed to significantly enhance military veterans' entrepreneurship passion and their business awareness, which more likely leads to success in starting their own businesses (Kerrick et al., 2014; Yu et al., 2021).

However, Olawuyi and Nwude (2023: 510) on their part observe divided opinion among respondents (trainees) about the effectiveness of their training at the NAFRC, but most of their respondents do not see value in the training and the authors affirm that '… considerable gaps still exist in the ability of ex-participants to transform into successful entrepreneurs after retirement despite their training'. The first question relating to the extent to which the pre-retirement entrepreneurial and vocational trainings at NAFRC impact entrepreneurial knowledge and skills of the veterans in Nigeria is thus unravelled.

The second question about how well the NAFRC is equipped to provide value to veterans in their training programme is dissected as follows. Ojo and Fakokunde (2021) observe that the NAFRC lack the organizational capacity to check and appraise the outcomes of its programme. The authors believe that monitoring and evaluation (M&E) are needed to assess the training efficiency of NAFRC's entrepreneurship and skills training and suggest that M&E should be incorporated into the design of NAFRC's training curriculum to achieve better outcomes. Furthermore, Ojo and Fakokunde (2021) are of the view that the introduction of new initiatives at NAFRC is not often driven by trainees' interest but rather depends on the impulses of the commandants. The authors declare that 'successful ideas and innovations are customer-centric, that is, value creation or customer value has to be from the perspectives of the customers (in this case, the trainees)' (Ojo and Fakokunde, 2021: 238). The view is also expressed by other researchers that the NAFRC curriculum is not robust enough in terms of duration and method of delivery. For instance, Olawuyi and Nwude (2023) discovered that many of the trainees were not computer literate, and there was not enough time to learn sufficiently during the six-month course. The authors thus suggest that the NAFRC should extend the duration for better learning and practices. In addition, Olawuyi and Nwude (2023: 508) express the view that NAFRC does not have 'both the capacity (i.e. current ability in NAFRC) and capability (i.e. the level of the ability of the trainers)'.

Furthermore, although the data provide evidence that entrepreneurship training is significant for veterans during their transition. However, Ojo and Fakokunde (2021) claim that the process of M&E in NAFRC appears insubstantial, as the mechanisms for systematic collection of data for evaluation and monitoring are weak. The authors further assert that although the centre has a course telephone directory for each cohort group, it is undeniable that no coherent system of follow-up exists in the NAFRC. Ojo and Fakokunde

(2021) also proclaim that the trainees have no access to funding after the completion of their training at NAFRC and that the gratuity and emoluments paid at retirement are often not adequate to start a viable business at retirement. The authors thus recommend that a careful career counselling and guidance regime tailored to take account of veterans' needs and nuances must be established to enable resources to be optimally directed and maximize the benefits of NAFRC's entrepreneurial training programme.

Conclusion and Recommendations

The failure of small businesses has been attributed to commencing businesses without taking entrepreneurship training (Ladzani and Van Vuuren, 2002). The importance of entrepreneurship training for the Nigerian military veterans cannot be overstressed, as many scholars have established. Invariably, entrepreneurship training helps an individual to cultivate entrepreneurial skills, acquire knowledge associated with entrepreneurship, learn the process of becoming an entrepreneur, enhance the capacity to identify business opportunities, and start a business enterprise (Henry et al., 2005; Hytti and O'Gorman, 2004; Tittel and Terzidis, 2020).

Veteran entrepreneurship represents one exceptionally engaging and socially advantageous self-employment option for retired military personnel, but it is not a panacea for veteran development and in no way absolves policymakers from their broader responsibility to address the needs of retired military personnel comprehensively and sustainably. In essence, the success of veteran entrepreneurship rests on a robust entrepreneurial training schedule that is adequately monitored for its merits, opportunities and challenges. Veteran entrepreneurship training must also be supplemented by the application of commonly underpinning support measures (e.g. refresher courses, access to funding, etc.). In other words, customized entrepreneurship ecosystems must be formulated to help veteran entrepreneurs overcome challenges and make an impact in life after retirement from military service. Overall, entrepreneurial training plays an instrumental role in preparing members of the armed forces for self-reliance in the post-retirement era.

Recommendations

There is a need to expand the veteran entrepreneurship training ecosystem in Nigeria to include other capable and interested partners, such as non-governmental organizations (NGOs), higher institutions, etc. For instance, entrepreneurship training for the military in Europe and America is not conducted solely by military institutions. Local, national and regional entrepreneurship training institutions, private institutions and the business community are involved to ensure wide coverage of such training (Tar and Wapmuk, 2021). It is essential to encourage interaction with the business community and nurture frequent networking interactions.

Likewise, it is important to emphasize the need for greater interdisciplinary research focusing on military entrepreneurship training and veteran entrepreneurship to inform and expand theorizing and new policy development in supporting military veterans. Thus, the Nigerian military authorities should facilitate constant collaboration with universities and research institutes in researching various aspects of military entrepreneurship, including veteran entrepreneurship.

Monitoring and evaluation (M&E) are needed to assess the training efficiency of NAFRC's entrepreneurship and skills training. M&E should also inform the design and mix of NAFRC training policies by identifying those features that lead to desirable outcomes. In essence, evaluation is fundamental to NAFRC's accountability. Furthermore, it has been suggested that effective entrepreneurship education programmes for veterans will signal the success of veteran entrepreneurship policies and support the expansion of such initiatives to other transitioning groups (Tihic, 2024).

References

Adekiya, A.A., and F. Ibrahim (2016). 'Entrepreneurship Intention Among Students. The Antecedent Role of Culture and Entrepreneurship Training and Development', *International Journal of Management Education*, 14(2): 116–32.

Afolabi, M.O., F.A. Kareem, I.O. Okubanjo, O.A. Ogunbanjo and O.O. Aninkan (2017). 'Effect of Entrepreneurship Education on Self-Employment Initiatives Among Nigerian Science and Technology Students', *Journal of Education and Practice*, 8(15): 44–51.

Akinnawo, T. (2013). *Framework and Guidelines for Entrepreneurship Development as a Sustainable Employment Generation Strategy in Nigeria*. Lagos: African Consulting Professionals Ltd.

Al-Awlaqi, M.A., A.M. Aamer and N. Habtoor (2021). 'The Effect of Entrepreneurship Training on Entrepreneurial Orientation: Evidence from a Regression Discontinuity Design on Micro-Sized Businesses', *International Journal of Management Education*, 19(1): 100267. Available at: https://doi.org/10.1016/j.ijme.2018.11.003

Audet, J. (2000). 'Evaluation of Two Approaches to Entrepreneurial Education Using an Intention-Based Model of Venture Creation', *Academy of Entrepreneurship Journal*, 6(1): 58–63.

Azim, M.T. (2013). 'Entrepreneurship Training in Bangladesh: A Case Study on Small and Cottage Industries Training Institute', *Life Science Journal*, 10(12s): 188–201.

Bhuian, S., O. Richard and H. Shamma (2012). 'Entrepreneurial Orientation and Organisational Performance: The Role of Managerial Traits', *J. for International Business and Entrepreneurship Development*, 6: 203–23. Available at: https://doi.org/10.1504/JIBED.2012.049797.

Brown, C. (1999). 'Teaching New Dogs New Tricks: The Rise of Entrepreneurship Education in Graduate Schools of Business', *DIGEST*, 99(2): 1–4.

Brown, C.R. (2011). 'Illuminating the Black Box of an Entrepreneurship Education Program: The Case of the Enterprise & You Program.' PhD Thesis. Available at: https://pdfs.semanticscholar.org/cf96/457c694d2184e8b39ed2f01690639dce8b4b.pdf

Buli, B.M. (2017). 'Entrepreneurial Orientation, Market Orientation and Performance of SMEs in the Manufacturing Industry: Evidence from Ethiopian Enterprises', *Management Research Review*, 40(3): 292–309.

Buli, B.M., and W.M. Yesuf (2015). 'Determinants of Entrepreneurial Intentions: Technical-Vocational Education and Training Students in Ethiopia', *Education+Training*, 57 (8/9): 891–907. Available at: https://doi.org/10.1108/ET-10-2014-0129.

Cater, J., and M. Young (2020). 'U.S. Veterans as Emerging Entrepreneurs: Self-Efficacy, Intentions and Challenges', *Journal of Developmental Entrepreneurship*, 25(1): 2050012. Available at: https://doi.org/10.1142/S1084946720500120

Chang, A.Y., and Y. Xu (2023). 'Decoding Underperformance of Entrepreneurship at the Bottom of the Pyramid: A Literature Review of the Field', *New England Journal of Entrepreneurship*, 26(2): 88–106.

Cooper, S., C. Bottomley and J. Gordon (2004). 'Stepping Out of the Classroom and Up the Ladder of Learning: An Experiential Learning Approach to Entrepreneurship Education', *Industry & Higher Education*, 18(1): 11–22.

Crecente, F., M. Sarabia and M. Teresa Del Val (2021). 'The Hidden Link Between Entrepreneurship and Military Education', *Technological Forecasting and Social Change*: 163. Available at: https://doi.org/10.1016/j.techfore.2020.120429.

Davidsson, P. (2003). 'The Domain of Entrepreneurship Research: Some suggestions', in J. Katz and D. Shepherd (eds), *Advances in Entrepreneurship, Firm Emergence and Growth*, Vol. 6, 315–72. Oxford: Elsevier/JAI Press.

Do Paço, A., J. Ferreira M., M. Raposo, R.G. Rodrigues and A. Dinis (2015). 'Entrepreneurial Intentions: Is Education Enough?' *International Entrepreneurship and Management Journal*, 11(1): 57–75. Available at: https://doi.org/10.1007/s11365-013-0280-5

Elert, N., F.W. Andersson and K. Wennberg (2015). 'The Impact of Entrepreneurship Education in High School on Long-Term Entrepreneurial Performance', *Journal of Economic Behaviour & Organisation*, 111: 209–23.

Fayolle, A. (2007). *Handbook of Research in Entrepreneurship Education – A General Perspective*, Vol.1. Aldershot: Edward Elgar.

Fayolle, A., and B. Gailly (2015). 'The Impact of Entrepreneurship Education on Entrepreneurial Attitudes and Intention: Hysteresis and Persistence', *Journal of Small Business Management*, 53(1): 75–93. Available at: https://doi.org/10.1111/jsbm.12065

Feder, E.S., and R.D. Nitu-Antonie (2017). 'Connecting Gender Identity, Entrepreneurial Training, Role Models and Intentions', *International Journal of Gender and Entrepreneurship*, 9(1): 87–108.

Fiet, J.O. (2000a). 'The Theoretical Side of Teaching Entrepreneurship', *Journal of Business Venturing*, 16: 1–24.

Fiet, J.O. (2000b). 'The Pedagogical Side of Entrepreneurship Theory', *Journal of Business Venturing*, 16: 101–17.

Fiet, J.O. (2002). *The Systematic Search for Entrepreneurial Discoveries*. Westport, CN: Quorum.

Gendron, G. (2004). 'Practitioners' Perspectives on Entrepreneurship Education: An Interview with Steve Case, Matt Goldman, Tom Golisano, Geraldine Lay Bourne, Jeff Taylor and Alan Webber', *Academy of Management Learning and Teaching*, 3(3): 302–14.

Gibb, A.A. (1993). 'The Enterprise Culture and Education: Understanding Enterprise Education and Its Links with Small Business, Entrepreneurship and Wider Educational Goals', *International Small Business Journal*, 3: 11–34.

Henry, C., F. Hill and C. Leitch (2005). 'Entrepreneurship Education and Training: Can Entrepreneurship Be Taught?' *Education + Training*, 47: 98–111. Available at: https://doi.org/10.1108/00400910510586524.

Hytti, U., and C. O'Gorman (2004). 'What is "Enterprise Education"? An Analysis of the Objectives and Methods of Enterprise Education Programs in Four European Countries', *Education and Training*, 46(1): 11–23.

Kerrick, S.A., D. Cumberland, M. Church-Nally and B. Kemelgor (2014). 'Military Veterans Marching Towards Entrepreneurship: An Exploratory Mixed Methods Study', *International Journal of Management Education*, 12(3): 469–78.

Kirby, D.A. (2004). 'Entrepreneurship Education: Can Business Schools Meet the Challenge?' *Education+Training*, 46: 510–19.

Klandt, H., and C. Volkmann (2006). 'Development and Prospects of Academic Entrepreneurship Education in Germany', *Higher Education in Europe*, 31(2): 195–208. Available at: https://doi.org/10.1080/03797720600940880

Kulmie, D., H.M. Sheikh, M.B. Abdi, M. Abdulle and A. Ali (2023). 'Entrepreneurship Training, Job Creation and Youth Empowerment', *Asian Social Science*, 19: 111. Available at: https://doi.org/10.5539/ass.v19n6p111.

Ladzani, M., and J. Vuuren (2002). 'Entrepreneurship Training for Emerging SMEs in South Africa'. *Journal of Small Business Management*, 40: 154–61. Available at: https://doi.org/10.1111/1540-627X.00047.

Liman, A.S. (2019). 'From the Commandant's Desk', *Hope* (NAFRC Magazine. Publication of NAFRC), 1: 3.

Low, M. (2001). 'The Adolescence of Entrepreneurship Research: Specification of Purpose', *Entrepreneurship Theory and Practice*, 25(4): 17–26.

Mani, K. (2007). 'Militaries in Business: State-Making and Entrepreneurship in the Developing World', *Armed Forces & Society*, 33(4): 591–611.

Maune, A. (2023). 'Role of Military in the Entrepreneurial Ecosystem.' Newsday. Available at: https://www.newsday.co.zw/theindependent/opinion-analysis/article/200011603/role-of-military-in-the-entrepreneurial-ecosystem

McKenzie, B. (2005). 'Collecting Oral Histories for Entrepreneurship Research', *New England Journal of Entrepreneurship*, 8(1): Article 6. Available at: https://digitalcommons.sacredheart.edu/neje/vol8/iss1/6

McMullan, W.E., and A. Cahoon (1979). 'Integrating Abstract Conceptualising with Experiential Learning', *The Academy of Management Review*, 4(3): 453–8.

Morgan, T.R., A. Rapp, R. Glenn Richey Jr. and E. Ellinger (2014). 'A Marketing Culture to Service Climate: The Influence of Employee Control and Flexibility', *J. Serv. Mark.*, 28(6): 498–508.

Murphy, G.B., J.W. Trailer and R.C. Hill (1996). 'Measuring Performance in Entrepreneurship Research', *Journal of Business Research*, 36(1): 15–23. Available at: https://doi.org/10.1016/0148-2963(95)00159-X

Mwasalwiba, E.S. (2010). 'Entrepreneurship Education: A Review of Its Objectives, Teaching Methods, and Impact Indicators', *Education+training*, 52(1): 20–47. Available at: https://doi.org/10.1108/00400911011017663

O'Connor, A. (2012). 'A Conceptual Framework for Entrepreneurship Education Policy: Meeting Government and Economic Purposes', *Journal of Business Venturing*, 28(4): 546–63.

Ojo, S. (2017). 'Interrogating Returnee Entrepreneurship in the Nigerian Context', *Journal of Enterprising Communities: People and Places in the Global Economy*, 11(5): 590–608. Available at: https://doi.org/10.1108/JEC-07-2016-0025

Ojo, S. (2021). 'Investigating Entrepreneurship Among Nigerian Retired Military Veterans', in S. Ojo (ed.), *Global Perspectives on Military Entrepreneurship and Innovation*, 119–47. Hershey: IGI Global. Available at: https://doi.org/10.4018/978-1-7998-6655-8

Ojo, S., and M.O. Fakokunde (2021). 'Military Enterprise and Entrepreneurship: A Case Study of the Nigerian Armed Forces Resettlement Centre', in S. Ojo (ed.), *Global Perspectives on Military Entrepreneurship and Innovation*, 216–47. Hershey: IGI Global. Available at: https://doi.org/10.4018/978-1-7998-6655-8

Olawuyi, I.B., and C. Nwude (2023). 'Nigerian Armed Forces Resettlement Centre and the Preretirement Entrepreneurship Training of Veterans' Occupation', *International Journal of Institutional Leadership, Policy and Management*, 5(4): 491–514.

Olokundun, M., F. Hezekiah, I. Stephen and I. Fred (2014). 'An Assessment of the Taught Entrepreneurship Program in Nigerian Secondary Schools', *Merit Research Journal of Education and Review*, 2(11): 257–75.

Rauch, A., and M. Frese (2007). 'Born to Be an Entrepreneur? "Revisiting the Personality Approach to Entrepreneurship"', in J.R. Baum, M. Frese and R.A. Baron (eds), *The Psychology of Entrepreneurship*. The Organisational Frontiers Series, 41–65. Mahwah: Lawrence Erlbaum.

Rezaei, J., and R. Ortt (2018). 'Entrepreneurial Orientation and Firm Performance: The Mediating Role of Functional Performances', *Management Research Review*, 41(7): 878–900. Available at: https://doi.org/10.1108/MRR-03-2017-0092

Sánchez, J.C. (2012). 'Entrepreneurial Intentions: The Role of the Cognitive Variables', in T. Burger-Helmchen (ed.), *Entrepreneurship – Born, Made and Educated*, 27–50. Rijeka: InTech.

Tar, U., and S. Wapmuk (2021). 'Entrepreneurial Training for the Nigerian Armed Forces and Its Significance in Post-Retirement Era: Opportunities and Challenges for Self-Reliance', in S. Ojo (ed.), *Global Perspectives on Military Entrepreneurship and Innovation*, 45–66. Hershey: IGI Global. Available at: https://doi.org/10.4018/978-1-7998-6655-8

Tihic, M., A. Pritchard, A. McKelvie and R. Maury (2024). 'Entrepreneurship Education and its Role in Transitional Entrepreneurship as Veterans Transition from Military to Civilian Life', *Entrepreneurship Education and Pedagogy*, 8(3): 424–51. Available at: https://doi.org/10.1177/25151274241232357.

Tittel, A., and O. Terzidis (2020). 'Entrepreneurial Competences Revised: Developing a Consolidated and Categorized List of Entrepreneurial Competences', *Entrepreneurship Education*, 3: 1–35. Available at: https://doi.org/10.1007/s41959-019-00021-4.

Usman, E. (2011). 'Armed Forces Resettlement Centre Graduates 149 Retiring Servicemen.' Vanguard. Available at: https://www.vanguardngr.com/2011/12/armed-forcesresettlement-centre-graduates-149-retiring-servicemen/

Usman, E. (2017). 'NAFRC Trains 403 Retiring Soldiers.' Vanguard. Available at: https://www.vanguardngr.com/2017/12/nafrc-trains-403-retiring-soldiers/

Usman, E. (2018). 'Military Personnel Retire Says NAFRC Commandant.' Vanguard. Available at: https://www.vanguardngr.com/2018/06/320-military-personnel-retire-says-nafrccommandant/

Usman, E. (2019). '35 Middle Cadre Military Personnel Undergo Training on Entrepreneurship, Mgt.' Vanguard. Available at: https://www.vanguardngr.com/2019/01/35-middle-cadre-military-personnel-undergo-training-on-entrepreneurship-mgt/

Usman, E. (2020). '342 Military Officers Retire in June.' Vanguard. Available at: https://www.vanguardngr.com/2020/06/342-military-officers-retire-in-june

Wada, I. (2020). 'Senate Committee Lauds Lar for Judicious Use of NAFRC Funds.' *Guardian*. Available at: https://guardian.ng/news/senate-committee-lauds-lar-for-judicioususe-of-nafrc-funds/

Wennekers, A.R.M., and A.R. Thurik (1999). 'Linking Entrepreneurship and Economic Growth', *Small Business Economics*, 13: 27–55.

Woollard, D., M. Zhang and O. Jones (2007). 'Creating Entrepreneurial Universities: Insights from a New University Business School', *Institute for Small Business & Entrepreneurship*, 7–9: 1–20.

Yohana, C.I.D., and O. Ugboaja (2019). Cover Story. *Hope* (NAFRC Magazine. Publication of NAFRC), 1: 33.

Yu, H., Y. Gao, J. Liu and Q. Huang (2021). 'Prelude to Military Entrepreneurship in China: A Retrospective View', in S. Ojo (ed.), *Global Perspectives on Military Entrepreneurship and Innovation*, 80–99. Hershey: IGI Global. Available at: https://doi.org/10.4018/978-1-7998-6655-8

Yusuf, L., and M.S. Minai (2016). 'Entrepreneurial Training and Career Path of Retired Military Personnel as Entrepreneurs in Nigeria', *International Journal of Sciences, Basic and Applied Research*, 28(3): 217–30.

13

Impact of Monetary Policy on Entrepreneurial Financing in Nigeria

Alfa Yakubu

Entrepreneurship plays a critical role in driving economic growth, job creation and innovation in developing economies such as Nigeria. Access to finance remains one of the most significant challenges faced by entrepreneurs, with monetary policy exerting considerable influence on the cost and availability of credit. Understanding how monetary policy affects entrepreneurial financing is therefore essential for promoting enterprise development and sustaining inclusive economic growth.

This chapter examines the relationship between monetary policy and entrepreneurial financing in Nigeria over the period 1990–2023, using annual data obtained from the Central Bank of Nigeria's Statistical Bulletin (2024). The analysis is conducted within the framework of the autoregressive distributed lag (ARDL) model, which allows for the exploration of both short-run and long-run dynamics.

The chapter seeks to provide empirical evidence on whether key monetary policy instruments – such as lending rates, the monetary policy rate and broad money supply – facilitate or constrain entrepreneurial financing in Nigeria. By focusing on this relationship, the research contributes to ongoing debates on how monetary policy can be effectively aligned with the broader goal of promoting entrepreneurship and economic diversification in a developing country context.

The power to conduct monetary policy in a country is usually vested in the Central Bank of the country. Thus, the Central Bank of a country formulates monetary policies that could affect the business environment, economic agents and the overall economy. The policy is conducted by the bank through the Open Market Operations (OMOs) or deliberate change of interest rates and reserve requirements to achieve a set target. The OMOs involve the buying and selling of government securities to regulate liquidity in the economy. For example, during inflationary pressure characterized by excess liquidity in the economy, the Central Bank could sell government securities through the open market (Alfa, 2019). As buyers of the securities make payment to the government account, the amount of liquidity in the economy is gradually mopped up. This policy of the Central Bank, which is directed towards mopping up excess liquidity in the economy, is referred to as the contractionary monetary policy.

Also, monetary policy variables such as interest rate, reserve requirements and liquidity ratio could be reduced to stimulate the economy especially during recession or economic meltdown to stimulate the economy. For example, a lowering of interest rates could make borrowing cheaper and encourage investment and consumption in the economy (Alfa and Haladu, 2023). Similarly, when the Central Bank reduces the reserve requirements of commercial banks, it allows the banks to lend more and create more money in the economy. This policy of the Central Bank, which is directed towards injecting more money into the economy, is referred to as the expansionary monetary policy.

Monetary policy plays a vital role in shaping the economic environment for entrepreneurship. By entrepreneurship, it meant activities that involve the creation or extraction of economic value through innovative ideas, goods, services, or business models (Jackson and Madison, 2021). Entrepreneurial activities are fundamentally born out of innovative development of goods and services (Schumpeter, 1934). Progressively, the activities grow with ideas and innovations with consciously calculated risks and development of new business prospects (Ofili, 2014).

Entrepreneurial financing involves securing the necessary capital by an entrepreneur to start, operate and grow a new business venture. The business may start small, but over time, begin to grow alongside the entrepreneurs (the initiators of the business). The growth of the entrepreneur precipitates more experience for him/her, creates employment, increases investments, raises the standard of living, promotes effective and efficient functioning of the business, alleviates poverty, etc. (John and Ibenta, 2017).

The funding of entrepreneurs depends on the type of monetary policy adopted in a country. In other words, the monetary policy adopted by the monetary authorities determines how fast or slow the growth rate of entrepreneurs in that country is. If the policy is contractionary, the entrepreneurs will be starved of funds to run the business. This implies that the entrepreneurs will not have enough money to run the business, and the growth rate will be minimal (Damieibi and Hyginus, 2021). But if the policy is expansionary, then the entrepreneurs will have enough funds to run and grow their business. Expansionary policy of monetary authorities means that the monetary authorities will reduce their monetary policy rate (MPR); monetary authorities will also push out money into the economy through the purchase of Treasury bills and OMOs, reducing their liquidity ratio and increasing the loan-to-deposit ratio.

One of the core goals of monetary policy is to promote sustainable economic growth and full employment. Thus, by ensuring stable financing conditions, monetary policy can support long-term investment in infrastructure and innovation. Therefore, in line with United Nations development goals, inclusive monetary policies that ensure credit access for marginalized communities help reduce income and wealth disparities. For example, interest rate adjustments can encourage investment and entrepreneurship, create jobs and support decent work.

In Nigeria, monetary policy directly affects the accessibility and affordability of financing for entrepreneurs through changes in interest rate, inflation, exchange rate and liquidity. For example, high interest rates discourage borrowing, making it difficult for entrepreneurs to secure affordable financing. When the Central Bank of Nigeria (CBN) increases the MPR, commercial banks raise lending rates, thereby reducing access to credit for entrepreneurs (Alfa et al., 2020). Similarly, inflation erodes the purchasing power of entrepreneurs and increases operational costs. A tight monetary policy aimed at curbing inflation may lead to reduced money supply, limiting available funds for business expansion. Furthermore, exchange rate fluctuations impact the cost of imported raw materials and equipment. A stable monetary policy helps entrepreneurs plan better and mitigate foreign exchange risks.

Monetary policy decisions regarding interest rates have a direct impact on the entrepreneurship landscape (Zhao and Li, 2021). Lower interest rates can stimulate borrowing for business expansion and innovation, fostering entrepreneurship. Reserve requirements set by the central bank affect the liquidity of commercial banks in Nigeria. Lower requirements can increase the availability of funds for lending to entrepreneurs and businesses. The central bank's OMOs influence the money supply. Proper management of these operations can help stabilize the economy and create a conducive environment for entrepreneurship. Monetary policies that ensure easy access to financing through the banking sector can significantly benefit entrepreneurs in Chengdu, promoting business growth.

Monetary policy also aims to control inflation, which is crucial for entrepreneurial sustainability (Stoica et al., 2020). Stable prices encourage investment and entrepreneurship by reducing uncertainty. Chengdu's export-oriented economy is impacted by exchange rate policies. A stable exchange rate can benefit entrepreneurs by enhancing predictability in international trade. Unfortunately, despite policies by the monetary authority in Nigeria to finance entrepreneurial performance, entrepreneurial activities in the country continue to be at a low ebb. Many entrepreneurs, especially startups, still struggle to access traditional financing from banks due to a lack of credit history, collateral or business track record. Even when financing is available, interest rates and repayment terms can be restrictive, making it difficult for business entrepreneurs to manage cash flow (Alfa, 2020). Banks and financial institutions often require extensive documentation, a solid business plan and proof of profitability, which can be hard for new businesses to provide. These factors have hindered the growth of entrepreneurship in Nigeria. Against this backdrop, this study examines monetary policy and entrepreneurial financing in Nigeria.

Literature Review

Various perspectives have been used to describe the concept of entrepreneurship. According to Isoboye and Ihenetu (2021), entrepreneurship is the process of designing, launching and running a new business, which is more often than not, initially a small business. The business, though, starts small, but with time begins to grow alongside the entrepreneurs (the initiators of the business). The growth of the entrepreneur precipitates more experience, creates employment, increases investments, raises the standard of living, promotes effective and efficient functioning of the business, and alleviates poverty, etc. (John and Ibenta, 2017). Entrepreneurial activities are fundamentally born out of innovative development of goods and services (Okafor and Onebunne, 2012; Ifionu and Akinpelumi, 2017). Progressively, the activities grow with ideas and innovations with consciously calculated risks and development of new business prospects (Ofili, 2014).

Manta (2022) describes entrepreneurial financing as the process of acquiring and managing financial resources to start, grow and sustain a new business venture. Entrepreneurs need capital at different stages of their business journey, from idea development to scaling operations. Since startups often lack collateral or a proven track record, they rely on a mix of funding sources tailored to their risk profile and growth potential. According to Metrick and Yasuda (2021), entrepreneurial financing is a specialized branch of finance that focuses on funding mechanisms, investment decisions and capital management for entrepreneurial ventures, particularly startups and high-growth businesses. These definitions highlight that entrepreneurial financing involves securing and managing funds for new ventures, considering risk, growth and investment strategies.

On the other hand, monetary policy is a conscious action undertaken by the monetary authorities to change or regulate the availability, quantity, cost or direction of credit in any economy in order to achieve a stated economic goal (Nzotta, 2004; Ihenetu, 2021). It is the combination of discretionary measures designed to regulate and control the money supply in an economy by the monetary authorities with the view of achieving a desired macroeconomic goal. The goals of monetary policy are to reduce inflation, reduce unemployment, stabilize the exchange rate, stabilize the price level, and accelerate economic growth and development and balance of payment equilibrium (CBN, 2020).

Theoretical Review

This study is anchored on the Resource-Based Theory (RBT) of Entrepreneurial Finance, rooted in Barney (1991) and reformulated by Subramanian (2010). The theory suggests that a firm's competitive advantage stems from its unique and valuable resources, and that monetary policy can impact entrepreneurial finance by influencing access to capital and overall economic conditions, impacting the ability of entrepreneurs to leverage their resources.

According to Isoboye and Ihenetu (2021), the main focus of the theory is that resources available for entrepreneurs are very scarce, hence the need to develop a strategy to gain a competitive advantage and enhance organizational performance. The theory assumes that firms' competitive advantage and subsequent performance originate in the resources and capabilities the firm controls. One of the scarce resources that hampers the growth of entrepreneurs is funds. The entrepreneurs are hungry for financial resources to stimulate their growth. Scarcity of funds stifled the growth of entrepreneurs. Expansionary monetary policy provides the opportunity for entrepreneurs to secure funds to grow their business. The policy will make funds available to entrepreneurs in every sector of the economy to boost their businesses and grow.

Empirical Review

Kumar, Shahbaz and Idris (2023) examine the relationship between monetary policy and entrepreneurship growth and development in Chengdu, China, using the survey method. Findings show that lower interest rates can stimulate borrowing for business expansion and innovation, while access to finance becomes more accessible. Stable inflation and exchange rates reduce uncertainty for entrepreneurs, encouraging long-term investments. The study also noted that monetary policy in Chengdu, China, has a significant impact on entrepreneurship growth and development. Lower interest rates resulting from accommodative monetary policies stimulate borrowing for business expansion and innovation, promoting entrepreneurship.

Mehar and Al-Faryan (2022) examine the role of monetary policy in the creation of new business entities and the enhancement of external trade. Using data from 105 nations collected over 20 years, a statistical model was developed based on two simultaneous equations. The results of this research may be used as a benchmark for policymakers to gauge the health of the private sector's access to credit. New company formation, exports, interest rates and private sector financing are all examined in connection with one another, as are a number of other factors. It was also shown that foreign direct investment is a useful supplement to trade in external goods.

Isoboye and Ihenetu (2021) evaluated the effect of monetary policy on entrepreneurial growth in Nigeria using secondary data collected from the CBN statistical bulletin (2023). Ex post facto design was employed for the study. An autoregressive and distributive lag model was adopted for the analysis of the data. The findings showed that the MPR, the reasury bill rate, the liquidity ratio and the loan-to-deposit ratio had no significant effect on entrepreneurial growth in Nigeria, but the combination of these variables had a positive and significant effect on entrepreneurial growth in Nigeria during the period of the study. The coefficients of these variables were positive, which suggested a positive drive on entrepreneurial growth in Nigeria.

Jackson and Madison (2021) examine the relationship between entrepreneurial financing and monetary policy in the United States using the statistical calibration approach. The result of calibration shows that the monetary policy transmission channel is strong and that there are substantial interactions between the frictions faced by entrepreneurs and the strength of the transmission and pass-through of monetary policy. There was a quantitatively significant transmission channel with a one percentage point increase in the nominal interest rate decreasing sectoral output by 5.3 per cent.

Kumar, Acharya, and Ho (2020) evaluate the effect of monetary policy and entrepreneurial growth in New Zealand using an autoregressive and distributed lag model. Findings show that the combination of the MPR, the treasury bill rate, the liquidity ratio and the loan-to-deposit ratio had a positive and significant effect on entrepreneurial growth in New Zealand. These factors all had positive coefficients, which pointed to a constructive influence on New Zealand's burgeoning startup scene.

Satti, Mahalik and Shahbaz (2019) examine the effects of monetary policy measures on economic growth in Kazakhstan. Questionnaire responses were utilized as the main data, while other sources were consulted for secondary data. All the secondary information came from records kept by the Kazakhstan National Bureau of Statistics and the Kazakhstan Central Bank over the course of seven years. Multiple regression analysis was used to conclude the associations between the dependent and independent variables. A regression and correlation study showed a positive and statistically significant relationship between money supply and economic expansion. The expansion of the economy, as measured by the GDP, was shown to be negatively correlated with interest and exchange rates. The results also showed that the cash reserve ratio was positively related to GDP growth.

Methodology

Sources and Nature of Data

The study uses annual time series secondary data covering 1990–2023. The data were collected on lending rate (LDR), MPR, broad money supply (M2) and entrepreneurial financing (ENF). Data for all the variables were obtained from the Central Bank of Nigeria's Statistical Bulletin (2024). LDR, MPR, and broad money supply (M2) were the explanatory variables, while entrepreneurial financing is the dependent variable. In this study, the lending rate is the cost of a loan to customers set by commercial banks. It is measured in percentage. The MPR is the minimum rate at which monetary authorities lend to the deposit money bank. The deposit money banks now add their own percentage to the one given to them by the monetary authorities. It is expressed as a percentage. Broad money supply, M2, is demand deposits in the economy and other easily convertible assets, such as savings accounts and time deposits, providing a broader view of liquidity than narrow money measures. It is measured in Naira. In this study, the log of M2 was taken in order to correct for heteroscedasticity.

Model Specification

This study uses the ARDL model to examine the impact of the explanatory variables on the dependent variable. The model was adapted from the work of Isoboye and Ihenetu (2021), with the main difference in the choice of variables. While Isoboye and Ihenetu (2021) used entrepreneurial growth, treasury bills, monetary policy rate and liquidity ratio, this study retains LDR and MPR but replaces other variables with broad money supply (M2) and entrepreneurial financing (ENF). This was done to align with the objective of this study. The ARDL model of this study is given as:

$$ENFt = \alpha_0 + \sum_{i=0}^{n} \alpha_1 ENF_{t-i} + \sum_{i=0}^{n} \alpha_2 LDR_{t-i} + \sum_{i=0}^{n} \alpha_3 MPR_{t-i} + \sum_{i=0}^{n} \alpha_4 M2_{t-i} \mu.$$

Where:

ENT = Entrepreneurial financing
INT = Lending rate
MPR = Monetary policy rate
M2 = Broad money supply

The parameters $\alpha_1, \alpha_2, \alpha_3, \alpha_4,$ represent the long-run parameters. The null hypothesis of the model is:

$H_0 : \alpha_1 = \alpha_2 = \alpha_3 = \alpha_4 = 0$ (There is no long-run relationship among the variables)

$H_1 : \alpha_1 \neq \alpha_2 \neq \alpha_3 \neq \alpha_4 \neq 0$ (There is a long-run relationship among the variables)

To test the hypothesis stated above, the first step is to calculate the F-statistic and compare the result with the critical value tabulated by Pesaran and Shin (1999) and Pesaran and Weeks (2001). If the test statistic exceeds the upper critical value, the null hypothesis of a no long-run relationship can be rejected regardless of whether the underlying order of integration of the variables is 0 or 1. Similarly, if the test statistic falls below a lower critical value, the null hypothesis is not rejected. However, if the test statistic falls between these two bounds, the result is inconclusive. When the order of integration of the variables is known and all the variables are I(1), the decision is made based on the upper bound. Similarly, if all the variables are I(0), then the decision is made based on the lower bound.

In the second step, if there is evidence of a long-run relationship (co-integration) among the variables, the long-run model in equation (1) is estimated. If the study finds no evidence of a long-run relationship, then the error correction model (ECM) will be estimated. The ECM indicates the speed of adjustment back to long-run equilibrium after a short-run disturbance. The standard ECM model is the short-run model and is given as:

$$ENFt = c + v(ECM)_{t-1} + \sum_{i=0}^{n} \beta_1 ENF_{t-i} + \sum_{i=0}^{n} \beta_2 LDR_{t-i} + \sum_{i=0}^{n} \beta_3 MPR_{t-i} + \sum_{i=0}^{n} \beta_4 M2_{t-i} + \Upsilon_t$$

The second equation represents the short-run dynamics of the model, whereas the parameter v represents the error correction coefficient.

Results and Discussions of Findings

Table 13.1 shows the result of the test of stationarity using the Augmented Dikey-Fuller (ADF) unit root tests option. The test was conducted with an intercept but no trend. This is because when intercept and trend were included in the test, the intercept was found to be statistically significant, while the trend was found to be statistically

Table 13.1 Unit Root Test of Stationarity; H_0: The Series Has a Unit Root

Variables	ADF Levels	ADF 1st Difference	Remarks
ENF	−1.957[]	−4.320[]	I (1)
LDR	−2.752[]	−6.689[]	I (1)
MPR	−3.086[]*	– – –	I (0)
M2	−2.118[]	−4.359[]	I (1)

ADF Critical Value at 5% = −2.957

* *Indicates significant at 5%*

[] Indicates that no lag length was included in the tests.

Source: Computed by the researcher using EViews 12.

Table 13.2 Result of Lag Selection for Bound Co-Integration Test

Lag	LogL	LR	FPE	AIC	SC	HQ
0	-1150.078	NA	3.05e+28	76.93851	77.12534	76.99828
1	-1056.100	156.6300*	1.71e+26*	71.73998*	72.67411*	72.03881*
2	-1043.717	17.33574	2.31e+26	71.98113	73.66257	72.51904
3	-1032.806	12.36608	3.85e+26	72.32038	74.74912	73.09736
4	-1014.702	15.68988	4.80e+26	72.18014	75.35618	73.19618

Source: Researcher's computation using EViews 12.

insignificant. The result reveals that ENF, LDR, and M2 are non-stationary at levels because the ADF calculated values for the variables are less than the critical value at the 5 per cent level of significance. However, the variable becomes stationary at first difference, implying that they are integrated of order one. But MPR is stationary at levels, because the ADF calculated values for MPR are greater than the critical value at the 5 per cent level of significance. This implies that MPR is integrated of order zero. Therefore, since the variables are integrated of different orders, the data set has met the necessary condition for the ARDL model.

Before carrying out the bound co-integration test, it is necessary to determine the appropriate lag length for the test. The optimal length of lag selection for the co-integration test, based on the five information criteria, is reported in Table 13.2. From Table 13.2, all five information criteria suggest that a lag length of one is optimal for the test. Consequently, this study used a lag length of one for the test of co-integration and the subsequent diagnostic tests.

Co-integration is a way of reconciling the short-run and long-run equilibrium relationship among the variables of the study. Since the variables are confirmed to be non-stationary, their linear combination is expected to give a stationary result in the long run. The result of F-bound co-integration in Table 13.3 revealed that the F-statistic

Table 13.3 Result of Bound Co-Integration Test

Test Statistic	Value	Significant	I(0)	I(1)
			Asymptotic: n = 1000	
F-statistic	3.684	10%	2.37	3.2
K	3	5%	2.79	3.67
		2.5%	3.15	4.08
		1%	3.65	4.66
Actual Sample Size	33		Finite Sample: n = 35	
		10%	2.618	3.532
		5%	3.164	4.194
		1%	4.428	5.816
			Finite Sample: n = 30	
		10%	2.676	3.586
		5%	3.272	4.306
		1%	4.614	5.966

Source: Researcher's computation using EViews 12.

is 3.68, which is greater than the 5 per cent and 10 per cent asymptotic critical values. Therefore, the null hypothesis of no co-integration is rejected while the alternative hypothesis of the presence of co-integration among the variables is accepted. Based on the result in Table 13.4, it can be concluded that the variables of the study have a long-run equilibrium relationship. Specifically, it could be inferred from the result that ENF in the current year had an equilibrium relationship with lending rate, MPR and broad money supply, which kept them in proportion to each other in the long run for the period under study.

Table 13.4 shows the result of the long-run ARDL model. The result shows that LDR has a negative and statistically significant impact on ENF over the period of the study. A one per cent increase in LDR decreases ENF by about 0.61 per cent. This conforms to the apriori expectation. This is because an increase in the cost of borrowing is likely to discourage entrepreneurs from borrowing and hence reduce their business finance. That is, an increase in lending rates (interest rates) generally decreases entrepreneurial finance by making it more expensive for entrepreneurs to borrow money, potentially leading to reduced investment, slower growth and difficulty in securing capital. However, this finding disagrees with Isoboye and Ihenetu (2021), whose study revealed a positive impact of lending rate on entrepreneurial growth in Nigeria.

Like LDR, MPR has a negative impact on ENF over the period of the study. The result in Table 13.4 shows that a one per cent increase in MPR decreases ENF by about 0.57 per cent. This also conforms to the apriori expectation. Higher MPR leads to higher interest rates or borrowing costs. This can discourage entrepreneurs from

Table 13.4 Result of Long-Run ARDL Model Dependent Variable: ENF

Variable	Coefficient	Std. Error	t-Statistic	Prob.
LDR	−0.608	0.184	−3.666	0.016
logM2	1.382	0.670	1.889	0.049
MPR	−0.567	0.153	−3.694	0.015
C	−12.65	11.22	−1.127	0.269

Source: Researcher's computation using EViews 12.

taking on new projects or expanding existing ones, as the cost of financing investments becomes too high. This agrees with Mehar and Al-Faryan (2022).

However, the log of money supply (logM2) has a positive elasticity. This implies that the elasticity of ENF increases with an increase in log M2 and is fairly elastic. This is as expected and agrees with Jackson and Madison (2021). An increase in money supply can indirectly facilitate entrepreneurial finance by lowering interest rates, making it easier for businesses to secure loans and access capital, and potentially stimulating economic activities in the country.

The result of the short-run ARDL model is shown in Table 13.5. Unlike the long-run ARDL model in Table 13.4, the short-run ARDL model in Table 13.5 was estimated at the first difference of the variables. The result reveals a negative error correction term (ECMt), as anticipated, which is statistically significant. The negative sign implies that there is an adjustment from the short-run to the long-run equilibrium among the variables of the study. That is, the system is responsive to deviations from equilibrium such that if the short-run variables (LDR, MPR, M2 and ENF) deviate from equilibrium, they have the tendency to re-adjust back to equilibrium. The coefficient of ECMt indicates an annual level of adjustment from long-run disequilibrium of about 0.377 per cent per annum. This means that in the current year, about 37 per cent of the disequilibrium errors, which occurred in the previous years, are corrected.

However, unlike the long-run results, all the short-run estimated coefficients are statistically insignificant, except for money supply. The result shows that a one per cent increase in LDR decreases ENF by 0.17 per cent. This conforms to apriori expectation and supports the long-run result reported in Table 13.4. Similarly, MPR has a negative impact on ENF. The result shows that a 1 per cent increase in MPR decreases ENF by 0.15 per cent. This conforms to apriori expectation and supports the long-run result reported in Table 13.5. Similarly, like the long-run result, M2 increases ENF with an elasticity coefficient of about 3.7. This conforms to apriori expectation and supports the long-run result reported in Table 13.4.

Table 13.6 shows the post-estimation statistics for the variables of the study. The serial correlation LM test has a probability value of 0.1684, which is greater than 0.05. This suggests that there is no autocorrelation in the model. Similarly, the probability value for the test of heteroskedasticity is 0.540, implying that there is no heteroskedasticity in the model. Furthermore, the normality plot reported in Figure 13.1 shows that the Jarque-Bera value and its probability are 0.748 and 0.688, respectively. Hence, the null hypothesis that the error terms of the data used in the study are normally distributed

Table 13.5 Result of Short-Run ARDL Model

Variable	Coefficient	Std. Error	t-Statistic	Prob.
D(LDR)	−0.178	0.550	−0.323	0.7486
LOGM2	3.661	1.509	2.427	0.0222
D(MPR)	−0.150	0.359	−0.418	0.6790
ECMt	−0.377	0.097	−3.896	0.0006

Source: Researcher's computation using EViews 12.

Table 13.6 Result of Post-Estimation Statistics

Breusch-Godfrey Serial Correlation LM Test			
F-statistic	2.007220	Prob. F(1,26)	0.1684
Obs*R-squared	2.365042	Prob. Chi-Square(1)	0.1241
Autoregressive Conditional Heteroskedasticity (ARCH) Test			
F-statistic	3.378140	Prob. F(1,30)	0.0540
Obs*R-squared	3.075278	Prob. Chi-Square(1)	0.0535

Source: Researcher's computation using EViews 12.

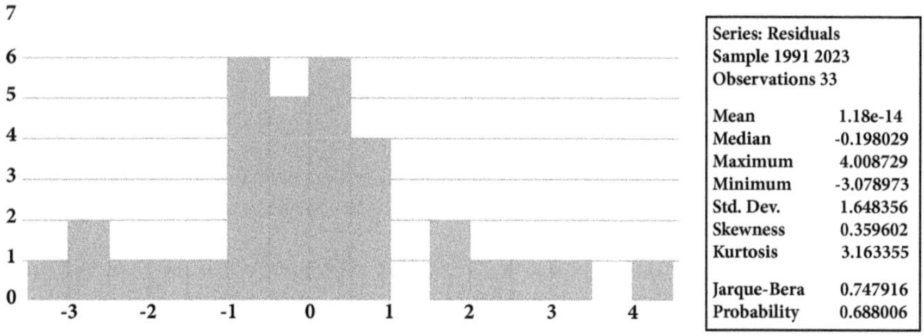

Figure 13.1 Test of Normality.
Source: Researcher's computation using EViews 12.

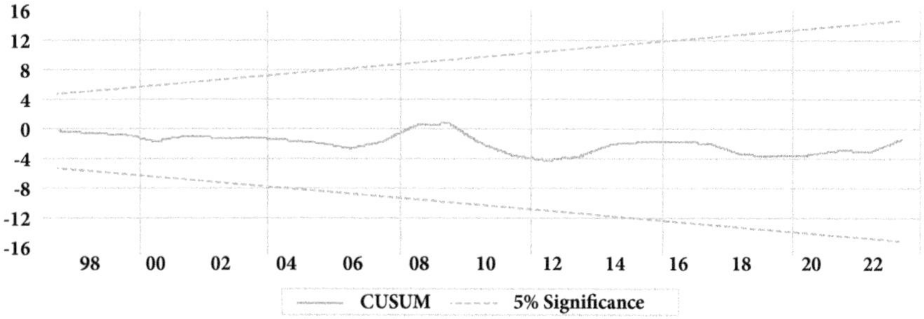

Figure 13.2 Test of Stability.
Source: Researcher's computation using EViews 12.

cannot be rejected. Furthermore, the result passed the test of stability. This is because the CUSUM plot reported in Figure 13.2 does not cross either of the 5 per cent critical lines. Therefore, it could be concluded that the estimated parameters for the study are stable for the period under investigation.

Conclusion and Recommendations

Findings from this study reveal that monetary policy impacts on entrepreneurial financing in Nigeria, both in the short run and in the long run, but is significant only in the long run. Specifically, the findings show that lending rate and MPR have negative impacts on entrepreneurial financing both in the short run and in the long run. Hence, the study concludes that a high lending rate is likely to discourage borrowing, thereby reducing the financial strength of the entrepreneurs in the country. However, broad money supply has a positive impact on entrepreneurial financing both in the short run and in the long run. The study, therefore, concludes that entrepreneurial financing is enhanced when there is enough liquidity available in the economy. Based on the findings, the study recommends that the monetary authorities keep the MPR and lending rate as low as possible in order to encourage entrepreneurs to borrow more for investment in Nigeria. Also, expansionary monetary policy should be used to inject more money into the economy.

References

Alfa, Y. (2019). 'Long-Run Impact of Interest Rate, Exchange Rate and Inflation on Private Sector Investment in Nigeria', *Confluence Journal of Economics and Allied Science*, 2(1): 1–15.

Alfa, Y., and H. Gambo (2023). 'Interest Rate Channel of Monetary Transmission and Real Sector Output in Nigeria', *Journal of Arid Zone Economy*, 2(2): 117–32.

Alfa, Y., A. Ugah and S. Ayodeji (2020). 'Impact of Money Supply on Economic Growth in Nigeria: Evidence from Vector Autoregressive Model', *Bingham Journal of Economics and Allied Studies (BJEAS)*, 4(2): 47–62.

Barney, J. (1991). 'Firm Resources and Sustained Competitive Advantage', *Journal of Management*, 17(1): 99–120.

Central Bank of Nigeria (CBN) (2020). *Monetary Policy Implementation Framework*. Abuja: Central Bank of Nigeria.

Ihenetu, H.I. (2021). 'Money Market Instruments and Real Sector Development in Nigeria', *Global Journal of Research in Business Management*, 1(1): 24–9.

Isoboye, J.D., and H.I. Ihenetu (2021). 'Monetary Policy and Entrepreneurial Growth in Nigeria', *African Journal of Business and Economic Development*, 1(10): 167–76.

Jackson, P., and Madison, F. (2021). 'Entrepreneurial Finance and Monetary Policy'. Available at: https://static1.squarespace.com/static/5d220f706f941b0001d943ac/t/601b6639acc8534bedd001df/1612408382338/EF_02032021.pdf

John, E.I., and S.N. Ibenta (2017). 'Financial Deepening and Entrepreneurial Growth in Nigeria', *Research Journal of Finance and Accounting*, 8(20): 40–51.

Kumar, D.Q., P.Z. Shahbaz and S.Z. Idris (2023). 'Monetary Policy and Entrepreneurship Growth and Development in Chengdu, China', *Journal of Entrepreneurship & Project Management*, 7(10): 14–21.

Kumar, V., S. Acharya and L.T. Ho (2020). 'Does Monetary Policy Influence the Profitability of Banks in New Zealand?' *International Journal of Financial Studies*, 8(2): 35. Available at: https://doi.org/10.3390/ijfs8020035

Manta, O. (2022). 'Entrepreneurial Financing, Financial Instrument for the Mountain Economy'. Available at: https://ssrn.com/abstract=4313097 or http://dx.doi.org/10.2139/ssrn.4313097

Mehar, M.A., and M.A.S. Al-Faryan (2022). 'Effects of Monetary Policy on Business Startups and Trade Activities: Global Empirical Evidences', *Theoretical Economics Letters*, 12(6): 1825–44. Available at: https://doi.org/10.4236/tel.2022.126098

Metrick, A., and A. Yasuda (2021). *Venture Capital & the Finance of Innovation*. Princeton, NJ: Princeton University Press.

Nzotta, S.M. (2004). *Money, Banking and Finance Theory and practice*. Nigeria: Jude Hudson.

Ofili, O.O. (2014). 'Challenges Facing Entrepreneurship in Nigeria', *International Journal of Business and Management*, 9(12): 258–74.

Okafor, R.G., and I. Onebunne (2012). 'Review of Financial Challenges of Nigerian Entrepreneurs in an Attempt to Reduce Financial Institutions Risk Perception Index of Small Firms: Evidence from Survey Data', *Developing Country Studies*, 2(11): 197–204.

Pesaran, M.H., and Y. Shin (1999). 'An Autoregressive Distributed Lag Modelling Approach to Cointegration Analysis', in S. Strom (ed.), *Econometrics and Economic Theory in the 20th Century*: The Ragnar Frisch Centennial Symposium, 371–413. Cambridge: Cambridge University Press.

Pesaran, M.H., and M. Weeks (2001). 'Non-Nested Hypothesis Testing: An Overview', in B.H. Baltagi (ed.), *A Companion to Theoretical Econometrics*, 279–309. Oxford: Wiley.

Satti, S.L., M.K. Mahalik and M. Shahbaz (2019). 'Dynamics of Income Inequality, Finance and Trade in Kazakhstan: Empirical Evidence from a New Transition Economy with Policy Prescriptions', Melbourne, Victoria: Monash University, Department of Economics.

Schumpeter, J.A. (1934). *The Theory of Economic Development*. Cambridge, MA: Harvard University Press.

Stoica, O., A. Roman and V.D. Rusu (2020). 'The Nexus Between Entrepreneurship, Monetary Policy and Economic Growth: A Comparative Analysis on Groups of Countries', *Sustainability*, 12(3): 1186. Available at: https://doi.org/10.3390/su12031186

Subramanian, K. (2010). *A Resource-Based Theory of Entrepreneurial Finance*. SSRN. Available at: https://ssrn.com/abstract=1562554 or http://dx.doi.org/10.2139/ssrn.1562554.

Zhao, J., and T. Li (2021). 'Social Capital, Financial Literacy, and Rural Household Entrepreneurship: A Mediating Effect Analysis', *Frontiers in Psychology*, 12: 724605. Available at: https://doi.org/10.3389/fpsyg.2021.724605

Part VI

Comparative Cases/International Partnerships/Alliances

14

Military Entrepreneurship in India and Nigeria: A Comparative Review and Future Research Agenda

Shaju Meetna and Sanya Ojo

The connection and complementarity between the Nigerian military and the Indian military establishments run deeper in many aspects than ordinarily envisaged. Both shared the same experience in their origin, training and standards through the British colonization episode. This complementarity is appraised in the chapter through a review of military entrepreneurship formation and practices in both India and Nigerian military establishments. Attention is also paid to issues such as the contextual parallel between the military entrepreneurship of both countries and the influence the national culture of each country has on their entrepreneurship cultures. A comprehensive literature review of military entrepreneurship in both countries is undertaken to interrogate these issues.

Entrepreneurship as an aggregated concept is delineated, in this chapter, as a context-dependent socio-economic process of discovering or creating, evaluating and exploiting new opportunities by individuals through which new business ventures can be initiated, such that value is generated to the society (Baron and Shane, 2008; Bruyat and Julien, 2000; Shane and Venkataraman, 2000). The multi-dimensionality and complexity of entrepreneurship is thus revealed in this all-embracing contemporary understanding of the concept, which reflects the primary ways the concept manifests itself in people's lives and society beyond its orthodox meaning.

Entrepreneurs have a very important and specific function in the economy; they engender relatively much employment creation, productivity growth and produce and commercialize high-quality innovations; they are more satisfied than employees; entrepreneurial firms produce important spillovers that affect regional employment growth rates of all companies in the long run; and many more (Praag and Versloot, 2007). In the literature of entrepreneurship, scholars have so far identified multiple forms of entrepreneurships like social entrepreneurship (Bloom and Smith, 2010; Ghauri et al., 2014), educational entrepreneurship (Kourilsky, 2001), military entrepreneurship (Maune, 2023; Mani, 2007; Ojo, 2021), veteran entrepreneurship (Kedia, 2019; Ojo, 2023), and many more. In all these, military entrepreneurship is a relatively new field of academic inquiry that investigates how entrepreneurial traits like adaptability, innovation, and leadership are developed and applied within military contexts (Brömmelhörster and Paes, 2004).

This chapter explores the possibilities around military entrepreneurship with special reference to India and Nigeria. Both countries, as former British colonies, share structural similarities in their military organizations but differ significantly in socio-economic and cultural frameworks. These distinctions create an intriguing basis for our comparative analysis.

Military systems contribute largely to the complex of state power. However, the existing capability of regional and global stabilization and control refers to military practices and capabilities. It is the framework that endows a state with the ability to align its military dimension with the ongoing dynamics of a region and beyond and operate upon its system to achieve security, stability and sustainable development. While there are significant differences between an advanced military state and those that are on the threshold of military industrial development, the aim of this paper, therefore, is to make a comparative analysis between the military systems of two nations and subsequently bring out the relevance of military entrepreneurship that has emerged as a product of the complex of political, economic and military equations alongside suitable recommendations.

While India's military entrepreneurship often focuses on technology-driven solutions, such as defence startups under the *Atmanirbhar Bharat* (self-reliant India) initiative, Nigeria's military entrepreneurial initiatives frequently address local socio-economic issues, such as community security and disaster management. In this context, our study adopts a narrative review approach through the analysis of existing literature, military records and government policies. The focus is on identifying patterns in entrepreneurial practices, cultural influences and policy frameworks in India and Nigeria. The narrative review includes a search of peer-reviewed journal articles, policy reports and organizational reviews found through database searching as well as the grey literature. Grey literature includes unpublished theses, conference proceedings, government reports, unpublished trial data and more (Goldacre, 2011).

It is necessary to note that, in this paper, some contiguous terms and expressions were used interchangeably broadly to keep in line with the literature from which they are extricated. Such terms include military entrepreneurship and veteran entrepreneurship. The intention is not to equate 'military entrepreneurship' with 'veteran entrepreneurship' since it is understood that the latter is a subset of the former, as clarified in Ojo (2021). The rest of the chapter is organized into four sections. The first two sections provide the conceptual foundation and the contextual framework, respectively. The third section articulates the discussion, and the final section consists of a conclusion and recommendations.

Conceptual Analysis

Military and Entrepreneurship

Building on Samuel Huntington's *Soldier and the State* (1957), modern militaries are recognized as state-centric institutional entities with collective objectives and professional norms. Their motivations are inherently corporate rather than individual. Economists like Joseph Schumpeter highlight that entrepreneurship involves innovating methods of production or reallocating resources in creative ways, for example, establishing a new market, acquiring new resources, or reorganizing an economic sector (Schumpeter, 1983: 66). The critical question is what makes militaries take on entrepreneurial approaches, and why does it matter?

The theories best placed to answer these questions come out of civil-military relations and international relations. In the space of civil-military relations, studies on developing areas have explored what could be defined as 'commercial preserve' military entrepreneurship. It indicates the idea that armed forces have embraced economic enterprises to increase resources to the institution (Brömmelhörster and Paes, 2004: 13). The scale and character of such activities, the capital obtained and their political legitimacy may differ greatly. In the twentieth century, militaries raised resources through corporations, welfare foundations and unit-level business ventures. In some cases, political leaders openly promote autonomy among militaries, as China did in the 1980s (Mulvenon, 2001). Typically, such activities arise to compensate for state and private sector limitations or to supplement inadequate defence budgets (Brömmelhörster and Paes, 2004).

In contrast, international relations (IR) scholars have focused on the state-level implications of military entrepreneurship, taking what can be referred to as a 'grand strategy' approach. Such an approach highlights how military procurement needs can spur technological and industrial development, thereby increasing state power. Contemporary militaries are state actors with strategic foresight, being at the same time patrons and consumers of new technologies and often creating new economic industries. These examples show that even gigantic bureaucracies can innovate (Snyder, 1984; Smith, 1985; Rosen, 2005). Armies try to gain a strategic edge over competitors by inventively and tactically controlling resources, sometimes in revolutionary innovations with long-lasting effects (Shimshoni, 1990–1991: 189). One example is Fordism, the production of the same items in large quantities to maximize output, which was first implemented in the US Army's armaments industry during the nineteenth century but then diffused into the private sector (Smith, 1985: 11). Military innovations may not always work or be intended but 'the IR literature places value on an analysis of such dynamics'.

The concept of military entrepreneurship is often used rather loosely to describe a host of profit-driven activities engaged in by armed groups, including the business of private security companies that mushroomed in the post–Cold War period. However, if this concept is to be useful as a stepping stone for theoretical development and cross-country comparison, it needs to be defined precisely and narrowly. A strong conceptual framework that captures the institutional nature of the military should, at the same time, capture the innovative aspect that is associated with entrepreneurship.

Military entrepreneurship involves fostering innovative practices within military organizations to address emerging challenges, optimize resources, and support national development (Dyer, 2021). Acting in an institutional rather than individual capacity, military entrepreneurs operate within legal and political frameworks – a crucial distinction separating legitimate activities from illicit ventures. Institutional and legal aspects of military economic activities lend credibility to their claims. This definition, therefore, excludes more routine profit-driven activities by emphasizing innovation. For example, security services only become entrepreneurial insofar as they include the creation of new goods or markets, like the commercialization of military-trained security forces.

Relevance of Military Skills for Civilian Employment

Kleykamp (2009) contends that militarily acquired competencies, such as administrative skills, human resources, logistics, technical services and financial planning, are sought after in civilian employment, all of which are variant forms of human capital. While combat skills per se are not transferable to the civilian world, indirect benefits of service in combat units, such as discipline, physical fitness, cohesion, and the ability to work in teams, are highly valued. To these, Kelty et al. (2010) add responsibility, health, constant training, self-improvement, and community and civic engagement.

Traits such as strategic planning, resourcefulness and resilience are nurtured through rigorous military training and real-world operational experience. Despite the apparent relevance of these military-spawned skills in the civilian workplace, Jelusic (2006) finds that it may be difficult to bring them to bear because military personnel are unaccustomed to using their own initiative. In the context of entrepreneurship, the lack of initiative makes any entrepreneurial activity an impossibility. In a study based on in-depth interviews with members of the South African National Defence Force, Kramm and Heinecken (2015: 130) conclude that 'military culture is in many ways an antithesis to civilian life', though many skills acquired in the technical and support branches increase the ex-serviceman's likelihood of employment in the private sector.

In an investigation into the impact of military work experience on civilian labour market outcomes, Baert and Balcaen (2013) are far more inclusive in defining military experience. Rather than considering only military skills and the more broadly defined fringe benefits, such as discipline and the ability to work in teams, they include social capital due to a particular military–social network, the screening process undergone for physical and psychological traits required for acceptance into certain military units and the image of the armed forces in the region. While none of these are provided by the military, former servicemen may benefit greatly from them in subsequent employment or in overcoming the challenges involved in establishing an entrepreneurial venture. Nevertheless, some of the acquired vocational skills and experiences in the military service help veteran entrepreneurs to grow their self-assurance in forming their business enterprises (Ojo, 2021b). This is consistent with the view that knowledge and experience gathering is important to create necessary self-confidence in the individual before embarking on a business venture (Gomezelj and Kusce, 2013).

Screening for various characteristics necessarily distinguishes members of a particular group from the general population. In a study (Johnson, 1999) of personality characteristics of third-year midshipmen at the US Naval Academy, they were found to be ranked higher in ambition (initiative, competitiveness and leadership potential), sociability (extroversion, gregariousness and need for social interaction), intellectance (imagination, creativity and curiosity) and school success (interest in and commitment to learning and education) than the general population. On the other hand, they were found to rank lower than the general population in adjustment (confidence, self-esteem and composure), likability (warmth, charm and relationship maintenance) and prudence (responsibility, self-control and conscientiousness). Further, it is observed that the eight leadership principles of military training are the same principles that are essential for being a successful entrepreneur (Kiyosaki, 2015: 2).

Cultural Influences on Entrepreneurship

Entrepreneurial activity is largely affected by various economic, cultural, political and technological factors (Wennekers, 2006). These factors help in clarifying the cross-national differences in terms of the rate and intensity of entrepreneurial activity. Nevertheless, the effect of culture and value systems across countries is extensive. Some seminal studies (e.g. Hofstede, 1980; Lynn,1991; Shane,1993) have already propagated the importance of culture and presented various scales to measure the variation across nations. In particular, Hofstede's cultural dimensions theory (1980) has provided a foundation for the understanding of how cultural values impact entrepreneurship. For example, societies with low uncertainty avoidance are likely to encourage entrepreneurship because they embrace risk-taking and innovation. In contrast, high uncertainty avoidance cultures tend to suppress entrepreneurship because of their desire for stability and predictability (Hofstede, 2001). Individualistic cultures that emphasize personal achievement and autonomy tend to have higher rates of entrepreneurial activity than collectivist cultures, which stress group cohesion and conformity (Hayton et al., 2002). Cultural values are, therefore, crucial in determining how individuals perceive entrepreneurial opportunities and the risks surrounding them.

Social norms and institutional frameworks within a culture also shape entrepreneurial ecosystems. For instance, high-power distance cultures may limit entrepreneurship by promoting hierarchical structures and denying resources to those at the lower end of the social spectrum (Shane, 1993). On the other hand, low-power distance cultures are more likely to promote egalitarianism and, therefore, provide wider access to entrepreneurial opportunities. Furthermore, cultural long-term orientation may have implications for the sustainability and growth of entrepreneurial ventures since long-term oriented cultures tend to be more strategic in planning and persistent (Hofstede, 2001). These cultural dimensions underscore the complex interplay between societal values and entrepreneurial success, highlighting the need for culturally adaptive entrepreneurial policies and practices to foster innovation and economic development.

Contextual Re-Articulation

India–Nigeria Relationship

Relations between Nigeria and India have their roots in British colonialism. Both had shared colonial experiences, having been former colonies of Britain (Mehra and Yaruingam, 2015). The two countries, though in different geopolitical regions, are comparatively linked in several arenas spanning politics, socio-cultural and economic platforms. For instance, in the fields of politics and socio-economics, both India and Nigeria are the largest democracies and the largest economies in their respective regions (Cohn, 2013). Both countries are multi-religious, multi-lingual, multi-ethnic and plural societies, and their demography and economy provide immense market opportunities and a huge pool of human resources. Nigeria, one of India's largest suppliers of crude oil, is India's largest trading partner in Africa. India's multiple cleavages of religion, caste, tribe, region and language slicing across each other are considered a good example of a society with cross-cutting cleavages that help in achieving political stability due to its diversity. Whereas Nigeria's multiple cleavages of linguistic, religious and ethnic differences that overlap one another and coincide with regional boundaries are considered overlapping cleavages, which have compromised its political stability (Cohn, 2013).

In the military arena, the connection and complementarity between the Nigerian military and the Indian military establishments run deeper in many aspects than ordinarily envisaged. Both shared the same experience in their origin, training and standards through the British colonization episode. For instance, to achieve standardization of the British imperial forces across the British Empire, there was a uniformity in education, training and structure of the armed forces throughout the empire. Also, after the Second World War, the UK, in an attempt to create a closer military, offered to train cadets from around the British Empire at the Royal Military Academy, Sandhurst (RMAS), the elite army officer training school in the UK. With this training process, the UK sought to inculcate shared norms and values and cement personal relationships with members of military elites abroad (Eck and Ruffa, 2022). As such, it was easier for forces of different nations in the empire (including many African countries) to work together. For instance, the British imperial colleges were heavily staffed by the British and Indian military instructors. For example, the Nigerian Defence Academy follows the pattern of the similar National Defence Academy in India, and its initial trainers were mostly officers in the Indian Army, and the Nigerian Defence Academy's first commandant was an Indian Army Brigadier, M.R. Varma.

The Second World War incident marked a period of comradeship and sharing of experiences between Indian soldiers and Nigerian soldiers, and both countries also established contact through the migration of indentured labourers from India who were part of the British colonial ventures to Nigeria (Osondu-Oti, 2019). Indian experts were sent to Nigeria under the Indian Technical and Economic Co-Operation (ITEC) agreement from 1971 to assist in the training of Nigerian professionals (Kura, 2009). According to PwC (2022), Nigerians and Indians are highly entrepreneurial people with a strong appetite for risk-taking and a can-do spirit. Over the years, both countries have developed promising entrepreneurial ecosystems and have been on a similar trajectory of entrepreneurial advancement in recent times.

Entrepreneurship in the Indian Context

The Indian economy has many unique characteristics that continue to puzzle scholars and policymakers, especially when it is compared to the economies of the other Asian counterparts (Bhagavatula et al., 2019). In the twenty-first century, the Indian economy, described as an 'entrepreneurial economy' and the pillar of global connectivity, has become so crucial as to be indispensable (Audretsch and Thurik, 2001). Studies on entrepreneurship in the Indian context are much more warranted. Further, for several years, the number of tech startups in India (estimated at 7,200–7,700 between 2013 and September 2018), as well as the number of startups that have achieved substantial market capitalization, have increased rapidly (NASSCOM, 2018). According to CB Insights (2018), India ranks fourth in the world in terms of the number of unicorns (startups that achieved a market capitalization of more than US$1 billion).

Today, India's innovation and entrepreneurship ecosystem is one of the largest in the world, with global integration in terms of technology, financing, human capital and administration (Bhagavatula et al., 2019). Evidence of true innovation capabilities in the Indian entrepreneurship ecosystem began to appear about two decades after the initial establishment of the Bangalore cluster. Scholars such as Parthasarathy and Aoyama (2006), as well as Prabhu and Jain (2015), contend that Indian entrepreneurship and innovation, unlike their counterparts, have been characterized as frugal (Prahalad, 2012), flexible (Sarasvathy, 2001) and inclusive (George et al., 2015) in approach.

Nonetheless, some problems are prevalent in all entrepreneurial sectors around the world, regardless of the country's stage of growth. Cash flow management, marketing strategy and legal complications are just a few of them. Some challenges are, however, isolated to the entrepreneurs in developing countries such as India. These problems include the orthodox mindset of Indian society, inefficient education system, red-tapism and bureaucratic corruption, to name a few (Sharma, 2021). In the context of veteran entrepreneurship, Kumar and Jain (2021) enumerated nineteen challenges that are commonly encountered by veteran entrepreneurs in India. These challenges relate to conceptualizing and implementation and sustenance of the business plan, creation of infrastructure, human capital management, finance management, and product and service management.

Military Entrepreneurship in India

The Global Firepower Index for 2023 reports India to be the fourth world power in terms of its military supremacy with a combined 26,05,000 active and reserve personnel (Global Firepower, 2023). However, with an intention to maintain a youthful profile, more than 70,000 personnel of the Indian military (including army, air force, and navy) are released from the service on an annual basis (Maharajan and Krishnaveni,

2016). This normally happens in the age bracket of 30–40 for personnel below officer rank (PBOR) and officers of short service commission (SSC) cadre with a label of retirees or ex-servicemen or veterans. However, since most of the retired military personnel go ahead with a second career on completion of their military service, the term 'retirement' cannot be used in its literal sense for them (Ojo, 2023). Notably, many veterans, in their transition to civilian life, may focus on self-employment as a viable option in seeking work (Blass and Ketchen, 2014). However, providing such opportunities becomes a challenge in a country like India with a developing economy and the world's second-largest population.

A military person's readiness to embrace such a venture is questionable, per se. In India, though many of the veterans adopt entrepreneurship for their life's second innings (Kedia, 2019), it is also to be noted that the prolonged indoctrination to military life often hinders veterans from developing entrepreneurship qualities (Maharajan and Krishnaveni, 2016). On the flip side, there are also mentions that proper guidance and groundwork may help veterans become successful in entrepreneurship (Maharajan and Subramani, 2014).

Entrepreneurship in the Nigerian Context

Like many other countries in the world, the Nigerian governments strive to encourage and support entrepreneurship in the country, such that many schemes were initiated to stimulate entrepreneurship at all strata of the economy in recognition of the importance of entrepreneurship and enterprise in creating employment. Successive governments established several agencies to promote the growth of the small business sector including the National Directorate of Employment (NDE), the Small and Medium Enterprises Development Agency (SMEDAN), the Central Bank of Nigeria's (CBN) Entrepreneurship Development Centres (EDCs), the Micro-Finance Policy, the Venture Prize Competition, NYSC Entrepreneurship Training Programmes, Youth Enterprise with Innovation in Nigeria (YouWIN!), Youth Initiative for Sustainable Agriculture in Nigeria (YISA), Subsidy Reinvestment and Empowerment Program (SURE-P), Graduate Intern-ship Scheme (GIS), Africa Youth Empowerment Nigeria (AYEN), Youth Entrepreneur Support Program (YES-P), N-Power Empowerment Program, and many more (Omeje et al., 2020).

Despite all these efforts, SMEs continue facing challenges, such that many of them struggle to survive or stop trading after a short while (Kayode and Ilesanmi, 2014). Adebizi and Gbegi (2013) argue that 80 per cent of SMEs fail within the first five years of establishment. Some of the reasons adduced to SMEs' failure in Nigeria include lack of access to finance (Ozioma-Eleodinmuo, 2015; Gbandi and Amissah, 2014; Akinola and Iordoo, 2013), crime, inadequate infrastructure, corruption and regulations (Ekpo and Bassey, 2016; Bah and Fang, 2015; Alarape, 2014). Other significant reasons include mismanagement, incompetence, official malfeasance, ineffective supporting mechanisms and the general poor socio-economic conditions (such as poverty) in Nigeria (Opara, 2011).

Military Entrepreneurship in Nigeria

The literature on veteran (or military) entrepreneurship in Nigeria is meagre as the field is just emerging. Only a handful of studies exist on the subject, and many of these focused on entrepreneurship training for retired or retiring military personnel. However, a few (e.g. Madichie and Ayasi, 2018; Ojo, 2023; Yusuf and Minai, 2016) who wrote on veteran entrepreneurship established that most of the military personnel in Nigeria only have military experience with limited real-life exposure, and they end up depending solely on their pension income. Due to the rising cost of living, with the salary they are getting from their pension, they are not able to cope with the financial challenges arising upon retirement from active service (Ojo, 2023; Yusuf and Minai, 2016). Hence, many of Nigeria's veterans are retiring into entrepreneurship. In one sense, they serve the country by protecting it when they are on active duty. Upon retirement, they decide to serve the economy in the guise of veteran entrepreneurship. Whereas Madichie and Ayasi (2018) have circumstantial evidence that seems to point to veteran entrepreneurs not having fared well in business, Ojo (2023) bases this more on the retirees' conditions of retirement.

Nigerian veteran entrepreneurs often benefit from their military background and training in their business ventures. However, many of them are challenged in fully adapting to the less structured civilian environment in which they operate, in contrast to the highly structured military setting they retired from and are familiar with. Furthermore, the valuable skill sets they acquired in the military that help their entrepreneurial engagement could also generate an impediment for them. For instance, the rigidity and stern bearing associated with military training could be a source of tension between veteran entrepreneurs and their staff or customers (Ojo, 2021).

Discussion

Arising from the review in the preceding sections, the following narratives itemizing the military entrepreneurship in India and Nigeria on a comparative basis are offered.

Shared Foundations and Divergent Applications

Both nations share a colonial military legacy that emphasized discipline, strategic thinking and adaptability. However, their socio-economic contexts have led to different applications. India leverages its military entrepreneurship for defence innovation, contributing to global technology markets (Gupta, 2022). In Nigeria, military entrepreneurship often addresses grassroots development needs, such as empowering local communities through small-scale entrepreneurial projects (Okafor, 2020).

National Culture and Military Practices

India's collectivist orientation fosters a collaborative approach to entrepreneurship, seen in its robust public-private partnerships in defence (Hofstede, 1980; Singh, 2021).

Conversely, Nigeria's emphasis on hierarchy and community support drives initiatives that prioritize social welfare, such as agricultural and infrastructural projects led by retired military personnel (Onuoha, 2013).

Challenges in Military Entrepreneurship

Both nations face challenges such as bureaucratic inertia, resource constraints and resistance to change. In India, the integration of cutting-edge technologies into traditional military structures is slow, while in Nigeria, limited funding and political instability hinder entrepreneurial efforts (Dyer, 2021; Okafor, 2020).

Opportunities for Mutual Learning

Cross-cultural exchanges could address these challenges by allowing both nations to learn from each other's strengths. India's success in defence technology startups can inspire similar ventures in Nigeria, while Nigeria's community-focused initiatives can provide insights for India's rural development projects.

Future Research Directions on Military Entrepreneurship

Findings from the comparative review suggest a number of insights for further study. First, examining the processes of military entrepreneurship in India and Nigeria can provide us with insights into the impact of colonial ties and cultural paraphernalia on veteran entrepreneurship in both countries. In doing so, there is value added to studying the differences in military entrepreneurship support systems across countries with a shared history of colonization. Second, these findings help to inform current policies and debates around military entrepreneurship in India and Nigeria.

Furthermore, future research on military entrepreneurship may explore several promising avenues that would deepen understanding and enhance the theoretical and practical contributions of the field. For instance, one critical direction involves looking into the role of military entrepreneurship in fostering national economic development, particularly in developing nations like India and Nigeria. Although past literature confirms the indispensable role of the retired military men in entrepreneurial endeavours, future studies are called to conduct an assessment to establish if military entrepreneurial initiative plays any role in socio-economic stability, as well as contributing to the creation of more employment (Okafor, 2020; Ojo, 2023). Long-term longitudinal studies might measure whether these ventures are sustainable and scalable in the long term. Relevant studies on comparative national analyses between India and Nigeria, which posit different socio-economic contexts, might provide insights into how military culture matters in entrepreneurial outcomes under varying political and economic contexts.

The intersection of military entrepreneurship and technological innovation would be another key area of future research. Defence startups in India, for example, under the self-reliant initiative of Atmanirbhar Bharat (Self-reliant India), have shown the possibility of military-driven technological development (Gupta, 2022). How military entrepreneurship leads to innovation in other sectors, such as healthcare, logistics and disaster management, could be another future direction for research. In addition, research regarding the impact of public-private partnerships on stimulating innovation in the military can provide insight into how collaborative ventures enhance the capacity of national defence while contributing to economic growth as well (Singh, 2021). Future research should address specific peculiarities of military entrepreneurs concerning bureaucratic inertia, lack of resources and political turbulence, which may also contribute towards developing strategies for alleviating these barriers for enhanced progress in military entrepreneurship within the national development policy scope.

Future studies may also focus on the social and cultural factors that influence military entrepreneurship, especially in transitioning from military life to civilian life. The research can go into finding out how the discipline and the adaptability developed due to military service can translate to entrepreneurial success, and how it could be started in retired serving personnel. For example, one can take up questions like how training programmes aimed at entrepreneurship, especially specifically for veterans and how these in turn affect their business's success rates (Kleykamp, 2009).

Moreover, the importance of social networks, mentorship and access to capital for supporting veteran-owned enterprises will be useful information for policy and military establishments. An analysis of these socio-cultural dimensions would give a very panoramic view of military entrepreneurship and its contribution to greater development within society. Finally, further research would help determine the additional role that military entrepreneurship might play in spurring innovation, economic resilience and sustainable development and promote mutual learning among nations about this nascent field.

Conclusion and Recommendations

Military entrepreneurship in India and Nigeria is a fusion of common colonial heritages and unique socio-economic conditions, contributing to national development. In India, it is linked to the growth of technological innovation and defence industries; in Nigeria, it caters to grassroots economic needs through grassroots initiatives. Yet, notwithstanding these differences, both have common problems, such as resource limitations, bureaucratic inertia and political instability. Such barriers demand focused policies, more public-private partnerships and specialized training for exiting military members.

It is clear from the literature that military entrepreneurship (i.e. veteran entrepreneurship), wherever it is practiced, highlights certain traits that are inculcated into military personnel during their service years. Such traits include discipline, resilience, perseverance, adaptability, overcoming hurdles, risk appetite, team leadership and focused mission orientation. These traits are considered valuable to veteran entrepreneurs in running their businesses since a person with good officer-like qualities will be able to make a good entrepreneur (Kumar and Jain, 2021; Ojo, 2023).

Taken together, the Indian and Nigerian cases – both civilian and military – illustrate the paradox of entrepreneurship in emerging economies. On one hand, it is celebrated as a vehicle for empowerment, job creation and innovation, supported by government programmes and the resilience of individuals. On the other hand, deep-rooted institutional, structural and socio-economic challenges undermine sustainability. Whether among civilian entrepreneurs or military veterans, the transformative potential of entrepreneurship remains constrained until these systemic barriers are effectively addressed.

Given the findings in this paper, it will be valuable for policy-makers in both countries to use existing military exchange/bilateral platforms to promote issues around veteran entrepreneurship in their deliberations. Additionally, entrepreneurship workshops and conferences could be organized for veteran entrepreneurs of both countries to meet and network regularly.

References

Adebisi, J.F., and D.O. Gbegi (2013). 'Analysis of Tax Morale and Tax Compliance in Nigeria', *Journal of Finance and Management in Public Services*, 11(1): 85–98.

Akinola, A.O., and Iordoo, D.A. (2013). 'The Effect of Nigerian Capital Market on the Micro, Small and Medium Scale Enterprises (MSMEs) in Nigeria', *Journal of Finance and Accounting*, 4(7): 1–14.

Alarape, A.A. (2014). 'Entrepreneurial Orientation and the Growth Performance of Small and Medium Enterprises in Southwestern Nigeria', *Journal of Small Business & Entrepreneurship*, 26(6): 553–77. Available at: https://doi.org/10.1080/08276331.2014.892308

Audretsch, D.B., and A.R. Thurik (2001). 'What Is New About the New Economy: Sources of Growth in the Managed and Entrepreneurial Economies', *Industrial and Corporate Change*, 10(1): 267–315.

Audretsch, D.B., M.A. Carree and A.R. Thurik (2001). '*Does Entrepreneurship Reduce Unemployment?*' Tinbergen Institute discussion paper No. 01-074/3.

Baert, S., and P. Balcaen (2013). 'The Impact of Military Work Experience on the Hiring Decisions of Employers', *Journal of Labor Studies*, 30(2): 43–55.

Bah, E., and L. Fang (2015). 'Impact of the Business Environment on Output and Productivity in Africa', *Journal of Development Economics*, 114(C): 159–71.

Baron, R., and S. Shane (2008). *Entrepreneurship: A Process Perspective*. Mason (Ohio): Thomson/South-Western.

Bhagavatula, S., R. Mudambi and J.P. Murmann (2019). 'Innovation and Entrepreneurial Ecosystems in India: An Analytical Perspective', *International Journal of Entrepreneurial Behaviour & Research*, 25(3): 342–65.

Blass, F.R., and D.J. Ketchen (2014). 'So, You Want to Be an Entrepreneur? Lessons from the Entrepreneurship Bootcamp for Veterans with Disabilities', *Business Horizons*, 57: 5–9. Available at: https://doi.org/10.1016/j.bushor.2013.09.006

Bloom, P.N., and B.R. Smith (2010). 'Identifying the Drivers of Social Entrepreneurial Impact: Theoretical Development and an Exploratory Empirical Test of SCALERS', *Journal of Social Entrepreneurship*, 1(1): 126–45.

Brömmelhörster, J., and W.-C. Paes (2004). *The Military as an Economic Actor: Soldiers in Business*. New York: Palgrave Macmillan.

Bruyat, C., and P. Julien (2000). 'Defining the Field of Research in Entrepreneurship', *Journal of Business Venturing*, 16: 165–80.

CB Insights (2018). *The Global Unicorn Club: Private Companies Valued at $1B+*. CB Insights. Available at: https://www.cbinsights.com/

Cohn, C. (2013). 'India and Nigeria: Similar Colonial Legacies, Vastly Different Trajectories: An Examination of the Differing Fates of Two Former British Colonies', *Cornell International Affairs Review*, 7(1): 18–30.

Dyer, J. (2021). 'Military Innovation and Entrepreneurship: Strategic Imperatives in a Volatile World', *Defense Studies Journal*, 28(3): 201–23.

Eck, K., and C. Ruffa (2022). 'Military Training and Decolonisation in the British Empire', *Journal of Imperial and Commonwealth History*, 51(1): 156–81. Available at: https://doi.org/10.1080/03086534.2022.2084937

Ekpo, I.C., and E.A. Bassey (2016). 'Corruption and Economic Growth in Nigeria: The Role of Private Sector', *Journal of Development and Economic Policies*, 18(1): 72–88.

Gbandi, E.C., and G. Amissah (2014). 'Financial Options for Small and Medium Enterprises (SMEs) in Nigeria', *European Scientific Journal*, 10(1): 327–40.

George, G., A.M. McGahan and J. Prabhu (2015). 'Innovation for Inclusive Growth: Towards a Theoretical Framework and a Research Agenda', *Journal of Management Studies*, 52(1): 1–25.

Ghauri, P., M. Tasavori and R. Zaefarian (2014). 'Internationalisation of Service Firms Through Corporate Social Entrepreneurship and Networking', *International Marketing Review*, 31(6): 576–600.

Global Firepower (2023). 'Military Strength Ranking'. Global Firepower. Available at: https://www.globalfirepower.com

Goldacre, B. (2011). *Battling Bad Science*. TED. Available at: https://www.ted.com/talks/ben_goldacre_battling_bad_science

Gomezelj, D.O., and I. Kusce (2013). 'The Influence of Personal and Environmental Factors on Entrepreneurs' Performance', *Kybernetes*, 42(6): 906–27.

Gupta, A. (2022). 'Defense Startups and India's Atmanirbhar Bharat: Opportunities and Challenges', *Journal of Defense Innovation*, 19(4): 56–78.

Hayton, J.C., G. George and S.A. Zahra (2002). 'National Culture and Entrepreneurship: A Review of Behavioural Research', *Entrepreneurship Theory and Practice*, 26(4): 33–52. Available at: https://doi.org/10.1177/104225870202600403

Hofstede, G. (1980). *Culture's Consequences: International Differences in Work-Related Values*. Beverly Hills, CA: Sage.

Hofstede, G. (2001). *Culture's Consequences: Comparing Values, Behaviours, Institutions, and Organisations Across Nations* (2nd ed.). Thousand Oaks, CA: Sage.

Huntington, S.P. (1957). *The Soldier and the State: The Theory and Politics of Civil-Military Relations*. Cambridge, MA: Harvard University Press.

Jelusic, L. (2006). 'Conversion of the Military', in G. Caforio (ed.), *Handbook of the Sociology of the Military*, 345–60. New York: Springer.

Johnson, J.W. (1999). 'Personality Characteristics of Third-Year Midshipmen at the U.S. Naval Academy', *Journal of Personality Assessment*, 73(3): 392–405.

Kayode, K.B., and A.O. Ilesanmi (2014). 'Determinants of Factors Influencing Capacity of Small and Medium Enterprises (SMEs) in Employment Creation in Lagos State,

Nigeria', *International Journal of Financial Research*, 5(2): 133–41. Available at: https://doi.org/10.5430/ijfr.v5n2p133

Kedia, S. (2019). 'With This Organisation's Help, Indian Army Veterans Are Becoming Entrepreneurs.' Social Story. Available at: https://yourstory.com/socialstory/2019/03/indian-army-veterans-turn-entrepreneurs-8icuu43y47

Kelty, R., M. Kleykamp and D.R. Segal (2010). 'The Civilian-Military Gap in the United States: Does It Exist, Why, and Does It Matter?' *Armed Forces & Society*, 36(2): 203–29.

Kiyosaki, R.T. (2015). *8 Lessons in Military Leadership for Entrepreneurs*. Scottsdale, AZ: Plata Publishing.

Kleykamp, M. (2009). 'Military Service and the Transition to Entrepreneurship: Exploring the Role of Military-Acquired Skills', *Journal of Labor Studies*, 28(2): 67–89.

Kourilsky, M.L. (2001). 'The Education of Entrepreneurs: A Blueprint for the 21st Century', *Journal of Business Venturing*, 16(1): 275–96.

Kramm, N., and L. Heinecken (2015). 'We Are Different Now? The Effect of Military Service on Youth Reintegration and Employment in South Africa', *African Security Review*, 24(2): 122–37.

Kumar, M.V., and R.K. Jain (2021). 'Study of Challenges Encountered by Indian Military Veteran Entrepreneurs During Their Entrepreneurial Journey', *Journal of Emerging Technologies and Innovative Research*, 8(5): 75–82.

Kura, S.B. (2009). 'Nigeria-India Economic, Political and Socio-Cultural Relations: Critical Reflections for Continuous Mutual Co-operation', *International Journal of Asia Pacific* Studies, 5(1): 1–31.

Lynn, R. (1991). *The Secret of the Miracle Economy: Different National Attitudes to Competitiveness and Money*. Exeter: Social Affairs Unit.

Madichie, N.O., and K. Ayasi (2018). 'Entrepreneurial Opportunities and Challenges for Retired Senior Military Officers in Nigeria', in L.P. Dana, V. Ratten and B. Honyenuga (eds), *African Entrepreneurship. Palgrave Studies of Entrepreneurship in Africa*, 131–51. Cham: Palgrave Macmillan.

Maharajan, K., and B. Subramani (2014). 'A Critical Study on the Resettlement Problems of Air Force Ex-Servicemen in India: Evolving Management Strategies', *International Journal of Research in Management Sciences*, 2: 13–23.

Maharajan, K., and R. Krishnaveni (2016). 'Managing the Migration from Military to Civil Society: Motivation Model for Socioeconomic Needs in Resettlement of Veterans in India', *Armed Forces & Society*, 42(3): 605–25.

Mani, K. (2007). 'Militaries in Business: State-Making and Entrepreneurship in the Developing World: State-Making and Entrepreneurship in the Developing World', *Armed Forces & Society*, 33(4): 591–611. Available at: https://doi.org/10.1177/0095327X06291348

Maune, A. (2023). 'Military Entrepreneurship: An Emerging Research Domain', *International Journal of Entrepreneurship and Innovation Management*, 7(2): 45–67.

Mehra, N., and A.S. Yaruingam (2015). 'India-Nigeria Relations (from Historical Friends to Strategic Partners)', *International Journal of Political Science and Development*, 3(5): 232–9.

Mulvenon, J.C. (2001). *Soldiers of Fortune: The Rise and Fall of the Chinese Military-Business Complex, 1978–1998*. Armonk, NY: M.E. Sharpe.

NASSCOM (2018). 'Indian Tech Start-Ups: Ecosystem for Inclusive Growth', NASSCOM. Available at: https://nasscom.in/product/94

Ojo, S. (2021a). 'Military Enterprises and Entrepreneurship: A Critical Perspective', in S. Ojo (ed.), *Global Perspectives on Military Entrepreneurship and Innovation*, 14–44. Hershey: IGI Global. Available at: https://doi.org/10.4018/978-1-7998-6655-8

Ojo, S. (2021b). 'Investigating Entrepreneurship Among Nigerian Retired Military Veterans', in S. Ojo (ed.), *Global Perspectives on Military Entrepreneurship and Innovation*, 119–47. Hershey: IGI Global. Available at: https://doi.org/10.4018/978-1-7998-6655-8

Ojo, S. (2023). 'Exploring Veteran Entrepreneurship in Nigeria', *Journal of Enterprising Communities: People and Places in the Global Economy*, 17(3): 644–63. Available at: https://doi.org/10.1108/JEC-10-2021-0148

Okafor, I. (2020). 'Military Entrepreneurship and Community Development in Nigeria: Challenges and Prospects', *African Journal of Economic Studies*, 12(2): 78–95.

Omeje, A.N., A. Jideofor and M.O. Ugwu (2020). 'Youth Empowerment and Entrepreneurship in Nigeria: Implication for Economic Diversification', *Sage Open*, 10(4). Available at: https://doi.org/10.1177/2158244020982996

Onuoha, C. (2013). 'The Cultural Dynamics of Entrepreneurship in Africa: A Focus on Nigeria' *Journal of African Studies*, 15(1): 45–60.

Opara, J.O. (2011). 'Factors Constraining the Growth and Survival of SME in Nigeria: Implications for Poverty Alleviation', *Management Research Review*, 34(2): 156–71. Available at: https://doi.org/10.1108/01409171111102786

Osondu-Oti, A. (2019). 'An Appraisal of India-Nigeria Historical and Contemporary Relations', *Alternation Special Edition* No 15 (2015): 102–26. ISSN 1023-1757.

Ozioma-Eleodinmuo, P. (2015). 'Analysis of Entrepreneurship Policy for Small and Medium Scale Enterprise in Aba, Abia State Nigeria', *Journal of Economic Development, Management, IT, Finance and Marketing*, 7(1): 47–60.

Parthasarathy, B., and Y. Aoyama (2006). 'From Software Services to R&D Services: Local Entrepreneurship in the Software Industry in Bangalore, India', *Environment and Planning A*, 38(7): 1269–85. Available at: https://doi.org/10.1068/a37247

Praag, C.M., and P.H. Versloot (2007). 'What Is the Value of Entrepreneurship? A Review of Recent Research', *Small Business Economics*, 29(4): 351–82.

Prabhu, J., and S. Jain (2015). 'Innovation and Entrepreneurship in India: Understanding Jugaad', *Asia Pacific Journal of Management*, 32: 843–68.

Prahalad, C.K. (2012). 'Bottom of the Pyramid as a Source of Breakthrough Innovations', *Journal of Product Innovation Management*, 29(1): 6–12.

PwC (2022). 'Nigeria – India. Learnings from Two Large Democracies'. PwC. Available at: https://www.pwc.com/ng/en/assets/pdf/india-nigeria-connectivity1.pdf

Rosen, H.S. (2005). 'Entrepreneurship and Taxation: Empirical Evidence', in C. Keuschnigg (ed.), *Venture Capital, Entrepreneurship and Public Policy*, 251–80. Cambridge, MA: MIT Press.

Sarasvathy, S.D. (2001). 'Causation and Effectuation: Towards a Theoretical Shift from Economic Inevitability to Entrepreneurial Contingency', *Academy of Management Review*, 26(2): 243–63.

Schumpeter, J.A. (1983). *The Theory of Economic Development: An Inquiry into Profits, Capital, Credit, Interest, and the Business Cycle*. New Brunswick, NJ: Transaction.

Shane, S. (1993). 'Cultural Influences on National Rates of Innovation', *Journal of Business Venturing*, 8: 59–73.

Shane, S., and S. Venkataraman (2000). 'The Promise of Entrepreneurship as a Field of Research', *Academy of Management Review*, 25(1): 217–27.

Sharma, A. (2021). 'Entrepreneurship in India: Challenges, Policy Efforts and Potential', *International Journal of Social Science and Economic Research*, 6(10): 3954–65.

Shimshoni, J. (1990–1). 'Technology, War, and Peace: The State and Military Affairs in the Twentieth Century', *Journal of Strategic Studies*, 13(1): 1–22. Available at: https://doi.org/10.1080/01402399008437494

Singh, R. (2021). 'Public-Private Partnerships in Indian Defence Innovation: A Critical Analysis', *Indian Journal of Strategic Studies*, 34(2): 67–89.

Smith, M.R. (1985). *Military Enterprise and Technological Change: Perspectives on the American Experience*. Cambridge, MA: MIT Press.

Snyder, J. (1984). *The Ideology of the Offensive: Military Decision Making and the Disasters of 1914*. Ithaca, NY: Cornell Studies in Security Affairs.

Wennekers, S. (2006). *Entrepreneurship at Country Level: Economic and Non-Economic Determinants*. ERIM: Rotterdam.

Yusuf, L., and M.S. Minai (2016). 'Entrepreneurial Training and Career Path of Retired Military Personnel as Entrepreneurs in Nigeria', *International Journal of Sciences: Basic and Applied Research*, 28(3): 217–30.

15

War Entrepreneurship: Analysing the Wagner Group's Military Activities in Africa

Sanya Ojo

The focus of this chapter is on war entrepreneurship using the prism of private military companies (PMCs) in general and the activities of the Wagner Group in particular. PMCs' operations are increasingly taking place in many parts of Africa that are experiencing turmoil and violent conflict situations. The term entrepreneurship is leveraged in many contexts, across institutions, private industry and public agencies. Entrepreneurship is everywhere and has become a part of the lexicon of a diverse set of public and private entities (Jeffrey et al., 2018). Its diversity is apparent in several research streams, and its reach is broad and can branch in many profitable directions. An important branch of the entrepreneurship field that is increasingly gaining attention is military entrepreneurship, which speaks to the entrepreneurial activities within the military ecosystem (Ojo, 2021). Embedded within this ecosystem are the various aspects of business ventures around warfare – or to put it aptly – war entrepreneurship. War entrepreneurship unifies different enterprises conducted during conflict and war situations in a society. Many businesspeople who engaged in selling arms or military expertise and support applied all the attributes of entrepreneurs and entrepreneurial spirit in their dealings. Thus, under the rubric of war entrepreneurship, this chapter looks at the activities of the Wagner Group, a Russian-based PMC in Africa, as a demonstration of war entrepreneurship. Also, the benefits accruing to Russia, as an entrepreneurial state and through Wagner's operations are evaluated.

According to Arduino (2024), history has shown that Africa serves as a lucrative arena for mercenaries (private bands of soldiers) due to various factors. These factors include (a) the prevalence of low-intensity conflicts that reduce the risks to mercenaries' lives compared to full-scale wars like in Ukraine, (b) the continent's abundant natural resources that are prone to exploitation, and (c) pervasive instability that allows mercenaries to operate with relative impunity. Many parts of the African continent are witnessing violent conflicts, including Islamic fundamentalism, banditry, struggle for resources, ethnic-derived battles, and others, in which PMCs are engaged. The Wagner Group has been recorded to operate in some African countries, such as Sudan, South Sudan, Libya, Mali, the Central African Republic (CAR), Burkina Faso, Niger, and Chad (Walsh, 2022). Wagner wielded both hard power (coercive) and soft power (persuasive) operations in Africa. Beyond the security work Wagner handles for governments (e.g. protection of sensitive natural resource extraction sites), the group's network also engages in disinformation campaigns by paying people to attend protests and write pre-approved stories in the local press (Gedeon, 2023). From Libya to Sudan to Madagascar to the CAR, the Wagner Group is making inroads by building cultural hubs – complexes to host meetings and events, establishing military bases and making money out of those activities.

Consequently, this paper, aside from tracking the incursion of the Wagner Group in Africa, offers a critical evaluation of its role, the legitimacy of its existence and the entrepreneurial bases for services offered. Furthermore, the paper takes a look at Russia's (Wagner's principal) strategic economic and socio-political impact on the African countries in which Wagner operates. The Wagner Group's involvement in Africa (and elsewhere) is a relatively new phenomenon and is generating research interest in several academic fields. Interrogating the space of war entrepreneurship, using Wagner's template, will add new insight and enrich the field of entrepreneurship. It is important to focus on new areas of research related to entrepreneurship that have not yet been fully explored (Kuhn and Galloway, 2015; Ratten, 2023). According to Ratten (2016), this will enable entrepreneurship to be contextualized and stimulate more research efforts.

Against this background, this chapter builds on the existing literature to explore the features of war entrepreneurship, from the Wagner Group's peculiarities through two questions: (1) To what extent is war entrepreneurship engaged in Wagner's activities in Africa? (2) What effect do Wagner's activities have on political and socio-economic development in Africa? The rest of the paper is arranged into five sections: the first is the conceptual appraisal, the second enunciates the contextual audit, the third describes the methodology, the fourth shows the findings and analysis and the fifth presents the discussion, recommendations and conclusion.

Conceptual Appraisal

Enterprises, Conflicts and Wars

Earning income from warfare is as old as time, and there have been individuals and organizations supplying weapons to ready militaries and subsequently profiting from wars. Individuals, for instance, as mercenaries, are known to sell their services for hire to fight in other people's wars. Likewise, private sector organizations have been deeply involved in all facets of war and conflict throughout history. According to Nimkar (2009), the first private military band was hired in 1294 BC to fight in the battle of Kadesh between Egypt and the Hittites. However, the first modern PMCs emerged shortly after the Cold War (Shearer, 2005). Presently, the private military and security industry represents the modern and commercialized provision of military and security services that are increasingly outsourced in wars and violent conflicts around the world. The face of the private sector military and security industry is recognized in

PMCs that operate in conflict zones and are often tagged the 'invisible army'. PMCs represent a global industry worth more than $100 billion and have continued to grow amid increasing and diversifying security threats (Klaassen, 2023: 5).

War Entrepreneurship

War entrepreneurship describes the facets of business enterprises integrated in a war (and/or violent conflicts more broadly) situation. War entrepreneurship is in many ways ensconced within the general entrepreneurship trope. Shane and Venkataraman (2000) define entrepreneurship as an analysis of how, by whom and with what consequences opportunities to produce future goods and services are discovered, evaluated and exploited. Invariably, an entrepreneur is innovative, as he/she must, first, perceive and create new opportunities. Second, an entrepreneur operates under unpredictability, as well as introducing merchandise for sale, deciding on the venues, and forming and using means/assets. Third, an entrepreneur manages his/her business and competes with others for a stake in the market (Wennekers and Thurik, 1999). Furthermore, Shane (2003) contends that environmental factors can affect the entrepreneurial process in various ways. Hence, in as much as entrepreneurs, according to Baumol (1990: 987), are 'persons who are ingenious and creative in finding ways that add to their own wealth, power, and prestige', entrepreneurial talent may be directed not only to productive activities but also to unproductive (e.g. rent seeking) or destructive (e.g. illegal) activities (Brück et al., 2013). Weapons and soldiers must be accumulated to wage wars; hence, entrepreneurial skills are needed to organize weapons, ammunition, and other war materials, and the willingness to bear risk to significantly generate income/profits. It is instructive to recall Ramoglou and Gartner (2022) contention that the entrepreneurial process is about opportunities that must be created or discovered, then exploited and finally realized. Profits, the ultimate goal of war entrepreneurship (or any other business venture), are made from enterprises that supply material and resources to prepare armies. Important tasks of a state and directing an army, such as supplying, transporting, coordinating, map making, arms and munition making, weapons and personnel for hire, and many more, are undoubtedly lucrative for entrepreneurs involved in the business of war. Making profits out of warfare is an enduring and long-standing reality, as there are always firms supplying hardware to prepare militaries and subsequently profit from war and violent conflicts. For example, private entrepreneurs supplied the government military with much of its food requirements during the Mozambican 18-year civil war (Addison, 2001).

Impact of War on Entrepreneurship

Some studies have investigated how entrepreneurs are affected by war. Many of those studies (e.g. Mason, 1966; Overton, 1986; Duménil et al., 1993; Jackson and Worthen, 2002; Cheung, 2016; Barker, 2017) seem to suggest a positive correlation between war and entrepreneurial activity. The positive association reflects a widespread belief that war may promote economic growth; for instance, Syrtseva et al.'s (2022) study in Ukraine indicates that entrepreneurship is promoted in the conditions of war through innovation. Yet, other studies (e.g. Yasuyuki, 1996; Arnold, 1999; Baten and Schulz, 2005) firmly contend that war hurts economic growth in any society. For instance, Audretsch et al. (2023) find that the Russia-Ukraine war negatively impacts entrepreneurial activity through reduced Small and Medium Enterprises (SMEs) birth rates and increased SME closures. Audretsch et al. (2023) also argue that the evidence that war diminishes entrepreneurial activity is striking because the benefits of entrepreneurship often materialize only in a few years, implying that the post-war economic recovery will be more dampened in countries that rely to a greater extent on their entrepreneurs.

From both sides of the contestation, one could infer that just as war influences business and entrepreneurship, conversely, entrepreneurship influences war. The phenomenon of the military-industrial complex (Avlon, 2017), which highlights the influence of firms on governments towards continued or increased military spending, also supports the arguments on both sides of the divide. The competitive advantages (e.g. provision of needed armament) conferred by the military-industrial complex are moderated by the negative externalities (e.g. warmongering, capturing the policy-making process) that the military-industrial complex generates (DeVore, 2020).

Private Military Companies (PMCs)

PMCs are profit-driven organizations that provide professional services intricately linked to warfare. They offer both armed and unarmed military services in high-threat environments for a range of clients, including national governments, multinational companies, and international organizations (Schreier and Caparini, 2005). As corporate bodies, PMCs' military skills and specialities include tactical combat operations, strategic planning, intelligence gathering and analysis, logistical and operational support, troop and personnel training and military technical assistance. The global private military services market size was valued at USD241 billion in 2021 and is expected to reach USD366.8 billion by 2028 (Vantage Market Research, 2022). Some of the firms are publicly traded on major stock exchanges, and they market themselves as flexible tools to accomplish the security goals of their clients around the world. Some popular PMCs include Executive Outcomes (South Africa), Sandline (UK), Wagner Group (Russia), Military Professionals Resource Incorporated (MPRI) (USA), Vinnell and Military Professional Resources Inc. (USA), G4S and Keeni-Meeny Services (UK), and Lordan-Levdan (Israel).

There are varied appellations in the industry of private military service. Commonly applied abbreviations include PMCs, PSCs (private security companies), PSP (private security providers), and PMSCs (private military and security companies); these are only a few examples of synonyms used to describe private military organizations. Some of these appellations refer exclusively to those having military services as their specific area of expertise, and some to those focusing on providing security services. In addition, academic research once used typologies that categorized types of firms based on their proximity to the battlefield. Nonetheless, while distinguishing between PMCs and PSCs may work in theory, it remains difficult in practice. Military contractors or firms develop different profiles based on the types of services they offer and their clients. Most opt to call themselves 'security' companies to deflect negative connotations associated with the term 'military' (Birthe, 2014: 76).

Generally, the United Nations (2018) describes a private military and security company as a corporate entity that provides, on a compensatory basis, military and/or security services by physical persons and/or legal entities. Many of these PMCs (e.g. ArmorGroup and Blackwater) are legally established corporate entities and are usually registered with the International Stability Operations Association (ISOA) (Klaassen, 2023). In this sense, PMCs are widely regarded as a legal intermediary between professional soldiers and national governments (Klaassen, 2023). However, there is the perception in the public space that PMCs are nothing but mercenaries. Mainstream media and public statements often employ the terms 'mercenaries', 'private military contractors', and 'private military companies' interchangeably. Nevertheless, the boundary between mercenary and PMC activities is often obscured. Whilst the services of PMCs are mostly regarded as legal and/or legitimate, the use and recruitment of mercenaries are prohibited by international law according to the 1989 International Convention against the Recruitment, Use, Financing and Training of Mercenaries (Taulbee, 1985).

The African Union's Convention for the Elimination of Mercenaryism in Africa is also against the use of mercenaries (OAU, 1985). There are notable differences between PMCs and mercenaries. For example, conventional mercenaries usually use lighter arms than professional PMCs. The latter have access to more complex and heavy military equipment such as tanks, helicopters, planes and sophisticated firearms as compared to mercenaries whose resources are often limited to small arms (Legal Assistant, 2020). Additionally, mercenaries are largely used in front-line combat while PMCs serve a variety of purposes, including in the areas of intelligence gathering, logistics, transportation, security, networks, and direct combat (Tekingunduz, 2018). Ultimately, PMCs' personnel are not considered mercenaries, but rather employees within a regulated and legal industry.

The industry's service is broadly classified into three types: (1) military provider firms, (2) military consulting firms, and (3) military support firms. These categories could be further reclassified under four rubrics of services provided using the 'tip of the spear' analogy. The first is the offensive combat services, which arguably is the most controversial category of PMCs' contracts. Offensive combat involves services located at the very tip of the spear. The second is the military and security expertise services, which is a category of PMCs' services characterized by the provision of high-level strategic or technical capabilities to military and/or security forces. It involves unarmed contractors unauthorized to use physical force (Tonkin, 2011). The third is armed security services, which involves various types of activities undertaken by means of physical protection of persons or property during armed conflict. The fourth category is the military support services, which is the largest sector within the private military service industry. Contracts under this category are generally considered to be the least questionable ones offered by PMCs (Macías, 2014).

The services of PMCs are sought by a variety of patrons such as

> failing government trying to prevent the imminent capture of its capital, a regional power planning for war, a ragtag militia looking to reverse its battlefield losses, a peacekeeping force seeking deployment support, a weak ally attempting to escape its patron's dictates, a multinational corporation hoping to end constant rebel attacks against its facilities, a drug cartel pursuing high-technology military capabilities, a humanitarian aid group requiring protection within conflict zones, and the world's sole remaining superpower searching for ways to limit its military costs and risks.
>
> (Singer, 2001: 186)

In other words, PMCs' clients include countries, armed groups, business enterprises, the UN (United Nations), and NGOs (Non-governmental Organizations) – even the International Committee of the Red Cross (ICRC) has occasionally resorted to private security firms to protect its premises.

Industry experts claim PMCs are more cost-effective due to the absence of long-term obligations to the institution (clients) and timely response (rapid mobilization) than the military (Efflandt, 2014). For instance, the conflicts in Angola and Sierra Leone are conspicuous examples in which Executive Outcomes (a South African-based PMC) was contracted by the two countries to assist in bringing their respective internal conflicts to an end and stabilize the region when national military capacities were limited; and they did so with great success (Shearer, 2005). Also in 2015, to combat insurgency in the northern part of Nigeria, the government contracted Specialized Tasks, Training, Equipment, and Protection (STTEP), a PMC founded by South African Defence Force veterans, for a three-month contract to help the Nigerian military build a counterinsurgency 'strike force', specifically the 72 Mobile Strike Force (Nielsen, 2016). The contemporary demand surge for PMCs' services, particularly on the African continent, is partly traceable to the effects of the withdrawal of foreign patronage occasioned by the end of the Cold War (Howe, 1998). Kaldor (2012) affirms that due to the reduced interest of Western powers in the developing world since the end of the Cold War, many fragile or failing states have emerged, unable to maintain strong armed forces to match new threats and maintain internal order. On the supply side, the end of the Cold War, the fall of the apartheid regime in South Africa, and the consequent military downsizing that followed created a large pool of highly trained military personnel for hire (Higate and Utas, 2017). The collapse of Gaddafi's Libyan government and the subsequent proliferation of arms and armed groups in the Sahel region also aided PMCs' recruitment drives (Brahimi, 2021).

Nonetheless, as non-state actors, both mercenaries and PMCs can severely subvert a country's legitimacy and long-term security. The UN Working Group on the use of mercenaries has established a correlation between the presence of foreign fighters (including both mercenaries and PMCs) and an increase in human rights abuses. PMCs are reported to have engaged in 'direct participation in hostilities', even in situations where there is no armed conflict, 'posing grave threats to human rights' (United Nations, 2018). Also, it is crucial to recognize that PMCs have a vested interest in perpetuating regional conflict to remain in business. In sum, while the use of PMCs may be operationally effective in restoring short-term order in conflict zones, they can also threaten the long-term stability and legitimacy of state governments and militaries (Klaassen, 2023).

Furthermore, issues relating to incomplete information and monitoring problems generally accompany the outsourcing of military service to PMCs. The issues of incomplete information are particularly intensified in the military field because few clients (e.g. NGOs and Multinational firms) have experience in contracting with security agents. In most cases, there is either little oversight or a lack of clearly defined requirements, or both and in the murky situation of war, getting full information becomes extremely difficult. The problem of proper monitoring is exacerbated because of the nature of PMCs, which are usually autonomous and thus require extraterritorial monitoring. The monitoring problem is also manifested in the danger that PMCs may not perform their missions optimally as they have incentives not only to prolong their contracts but also to avoid taking undue risks that might endanger their corporate assets. This could result in a protracted conflict, which perhaps could have been avoided if the client had built up its military forces or more closely monitored its hired PMC. Adams (1999) argues that this was certainly true of mercenaries in the Nigerian civil war of the 1970s, and that this might also be the case with PMCs in the Ethiopia-Eritrea conflict in 1997–99. The wars in both cases were needlessly prolonged. Moreover, the customer may not be the consumer, as some states, for example, pay PMCs to supply personnel on their behalf to international organizations. In addition, PMCs may be tempted to cut corners to boost their bottom line and increase their profit.

Taken together, PMCs are highly organized businesses, driven by business profit rather than individual profit, and they operate legally on the open global market. PMCs offer services within a significantly broad spectrum, sometimes to multiple clients at the same time, and usually interlinked to other industries (e.g. corporate holdings and financial markets). All these generally provide them with some degree of legitimacy. Apart from Russia's Wagner Group, other PMCs operating on the African continent include the Dyck Advisory Group (DAG) – a South African security firm, CACI and Academi – USA, Secopex – France, Aegis Defence Services and G4S – Great Britain, Omega Consulting Group – Ukraine, Asgaard and Xeless – Germany (Cascais and Koubakin, 2022).

The Wagner Group and Its Activities in Africa

The Wagner Group is a PMC of Russian origin, also described as the Africa Corps in Africa (Bobin and Le Cam, 2023) because of its connection with the Russian Ministry of Defence (MoD) or Russia's military intelligence agency, the GRU (Higgins and Nechepurenko, 2018). Established by a Russian businessman, Yevgeny Prigozhin, the Wagner Group is a complex network of businesses and mercenary groups with a strong tie to the Russian military and intelligence community. Its personnel strength in Africa is estimated to be about five thousand members, consisting of ex-Russian soldiers, convicts, and foreign nationals (Rampe, 2023). The Wagner Group's operations sit at the heart of a complex web of geopolitical ambitions, covert operations and influence peddling. Currently, Wagner is very active in the CAR, Libya, Mali and Sudan, all of which have a strained relationship with the West due to colonial legacies and inherent political differences. The group's services vary based on the needs of its clients, which include rebel groups and regimes, and its funding ranges from direct payment to resource concessions.

The group has operated in several African countries since 2017, often providing its clients with direct military support and associated security services coupled with propaganda activities (Rampe, 2023). Wagner's use of domestic disinformation targeting opposition political actors and pro-democracy activists has been documented in many African countries (e.g. Africa Centre for Strategic Studies, 2021). Wagner operations in Africa consist of (1) Combat operations (supporting governments' clients in combat operations against rebel groups, and vice versa), (2) Security and training support (acting as a security service for vulnerable regimes) and (3) Disinformation campaigns (using the media, social media, and troll farms to promulgate anti-Western messages) (Rampe, 2023).

The Wagner Group, with thousands of personnel in arm, has become one of Russia's most influential foreign policy tools. On the cultural side, Russia is recording some gains. For instance, the Russian language has been made compulsory in the school curriculum in the CAR (Flanagan, 2022). This enables those at the top of the dominant elite few to easily direct their people's thinking and, therefore, shape the world they control. The group has been deployed on the battlefields of Syria and Ukraine, where its involvement has been hugely significant.

Historically, Africa has served as a lucrative arena for mercenaries due to several factors. These include the prevalence of low-intensity conflicts, which reduces the risks to mercenaries' lives compared to full-scale wars, like in Ukraine. Also, Africa's abundant natural resources are prone to exploitation, and pervasive instability on the continent enables mercenaries to operate with relative impunity (Arduino, 2024). Consequently, several PMCs have cause to operate in Africa. However, the particular attraction of Wagner to state clients in Africa seems to be its low-cost billing. For instance, highly qualified experts from other PMCs cost between $15,000 and $25,000 per person per month compared to the meagre pay a lower-rank Wagner soldier receives, which is between 120,000 and 300,000 roubles per month ($1,800 – $4,700) (Sauer, 2019). The next section provides an audit trail of the Wagner Group's activities in some African countries.

Contextual Audit

This section offers a contextual appraisal of Wagner's operations, which consist of both hard and soft power projection in African countries identified in the literature.

Burkina Faso

Burkina Faso has always denied the allegation that the Wagner Group was hired to help fight insurgency in the country (Sy, 2022), even in the face of people waving Russian flags in celebration of the military coup in September 2022 (Wilkins, 2022). Yet, on 24 January 2024, 100 Russian mercenaries (a.k.a. Africa Corps) arrived in Burkina Faso to provide security, including for President Traoré (Lechne, 2024). The Africa Corps, which metamorphosed from Wagner, are regarded as 'military specialists' bearing equipment and weapons to train Burkinabe troops and patrol dangerous areas (Hoije, 2024). According to the Ghanaian President, Nana Akufo-Addo, a mine in southern Burkina has been allocated to the Wagner Group as a form of payment for their services (Irish, 2022). Like in Mali, Burkina Faso's armed forces are involved in fighting to curb al-Qaeda and ISIS-linked Islamist' terrorists in the country (Adeoye, 2023).

Central African Republic (CAR)

The Wagner Group's activities are also recorded in CAR. The Group deployed its personnel to the country under the pretence of protecting lucrative mines and supporting the CAR government, particularly, providing close protection for the president, Faustin-Archange Touadéra (Kharief, 2018). Also, the presence of Wagner (up to 1400 personnel in 2018) in the CAR was ostensibly to fill the security vacuum left after France's withdrawal. Cases of human rights abuses trailed Wagner's activities in the CAR, and the Group has been accused of exacerbating the conflict in the country (France 24, 2021). The Wagner Group was also reported to be deeply involved in the mining of precious stones in the CAR (Security Service of Ukraine, 2018). Reportedly, Wagner has taken advantage of weak institutions and a weak army to perfect 'a blueprint for state capture', and focusing on four pillars: political, economic, information, disinformation and propaganda, and the military (Adegoke, 2023).

Chad

The presence of Wagner in Chad is not as orchestrated as in other parts of the Sahel region. However, it has been reported that the USA government shared intelligence with the Chadian government of Wagner, working with Chadian rebels to destabilize the government, and possibly plotting to kill the country's president and other top government officials (Faucon, 2023). Wagner has, allegedly, provided material and operational support to local rebels seeking to destabilize and possibly overthrow the government of Chad's interim president, Mahamat Idriss Déby Itno (Stronski, 2023). The fear has been expressed that Wagner mercenaries already present in surrounding countries such as Libya, Sudan, and the CAR could be used to destabilize Chad (Chason, 2023).

Ghana

The Wagner Group usually creates a group of media outlets that are either operated in Russia or elsewhere to provide favourable coverage that is often pro-Russian and anti-West in exchange for financial support. Such an establishment (troll farm) has been reported in Accra, Ghana, where employees have worked on disinformation campaigns related to the USA elections, focusing on racial issues and dividing voters (Banco et al., 2020). Young Ghanaians are paid, housed in a private apartment and are given mobile phones to post online topics ranging from racial issues, LGBT and police brutality and often displaying anger towards white Americans. The goal is, allegedly, to inflame divisions among Americans and provoke social unrest. The language and images used in the posts – on Twitter, Facebook and Instagram – are sometimes graphic (CNN, 2020). For instance, according to CNN (2020), Wagner's trolls attempted to poison the political atmosphere in the USA ahead of the 2020 presidential elections by the use of a better-disguised and more targeted, harder to identify and track disinformation campaign strategy. This Wagner Group's operation was managed by an organization called Eliminating Barriers for the Liberation of Africa in Ghana.

Ghana is not the only African country where Wagner operates its misinformation campaigns. For instance, CNN (2020) alluded to Wagner's covert operations in Nigeria, establishing physical disinformation infrastructures in South Africa (Whitman, 2023), and ensuring victory for Mnangagwa in the 2018 Zimbabwe presidential election (Launder, 2024). The waving of Russian flags by protesters during the August #endbadgovernance protest in Nigeria has been attributed to Russian (and Wagner by extension) influence (Abdullahi, 2024).

Libya

The Wagner Group's presence in Libya was first reported in October 2018, with bases set up in Benghazi and Tobruk in support of Field Marshal Khalifa Haftar, leader of the Libyan National Army (LNA). Wagner provided training and support to Haftar's forces and was alleged to be using banned land mines and booby traps in Libya (Human Rights Watch, 2022a). Since entering combat operations in Libya, Wagner's presence there has swelled to roughly 2,000 mercenaries (Uniacke, 2022). The Wagner Group has been accused of committing human rights abuses against the Libyan people and intensifying ongoing instability (Ibrahim and Ochieng, 2023). Also, it has been argued that the objectives of Wagner in Libya have been mainly for financial gain through access to oil revenues and to facilitate easy access to other African countries (Holleis and Katamadze, 2024).

Madagascar

Wagner's engagement in the country is largely in political interference, particularly in the 2018 presidential election, when a group of Russian political strategists descended on the country. Wagner-linked political agents are said to have provided direct financial and strategic support to contestants that were considered friendly to Russia (Baker and Bullock, 2023). In the effort to influence election outcomes, the Wagner group was said to have spent $15 million (USD) (Proekt, 2019) to secure mining concessions, facilitate access by Russian investors to other areas of Madagascar's economy, and uphold existing bilateral arrangements, especially on defence issues (Lauder, 2024).

Mali

To execute its war against terrorism, Mali engaged the services of the Wagner Group in 2021, with the latter supplying military hardware and personnel towards prosecuting the war and providing protection for government officials. Like in other African countries that seek Wagner's services, Mali's valuable natural resources, such as timber, gold, uranium, and lithium, are expected to be exploited to cover Wagner's operational costs (Inwood and Tacchi, 2024). It was also reported that the government paid around $10.8 million a month for services Wagner rendered in 2021 (Reuters, 2023).

However, the brutality of the Wagner Group in their operations in Mali has been spotlighted by the Human Rights Watch (2022b) who, on 5 April 2022, published a report accusing Malian soldiers and Wagner of executing around 300 civilians between 27 and 31 March 2022, during a military operation in Moura, in the Mopti region, known as a hotspot of Islamic militants (Akinwotu, 2022). It was also reported that between December 2021 and June 2023, 298 instances of political violence involving Wagner, including civilian targeting, mass killings, abductions, cattle theft, extortion and looting, were recorded (Bergengruen, 2023). Furthermore, the effectiveness of Wagner's operation in Mali has been questioned. For instance, according to the UN Panel of Experts for Mali, the insurgency rate in the country has almost doubled in less than a year between 2022 and 2023 (US Department of State, 2024).

Mozambique

The Wagner Group was reported to have been contracted by the government of Mozambique to provide technical and tactical assistance to the Mozambique Defence Armed Forces (FADM) and was stationed in the Cabo Delgado province to quell an intensifying insurgency (Sauer, 2019). This insurrection was associated with the Islamic State's Central African Province (ISCAP). However, Wagner was unable to perform effectively due to reasons such as a lack of cultural understanding and unfamiliarity with the dense jungle terrain, which severely hindered their capability to counteract the insurgents effectively. Also, there were frictions between Wagner forces and the Mozambican military, which aggravated the situation as each side condemned the other's preparedness and conduct (Baghai, 2024).

Sudan

The Wagner Group's presence in Sudan is noted in a number of reports (e.g. CNN, 2023; BBC, 2023). The group has been supplying Sudan's Rapid Support Forces (RSF) with missiles to aid their fight against the country's army (CNN, 2023). Wagner's activities in Sudan include lucrative mining concessions given to the Group near the town of Abidiya, in Sudan's northeastern gold-rich area and helping in Russia's attempts to build a naval base on the Red Sea. The Wagner Group used western Sudan's Darfur region as a staging point for its operations in other neighbouring countries of the CAR, Libya and parts of Chad (Walsh, 2022).

The atrocities committed by Wagner in Sudan include the killing of scores of Sudanese miners working in artisanal gold mines along the border between Sudan and the CAR, and the looting of Sudan's rich gold mines (US Department of State, 2024). Furthermore, the Wagner Group was involved in disinformation campaigns in Sudan through its own media narratives to project its position (BBC, 2023). For example, the network connected to Wagner's founder, Prigozhin, hired locals in Sudan to run numerous undetectable disinformation campaigns, promoting Russia as a friend of Sudan (Africa Centre for Strategic Studies, 2021).

Methodology

The methodological root of this paper is a set of dialectical principles, which facilitated the identification of essential characteristics of the processes under study, the forms of their manifestation and development trends. The literature review aimed to integrate diverse works into the PMCs and war entrepreneurship discourse. Therefore, the author, based on the advice given by Clark et al. (2021) and Fisch and Block (2018), sought to gain insights from the dominant views that have traversed synchronous fields of war entrepreneurship and Wagner's activities on the continent of Africa. To achieve this goal, articles were sourced through the following steps. First, titles, abstracts and keywords in the academic research databases, such as 'JSTOR', 'Web of Science', 'Google Scholar', and 'Scopus' databases, were searched using key terms associated with entrepreneurship, war/conflict, PMCs and the Wagner Group. Afterwards, journal publisher databases (Elsevier, Emerald, SAGE, Springer, Taylor & Francis, Wiley) and other internet sources were probed for further publications. In other words, multiple search iterations were run, using Category 1 terms associated with war entrepreneurship, with Category 2 terms associated with Africa/conflicts, and Category 3 terms associated with Wagner. This broad-based search generated over 2,500 items.

Method

The method adopted was a three-step systematic literature review approach. First, appropriate search keywords were determined. Second, all relevant papers and publications that have a significant focus on war entrepreneurship and the Wagner Group were identified, and third, the identified papers/publications were analysed and structured (Tranfield et al., 2003). According to Cochrane Collaboration (2005: 45), a systematic literature review is: '[a] review of a formulated question that uses systematic and explicit methods to identify, select, and critically appraise relevant research and to collect and analyse data from the studies included in the review'. Statistical methods (meta-analysis) may or may not be used to analyse and summarize the results of the included studies. Systematic reviews are deemed the gold standard for extant literature review activities (Boland et al., 2017) as they follow well-defined, logical and transparent ways of synthesizing findings. Therefore, current publications are surveyed to provide answers to the pre-set research questions and achieve the stated objectives.

Findings and Analysis

The collected data reveal two main tracks in war entrepreneurship that could be considered from the micro and macro perspectives. The micro level is rooted in the entrepreneurial activities of PMCs, and the macro level is based on the geopolitics of entrepreneurship. Whilst the Wagner Group's activities in Africa are interrogated as the micro level, the subterranean economic and political benefits Russia acquired from Wagner's pay-offs in Africa represent the macro level. These two aspects are discussed below.

Entrepreneurship in War and Conflict Situations

Considering that entrepreneurs always find creative ways to grow their wealth, power and prestige, and their entrepreneurial talent may be directed not only to productive activities but also to unproductive and destructive activities (Baumol, 1990), Wagner's operations fall well within the ambit of entrepreneurship. In almost every African country in which it operates, Wagner was reported to have secured valuable natural resources, using these to not only cover costs but also extract significant revenue. Wagner's modus operandi follows a pattern: Military interference, active measures, disinformation and pay-off. The pattern is well established, and the record of success is remarkable: destabilize wherever possible, for fun and profit (Whitman, 2023). Ostensibly, Wagner 'sustains' its patrons (e.g. African regimes) through military action in return for access to mineral resources (e.g. gold in the Sahel) as payment for services rendered.

It appears Wagner uses all forms of tactics in its pursuit of entrepreneurial gains, comprising both hard and soft power projection. It could be argued that Wagner's grey zone operations, i.e. strong disinformation campaigns, have denied African governments and people the ability to make informed choices. Invariably, the damage done by disinformation may have longer-lasting and more harmful effects than a transient military escapade (Whitman, 2023). Consequently, the overlapping elements of Wagner's military action and disinformation work in tandem to achieve set objectives.

On the morality angle, Wagner's gains from war and conflict situations might be seen as largely unproductive and destructive to its host country. However, the theory of unproductive/destructive entrepreneurship, supported by authors such as Desai et al. (2013; Acs et al., 2013), and Collins et al. (2016), underscores the fact that entrepreneurship is not a wholly inherently economically healthy activity and can be allocated among productive, unproductive and destructive forms. When unproductive and destructive entrepreneurship comes in association with PMCs' activities, war entrepreneurship emerges. PMCs (such as Wagner) may directly or indirectly profit from unproductive entrepreneurship. War/conflict situations can both grease and sand the wheels of business, but in the case of Wagner's enactment of war entrepreneurship, it seems to only support entrepreneurial activity based on rent-seeking, co-ownership and state capture.

Entrepreneurship and Geopolitics

The data analysis in this section enables reflections and critical articulation of the geopolitics of the contemporary entrepreneurial state and its connotation economically and political. Geopolitics, regarded as the convergence of geography, economics and politics and its influences on events, is shaped by geographic location, resources (natural and artificial), demographics and people factors, and relationships with other countries (Bronshtein, 2011). The state can act entrepreneurially (Mazzucato, 2011), and entrepreneurial states are countries that seek to gain the support of others in pursuit of their perceived interests in the international system (Ravenhill, 2018).

The interplay between entrepreneurship and geopolitics is indicated in the economic benefits Russia seems to be getting from the accrual of incomes (e.g. in the form of mining rights) generated from Wagner's clients in Africa. It is largely accepted that the Russian state delegates its monopoly over organized violence to the Wagner Group, in a kind of symbiotic arrangement in which both parties accrued significant benefits (financial and non-financial). For instance, the Wagner Group provides a private alternative for Russia to project power with prestige and reduced risks in Africa (Murphy, 2024). Allegedly, some of Wagner's illicit gold trade dealings in Africa have been used to bolster Moscow's gold reserves, enabling the circumvention of economic sanctions imposed due to the Ukraine conflict (Mustaffa, 2023). Relatedly, Russia was reported to have extracted \$2.5bn (£2bn) worth of gold from Africa in the past two years, which is likely to have helped fund its war in Ukraine, according to the Blood Gold Report (Inwood and Tacchi, 2024). Russia seems to be offering governments in Africa a 'regime survival package' in exchange for access to strategically important natural resources, for instance, the three West African states with close links to Wagner – Mali, Niger and Burkina Faso – have all experienced military takeovers in recent years (Inwood and Tacchi, 2024) and have signed mining concessions with Russia proxy – Wagner.

Invariably, through the activities of Wagner, the Russian state has been able to operate within the sub-threshold conflict space on the continuum of operations between peace and war (also alluded to as the concept of operations other than war (OOTW)). This space is designed to prevent a conflict from escalating to all-out war, but to facilitate the accomplishment of geopolitical objectives (Lauder, 2024). The sub-threshold conflict zone is based on the key assumption of structural subversion, which involves the employment of all elements of national power to undermine the integrity of the target state and to set conditions for state capture (i.e. systematic dependence and exploitation) and the seizure of state power (Lauder, 2024; Lauder et al., 2020). Inevitably, Russia has been able to exploit these conditions for state capture to extract benefits that can be considered entrepreneurial gains from Wagner's activities.

Generally, scholars of geopolitics have often overlooked the critical role played by entrepreneurship in shaping global affairs. A profound understanding of geopolitics is crucial for navigating an increasingly complex global economic space. Issues relating to trade disputes, sanctions, political instability and regional conflicts can have direct and indirect impacts on business, supply chains, market access, investment events, and consumer behaviour (Broshtein, 2011).

Discussion, Implication and Conclusion

Unproductive and Destructive Entrepreneurship

Entrepreneurial activity is often viewed as bringing about universally positive benefits, such as reducing poverty and transforming communities (Sutter et al., 2019). Nonetheless, Baumol (1990) reminded us that entrepreneurs are ingenious and creative people who find ways to add to their wealth, power, and prestige in a manner that could be unproductive (e.g. rent seeking) or destructive (e.g. illegal). Thus, the illegal and destructive 'entrepreneurial activities' of the Wagner Group in places like the Central African Republic, Mali and Sudan have undermined democracies, violated human rights and extracted resources at the expense of their African hosts.

Dialectics of PMCs in Africa

There are different perspectives on the involvement of PMCs in the African security framework. On the positive side, a perspective considers PMCs to be useful actors seeking peace and stability on the African continent. Scholars (e.g. Shearer, 1999) in this school of thought argue that PMCs break cycles of violence in conflicts, particularly in areas where countries cannot provide security due to weak or under-equipped armies. Another perspective contends that PMCs often improve the low capacity of African military formations, which makes most of the military forces of Africa weak and vulnerable (Howe, 2001). Yet, on the negative side, the argument could be made that PMCs weaken the confidence, create tension and disruptions and low morale among the military forces where they operate in Africa or wherever. The friction between Wagner forces in Ukraine and the Russian military (Murphy, 2024) bears witness to this assertion. Furthermore, PMCs such as the Wagner Group are plunderers of mineral resources, perpetrators of human rights abuses and have the penchant to prolong conflicts to satisfy their interests wherever they operate.

Russian Imperialism

The Russian state association with Wagner's operations in Africa could be considered imperialism because Russia is changing the power balance in its favour, at the expense of the UK and France (the erstwhile Africa's dominant colonial masters). On closer observation, most of the crimes the Wagner Group has been accused of and sanctioned for are not sui generis. It is most likely that the real issue is that Russia, as a country, is projecting its national interest on the African continent at the expense of the USA and the former colonial powers. Russia (through Wagner) is gradually becoming the guarantor of fragile regimes on the African continent. The Russian state seems to be using extraordinary tools to reach its goals of garnering influence in Africa. Russia lacks the resources to garner influence to compete with others in terms of infrastructure projects, economic development, trade ties and humanitarian initiatives in Africa. But the activities of the Wagner Group act as a costless tactic to ensure

Russia's presence and influence in Africa (Anisova, 2023). Tangentially, the cordial relationship between Russia and China, and their collective inroads on the African continent, in particular, point to a progressive decline in the relevance of Europe and America to Africa. If regimes can secure financial assistance from China and military assistance (in the form of PMCs) from Russia, they will have less need for the USA and its allies. Ultimately, the attraction to Russia (through Wagner activities), especially by the francophone countries of the Sahel, is understandable in the context of their new policies to 'decouple' from Western alliances and friendships.

Russian appears to have cleverly sparked subliminal overtones (using social media), matching Pan-African and anti-colonial sentiments of the pre-independence eras, 1960s and 1970s. According to the Africa Centre for Strategic Studies (2024), Africa has been exposed to many transnational disinformation campaigns, mostly sponsored by external state actors attempting to assert influence on the continent. In particular, Russia (through the Wagner Group) and China are alleged to be the chief culprits in the disinformation campaign that is engineered to advance their geostrategic interests. The disinformation narratives are shaped to undermine democratic processes, promote coups in Africa, stoke anti-Western and anti-UN sentiment and spread confusion about climate change science, among others (Africa Centre for Strategic Studies, 2024). Wagner's services enable Russia to pursue policies in tough parts of the world with the distance and comfort of plausible deniability (e.g. Niekerk, 2002).

Summary and Implications

The chapter highlights the concept of war entrepreneurship from the prism of PMCs. War and conflict situations provide a template to interrogate the notion of war entrepreneurship using the activities of the Wagner Group (a PMC) on the African continent. Wagner's activities through both hard coercive power and soft persuasive power are calibrated to state capture and resource plundering, and on many occasions, Wagner's involvement in Africa has resulted in alleged human rights violations and exacerbated regional insecurity. The chapter also illustrates the vital role played by Russia (Wagner's principal) as an entrepreneurial state in geopolitical affairs and particularly in shaping events in Africa.

Following Baumol's (1990) treatise on unproductive and destructive entrepreneurship, it is understandable that people, organizations and states extract entrepreneurial gains from adverse conditions of war and conflict. PMCs and individuals, such as arms dealers or weapon traders, will make war as their profitable business. As we know, war is the worst and horrific type of human interaction; however, it is difficult to make a judgment call on war entrepreneurship, as choosing between ethics/morality and business could be tough. Making profits out of war is an ancient phenomenon. There were, and will always be, enterprises constantly supplying materials to prepare armies and consequently profit from war. Organizations and individual businesspeople have become aware that conflicts and war situations are undoubtedly lucrative. Warmongers who propagate and influence patriotic and despotic war-peddling around the world make several million dollars in profit. Unfortunately, these profits are made from devastation, suffering and the deaths of people who are mostly vulnerable and innocent.

In terms of implication, it is clear that the activities of PMCs, whilst straddling both the public and private spheres, also breach the distinction between civilians and combatants' lines with serious implications on the cardinal principles of International Humanitarian Law (Sossai, 2017). PMCs' operations, as can be derived from the data, indicate a possible erosion of sovereignty of some of the African countries in which they operate and thus, can be seen as re-colonizing forces. The patronage of PMCs may ultimately weaken existing security structures, making African states more vulnerable. The point must be made that the increased deployment of PMCs, particularly during the Global War on Terror, shows they are actively and passively contesting the state military profession's jurisdiction over its core task, that is, the authority to use lethal force as the agent of the state. At any rate, PMCs (such as the Wagner Group) may not be able to deliver sustainable peace, for instance, the conflicts in the Sahel states (e.g. Mali, Burkina Faso) are protracting with no end in sight.

While the chapter covers a lot of ground, there is room for further studies to investigate the concepts of war entrepreneurship and entrepreneurial state more robustly. For example, the notion of entrepreneurial state has been firmly linked to a country's ability to act as a primary risk-taker in innovation-based investments (Mazzucato, 2013) in the literature. Nevertheless, in this paper, the concept is considered a country that seeks to gain the support of others in pursuit of its perceived interests in the international system (Ravenhill, 2018). These differing perspectives will need further exploration in terms of alignment or complementarity. In addition, Wagner's services to state clients in other regions (e.g. Europe) should be studied to understand how unproductive and destructive they are, particularly in terms of weakening the military forces, human rights abuses, resource plundering and state capture of the clients.

References

Abdullahi, M. (2024). 'Matters Arising: The Implications of Protesters Waving Russian Flags in Some Northern States.' The Cable. Available at: https://www.thecable.ng/matters-arising-the-implications-of-protesters-waving-russian-flags-in-some-northern-states/

Acs, Z.J., M.C. Boardman and C.L. McNeely (2013). 'The Social Value of Productive Entrepreneurship,' *Small Business Economics*, 40(3): 785–96.

Adams, T.K. (1999). 'The New Mercenaries and the Privatization of Conflict,' *Parameters*, 29(2): 103–16. Available at: https://doi.org/10.55540/0031-1723.1926

Addison, T. (2001). 'Reconstruction from War in Africa: Communities, Entrepreneurs and States.' WIDER Discussion Paper 2001/018. Helsinki: UNU-WIDER.

Adegoke, Y. (2023). 'Why Wagner Is Winning Hearts in the Central African Republic.' BBC News. Available at: https://www.bbc.co.uk/news/world-africa-67625139

Adeoye, A. (2023). 'Burkina Faso Calls Russia an Ally Amid Fight Against Sahel Insurgents.' *Financial Times*. Available at: https://www.ft.com/content/96765db5-69b3-46ee-8601-15f41cf25211

Africa Centre for Strategic Studies (2021). 'Domestic Disinformation on the Rise in Africa'. Available at: https://africacenter.org/spotlight/domestic-disinformation-on-the-rise-in-africa

Africa Centre for Strategic Studies (2024). 'Mapping a Surge of Disinformation in Africa'. Available at: https://africacenter.org/spotlight/mapping-a-surge-of-disinformation-in-africa

Akinwotu, E. (2022). 'Russian Mercenaries and Mali Army Accused of Killing 300 Civilians'. *Guardian*. Available at: https://www.theguardian.com/world/2022/apr/05/ussia-mercenaries-and-mali-army-accused-of-killing-300-civilians

Alami, I., A.D. Dixon, R. Gonzalez-Vicente, M. Babic, Seung-Ook Lee, I.A. Medby and N. Graaff (2021). 'Geopolitics and the "New" State Capitalism', *Geopolitics*, 27(3): 995–1023. Available at: https://doi.org/10.1080/14650045.2021.1924943

Anisova, K. (2023). 'Russian Inroads in Africa: Responsible Power Projection or Regional Instability Preservation'. The Security Distillery. Available at: https://thesecuritydistillery.org/all-articles/russian-inroads-in-africa-responsible-power-projection-or-regional-instability-preservation

Arduino, A. (2024). 'Wagner Group Is Now Africa Corps. What This Means for Russia's Operations on the Continent'. The Conversation. Available at: https://theconversation.com/wagner-group-is-now-africa-corps-what-this-means-for-russias-operations-on-the-continent-223253

Arnold, A.J. (1999). 'Profitability and Capital Accumulation in British Industry During the Trans War Period, 1913–1924', *Economic History Review*, 52(1): 45–68. Available at: https://doi.org/10.1111/1468-0289.00118

Audretsch, D.B., P.P. Momtaz, H. Motuzenko and S. Vismara (2023). 'War and Entrepreneurship: A Synthetic Control Study of the Russia-Ukraine Conflict', CESifo Working Paper No. 10466. Available at https://ssrn.com/abstract=4470386 or http://dx.doi.org/10.2139/ssrn.4470386

Avlon, J. (2017). 'The Military Industrial Complex Is Real and It's Bigger than Ever'. Daily Beast. Available at: https://www.thedailybeast.com/the-military-industrial-complex-is-real-and-its-bigger-than-ever

Baghai, C. (2024). 'The Failed Military Engagement of the Wagner Group in Mozambique'. Available at: https://christianbaghai.medium.com/the-wagner-group-in-mozambique-a-complex-engagement-with-lasting-implications-6a27b301ea0f

Baker, N., and C. Bullock (2023). 'How a Shadowy Russian Organisation Is Making Political and Economic Inroads Across Africa'. ABC. Available at: https://www.abc.net.au/news/2023-03-31/ussia-wagner-group-in-africa/102160936

Banco, E., S.A. Aarup and A. Carrier (2020). 'Inside the Stunning Growth of Russia's Wagner Group.' Politico. Available at: https://www.politico.com/news/2023/02/18/russia-wagner-group-ukraine-paramilitary-00083553

Barker, D. (2017). '"Business as Usual": The Impact of the Great War on the British Ceramics Industry', *Post-Medieval Archaeology*, 51(2): 209–60.

Baten, J., and R. Schulz (2005). 'Making Profits in Wartime: Corporate Profits, Inequality, and GDP in Germany During the First World War', *Economic History Review*, 58(1): 34–56. Available at: https://doi.org/10.1111/j.1468-0289.2005.00297.x

Baumol, W. (1990). 'Entrepreneurship: Productive, Unproductive, and Destructive', *Journal of Political Economy*, 98(5): 893–921.
BBC (2023). 'Wagner in Sudan: What Have Russian Mercenaries Been up to?' BBC News. Available at: https://www.bbc.co.uk/news/world-africa-65328165
Bergengruen, V. (2023). 'Despite Rift with Putin, the Wagner Group's Global Reach Is Growing.' *Time*. Available at: https://time.com/6300145/wagner-group-niger-future/
Birthe A. (2014). 'Private Military and Security Companies: A Review Essay', *Parameters*, 44(2): 75–80. Available at: https://doi.org/10.55540/0031-1723.2886.
Bobin, F., and M.L. Cam (2023). 'Africa Corps, Le nouveau label de la ussiae russe au Sahel' [Africa Corps, the New Label of the Russian Presence in the Sahel]. *Le Monde* (in French). Available at: https://jdarcvitre.basecdi.fr/pmb/opac_css/index.php?lvl=notice_display&id=426741 (retrieved 15 December 2023).
Boland A., G. Cherr and R. Dickso (eds) (2017). *Doing a Systematic Review: A Student's Guide*. London: Sage.
Brahimi, A. (2021). 'Libya Has a Mercenaries Problem. It's Time for the International Community to Step Up'. Atlantic Council. Available at: https://www.atlanticcouncil.org/blogs/menasource/ussi-has-a-mercenaries-problem-its-time-for-the-international-community-to-step-up/
Bronshtein, M. (2011). 'Estonia: Economics and Geopolitics'. Available at: http://www.accordsdepeche.com/fichiers/docs/bibli_07/343.pdf
Brück, T., W. Naudé and P. Verwimp (2013). 'Entrepreneurship and Violent Conflict in Developing Countries'. WIDER Working Paper 2013/028. Helsinki: UNU-WIDER.
Cascais, A., and R. Koubakin (2022). 'Mercenary Armies in Africa'. Deutsche Welle. Available at: https://www.dw.com/en/the-rise-of-mercenary-armies-in-africa/a-61485270
Chason, R. (2023). 'As Russians Plot Against Chad, Concerns Mount Over Important U.S. Ally'. *Washington Post*. Available at: https://www.washingtonpost.com/world/2023/04/23/chad-wagner-russia-leaked-documents
Cheung, C.W.M. (2016). 'Exploitative Learning and Entrepreneurial Opportunity Recognition of a Family Business in Hong Kong During and After the Second World War', *Journal of Entrepreneurship in Emerging Economies*, 8(3): 321–34.
Clark, W.R., L.A. Clark, D.M. Raffo and R.I. Williams (2021). 'Extending Fisch and Block's (2018) Tips for a Systematic Review in Management and Business Literature,' *Management Review Quarterly*, 71(1): 215–31.
CNN (2020). 'Russian Election Meddling Is Back – Via Ghana and Nigeria – and in Your Feeds'. CNN. Available at: https://edition.cnn.com/2020/03/12/world/ussia-ghana-troll-farms-2020-ward/index.html
CNN (2023). 'Exclusive: Evidence Emerges of Russia's Wagner Arming Militia Leader Battling Sudan's Army'. CNN. Available at: https://edition.cnn.com/2023/04/20/ussia/wagner-sudan-russia-libya-intl/index.html
Cochrane Collaboration (2005). 'Glossary Terms in the Cochrane Collaboration'. Cochrane. Available at: https://www.cochrane.org
Collins, J.D., J.S. McMullen and C.R. Reutzel (2016). 'Distributive Justice, Corruption, and Entrepreneurial Behaviour', *Small Business Economics*, 47(4): 981–1006.
Desai, S., Z.J. Acs and U. Weitzel (2013). 'A Model of Destructive Entrepreneurship: Insight for Conflict and Postconflict Recovery', *Journal of Conflict Resolution*, 57(1): 20–40.

DeVore, M. (2020). 'Military-Industrial Complexes and Their Variations', in W.R. Thompson (ed.), *Oxford Research Encyclopedia of Politics*. Oxford: Oxford University Press. Available at: https://oxfordre.com/politics/view/10.1093/acrefore/9780190228637.001.0001/acrefore-9780190228637-e-1876

Dumenil, G., M. Glick and D. Lévy (1993). 'The Rise of the Rate of Profit During World War II', *Review of Economics and Statistics*, 75(2): 315–20. Available at: https://doi.org/10.2307/2109437

Efflandt, S.L. (2014). 'Military Professionalism and Private Military Contractors', *Parameters*, 44(2): 49–60. Available at: https://doi.org/10.55540/0031-1723.2884.

Faucon, B. (2023). 'U.S. Intelligence Points to Wagner Plot Against Key Western Ally in Africa.' *Wall Street Journal*. Available at: https://www.wsj.com/articles/u-s-intelligence-points-to-wagner-plot-against-key-western-ally-in-africa-29867547

Fisch, C., and J. Block (2018). 'Six Tips for Your (Systematic) Literature Review in Business and Management Research', *Management Review Quarterly*, 68: 103–6.

Flanagan, J.F. (2022). 'Central African Republic Introduces Mandatory Russian for University Students'. *Times*. Available at: https://www.thetimes.co.uk/article/central-african-republic-introduces-mandatory-russian-for-university-students-nmpxsfxkb

France 24 (2021). 'UN Urges CAR to Cut Ties with Russia's Wagner Mercenaries Over Rights Abuses', France 24, 28 October 2021.

Friedman, H.H., and Friedman, L.W. (2009). 'The Global Financial Crisis of 2008: What Went Wrong?' SSRN. Available at: https://ssrn.com/abstract=1356193

Gedeon, J. (2023). 'Wagner and the Troll Factories'. Politico. Available at: https://www.politico.com/newsletters/weekly-cybersecurity/2023/06/26/wagner-the-troll-factories-00103598

Higate, P., and M. Utas (2017). *Private Security in Africa: From the Global Assemblage to the Everyday*. London: Zed Books.

Higgins, A., and I. Nechepurenko (2018). 'In Africa, Mystery Murders Put Spotlight on Kremlin's Reach'. *New York Times*. Available at: https://www.nytimes.com/2018/08/07/world/europe/central-african-republic-russia-murder-journalists-africa-mystery-murders-put-spotlight-on-kremlins-reach.html

Hoije, K. (2024). 'Russian Troops Begin Burkina Faso Deployment to Bolster Security.' Bloomberg. Available at: https://www.bloomberg.com/news/articles/2024-01-24/russian-troops-begin-burkina-faso-deployment-to-bolster-security?embedded-chec

Holleis, J., and M. Katamadze (2024). 'Libya: Russia's Wagner Group Makes Further Inroads'. Deutsche Welle. Available at: https://www.dw.com/en/libya-russias-wagner-group-makes-further-inroads/a-68394810

Howe, H.M (1998). 'Private Security Forces and African Stability: The Case of Executive Outcomes', *Journal of Modern African Studies*, 36(2): 307–31.

Howe, H.M. (2001). *Ambiguous Order: Military Forces in African States*. Boulder, CO: Lynne Rienner.

Human Rights Watch (2022a). 'Libya: Russia's Wagner Group Set Landmines Near Tripoli'. Human Rights Watch, 31 May 2022.

Human Rights Watch (2022b). 'Mali: Massacre by Army, Foreign Soldiers'. Human Rights Watch. Available at: https://www.hrw.org/news/2022/04/05/mali-massacre-army-foreign-soldiers

Ibrahim, N., and B. Ochieng (2023). 'Wagner's Network in Africa Faces Uncertain Future'. BBC News. Available at: https://www.bbc.co.uk/news/world-africa-66023041#:~:text=Wagner%20fighters%20have%20been%20accused%20of%20 widespread%20human,and%20booby%20traps%20in%20family%20homes%20around%20Tripoli.

Inwood, J., and J. Tacchi (2024). 'Wagner in Africa: How the Russian Mercenary Group Has Rebranded'. BBC News. Available at: https://www.bbc.com/news/world-africa-68322230

Irish, J. (2022). 'Burkina Faso Aware of the Dangers of Wagner Force – France'. Reuters. Available at: https://www.reuters.com/world/africa/burkina-faso-aware-dangers-wagner-force-france-2022-12-15

Jackson, R.A., and D.B. Worthen (2002). 'Retail Pharmacy Operations in World War II: A Profit and Loss Statement', *Pharmacy in History*, 44(4): 131–41.

Jeffrey, S., J.S. Hornsby, J.G. Messersmith, M. Rutherford and S. Simmons (2018). 'Entrepreneurship Everywhere: Across Campus, Across Campus, Across Communities, and Across Borders', *Journal of Small Business Management*, 56(1): 4–10.

Kaldor, M. (2012). *New and Old Wars. In Organised Violence in a Global Era*. Cambridge: Polity.

Kharief, A. (2018). 'Foreign Mercenaries in New Scramble for Africa and the Sahel'. Middle East Eye. Institute for Peace and Security Studies, Ethiopia. Available at: https://ipss-addis.org/wp-content/uploads/2023/12/Special-Policy-Report.pdf (retrieved 25 September 2024).

Klaassen, L. (2023). 'The Use and Regulation of Private Military Contractors: Lessons From Nigeria', *Institute for Peace and Security Studies*, 1(1): 1–16. Ethiopia. Available at: https://ipss-addis.org/wp-content/uploads/2023/12/Special-Policy-Report.pdf

Kuhn, K.M., and T.L. Galloway (2015). 'With a Little Help from My Competitors: Peer Networking Among Artisan Entrepreneurs', *Entrepreneurship Theory and Practice*, 39(3): 571–600.

Lauder, M. (2024). 'The Sword of No-Sword: Wagner Group Soft Power Operations in Africa'. Government of Canada. Available at: https://cradpdf.drdc-rddc.gc.ca/PDFS/unc467/p818009_A1b.pdf

Lauder, M.A., S. Waldman and J. McInnis (2020). 'Curating Dystopia: Russia's Application of Political Warfare and Structural Subversion in the Baltic States and Black Sea Region'. Defence Research and Development Canada, Reference Document, DRDC-RDDC-2020-D021.

Lechne, J.A. (2024). 'Is Africa Corps a Rebranded Wagner Group?' *Foreign Policy*. Available at: https://foreignpolicy.com/2024/02/07/africa-corps-wagner-group-russia-africa-burkina-faso

Legal Assistant (2020). 'Are Mercenaries Legal?' Laws 101 Resources, 15 April 2020. Available at: https://laws101.com/mercenaries-legal/accessed 9 August 2024

Macías, A. (2014). 'The Impact of PMSC on the Role of Today's Military', *Opera*, 12: 221–9.

Mason, B. (1966). 'Entrepreneurial Activity in New York During the American Revolution', *Business History Review*, 40(2): 190–212. Available at: https://doi.org/10.2307/3112329

Mazzucato, M. (2011). 'The Entrepreneurial State', *Soundings*, 49(49): 131–42.

Mazzucato, M. (2013). *The Entrepreneurial State*. London: Anthem.

Murphy, M. (2024). 'A Year After Mutiny, Kremlin Controls Wagner Remnants'. BBC News. Available at: https://www.bbc.com/news/articles/c4nn1p81q59o

Mustaffa, M. (2023). 'Shadows of the State: How Wagner Group Extends Russian Reach in Africa'. Lowy Institute. Available at: https://www.lowyinstitute.org/the-interpreter/shadows-state-how-wagner-group-extends-russian-reach-

africa#:~:text=Ostensibly%20a%20private%20military%20company,%20Wagner%20has%20not
Niekerk, P. (2002). 'The Business of War'. International Consortium of Investigative Journalists. Available at: https://www.icij.org/investigations/makingkilling/business-war/
Nielsen, L. (2016). 'Private Military Companies in Africa – The Case of STTEP in Nigeria', *Journal of World Development Studies*, 2(2): 1–14.
Nimkar, R. (2009). 'From Bosnia to Bagdad the Case for Regulating Private Military and Security Companies', *Journal of Public and International Affairs*, 8(1) 1–24.
Ojo, S. (2021). 'Military Enterprises and Entrepreneurship: A Critical Perspective', in S. Ojo (ed.), *Global Perspectives on Military Entrepreneurship and Innovation*, 17–44. Hershey: IGI Global. Available at: https://doi.org/10.4018/978-1-7998-6655-8 ISBN13: 9781799866558
Organisation of African Unity (1985). OAU Convention for the Elimination of Mercenarism in Africa. Available at: https://au.int/sites/default/files/treaties/37287-treaty-0009_-_oau_convention_for_the_elimination_of_mercenarism_in_africa_e.pdf
Overton, J. (1986). 'War and Economic Development Settlers in Kenya, 1914–1918', *Journal of African History*, 27(1): 79–103. Available at: https://doi.org/10.1017/S0021853700029212
Proekt (2019). 'Master and Chef: How Russia Interfered in Elections in Twenty Countries'. Proekt. Available at: https://www.proekt.media/en/article-en/ussia-african-elections/
Ramoglou, S., and W.B. Gartner (2022). 'A Historical Intervention in the "Opportunity Wars": Forgotten Scholarship, the Discovery/Creation Disruption, and Moving Forward by Looking Backward', *Entrepreneurship Theory & Practice*, 47: 1521–38.
Rampe, W. (2023). 'What Is Russia's Wagner Group Doing in Africa?' Council on Foreign Relations. Available at: https://www.cfr.org/articles/what-russias-wagner-group-doing-africa
Ratten, V. (2016). 'Female Entrepreneurship and the Role of Customer Knowledge Development, Innovation Outcome Expectations and Culture on Intentions to Start Informal Business Ventures', *International Journal of Entrepreneurship and Small Business*, 27(2–3): 262–72.
Ratten, V. (2023). 'Entrepreneurship: Definitions, Opportunities, Challenges, and Future Directions', *Global Business and Organisational Excellence*, 42(5): 79–90.
Ravenhill, J. (2018). 'Entrepreneurial States: A Conceptual Overview', *International Journal*, 73(4): 501–17.
Reuters (2023). 'Wagner's Global Operations: War, Oil and Gold'. Reuters. Available at: https://www.reuters.com/world/europe/wagners-global-operations-war-oil-gold-2023-08-24
Sauer, P. (2019). 'In Push for Africa, Russia's Wagner Mercenaries Are "Out of Their Depth" in Mozambique.' *Moscow Times*. Available at: https://www.themoscowtimes.com/2019/11/19/in-push-for-africa-russias-wagner-mercenaries-are-out-of-their-depth-in-mozambique-a68220
Schreier, F., and M. Caparini (2005). 'Privatising Security: Law, Practice and Governance of Private Military and Security Companies', Occasional Paper no. 6, DCAF, Geneva Centre for Security Sector Governance.
Security Service of Ukraine (2018). '"Covert activity of Russian mercenaries of Wagner's PMC in CAR should be subject of international investigation", says SBU Head Vasyl Hrytsak'. Security Service of Ukraine. Available at: https://web.archive.

org/web/20181222082056/https://ssu.gov.ua/en/news/1/category/2/view/5541#.ALOOs7PL.dpbs (archived from the original on 22 December 2018).
Shane, S. (2003). *A General Theory of Entrepreneurship: The Individual–Opportunity Nexus*. New Horizons in Entrepreneurship, Cheltenham: Edward Elgar.
Shane, S., and S. Venkataraman (2000). 'The Promise of Entrepreneurship as a Field of Research', *Academy of Management Review*, 25(1): 217–26.
Shearer, D. (1998). 'Outsourcing War', *Foreign Policy*, 112(1): 68–81.
Shearer, D. (1999). 'Private Military Force and Challenge for the Future', *Cambridge Review of International Affairs*, 13(1): 80–94.
Shearer, D. (2005). 'Outsourcing War', *Foreign Policy*, 84(2): 119–32.
Singer, P.W. (2001). 'Corporate Warriors: The Rise and Ramifications of the Privatized Military Industry', *International Security*, 26(3): 186–220.
Sossai, M. (2017). 'Combatting the Legal Side Effects of Privatized War. What Has Been Achieved, and What Still Needs to Be Done in International Legal Scholarship on Private Military and Security Companies', *Völkerrechtsblog*, 9 October. Available at: https://doi.org/10.17176/20171009-102744
Steele, G.R. (2007). *The Economics of Friedrich Hayek* (2nd ed.), London: Palgrave MacMillan.
Stronski, A. (2023). 'Russia's Growing Footprint in Africa's Sahel Region.' Carnegie Endowment for International Peace. Available at: https://carnegieendowment.org/research/2023/02/russias-growing-footprint-in-africas-sahel-region
Sutter, C., G. Bruton and J. Chen (2019). 'Entrepreneurship as a Solution to Extreme Poverty: A Review and Future Research Directions', *Journal of Business Venturing*, 34: 197–214.
Sy, L. (2022). 'Wagner Group: Burkina Faso Anger Over Russian Mercenary Link'. BBC News. Available at: https://www.bbc.com/news/world-africa-63998458
Syrtseva S., U. Ivaniuk, I. Fedotova, O. Hurina, O. Dovzhyk and O. Nazarenko (2022). 'Innovative Potential and Development of Ukrainian Small Enterprises During the War (2022–2023)', *Amazonia Investiga*, 11(58): 222–32. Available at: https://doi.org/10.34069/AI/2022.58.10.24
Taulbee, J.L. (1985). 'Mercenaries and Contemporary International Law', *California Western International Law Journal*, 15(2): 346.
Tekingunduz, A. (2018). 'Are Private Military Contractors Any Different from Mercenaries?' TRT World.
Tonkin, H. (2011). *State Control over Private Military and Security Companies in Armed Conflict*. Cambridge: Cambridge University Press.
Tranfield, D., D. Denyer and P. Smart (2003). 'Towards a Methodology for Developing Evidence-Informed Management Knowledge by Means of Systematic Review', *British Journal of Management*, 14(3): 207–22. Available at: https://doi.org/10.1111/1467-8551.00375
Uniacke, R. (2022). 'Libya Could Be Putin's Trump Card'. *Foreign Policy*. Available at: https://foreignpolicy.com/2022/07/08/wagner-group-libya-oil-russia-war
United Nations (General Assembly) (2018). 'Mercenaries, Private Military Contractors Can Destabilize Ruel of Law, Expert Tells Third Committee, amid Calls to End Racism, Respect Migrant Rights'. Seventy-Third Session, 39th and 40th Meetings.
United Nations (Human Rights Council) (2018). 'Mercenarism and Private Military and Security Companies'. United Nations Human Rights Special Procedures.

US Department of State (2024). 'The Wagner Group's Atrocities in Africa: Lies and Truth'. US Department of State. Available at: https://www.state.gov/the-wagner-groups-atrocities-in-africa-lies-and-truth/
Vantage Market Research (2022). 'Private Military Security Services Market Size Worth USD 366.8 Billion by 2028 | With stunning 7.2% CAGR, Says Vantage Market Research'. Global News Wire. Available at: https://www.globenewswire.com/en/news-release/2022/06/22/2466892/0/en/Private-Military-Security-Services-Market-Size-worth-USD-366-8-Billion-by-2028-With-stunning-7-2-CAGR-Says-Vantage-Market-Research.html
Walsh, D. (2022). '"From Russia with Love": A Putin Ally Mines Gold and Plays Favorites in Sudan'. *New York Times*. Available at: https://www.nytimes.com/2022/06/05/world/africa/wagner-russia-sudan-gold-putin.html
Wennekers, S., and R. Thurik (1999). 'Linking Entrepreneurship and Economic Growth', *Small Business Economics*, 13: 27–56. Available at: https://doi.org/10.1023/A:1008063200484
Whitman, D. (2023). 'Russian Disinformation in Africa: No Door on this Barn'. Foreign Policy Research Institute. Available at: https://www.fpri.org/article/2023/08/russian-disinformation-in-africa-no-door-on-this-barn
Wilkins, H. (2022). 'Pro-Russia Sentiment Grows in Burkina Faso After Coup'. VOA News. Available at: https://www.voanews.com/a/pro-russia-sentiment-grows-in-burkina-faso-after-coup/6416363.html
Yasuyuki, H. (1996). 'Japanese Companies' Inroads into Indonesia Under Japanese Military Domination'. Bijdragen Tot De Taal-, Land-En Volkenkunde, 152: 656–98. Available at: https://doi.org/10.1163/22134379-90003958

Index

www.ingramcontent.com/pod-product-compliance
Ingram Content Group UK Ltd.
Pitfield, Milton Keynes, MK11 3LW, UK
UKHW020220290926
15470UKWH00001B/298

9 781666 981230